STATE, SOCIETY AND CULTURE
EARLY INDIA 300 AD TO 900 AD

State, Society and Culture
Early India 300 AD to 900 AD

SHANKAR GOYAL

ADITYA PRAKASHAN
New Delhi

First Edition, 2022

ISBN 978-81-957640-0-6

Published by Aditya Prakashan, 2/18, Ansari Road,
New Delhi – 110 002.

Email: contact@adityaprakashan.com
Website: www.adityaprakashan.com

Printed at Replika Press Pvt. Ltd., Kundli (Haryana).

For my daughters
Meghna and Akshara
with immense love and affection

Preface

The collection of essays in this work is intended to draw the attention of scholars to some of the recent researches on various aspects of early Indian history and culture. They were, with some exceptions, delivered as lectures and later marginally changed for publication. 'Need of an Integral Approach to the Writing of Political History of South India', was the Valedictory Address to the South Indian History Congress held at University of Kerala, Thiruvananthapuram, in 2002; 'Harsha's Place in History', was delivered at the Department of History, University of Kerala, Thiruvananthapuram, in 2007; 'S.R. Goyal's Contribution to Historical Studies', was given at the Department of History, University of Kerala, Thiruvananthapuram, again in 2007; 'Bhakti Movement in South India', was the Presidential Address to the Cultural History Section of the South Indian History Congress held at Manonmaniam Sundaranar University, Tirunelveli, in 2009; 'The Ramtek Prabhāvatīguptā Memorial Fragmentary Stone Inscription', was given at the 16th World Sanskrit Conference, Silpakorn University, Bangkok, in 2015; 'The Madras School of Ancient Indian Historians', was the Presidential Address to the Historiography Section of the Tamilnadu History Congress held at Periyar University, Salem, in 2016; 'Harsha and Iran : The History of Relations in the Age of Harsha', was delivered in the panel of the Aligarh Historians Society at Jadavpur University, Kolkata, in 2016; 'Yuan Chwang's India', was delivered in the panel of the Aligarh Historians Society at Kerala University, Thiruvananthapuram, in 2017; and 'Revisiting the Inscriptions of Harsha', was given as Professor Ku. Si. Haridas Bhat Shashtipoorti Endowment Lecture at Sri Venkateswara University, Tirupati, in 2017.

All these papers, as well as others, are concerned with the sources, historiography, history, society and religion and art and culture and interpretation of various facets of early Indian history and culture. The interdisciplinary approach expressed in the paper 'Problems of the Decline of Classical Political Theory and Political History' is indicative of a new direction in historical research. This historiographical change has introduced many innovations in the study of early Indian history. The increasing interest in the historiography of early period is an indicator of the awareness of the role of ideology in historical interpretation.

April 26, 2022

Shankar Goyal

Contents

Abbreviations

ABORI	*Annals of the Bhandarkar Oriental Research Institute*, Poona.
AHD	*Ancient History of the Deccan*, by G. Jouveau-Dubreuil. Pondicherry, 1920.
AISIHC	*Ancient India and South Indian History and Culture*, Vol. I, by S. Krishnaswami Aiyangar. Poona, 1941.
AIU	*The Age of Imperial Unity*, ed. by R.C.Majumdar and A.D. Pusalker. Bombay, 1953.
ĀMMK	*Āryamañjuśrīmūlakalpa*, ed. and trans. by K.P. Jayaswal as *An Imperial History of India*. Lahore, 1934.
Arch. Sur. West. Ind./ASWI	*Archaeological Survey of Western India*.
ASI, AR	*Archaeological Survey of India, Annual Reports*.
Aspects	*Aspects of Indian History and Civilization*, by Buddha Prakash. Agra, 1965.
A V	*The Age of the Vākāṭakas*, ed. A.M. Shastri. New Delhi, 1992.
Bayana Hoard	*Catalogue of the Gupta Gold Coins in the Bayana Hoard*, by A.S. Altekar. Bombay, 1954.
BMC, AI	*Catalogue of Coins of Ancient India* (*in the British Museum*), by John Allan. London, 1936.
BMC, GD	*Catalogue of the Coins of the Gupta Dynasties and of Śaśāṅka, King of Gauḍa* (*in the British Museum*), by John Allan. London, 1914.
BSOAS	*Bulletin of the School of Oriental and African Studies*, London.
CA	*The Classical Age*, ed. by R.C. Majumdar and A.D. Pusalker. Bombay, 1962.
Coinage	*The Coinage of the Gupta Empire*, by A.S. Altekar. Varanasi, 1957.

Comp. Hist. Ind.	*A Comprehensive History of India*, Vol. II, ed. by K.A.N. Sastri. Calcutta, 1957; Vol. III, ed. by R.C. Majumdar and K.K. Dasgupta. New Delhi, 1981.
Corpus / CII	*Corpus Inscriptionum Indicarum.*
DKA	*The Purāṇa Text of the Dynasties of the Kali Age*, by F.E. Pargiter. Varanasi, 1962.
Eco. Life	*Economic Life of Northern India in the Gupta Period*, by S. K. Maity. Calcutta, 1958.
EHD	*Early History of the Deccan*, by R.G. Bhandarkar. Poona, 1927.
EHDPP	*Early History of the Deccan : Problems and Perspectives*, by A.M. Shastri. Delhi, 1987.
EHDY	*Early History of the Deccan*, by G. Yazdani. Oxford, 1960.
EHI	*Early History of India*, by V.A. Smith. Oxford, 1957.
EHNI	*Early History of North India*, by S. Chattopadhyaya. Calcutta, 1958.
EI	*Epigraphia Indica.*
GE	*The Gupta Empire*, by R.K. Mookerji. Bombay, 1948.
Giles, Travels	*The Travels of Fa-hsien*, by H.A. Giles. London, 1928.
HB	*Harsha and Buddhism*, by S.R. Goyal. Meerut, 1986.
HC	*Harshacharita*, by Bāṇabhaṭṭa.
HHAH	*History and Historiography of the Age of Harsha*, by Shankar Goyal. Jodhpur, 1992.
HIG	*A History of the Imperial Guptas*, by S.R. Goyal. Allahabad, 1967.
HIL	*A History of Indian Literature*, by M. Winternitz, 3 Vols. Delhi, 1981, 1983, 1985.
Hist. Ind.	*History of India, 150 A.D. to 350 A.D.*, by K.P. Jayaswal. Lahore, 1933.
HK	*History of Kanauj*, by R.S. Tripathi. Delhi, 1959.
IA	*Indian Antiquary*, Bombay.
IC	*Indian Culture*, Calcutta.
IE / Ind. Ep.	*Indian Epigraphy*, by D.C. Sircar. Delhi, 1965.
IG	*The Imperial Guptas : A Multidisciplinary Political Study*, by S.R. Goyal. Jodhpur, 2005.
IHQ	*Indian Historical Quarterly*, Calcutta.
IHR	*Indian Historical Review*, New Delhi.
IJPS	*The Indian Journal of Political Science*, Jodhpur.
IMC	*Catalogue of the Coins in the Indian Museum, Calcutta*, Vol. I, by V.A. Smith. Oxford, 1906.

INC	*Indian Numismatic Chronicle*, Patna.
JA	*Journal Asiatique*, Paris.
JAIH	*Journal of Ancient Indian History*, Calcutta.
JAOS	*Journal of the American Oriental Society*, New Haven (U.S.A.).
JAS	*Journal of the Asiatic Society*, Kolkata.
JASB	*Journal and Proceedings of the Asiatic Society of Bengal*, Calcutta.
JBBRAS	*Journal of the Bombay Branch of the Royal Asiatic Society*, Bombay.
JBORS	*Journal of Bihar and Orissa Research Society*, Patna.
JBRS	*Journal of the Bihar Research Society*, Patna.
JESHO	*Journal of the Economic and Social History of the Orient*, Leiden.
JESI	*Journal of the Epigraphical Soceity of India*, Mysore.
JIH	*Journal of Indian History*, Trivandrum.
JNSI	*Journal of the Numismatic Society of India*, Varanasi.
JOI	*Journal of the Oriental Institute*, Baroda.
JOR	*Journal of the Oriental Research*, Madras.
JPS	*Journal of Peasant Studies*, London.
JRAS	*Journal of the Royal Asiatic Society of Great Britain and Ireland*, London.
JRASB(L)	*Journal of the Royal Asiatic Society of Bengal : Letters*, Calcutta.
JUG	*Journal of the University of Gauhati*, Gauhati.
KCMP	*King Chandra and the Meharauli Pillar*, ed. by Munish Chandra Joshi, S.K. Gupta and Shankar Goyal. Meerut, 1989.
Life	*The Life of Hiuen-Tsiang*, by S. Beal. New Delhi, 1973.
MASI	*Memoirs of the Archaeological Survey of India.*
NHIP/ VGA	*A New History of the Indian People*, Vol. VI: *The Vākāṭaka-Gupta Age*, ed. by R.C. Majumdar and A. S. Altekar. Lahore, 1946.
Num. Chro. (*NC*)	*Numismatic Chronicle.*
Num. Suppl. (*NS*)	*Numismatic Supplement.*
PHAI	*Political History of Ancient India*, by H. C. Raychaudhuri. Calcutta, 1953.
PIHC	*Proceedings of the Indian History Congress.*
POC	*Proceedings of the All-India Oriental Conference.*
PSIHC	*Proceedings of the South Indian History Congress.*
QRHS	*Quarterly Review of Historical Studies*, Calcutta.

Records	*Si-Yü-Ki* or *Buddhist Records of the Western World*, by S. Beal. Delhi, 1969.
Sel. Ins./SI	*Select Inscriptions bearing on Indian History and Civilization*, Vol. I, ed. by D. C. Sircar. Calcutta, 1942.
SP, PMC	*Seminar Papers on the Chronology of the Punch-marked Coins*, ed. by A.K. Narain and Lallanji Gopal. Varanasi, 1966.
Studies	*Studies in Indian History and Civilization*, by Buddha Prakash. Agra, 1962.
Suc. Sat. Low. Dec.	*The Successors of the Sātavāhanas in the Lower Deccan*, by D. C. Sircar. Calcutta, 1939.
Travels	*On Yuan Chwang's Travels in India* (A Translation of Hsüan-tsang's *Hsi-Yü-Chi*), by T. Watters. Delhi, 1961.
Vākāṭaka Rājavaṁśa	*Vākāṭaka Rājavaṁśa kā Itihāsa tathā Abhilekha* (in Hindi), by V.V. Mirashi. Varanasi, 1964.
VIJ	*Vishveshvaranand Indological Journal*, Hoshiarpur.
VSH	*Vākāṭakas : Sources and History*, by A.M. Shastri. New Delhi, 1997.

Section I
Sources

ONE

Gupta Inscriptions : Discovery, Decipherment and Interpretation

Many inscriptions of the imperial Guptas, which are the main source of their history, were brought to light, deciphered and interpreted gradually in the last decades of the eighteenth and the early decades of the nineteenth century by the British scholars and their Indian colleagues. As the knowledge of ancient Indian scripts had been forgotten by the people of this country, the Britishers had to make a fresh start in this field. In the earlier stages their efforts met with success only in the sphere of medieval inscriptions which were written in scripts similar to those of modern vernaculars and were therefore easier to decipher. In 1785, Charles Wilkins read the Badal pillar inscription of the Pāla king Nārāyaṇapāla found in the Dinajpur District of Bengal[1] and Pandit Radhakant Sharma successfully deciphered the Topra-Delhi pillar inscription of the Chāhamāna king Vīsaladeva (Vigraharāja IV), dated V.S. 1220 (=1163 A.D.). But the Nagarjuni and Barabar cave inscriptions of the Maukhari king Anantavarman, though discovered in 1785 by J. H. Harrington, being written in a more archaic script, now called 'Gupta', defied the ingenuity of these early epigraphists for a pretty long time. However, Charles Wilkins, who laboured on them between 1785 and 1789, succeeded in reading almost half of the letters of the Gupta alphabet. But as at that time the attention of the scholars was mainly directed to the study of ancient Indian literature, the success of Wilkins could not be properly exploited for further progress. The decipherment of the Gupta script was resumed in 1834 when Captain Troyer read a part of the Allahabad pillar inscription of Samudragupta.[2] But the endeavours of W.H. Mill were attended with greater success. In 1837, he won fresh laurels when he deciphered the Bhitari record of Skandagupta.

[1] *Asiatic Researches*, II, 1790, p. 167.
[2] *JASB*, III, 1834, pp. 119-20.

The most notable success, however, was achieved by James Prinsep. Not only did he play a major role in the decipherment of the early Brāhmī script, but also successfully read a host of inscriptions of the Gupta period found at Delhi, Kahaum, Sanchi and Junagadh, as a result of which a table of the Gupta alphabet could be published in 1871.[3]

The early epigraphists naturally committed numerous errors in their decipherment and interpretation of the Gupta records, and in the absence of any independent evidence on the history of this dynasty, literary or otherwise, they had to grope in the dark for a long time in their efforts to locate it in time and space. For example, lines 25 and 26 of the Allahabad *Praśasti* of Samudragupta, one of the earliest Gupta records to be discovered, were translated in 1834 by Troyer as follows:

Of the great-grandson of *Sri Chandragupta*, the great Raja, of the grandson of the great Raja *Sri Yagnakacha*, of the son of the great Raja (Adhiraja) *Sri Chandragupta.*

Of the son of the daughter of *Lich-ch'ha Vikriti*, of the family of *Mahadivya Kumara*... of the great Raja, the supreme Raja (Adhiraja) *Sri Samudragupta.*[4]

Mill corrected the name of the grand-father of Samudragupta to Ghaṭotkacha[5] but was himself responsible for numerous other errors which, for a long time, coloured the vision of those who wrote on Gupta history. For instance, he translated the line 8 of the inscription as follows:

Whose mothers-in-law, formerly proud and addicted to highminded oppressions perpetually, having been by his own arm subdued with the sword of battle (viz. *Sanhāritā*) and the rest,... (line 18)...[6]

and commented that the mothers-in-law of Samudragupta 'appear to have been independent princesses whose daughters were thus won in battle by Samudragupta'. Mill also believed that a royal issue was expected at the date of the inscription. As regards the origin of the Gupta dynasty, he rejected the suggestion of the identity of Chandragupta, the father of Samudragupta, with Chandragupta Maurya on the ground that while the Mauryas were of Śūdra extraction, the house of Samudragupta belonged to the Solar race—an impression which he gathered from the faulty decipherment of the line 30 of the Allahabad record. However, he examined the possibility of Chandragupta, the father of Samudragupta, having been a scion of the Rāṭhora or Pratihāra or Chāhamāna dynasty but could not come

[3] S. R. Goyal, *A History of the Imperial Guptas*, Allahabad, 1967, pp. 2-3; idem, *The Imperial Guptas : A Multidisciplinary Political Study*, Jodhpur, 2005, pp. 29 ff.

[4] *JASB*, III, pp. 119-20.

[5] *Ibid.*, p. 267.

[6] *Ibid.*, p. 262.

to a satisfactory conclusion. "Our researches", he remarked, "for the subjects of this inscription in the records of Northern and Central India, seem to be hitherto unsuccessful, notwithstanding the various Chandraguptas that have appeared there. Of the name of Samudragupta, I have not yet seen any trace." Mill also believed that the king Dhanañjaya of the Allahabad *Praśasti* belonged to "the race of *Ugrasena*, i.e. most probably the celebrated king of Mathura so called, the father of *Cansa*, who was slain by *Crishna*."

This was the state of our knowledge of Gupta history in 1834. But the patient efforts of the epigraphists very soon laid its skeleton bare. An idea of the rapid progress in our knowledge may easily be had by a comparison of the notes of Mill published in 1834 the extracts from which we have just given, with the history of the Gupta dynasty in the *Bhilsa Topes* of General Cunningham published exactly two decades later. In this work General Cunningham suggested 319 A.D. as the initial year of the era used in the Gupta inscriptions, published a correct translation of the statement of Alberuni on the problem of the Gupta era, and gave a connected account of the history of the Gupta dynasty. He placed the accession of king Gupta in 319 A.D., of Ghaṭotkacha in 340, of Chandragupta I in 360, of Samudragupta in 380, and of Chandragupta II, Kumāragupta I and Skandagupta respectively in 400, 430 and 440. Further, he tried to reconstruct the history of the imperial Guptas after Skandagupta and, perhaps it was he who for the first time suggested that Lagrāditya (Śakrāditya), Budhagupta, Taktagupta (Tathāgatarāja), Bālāditya and Vajra, known from the Chinese sources, were the successors of Skandagupta and placed them in 452, 480, 510, 540 and 570 respectively. Furthermore, he identified the king Bālāditya of Yuan Chwang with Nara Bālāditya of coins. When we recall that at that time scholars generally believed that the Gupta dynasty ended with Skandagupta, that in 1860 Liston suggested that the power of the Gupta dynasty after Skandagupta was usurped by a family of a minister,[7] that in 1865 Henry Beveridge in his *A Comprehensive History of India*, Vol. I, merely referred to Samudragupta as a 'fanatic' who 'removed the seat of government from Kanauj' and established a dynasty 'which is held by those who follow the local tradition to have ruled for three or four hundred years', that Clark Marshman whose work *The History of India*, Vol. I, published in 1867, did not refer to the Guptas at all, and that even in 1888 Fleet in his *Corpus Inscriptionum Indicarum*, Vol. III, opined that Budhagupta was not connected with Skandagupta by direct descent, differentiated the Budhagupta of the Eran inscription from the Buddhagupta of Yuan Chwang, and came to the conclusion that Cunningham's suggestion as contained in the *Bhilsa Topes*, on the initial year of the Gupta era was the correct one, one cannot but

[7] *JASB*, VII, p. 38.

admire the brilliance and the creative imagination of the General. It was really unfortunate that Cunningham himself did not stick to his original views on the Gupta era and later accepted the then prevalent notion that the year 319 A.D. marked the extinction of the Gupta rule, and not its commencement. For example, in 1871 he ascribed, the date of the Kahaum inscription of Skandagupta to the Śaka era on the plea that it would accord best with the generally accepted view that the Gupta dynasty came to an end in 319 A.D.[8] and in 1880 accepted 166-67 A.D. as the initial year of the Gupta era.[9]

Be that as it may, the publication of J.F. Fleet's *Corpus Inscriptionum Indicarum*, Vol. III, in which he edited the inscriptions of the Imperial Guptas, the Later Guptas and some others, was a landmark in the progress of Gupta epigraphy. Its importance may easily be realized from the fact that even after more than a century of its publication and after more than fifty years of Independence it has not been replaced by a better work in English. The most which Indian scholarship has been able to do is the publication of its revised version prepared by D.R. Bhandarkar and edited, after the death of Bhandarkar, by B. Ch. Chhabra and G. S. Gai (1981). But in many ways the revised version of Fleet's work is inferior to the original one, for the new editors have deleted all the inscriptions of the dynasties which were contemporary of the imperial Guptas.

Among the works produced in the twentieth century which are notable for the inscriptions of the Vākāṭaka-Gupta age mention may first be made of D. C. Sircar's *Select Inscriptions bearing on Indian History and Civilization.*[10] But it does not provide summary or translation of the inscriptions in English. *The Corpus of Bengal Inscriptions* by R. R. Mukherji and S. K. Maity[11] is also a good volume and gives text and translation of all the inscriptions of the Gupta age found from Bengal at once place in about hundred pages. The *Nepalese Inscriptions in Gupta Characters*[12] by R. Gnoli, as its name indicates, contains Nepalese inscriptions of the Gupta age. In 1963, V.V. Mirashi brought out Volume V of the *Corpus Inscriptionum Indicarum* containing the inscriptions of the Vākāṭakas which had come to light by that time. The Vākāṭaka records which were discovered after the publication of this work are given (at least a detailed treatment of their contents and a discussion on their importance) by Ajay Mitra Shastri

[8] *ASI, AR*, I, pp. 93-94.
[9] *ASI, AR*, X, pp. 111 ff.
[10] Calcutta, 1942, second edn., 1965.
[11] Calcutta, 1967.
[12] Rome, 1956.

in *The Age of the Vākāṭakas* [13] and recently in *Vākāṭakas — Sources and History.*[14]

But the most important work on the inscriptions of the Guptas, Vākāṭakas and other contemporary powers is S. R. Goyal's *Guptakālīna Abhilekha* in Hindi published from Meerut in 1984. It contains text, translation, textual comments, comments on important passages and a discussion on the importance of each and every Gupta inscription and select inscriptions of other dynasties—the Vākāṭakas, Huṇas, Aulikaras, etc. What is more, it gives even meanings of all the difficult and important words occurring in an inscription. Naturally, it has been widely acclaimed as an important contribution to ancient Indian epigraphy.[15] On the other hand, Vasudeva Upadhyaya's *Gupta Abhilekha,*[16] which gives extremely faulty text and translations of Gupta epigraphs and is full of printing mistakes, has nothing to commend itself. Be that as it may, a replacement of Fleet's *Corpus,* III, in any language is still a *desideratum.*

[13] New Delhi, 1992, pp. 227-68.

[14] New Delhi, 1997, pp. 85-135; also see my *175 Years of Vākāṭaka History and Historiography,* Jodhpur, 2009, pp. 34-49.

[15] S.R. Goyal's another work *Ancient Indian Inscriptions : Recent Finds and New Interpretations* (Jodhpur, 2005) seeks mainly to acquaint the teachers and students with important ancient Indian inscriptions discovered in the last few decades.

[16] Patna, 1974.

TWO

Recent Epigraphs of the Vākāṭakas

More than five decades have passed since V. V. *Corpus of the Vākāṭaka Inscriptions* from Ootacamund in 1963 in which he gave a brilliant study of twenty-seven Vākāṭaka epigraphs along with a detailed introduction containing the political and cultural history of the dynasty which became the primary source-material and basis for future researches. After that till today fourteen more Vākāṭaka inscriptions have come to light.[1] Some of them discovered in this period have been published in well known periodicals, while some have not been published in detail or have been reported in rather obscure publications not easily accessible to historians. Here, I propose to discuss them as they throw new light on the history of the Vākāṭakas and underline the significant fact that their history needs rewriting.

Barring a couple of exceptions[2] all these Vākāṭaka epigraphs are copper plate charters. Three of them, one lithic and two copper plate grants, belong to the southern or Vatsagulma branch of the dynasty while the rest, one lithic and rest of the copper plate inscriptions, belong to the northern or main branch. They are all incised in box-headed variety of southern script and are composed in Sanskrit.[3] The copper plates are all multiplate charters.

[1] Cf. A. M. Shastri, *Early History of the Deccan*, Delhi, 1987, pp. 45-81; idem, *The Age of the Vākāṭakas*, New Delhi, 1992, pp. 227-68; idem, *Vākāṭakas—Sources and History* (henceforth *VSH*), New Delhi, 1997, pp. 85-135; S. R. Goyal, *Ancient Indian Inscriptions: Recent Finds and New Interpretations*, Jodhpur, 2005, pp. 210-25; Shankar Goyal, 'Vākāṭaka Itihāsa para Navīna Ābhilekhika aura Maudrika Prakāśa', app. in S. R. Goyal's *Dakshiṇa Bhārata kā Itihāsa*, Jodhpur, 1995, pp. III. 161-63. Also see Hans T. Bakker, *The Vākāṭakas: An Essay in Hindu Iconology*, Groningen, 1997; idem, *The Vākāṭaka Heritage: Indian Culture at the Crossroads*, Groningen, 2004; S.R. Goyal, *The Imperial Guptas : A Multidisciplinary Political Study*, Jodhpur, 2005.

[2] Hisse Borala and Ramtek inscriptions.

[3] Ramtek inscription is, however, engraved in nail-headed alphabet.

RECENT INSCRIPTIONS OF THE MAIN BRANCH

1. MANDHAL PLATES OF RUDRASENA II, YEAR 5

Incised on a set of four plates, this record was discovered in 1982 from a field at Mandhal, a village about seventy-five kms. from Nagpur. It mentions fifth year, evidently of the reign of Rudrasena II, the donor of the charter, and was written by Senāpati Vibhīshaṇa, who came to be known from this record for the first time. Before its discovery the fragmentary Deotek stone inscription of Rudrasena was regarded as the earliest known Vākāṭaka epigraph. But that did not provide definite evidence which could enable us to attribute it unhesitatingly to Rudrasena I or II. Be that as it may, now the present grant has become the earliest definitely attributable inscription of the main branch of the Vākāṭakas. Not only that, the length of Rudrasena II's reign has so far been conjecturally fixed variously by historians. But the present record, which was issued in the fifth year of his reign, shows that he ruled *at least* for five years.

Rudrasena II alone among the early Vākāṭaka rulers was a devout follower of Vaishṇavism. It is stated in this record that his authority was established by the grace of wheel-bearing god, i.e. Vishṇu.

2. MANDHAL PLATES OF PRAVARASENA II, YEARS 16 AND 17

Archaeological excavations at Mandhal have yielded three sets of Vākāṭaka copper plate inscriptions intact with their rings and seals. One of these charters belongs to Pravarasena II, and the rest to his grandson Pṛthivīsheṇa. This grant of Pravarasena II, which is incised on a set of five plates, was like the majority of his records, issued from Pravarapura, generally identified with modern Paunar in the Wardha district. The record contains two dates, separated from one another by about a year—one when the grant was made and the other when the charter was written and issued. Neither Narendrarāja nor his mother Ājñākabhaṭṭārikā, who is stated to have shared one-third of the merit accruing from the grant, is known from any other source. That they had some pretensions to royalty is indicated by the words *rāja* and *bhaṭṭārikā* respectively suffixed to their names. In case this Narendrarāja is identified with Narendrasena, son and successor of Pravarasena II, the inscription would give us the name of Pravarasena II's chief queen and Narendrasena's mother. But there can be no certainty about it.

3. MASOD PLATES OF PRAVARASENA II, YEAR 19

The set of five plates bearing this record was found while ploughing a field at the village of Masod of the Nagpur district. The grant was made at the request of the chief queen (*bhāryā-mahādevī*) who was, however, left unnamed. The Masod plates mention Senāpati Kātyāyana. He is also mentioned in the Pattan plates of the twenty-seventh year of Pravarasena II. According to A.M. Shastri, this fact coupled with a few other similar references would seem to indicate that there were different senāpatis appointed for the different regions of the kingdom.[4]

4. MIREGAON CHARTER OF THE REIGN OF PRAVARASENA II, YEAR 20

A grant of Prabhāvatīguptā engraved on a set of five plates is reported to have been found together with the ring and the seal at Miregaon of the Bhandara district. It was drafted by *amātya* (minister) named Chandra. The mention of the designation *amātya* in the Vākāṭaka kingdom is found only in this charter. The seal inscription of Miregaon charter describes Prabhāvatīguptā as the mother of two powerful kings. This information is of great historical value. In the present as well as in the Riddhapur charter she is styled *Vākāṭakānām Mahārāja-Śrī-Dāmodarasena-Pravarasena-jananī.* This expression has been variously interpreted by historians, and according to some, Dāmodarasena was just another, pre-coronation, name of Pravarasena (II), the reigning monarch, and that the name Pravarasena was assumed by him at the time of his coronation. If Dāmodarasena and Pravarasena were different personages, it has been argued, the title *mahārāja* should have been prefixed to Pravarasena also. But the use of the dual number in *vikrāntayoḥ* and *Vākāṭaka-narendrayoḥ* in the Miregaon charter leaves no room for doubt that they were separate persons, the latter following the former. A reference to Divākarasena, who was apparently the eldest son of Rudrasena II and Prabhāvatīguptā and consequently the rightful claimant to the throne, is out of question in the present context, for he remained a crown-prince or *yuvarāja* for full thirteen years as we learn from the Pune plates of Prabhāvatīguptā, and there is no evidence to indicate that he ever became a crowned king (*mahārāja*) in his own right. It is also worth noting in this connection that so far we have no definite indication that the Vākāṭakas followed the practice of adopting a new name at the time of coronation which was prevalent among some other dynasties. The present record has, therefore, made it necessary for modern historians to make a provision for the reign of Dāmodarasena in the chronology of the Vākāṭakas.

5. UNDATED RAMTEK PRABHĀVATĪGUPTĀ MEMORIAL FRAGMENTARY STONE INSCRIPTION OF THE REIGN OF PRAVARASENA II

The Ramtek Prabhāvatīguptā memorial fragmentary inscription was found engraved on two rectangular blocks of stone inside the *maṇḍapa* of the

[4] *VSH,* p. 91.

Kevala-Narasiṁha temple at Ramtek, usually identified with the famous Rāmagiri, mentioned in the *Meghadūta* of Kālidāsa. The record belongs to the reign of the Vākāṭaka king Pravarasena II and purports to record most likely the erection of the Kevala-Narasiṁha temple with the image of the man-lion (Narasiṁha) manifestation of Vishṇu by a daughter (name lost) of Prabhāvatīguptā to commemorate the latter.

The testimony of the extant portions of this highly fragmentary record clarify and elaborate numerous points of the Gupta-Vākāṭaka relations and the history of the Deccan. It makes it clear that Chandragupta indeed looked after the Vākāṭaka administration during the minority of Prabhāvatīguptā's sons.[5] It also shows that he was believed to have been a *Tri-samudra-nātha* (Lord of Three Oceans), a claim which, on the one hand, indicates that for sometime he exercised at least nominal suzerainty over the Vākāṭaka kingdom including almost whole of the Deccan and, on the other, tends to strengthen the testimony of the Meharauli record regarding the warlike activities of Chandra (generally identified with Chandragupta II) in south India.[6] The inscription also gives highly significant and interesting information that Ghaṭotkachagupta, a son of Chandragupta II, married his own niece (*bhāgineyī*) and obviously with the help of his Vākāṭaka in-laws revolted against the authority of his brother Kumāragupta I to whom he was owing allegiance till 435 A.D., the date of his Tumain inscription. The inscription also alludes to a reference that Ghaṭotkacha assumed the imperial title 'Rājarāja' obviously after raising the banner of revolt against Kumāragupta I. The fact that after his death his Vākāṭaka wife was forcibly (*balāt*) rescued by her brother and brought to the Vākāṭaka capital shows that the hand of the Vākāṭakas was behind the revolt of Ghaṭotkachagupta.[7]

6. INDORE PLATES OF PRAVARASENA II, YEAR 23

The last three plates of this grant had been known to historians for quite a long time, but its first plate was missing. But a few years ago this missing plate was found from Indore. It begins with the word *dṛshṭam* followed by a reference to the issuing place which is specified as *Tripuri-vāsaka*. According

[5] However, the epigraphic evidence cited in support of the Gupta influence on the Vākāṭakas does not prove the point. Cf. Shankar Goyal, 'Chandragupta II's Relations with the Vākāṭakas during the Regency of Prabhāvatīguptā', in *Proceedings of the South Indian History Congress*, Twenty-fourth Annual Session, Calicut, 2004, pp. 128-32.

[6] For a full discusion on the identity of the king mentioned in the Meharauli pillar inscription vide *King Chandra and the Meharauli Pillar*, eds. M.C. Joshi, S.K. Gupta and Shankar Goyal, Meerut, 1989, pp. 73-237.

[7] S. R. Goyal, *op. cit.*, 223-24; idem, *The Imperial Guptas*, pp. 315-17; idem, *A History of the Vākāṭaka-Gupta Relations*, Jodhpur, 2006, pp. 100-02.

to V.V. Mirashi, the term *vāsaka* here means *skandhāvāra* or *jayaskandhāvāra.* He opines that in the twenty-third year of his reign Pravarasena II was campaigning for victory over Madhya Pradesh and had occupied Tripurī. He has also connected this conjecture with the attack of the Pushyamitras.[8] But A.M. Shastri rejects this argument.[9] The remainder of the text on the plate forms the part of the genealogical account of the family well-known from other records.

7. YAWATMAL PLATES OF PRAVARASENA II, YEAR 26

Only two plates of this charter are available. They were rescued from a copper-smith of Yawatmal in Maharashtra. Its ring and the seal, like the rest of the plates (two or three), are missing. It was issued when Bāppadeva held the office of Senāpati. The Siwani and Wadgaon grants of Pravarasena II also inform us that Bāppadeva held the office of Senāpati respectively during the eighteenth and twenty-fifth years of his reign. The present record, therefore, indicates that he continued to enjoy this office during the twenty-sixth year as well. However, the present grant records only the renewal of an old grant. This is a rare instance of its kind in Vākāṭaka epigraphy, as all the remaining charters record fresh grants. Unfortunately, we have no information as to who was the original donor and what made it necessary to renew the grant. Further, this is the only example of the royal order in respect of the grant being addressed to the village as a whole, the rest of the charters contain orders addressed to government officials with jurisdiction over the granted villages and the administrative units of which they formed part. It is noticeable that the king's order regarding the grant recorded in the Pattan plates of Pravarasena II is also addressed to the village. But there it is described as headed by the Brāhmaṇas.

8. PAUNI PLATES OF PRAVARASENA II, YEAR 32

This set of four plates together with the ring on which they were strung and the seal were found at Pauni in the Bhandara district of Maharashtra. It was issued from Pravarapura when Mādhappa was Senāpati. As Mādhappa figures in the capacity of Senāpati in the Tigaon grant of the year 29 also, it would follow that he occupied this office at least from the twenty-ninth to the thirty-second year of Pravarasena II's reign. The importance of this record lies primarily in the fact that it supplies the latest date for the reign of Pravarasena II, that is, the thirty-second year.

[8] V.V. Mirashi, *Indological Research Papers*, Vol. I, Nagpur, 1982, p. 69.
[9] *VSH*, pp. 93-94.

9. MANDHAL PLATES OF PṚTHIVĪSHEṆA II, YEAR 2

The four plates bearing this record were recovered in the excavations at Mandhal. Before the discovery of these two grants, two copper plate inscriptions of Pṛthivīsheṇa II were known, namely the Balaghat and Mahurjhari plates. The present grant is the earliest dated record of Pṛthivīsheṇa II. It was issued from Rāmagiristhāna which is not referred to in any other hitherto known Vākāṭaka inscriptions. The genealogy given in this record up to Pravarasena II is practically the same as met with in the earlier records of the family and only a small portion relating to Narendrasena and his son and successor, Pṛthivīsheṇa II, has been added. But no regal title is applied to Narendrasena who is merely described as Pravarasena's son. At the time this charter was issued Vishṇudatta held the office of Senāpati, while the inscription was written by Sarvadatta. Its seal-inscription, refers to Pṛthivīsheṇa II as the good son (*satsūnu*) of Narendrasena, master of the royal fortune of the Vākāṭakas and as eager for conquests, and speaks of his rule as victorious.

10. MANDHAL CHARTER OF PṚTHIVĪSHEṆA II, YEAR 10

This charter, incised on a set of four plates, was issued from Beṇṇātaṭasthāna in the tenth regnal year of Pṛthivīsheṇa II. It was written by Śaradatta when Vishṇudatta was Senāpati. The combined evidence of the present and the preceding records shows that Vishṇudatta continued to occupy this office from at least the second to at least the tenth year of Pṛthivīsheṇa II's reign. Here, the post-Pravarasena II genealogical account of the family is found in a fully developed form. The present inscription also affords a new dimension to the problem by offering the reading of the phrase *pūrvv-ādhigata-guṇavad-dāyād-āpahṛta-vaṁśa śriyaḥ* which indicates that Narendrasena had at first succeeded to his family fortune, viz. throne, but was subsequently deprived of it by a *dāyāda* or *dāyādas.* The word *dāyāda* primarily means 'heirs to property', i.e., sons or brothers in relation to each other with a claim to inheritance. If we adopt this meaning, it would follow that Narendrasena was divested of his kingdom (or a part thereof) by his co-sharers (brothers or other close relations) during the later part of his career. It would suggest that the death of Paravarasena II was followed by a struggle for succession in which his son (or one of his sons) Narendrasena was at first successful, but at a subsequent stage some other *dāyāda* got an upper hand and seized the family fortune. This grant states that commands of Narendrasena were obeyed by the rulers of Kosalā (Chhattisgadh region), Mekalā (Amarkantak area) and Mālava[10] (Malwa) in the present state of Madhya Pradesh. The

[10] According to S. R. Goyal, Mālava janapada of Rajasthan (*op.cit.*, p. 216).

claim in regard to Mekalā may be substantiated on the assumption that the Bamhani plates make a veiled allusion to Narendrasena and that Bharatabala, the Pāṇḍava chief of Mekalā and the issuer of Bamhani plates, was a vassal of Narendrasena.[11] This charter also describes Pṛthivīsheṇa II as *magna-vaṁś-oddhartṛ*, 'resurrector of the sunken family'. This phrase is repeated in his Mahurjhari plates also.

11. MAHURJHARI PLATES OF PṚTHIVĪSHEṆA II, YEAR 17

The five-plate set grant together with the ring on which it is strung was found in a field adjacent to the Mahurjhari village near Nagpur. It was issued from Pṛthivīsamudra by Pṛthivīsheṇa II under the supervision of Senāpati Ravidatta. In this record the donor, Pṛthivīsheṇa II, is described, as in his Mandhal record of the year 10, as *magna-vaṁś-oddharttṛ*, 'resurrector of the sunken family'.

RECENT INSCRIPTIONS OF THE VATSAGULMA BRANCH

12. HISSE-BORALA STONE-SLAB INSCRIPTION OF DEVASENA, ŚAKA 380

The slab bearing this four-line inscription was found near the village of Hisse-Borala in Akola district. There has been some controversy about the interpretation of the initial portion of the inscription which is considerably damaged due to the breakage of the portion of the slab bearing it. But its main contents and purport are fairly clear.

The epigraph begins with the specification of date which is first indicated astronomically with reference to the position of the Saptarshis or Seven Bears and then in the Śaka era. The reading and interpretation of the astronomical portion are highly uncertain and consequently a subject of a wide difference of opinion among scholars. But the subsequent mention of Śaka 380 (=458 A.D.) is beyond doubt.

The object of the epigraph was to record that a lake named Sudarśana was constructed by a certain Āryya Svāmilladeva, an obedient servant (*ājñākara*) of the Vākāṭaka king Devasena, for the benefit of all the creatures, in Śaka 380 (=458 A.D.). This is the only lithic record and, for that matter, the only complete original inscription of Devasena, the penultimate member of the Vatsagulma branch, and by virtue of specifying a date in Śaka era, provides the so far only definite date in the history of the Vākāṭakas, for the rest of the Vākāṭaka records are dated in the years of individual reigns. It seems that Svāmilladeva, who was responsible for getting this inscription engraved and, of course, for the excavation of the (Sudarśana) lake mentioned in it, hailed from Gujarat where the Śaka era had been in use ever since its initiation. Be

[11] *Ibid.*

that as it may, the Hisse-Borala inscription provides a firm date for the chronology of the Vākāṭakas in general and of the Vatsagulma branch in particular. The naming of the newly constructed lake as Sudarśana is interesting. It may be recalled that the tank mentioned in the Ramtek Prabhāvatī memorial inscription was also given this name.[12]

13. BIDAR PLATES OF DEVASENA, YEAR 5

The original copper plates bearing this important record together with the ring which held them together as well as its seal are no longer traceable. But the original set was reportedly brought to an artist of Bidar by some villager of the Bidar district of Karnataka who, however, did not want to part with it. But the artist, realizing its historical and resultant monetary value, prepared its exact replica on iron plates of the same size and thickness with holes for the ring, as well as the seal, and sold it to the Birla Archaeological and Cultural Research Institute, Hyderabad, where it is presently deposited. The iron reproduction is so faithful, A.M. Shastri points out,[13] that it looks just like a xerox copy of present-day paper documents, and there is absolutely no reason to doubt its genuineness. Even otherwise no other complete copper plate charter of Devasena is known which could be used as the model so that there can be no question of anyone venturing a counterfeit.

The Bidar grant was issued from Vatsagulma (modern Wasim or Basim), the capital of the Vatsagulma branch of the Vākāṭakas, to which the issuer belonged. Its genealogical account begins with Vindhyaśakti (I) who is described as the first (*ādi*) *Dharma-mahārāja* of the Vākāṭakas. This account bears a close similarity to that found in the Thalner plates of Harisheṇa and apparently the former forms the basis of the latter. Vindhyaśakti's son Pravarasena I is described in the same manner as in the Wasim and Thalner plates including the application of the titles *Hāritīputra* and *Dharma-mahārāja.* Next mentioned are his son Sarvasena and Vindhyasena (the same as Vindhyaśakti II), Pravarasena (II) and Sarvasena, each succeeding king being the son of the preceding one. All these rulers are given the regal title Mahārāja, while the apparently more dignified title *Dharma-mahārāja* is reserved only for Vindhyaśakti I, Pravarasena I and Devasena, the issuer of this charter. The last named ruler is described, rather strangely, as the great-grandson of the son of Pravarasena's son, great-grandson of Sarvasena's son, grandson of Vindhyasena's son, grandson of Pravarasena and son of Sarvasena and is styled *Dharma-mahārāja.* This decription is met with in a summarized form in his son's Thalner grant.

[12] Shankar Goyal, 'Some Observations on the Ramtek Prabhāvatīguptā Memorial Fragmentary Stone Inscription', in *Proceedings of the Twenty-sixth Annual Session of the South Indian History Congress*, Bangalore, 2006, p. 26.

[13] *VSH*, p. 108.

The present record is Devasena's only known complete official record. Further, if it originally belonged to the Bidar region, it would indicate an extension of the dominions of the Vatsagulma branch of the Vākāṭakas into northern Karnataka. Only a little more southwardly expansion was needed so as to reach the Bidar region of Karnataka. The conjecture is supported by the Mudigere (Chikmagalur district, Karnataka) plates of the Kadamba king Siṁhavarman issued in his fifth regnal year which tell us that he was anointed by Sarvasena-mahārāja who was most likely no other than Sarvasena II of the Vatsagulma branch of the Vākāṭakas.[14]

14. THALNER GRANT OF HARISHEṆA, YEAR 3

A set of three plates on which this charter is incised along with the ring but without the seal were acquired by a copper-smith from a resident of Thalner in the Dhule district. It is the only known official record of Harisheṇa. Its genealogical account differs from its counterparts in other records in contents and nature. Like the above-mentioned Bidar grant the Thalner plates begin their account with Vindhyaśakti I describing him as the first (*ādi*) *dharma-mahārāja* of the Vākāṭakas. It seems as if Vindhyaśakti, who was ignored by all the earlier members of the dynasty whose records have come to us, was remembered reverentially, for some unknown reason during the reign of its last two kings. After him the Thalner plates describe Paravarasena I. But thereafter they skip over a number of the members of the Vatsagulma branch including Sarvasena I and his son Vindhyaśakti II, who is known from his Wasim plates (which for the first time brought this branch of the dynasty to light). In a strange manner it describes Harisheṇa, the donor, as the great-grandson of the grandson of the son of Pravarasena I, grandson of Sarvasena and son of Devasena. This description agrees with the genealogy reconstructed with the help of the Wasim plates of Vindhyaśakti II, the Bidar grant of Devasena and the Ajanta Cave XVI inscription of Harisheṇa's minister Varāhadeva. However, the name of Devasena's father, which was lost in the Ajanta inscription, is supplied by this record as well as the Bidar plates. He was Sarvasena whom we may call Sarvasena II in order to differentiate him from Sarvasena I, the founder of this branch of the Vākāṭakas. It is interesting to note that the titles *Dharma-mahārāja* and *Hāritīputra* are applied only to Pravarasena I, while his father Vandhyaśakti I is given only the first title. The rest of the kings including Harisheṇa are styled simply as *Mahārāja.*[15]

The executor of the grant was Svāmiladeva and it was written by Boppadeva. Whether this Svāmiladeva is to be identified with Svāmilladeva

[14] S. R. Goyal, *op.cit.*, p. 219.
[15] *Ibid.*, p. 220.

known as an officer of Devasena from the Hisse-Borala inscription and Bidar plates, cannot be determined. But the possibility cannot be ruled out.[16] Similarly, Boppadeva of the present grant may or may not be identified with Bāppadeva of the other inscription.[17]

[16] *Ibid.*

[17] Shankar Goyal, *175 Years of Vākāṭaka History and Historiography*, Jodhpur, 2009, p. 44.

THREE

The Ramtek Prabhāvatīguptā Memorial Fragmentary Stone Inscription

The Ramtek Prabhāvatīguptā memorial fragmentary inscription discovered a few years ago is of immense value for the history of the Vākāṭakas, a great power of the Deccan. It was found engraved on two rectangular blocks of stone inside the *maṇḍapa* of the Kevala-Narasiṁha temple at Ramtek, usually identified with the famous Rāmagiri, mentioned in the *Meghadūta* of Kālidāsa. A.P. Jamkhedkar[1], Hans Bakker[2], Harunaga Isaacson[3], A.M. Shastri[4] and S.R. Goyal[5] were the first scholars to study it.[6]

The record belongs to the reign of the Vākāṭaka king Pravarasena II and purports to record most likely the erection of the Kevala-Narasiṁha temple with the image of the man-lion (Narasiṁha)manifestation of Vishṇu by a daughter (name lost) of Prabhāvatīguptā to commemorate the latter.

The extant portion of the Ramtek Prabhāvatīguptā memorial inscription reads thus :[7]

[1] A.P. Jamkhedkar, 'A Newly Discovered Vākāṭaka Temple at Ramtek, District Nagpur', in *Shri C. Sivaramamurti Commemoration Volume*, ed. M.S. Nagaraja Rao, Delhi, 1987, pp. 217-23.

[2] Hans Bakker, *Ramtek*, Leiden, 1989, pp. 93-94; idem, 'The Antiquities of Ramtek Hill, Maharashtra', in *South Asian Studies*, V, 1989, pp. 79-102.

[3] Hans Bakker and Harunaga Isaacson, 'The Ramtek Inscriptions II : The Vākāṭaka Inscription in the Kevala-Narasiṁha Temple', in *BSOAS*, LVI, Part I, 1993, pp. 46-74.

[4] A.M. Shastri, *Early History of Deccan : Problems and Perspectives*, Delhi, 1987, Ch.5; idem, *Vākāṭakas — Sources and History*, New Delhi, 1997, pp. 125-35.

[5] S.R. Goyal, *Ancient Indian Inscriptions : Recent Finds and New Interpretations*, Jodhpur, 2005, pp. 221-25.

[6] On this, also see Shankar Goyal, 'The Ramtek Inscription', in *Epigraphic Studies*, Select Papers from the Panel on Epigraphy at the 16th World Sanskrit Conference, 2015, Sanskrit Studies Centre, Silpakorn University, Bangkok, Thailand, ed. D.P. Dubey, New Delhi, 2018, pp. 129-37.

[7] After S.R. Goyal.

1. [ज] यति सजलाम्बुदोदरो......मिति... चे समयैवि (र्वि)ताङ्गत...भयलोलदृष्टिर्मूं (र्ध्ना)...जमिस...
2. -प्रभवोद्गतवादेपि....प्योत्तमाङ्गैर्ब्बलयो [ऽ] क्रियन्त....चूडामणिभिर्नृ..... [तस्या] टवीप्रान्त....
3. - देवतेव प्रतिपूज्य...विचिन्त्य...वृद्धि....लस्य प्राज्याज्य [सि] क्तस्य शिखे [व]...... तां.....नाभ्युन्म [ता].....
4. तयो: क्रमादाह तल....प्रजाते.....न्विते....श्री [च] न्द्र...... [चा] मुण्डां नाम्नी [म्नीं] तन [यां]..... ल [दो] मि....
5. सदैव देवस्त्रिसमुद्रनाथस्स चन्द्रगुप्त:....र्ण्ण....प्त:....श्रीरु [द्र] सेनाय.......
6. सुदुर्ग्रहां राज्यधुरं समग्रां धुरन्धर [स्य]..... [सु] पुङ्गवस्य........ [घ] टोत्कचो नाम सुतो ...... मङ्गानल
7. ताम्भागिनेयीमथराजराजो दृ [ष्ट्वा] ..... वेश्मल [क्ष्मीं]..... [अ*] पास्य पाणिग्रहणं च [कार*] ..... देवेन्द्र त [नया*]—
8. शुद्धैर्वचोभिर्विदुषां म.... म्बुरुहेक्षणा..... [भू] न्धनौधैर्यशसा च लोकान्।......
9. तस्मिन्कदाचित्कमनीयरूपे ......[त] पुरन्दरेण ...... [प्समानां] भ्रातां बलात्तां गृह मानिना [य].....
10. तत्रैव यान्यान्मनुजेन्द्रपुत्री.... सवानका [र्षीत्*] ......यं....भागमेतं....
11. प्रभावतिस्वामिनं लोकना [थ] म [र्था] पुण्या (ण्य) मक्षयमुद्दिश्य ....जगदुत्त [म ? मि मं ?]...
12. सुदर्शनं तडागं च देवश्चैव सुदर्शनम् कदलीवाटकग्रामे कारयिता ...... वती..... तक्रेता पुण्यमुद्दिश्य
13. अर्ध्दं ब्रह्मार्पणं पुण्यं मातापितृभ्यो..... क्रयोद्भवम्॥ जगत्स्थिति सङ्हा (संहा) रकारणस्यामितो....
14. प्रासादं दयिता मातुर्विचिन्त्य तमशाश्वतम् मातुरेवसमुद्दिश्य पुण्यौधमधवर्ज्जिता। तिलात्तैलसङ्काश [चिराय].....
15. आलोकस्थायिनीं चैमाङ्कीर्तिम्प्रख्यापयिष्यता (न्त्या) तया .... गृही [तानं] तदाज्ञानुति वा [चिता ?] काष्य [ा ?] ज्जय.....

The Ramtek inscription is highly fragmentary. Its opening stanza is most probably an invocation to the man-lion (Narasiṁha) form of Vishṇu. The third stanza refers to a sovereign monarch whose feet were touched by the crest-jewels (*chūḍāmaṇi*) of numerous kings which served as his footstool (*pāda-pīṭha*). The description is obviously of the Gupta emperor Chandragupta II Vikramāditya who is mentioned by name in verse 9. The fifth stanza perhaps refers to his queen (name lost), most probably Kuberanāgā, mother of Prabhāvatīguptā. We learn from verse 7 that after sons (Sanskrit plural implying at least three) had been born to them (that is to Chandragupta II and Kuberanāgā) in succession, their younger sister was born whose name ended in *muṇḍā.* In case she was identical with Prabhāvatī it will have to be presumed that her name was changed after her marriage. It is also likely that she was different from Prabhāvatī who was married to the Vākāṭaka king Rudrasena II.

Verse 9 of the Ramtek record refers to Chandragupta (evidently Chandragupta II Vikramāditya) who had 'perfect character' (*paripūrṇa-vṛtta*), a 'god of gods' (*dai (de) va-deva*) and, what is most important historically, 'the lord of the three oceans' (*tri-samudra-nātha*). This stanza also seems to have contained a reference to the giving by Chandragupta II of his daughter to Rudrasena II in marriage. The name of this daughter, according to the Vākāṭaka records, was Prabhāvatīguptā.

The record next mentions some person who is described as bearing the entire burden of the great kingdom which was difficult to bear and as the best of the beasts of burden. He was obviously Chandragupta II who is believed to have looked after the Vākāṭaka kingdom after the death of his son-in-law Rudrasena II. Next is mentioned Chandragupta II's son Ghaṭotkacha, who is styled as 'Rājarāja' or 'king of kings'. The facts that he is mentioned after the reference to the marriage of probably Prabhāvatī, and after a gap of a stanza (verse 10) may perhaps indicate that he was born after the birth of Prabhāvatī (or after her marriage) and perhaps of a different queen. Verse 13, which is almost fully preserved, refers to his (Ghaṭotkacha's) sister's daughter (*bhāgineyī*), i.e. niece, and her marriage. She is described as the goddess of her house (*veśma-lakshmī*). Ghaṭotkacha is said to have done something about her marriage. The statement of the inscription (*pāṇigrahaṇam chakāra*) literally means that he actually married her. Such marriages were highly abhored in north India but were quite common (as they are at present) to the south of the Narmadā. As it is possible that Ghaṭotkacha was born after Prabhāvatī (how long after, one cannot say) or after her marriage there could have been no objection on the ground of the difference in his age and the age of his niece. Moreover, the possibility that his mother was different from Kuberanāgā, the mother of Prabhāvatī, might have made such a marriage somewhat easier. Be that as it may, this marriage must have strengthened the friendly relations of the two great ruling families.

Verses 14-16 of the Ramtek inscription probably referred to Ghaṭotkacha, and of these first and last are almost lost for historical purposes. The next verse most probably alludes to Ghaṭotkacha's death after which the brother of his wife (obviously Pravarasena II) brought back his widowed sister to his own house 'forcibly' (*balāt*).

After sometime another calamity took place. It was the death of Prabhāvatīguptā which must have occurred sometime after the twenty-third year of Pravarasena II's reign (the date of his Tirodi inscription, when he performed a pious act for his mother's merit). This event must have been described in verse 20 which is now completely lost. The next stanza refers to a pious act performed by the widow of Ghaṭotkacha in memory of her dead mother which was the execution of an image of 'the lord of the universe' (*loka-nātha*) and the erection of the temple christened Prabhāvatīsvāmin for housing it. The inscription next speaks of the excavation of a tank called Sudarśana. The rest of the contents of the inscription are not of much political importance.

The temple mentioned in this record was erected after Prabhāvatīguptā's demise by her daughter (name unknown) with the object of perpetuating her mother's memory. Now we learn from the Tirodi plates of her son Pravarasena II that she was alive at least up to his twenty-third regnal year. As, according to the Tumain inscription, till 435 A.D. Ghatoṭkachagupta was the governor of East Malwa under Kumāragupta I, his assumption of the title 'Rājarāja' (Emperor) (which he could do only after raising the banner of revolt against Kumāragupta I), the suppression of his revolt, his death and the bringing back of his widowed Vākāṭaka wife by her brother 'forcibly' (*balāt*), must have taken place in the years following 435 A.D. It was after all these events that the death of Prabhāvatī took place.

Thus, the testimony of the extant portions of this highly fragmentary record clarify and elaborate numerous points of the Gupta-Vākāṭaka relations and the history of the Deccan. It makes it clear that Chandragupta indeed looked after the Vākāṭaka administration during the minority of Prabhāvatīguptā's sons.[8] It also shows that he was believed to have been a *Tri-samudra-nātha* (Lord of Three Oceans), a claim which, on the one hand, indicates that for sometime he exercised at least nominal suzerainty over the Vākāṭaka kingdom including almost whole of the Deccan and, on the other, tends to strengthen the testimony of the Meharauli record regarding the warlike activities of Chandra (generally identified with Chandragupta II) in south India.[9] The inscription also gives highly significant and interesting information that Ghaṭotkachagupta, a son of Chandragupta II, married his own niece (*bhāgineyī*) and obviously with the help of his Vākāṭaka in-laws revolted against the authority of his brother Kumāragupta I to whom he was owing allegiance till 435 A.D., the date of his Tumain inscription. The inscription also alludes to a reference that Ghaṭotkacha assumed the imperial title 'Rājarāja' obviously after raising the banner of revolt against Kumāragupta I. The fact that after his death his Vākāṭaka wife was forcibly (*balāt*) rescued by her brother and brought to the Vākāṭaka capital shows that the hand of the Vākāṭakas was behind the revolt of Ghaṭotkachagupta.

[8] However, the epigraphic evidence cited in support of the Gupta influence on the Vākāṭakas does not prove the point. Cf. Shankar Goyal, 'Chandragupta II's Relations with the Vākāṭakas during the Regency of Prabhāvatīguptā', in *Proceedings of the South Indian History Congress*, Twenty-fourth Annual Session, Calicut, 2004, pp. 128-32.

[9] For a full discusion on the identity of the king mentioned in the Meharauli pillar inscription vide *King Chandra and the Meharauli Pillar*, eds. M.C. Joshi, S.K. Gupta and Shankar Goyal, Meerut, 1989, pp. 73-237.

FOUR

The Myth of the Vākāṭaka Coins

The Vākāṭakas were the greatest political power in the Deccan and central India in the fourth and fifth centuries A.D.[1] It is generally believed that they launched their political career somewhere in the Vindhyan region of Madhya Pradesh.[2] Later on, they shifted southwards as there was no scope for expansion in the north because of the growing power of the imperial Guptas and the Nāgas while in the Deccan there was no such potential power at that time. They carved out, in course of time, a substantial kingdom comprising the area of Madhya Pradesh to the south of the river Narmadā (viz., Betul-Chhindwara and Siwani-Balaghat region),[3] the Vidarbha-Khandesh-Marathwada region of Maharashtra and, perhaps, also some area of northern Karnataka in the proximity of Bidar,[4] the last one at a comparatively later stage of their career. Their neighbours, with whom they maintained more or less good,

[1] We, however, do not agree with the view of A. M. Shastri that the Vākāṭakas rose to power *with a pan-India image and impact* during the fourth-fifth centuries A.D. Cf. his *Vākāṭakas—Sources and History* (henceforth *VSH*), New Delhi, 1997, pp. 136, 149, 213. On this, also see Shankar Goyal, *The Classical Age : A Study in Feudalization*, New Delhi, 2022, Ch. 3.

[2] In a few Purāṇas the Vākāṭakas are mentioned along with central Indian dynasties and are styled as Vindhyakas or 'the Vindhyan people'. The first king of the dynasty is called by the meaningful name Vindhyaśakti, 'as powerful as the Vindhyas'.Cf. F. E. Pargiter, *The Purāṇa Text of the Dynasties of the Kali Age*, Oxford, 1913, Reprint, Varanasi, 1962, p. 50.

[3] As pointed out by A. M. Shastri, initially (up to the time of Pṛthivīsheṇa I) they controlled the Vindhyan region of Madhya Pradesh as well (*VSH*, p. 178).

[4] A copper-plate record of Devasena, the penultimate member of theVatsagulma branch of the dynasty, has been reported from Bidar and appears to record the grant of a village situated nearby. For details about this record cf. A.M. Shastri, *Early History of the Deccan : Problems and Perspectives*, Delhi, 1987, pp. 71-74.

but sometimes hostile relations during the course of their rule, included the imperial Guptas and the Nāgas in the north,[5] the Vishṇukuṇḍins in the eastern Deccan[6] and the Kadambas in the western Deccan.[7] According to some, they were at first on hostile terms with the Early Rāshṭrakūṭas of southern Maharashtra which later changed into cordiality.[8]

Excepting the Early Rāshṭrakūṭas, the neighbours of the Vākāṭakas, and also some other contemporary powers, some of them quite unimportant, are known to have left significant numismatic evidence of their regimes. Of them, the coins of the Guptas are numerous and varied in nature,[9] while the coins of the Nāgas,[10] Ikshvākus,[11] Vishṇukuṇḍins,[12] Kadambas,[13] Traikūṭakas, Bodhis[14] and Nalas,[15] are not so numerous and are artistically much inferior.

Till recently no coins of the Vākāṭakas themselves were known and

[5] In fact, there are only two matrimonial alliances involving the marriages of the Nāga and the imperial Gupta princesses with two Vākāṭaka kings that are mentioned in the inscriptions of the main branch. Yet another matrimonial alliance involving the marriage of a Vākāṭaka princess with a Gupta prince is known from the recently discovered Ramtek Prabhāvatīgyptā Memorial Stone Inscription in which it is said that Ghaṭotkachagupta, a son of Chandragupta II, married a daughter of his sister Prabhāvatīguptā (*bhāgineyī*), i.e. his own niece. However, the name of the mother of Ghaṭotkachagupta as well as of his Vākāṭaka wife are not known.

[6] Many Vishṇukuṇḍin inscriptions aver that king Vikramendravarman I had adorned by his birth the twin families of the Vishṇukuṇḍins and the Vākāṭakas.

[7] That the Kadamba king Siṁhavarman was anointed by the Vākāṭaka king Sarvasena II has been clearly stated in his Mudigere copper-plate grant of his fifth regnal year.

[8] V.V. Mirashi, *Corpus Inscriptionum Indicarum*, Vol. V : *Inscriptions of the Vākāṭakas*, Ootacamund, 1963, Intro., p. xxv.

[9] A.S. Altekar, *Catalogue of the Gupta Gold Coins in the Bayana Hoard*, Bombay, 1954; idem, *The Coinage of the Gupta Empire*, Banaras, 1957; S. R. Goyal, *An Introduction to Gupta Numismatics*, Jodhpur, 1994; Shankar Goyal, 'A.S. Altekar and the Bayana Hoard', *JNSI*, LXVII, 2005, pp. 80-84.

[10] H. V. Trivedi, *Catalogue of the Coins of the Nāga Kings of Padmāvatī*, Gwalior, 1957.

[11] R. Subrahmanyam, *A Catalogue of the Ikshvāku Coins in the Andhra Pradesh Government Museum*, Hyderabad, 1962.

[12] M. Rama Rao, *Vishṇukuṇḍin Coins in the Andhra Pradesh Government Museum*, Hyderabad, 1963.

[13] Cf. *VSH*, p. 136.

[14] E. J. Rapson, *Catalogue of the Coins of the Āndhra Dynasty, the Western Kṣatrapas, the Traikūṭaka Dynasty and the "Bodhi" Dynasty*, New Delhi, Reprint, 1975, pp. clviii-clix.

[15] 'The Edenga Hoard', cf. *JNSI*, I, pp. 29-30.

it was believed that they did not issue their own coins.[16] But of late A.M. Shastri (1990 and 1992), A. H. Siddiqui (1996) and Prashant P. Kulkarni (2001-2002) have claimed to have read on some small coins in base metal, with copper predominating, the broken legends such as *(Śrī-Ma)hārāja Pṛthivī*,[17] *(Na) rendra*,[18] *Jaya*,[19] *Vṛddhi*,[20] *Vṛddhaḥ*,[21] *Sarva(sena)*,[22]

[16] Among early historians it was only K. P. Jayaswal (*History of India : c. 150 A.D. to 350 A.D.*, Lahore, 1933, pp. 71-73, Pl. III) who believed that the Vākāṭakas had issued their own coins. He attributed some coins of north Indian fabric to the Vākāṭakas. The coin with the legend *Pravarasenasya* bears, according to Jayaswal, the date 76, and that having the legend *Rudra*, the date 100. Jayaswal referred these dates to the so-called Kalachuri-Chedi era commencing in 248 A.C., which, according to him, was really started by the Vākāṭakas. But Jayaswal's readings and interpretations have been disputed by other scholars. A. S. Altekar (*JNSI*, V, pp. 130-31) has shown that the coin attributed to Pravarasena is really of Vīrasena. The symbols which Jayaswal supposed to be the date 76 are really the branches of a tree in railing. As for the coins of Rudrasena I,what he took to be the letters *Rudra* is really the *triratna* symbol. The symbol supposed to denote the date 100 is clearly a *svastika*. As pointed out by V.V. Mirashi also (*op. cit.*,p. xiv), if Jayaswal's readings of the legends and dates and the identification of the era are correct, these coins may indicate the extension of the Vākāṭaka rule north of the Vindhyas during the reigns of the early Vākāṭaka rulers Pravarasena I and Rudrasena I. Again, even supposing that the readings of the dates on these coins are correct, they can not be referred to the era of 248 A.C. That era was not started by the Vākāṭakas and has not been used in dating any Vākāṭaka grants. All inscriptions of the Vākāṭakas are dated in regnal years. As a matter of fact, the era was introduced in Vidarbha after the downfall of the Vākāṭakas. Thus, according to Altekar and Mirashi, these coins can not be attributed to any Vākāṭaka king. Cf. Shankar Goyal, *The Classical Age : A Study in Feudalization*, pp. 72 ff.

[17] A. M. Shastri, 'Unique Coin of Vākāṭaka Pṛithivīsheṇa (II ?)', in *Indian Coin Society Newsletter*, No. 4, Nagpur, October 1990, p. 2.

[18] A.M. Shastri (ed.), *The Age of the Vākāṭakas*, New Delhi, 1992, pp. 287-88. Some copper coins of Narendrasena in the collection of R. C. Thakur have also been reported recently (H. D. Pathak and R. C. Thakur, 'Rare Variety Coins of Vākāṭaka Dynasty', *JNSI*, LXVII, 2005, pp. 85-87). These are found from Ujjain and Mahidapur which was included in the territory of the Vākāṭakas. According to Pathak and Thakur, the availability of the full legend *Narendra* on these coins removes the doubts of Shastri. Prashant P. Kulkarni also refers to a paper of Ellen M. Raven which brings to light a coin of Narendrasena with a better legend ('Coins of the Vākāṭakas', *Numismatic Digest*, Vol. 25-26, 2001-2002, p. 70).

[19] Shastri, *op. cit.*, p. 289.

[20] *Ibid.*, After A. M. Shastri Pathak and Thakur (*op. cit.*, pp. 85-86) have also claimed to have acquired some copper coins of *jaya* and *vṛddhi* legends which, according to them, were used for Pṛthivīsheṇa.

[21] *Ibid.*, pp. 289-90.

[22] A. H. Siddiqui, in *Oriental Numismatic Studies*, Vol. I,1996, pp. 99-105. But, according to Devendra Handa, the Editor of the Journal, "The coins attributed to the

Vijhasāti,[23] and *Pravara(se) nasya rā(jya ?).*[24] The coins published by Shastri have reportedly been found in the Wardha region which was included in the kingdom of the main branch of the dynasty and especially from Paunar which is believed to represent the site of their later capital, Pravarapura. The coins reported by Siddiqui were found in Nanded district and those of Kulkarni have been found from Paunar and Yawatmal regions respectively. Then, there are some other uniface coins found in Paunar, which appear to be closely allied with the coins attributed to the Vākāṭakas in respect of fabric and devices, but do not contain any legends.[25] Further, the discovery of the Vākāṭaka lead coins of two denominations from Paunar have also been reported recently.[26]

We, however, beg to differ with these scholars and believe that the Vākāṭakas did not strike any coins at all.

(1) We do not find any reference, direct or otherwise, to the Vākāṭaka coins in their fairly numerous inscriptions. Not that these inscriptions did not have any occasion to mention them; they could refer them in connection with the land-grants recorded in them. There is no reference to the coins of the Vākāṭakas in the inscriptions of the contemporary dynasties also.

(2) There is not a single word mentioning the Vākāṭaka coins in the contemporary literature and in the literature of the succeeding ages.

(3) The coins attributed to the Vākāṭakas have been studied by the above mentioned scholars with the help of those photographs only which were supplied to them by the coin-collectors; nobody seems to have ascertained whether these photographs are doctored or genuine. We have seen the photographs along with the paper entitled 'Vākāṭaka Coins from Washim Excavation' by Pradip Meshram and B. S. Gajbhiye submitted to the 90th Annual Conference of the Numismatic Society of India held at Santiniketan from December 1-3,2006, one of which seemed to us patently doctored. Here we would like to submit that for obvious reasons one should take the claim of the coin-collectors about the antiquity and genuineness of ancient coins in their possession with a grain of salt.

Vākāṭakas in this paper (of Siddiqui) do not admit of averred readings and differ in fabric, devices and palaeography from the Vākāṭaka coins published by Professor Shastri. ... The author has recalled Sebaka coins for similarities but seems to have missed the palaeographic evidence to consider the coins under consideration as the Vākāṭaka coins" (Editorial Note, p. 105). Also see Shankar Goyal, *Ancient Indian Numismatics : A Historiographical Study*, Jodhpur, 1998, pp. 183-84.

[23] Kulkarni, *op. cit.*, pp. 66-69.

[24] *Ibid.*, pp. 69-70.

[25] Shastri, *op. cit.*, p. 290.

[26] Kulkarni, *op. cit.*, pp. 74-75.

(4) As the coins, under discussion, bear no clear legend displaying the full name of any Vākāṭaka ruler, it will always remain debatable whether they may be indubitably attributed to the Vākāṭakas; legends and devices of these coins are only subtle, not definite, pointers to the identity of their issuers.

There is a marked difference in the attitudes of Shastri and Kulkarni on this problem. While reading the legends Shastri observed that "even though the Vākāṭakas had issued their own coins in cheap metals, earlier and contemporary costly metal coins also must have been in use for costlier transactions",[27] whereas, while referring to Shastri's readings, Kulkarni, opines that "as no coin bears a clear legend displaying the full name of any Vākāṭaka ruler; it was always debatable whether these coins could be attributed to the Vākāṭakas authoritatively"[28] and "now that a coin has come to light bearing the full name of the Vākāṭaka ruler Pravarasena, this wait has finally ended."[29] It is interesting to note that here Kulkarni himself doubts the readings of Shastri and claims that his own reading has finally settled the issue.

However, even if Shastri's conclusion is accepted the main question still remains unanswered, for we remain in the dark about those Vākāṭaka coins that served the purpose of costlier transactions in their kingdom. After all, what happened to them if at all they were issued ? Scholars like Shastri and Kulkarni adopt two contradictory positions : On the one hand, they opine that the Vākāṭaka period truly represented the classical or golden age, and on the other,explain the non-availability of their costlier coinage by arguing that earlier and contemporary costly metal coins were in circulation in the Vākāṭaka kingdom and they served the purpose of their costlier dealings. We, however, think that this whole reasoning is illogical. The conventional definition of a classical age is one where political culture, literature, architecture and fine arts reach a high level of excellence to form a standard for later times.[30] From this point of view there is nothing to prove that the Vākāṭaka period may be regarded as the golden age. Usually the age of the imperial Guptas is equated with the classical age of India but characteristics of their age such as the imperial ideal of the *chakravartin* rulers, the cultural florescence when norms or standard of values were laid down in different walks of life and the Smṛti law which formed the basis of socio-political organisation, were absent in the kingdom of the Vākāṭakas.

[27] *VSH*, p. 144.
[28] Kulkarni, *op. cit.*, p. 65.
[29] *Ibid.*
[30] Romila, Thapar, *A History of India*, Vol. I, New Delhi, 1966, p. 157.

As is well known, even silver and gold coins of the Vākāṭakas have not been found so far. Not only that the copper coins attributed to them are artistically inferior, minute in size, irregular in shape and light in weight. For a dynasty which ruled the Deccan for more than 250 years and the neighbour of which were the mighty imperial Guptas, who produced abundant coins in every type of metal, this fact is not easy to digest. This situation forced Shastri and Kulkarni not to elaborate their views on this issue.[31] Specially on the basis of the Mahāyāna caves of Ajanta and Śaiva sculptures of Mansar and Mandhal they think so. But all this must be seen as the extension of the Gupta influence on the Vākāṭaka territory. That this cultural florescence had its origins in the influence of the Gupta kings is also conceded by Walter M. Spink.[32] However, his observation that Indian classical culture reached the very highest point in its development during the reign of Harisheṇa who ruled from c. 460 to 477 A.D. is not correct as by the early years of his rule the Gupta dynasty was already on the course of disintegration.[33] Here he conveniently forgets that the traditions of any culture never die immediately; it takes centuries to loosen their impact in society. As shown by us elsewhere,[34] a cultural trend might have a long history before it finally emerges in a definite form and likewise might continue to exist in a changed form for some time even after it apparently ceased to exist. That being so, we may concede that the age of the Guptas marked the efflorescence and culmination of earlier tendencies many of which go back to the Maurya period and that much of its glory continued for about two centuries more after the fall of the Gupta empire. Similar is the view of Romila Thapar who in a recent study opines that "the classicism of the Gupta period is not an innovation emanating from Gupta rule but the culmination of a process that began earlier."[35] She is also of the view that in the Deccan and south India it was the post-Gupta period that saw the evolution of a high level of civilization.[36] We, therefore, feel that the observations of Shastri and Kulkarni are their wishful thinking only and nothing else; a deliberate attempt to prove the existence of the Vākāṭaka coins ! The present state of our

[31] *VSH*, pp. 137, 213 ; Kulkarni, *op. cit.*, p. 66.

[32] Walter M. Spink, 'The Vākāṭaka Caves at Ajanta and their Successors', in *Reappraising Gupta History for S. R. Goyal*, eds. B. Ch. Chhabra, P. K. Agrawala, Ashvini Agrawal and Shankar Goyal, New Delhi, 1992, p. 248.

[33] *Ibid.*

[34] Shankar Goyal, *Harsha : A Multidisciplinary Political Study*, Jodhpur, 2006, p. 239; idem, *The Classical Age : A Study in Feudalization*, p. 77.

[35] Romila Thapar, *The Penguin History of Early India*, New Delhi, 2003, p. 281.

[36] Thapar, *A History of India*, I, *op. cit.*, p. 136.

knowledge compels us to believe that the Vākāṭakas did not mint their own coins in any metal.[37] It is a well known fact that comparative paucity or complete non-availability of coins is generally taken as an indication of economic decline or backwardness.

The difficulty with Kulkarni seems to be that when he reads the legend of a coin he lets his imagination run wild and in his eagerness to suggest something which no one else had suggested earlier he overlooks other evidences which go against his suggestion. He has committed the same error here.[38] His theory of the existence of the Vākāṭaka coinage revolves around on a solitary copper coin, with the legend on the obverse and the humped bull on the reverse, which, according to him, belongs to Pravarasena II. The legend on this coin is in two lines and, though, the last two letters of both the lines are worn out, he restores it as *Pravara (se)/nasya rā(jya ?)*. But the legend of this coin may be interpreted differently. However, on the basis of his reading and device on the coin Kulkarni not only attributes all other copper and lead coins of questionable character, mentioned earlier, to the Vākāṭakas but also finds 'a common thread' in their execution.[39] After comparing the known weights of these coins he also finds that 'some metrology was intended' in making them.[40] Obviously, no comment is necessary on such observations. We would rather prefer to wait for some more discoveries of coins which may be attributed to the Vākāṭakas indubitably. But Kulkarni is keen to claim the credit of the discovery of the coins of the Vākāṭakas. Commenting on Shastri's reading of 1992 of the legend of a solitary copper coin of Pṛthivīsheṇa (II ?) he stated that "When Shastri wrote this paper the legned drawing was done by me and I felt that his eyesight was very weak at that time."[41] We take it as a most uncharitable comment on a scholar who is not alive. Mrs. Yogeshwari Shastri, the wife of late Professor A.M. Shastri, has told us that the eyesight of her husband did not deteriorate any further since the days he was a post-graduate student. We should also not forget that the eyesight of Shastri was good enough to read the inscriptions of the Vākāṭakas and other dynasties till he expired in 2002. Further, to the best of our knowledge, no numismatist of repute has

[37] For more details, see Shankar Goyal, *The Classical Age : A Study in Feudalization*, pp. 70-94; also, K. M. Shrimali, 'Some Aspects of the Economy of the Vākāṭakas', in Shastri (ed.), *op. cit.*, p.103.

[38] Cf. Shankar Goyal, 'Historiography of the Vākāṭaka-Gupta Relations', app. in S. R. Goyal, *A History of the Vākāṭaka-Gupta Relations*, Jodhpur, 2006, pp. 141-42.

[39] Kulkarni, *op. cit.*, p. 78.

[40] *Ibid.*, p. 75.

[41] *Ibid.*, p. 71. Shastri published this coin of Pṛthivīsheṇa (II ?) earlier in October 1990 also. Cf. fn. 17.

verified the genuineness of the coin attributed to Pravarasena II by Kulkarni. Therefore, if the name *(Śrī-Ma) hārāja Pṛthivī* is readable on the coin attributed by Shastri to Pṛthivīsheṇa and the coin indeed belongs to Pṛthivīsheṇa (I or II), Shastri should get the credit for discovering the first certain coin of a Vākāṭaka ruler, something which Kulkarni obviously does not like. Anyway, these two coins, even if the reading of their legends is accepted, can not conclusively prove that the Vākāṭakas had issued their own currency. After all, the question of the existence of the currency of an extensive kingdom, as the Vākāṭaka kingdom was, can not be decided by one or two copper coins.

But it can hardly be doubted that like any other state the Vākāṭaka kingdom also needed coins both in precious and non-precious metals. The coins in precious metals were needed for higher trade and land transactions. The inscriptions of the Vākāṭakas refer to such transactions. For example, the Indore plates of the twenty-third regnal year of Pravarasena II records the purchase and grant of half of a village (*vāṭaka*) by a merchant named Chandra.[42] The Ramtek fragmentary stone-slab inscription mentions the purchase of a piece of land by Prabhāvatīguptā's son for the construction of a temple called Prabhāvatīsvāmin and the excavation of a tank named Sudarśana in her memory.[43] Such transactions must have required costlier coins of silver or gold. Therefore, there could have been no paucity of silver coins in the Vākāṭaka kingdom. In ancient India coins issued continued to circulate in the market for centuries until they lost weight due to their use for a long time. It is a well known fact that punch-marked silver coins were in circulation till at least the early medieval period. They are referred to by the name *purāṇa* in inscriptions and literary works of the second century A.D.[44] and as *nīla-kāhāpaṇa* at least up to the fifth century A.D.[45] At a village called Chik Sandogi in the Kopal taluka of the Raichur district in Karnataka a hoard of 5,534 silver punch-marked coins was found in a copper pot bearing a Brāhmī label datable to about the third century A.D.[46] A hoard

[42] Mirashi, *op. cit.*, pp. 38-42; *VSH*, pp. 23-25.

[43] *VSH*, pp.125-35; S. R. Goyal, *Ancient Indian Inscriptions : Recent Finds and New Interpretatons*, Jodhpur, 2005, pp. 221-25.

[44] The name is mentioned in the Mathura inscription of the Kushāṇa king Huvishka and the *Manusmṛti* both of which are usually dated to the second century A.D.

[45] Buddhaghosha's *Samantapāsādikā* refers to the punch-marked silver coins as *nīla-kāhāpaṇa* for their bluish accumulation in course of time. Cf. C. D. Chatterjee, 'Some Numismatic Data in Pali Literature', *Buddhistic Studies*, ed. B. C. Law, Calcutta, 1931, Ch. XV; idem, 'Some New Numismatic Terms in Pali Texts', *Journal of the U. P. Historical Society*, VI, 1933, pp. 156-57.

[46] A. M. Shastri, his 'Presidential Address', *Proceedings of the Indian History Congress*, 1978, II, pp. 968-69; cf. also his *VSH*, p. 143.

of 440 silver punch-marked coins in association with an Indo-Sassanian coin in the Lucknow Museum show the popularity of these coins in the early medieval age.[47] V.S. Agrawala has very rightly concluded that the silver punch-marked coins and the *kārshāpaṇa* tradition continued right up to the medieval period.[48] The Sātavāhana silver coins might also have been in circulation in the Vākāṭaka territory as it was formerly under the Sātavāhanas. Quite a few Sātavāhana silver portrait coins have also been reported from Vidarbha.[49] The Western Kshatrapa coins were also highly valued and hoards and stray finds of these coins have been reported from various sties included in the Vākāṭaka kingdom. As far as Ranjangaon near Pune in Maharashtra, Petlurapalem in Andhra Pradesh and some places in Karnataka, hoards of Kshatrapa coins have been reported while stray coins and moulds for counterfeiting them have been reported from several ancient sites.[50] A treasure-trove of 36 silver coins of the Kshatrapas has also been reported from Dahigaon in the Malkapur taluka of district Buldhana in Maharashtra.[51] Further, the Gupta gold and silver issues must have been available in abundance. They have been reported from some sites in the Vākāṭaka territories, such as Harda (district Hoshangabad), Sakaur (district Damoh), Ganeshpur (district Jabalpur), Pattan (district Betul), Seoni (district Seoni), Ellichpur and Dhamori (district Amaravati), Khairtal (district Raipur), Tewar (district Jabalpur) and Bhandara (district Chanda).[52] The Traikūṭaka silver coins were also in use during this period as a hoard containing, *inter alia*, ten specimens of Dahrasena's coins has been reported at the village of Dahigaon in Malkapur taluka of the Buldhana district.[53] All these coins must have been in circulation during the Vākāṭaka period.

In view of the availability of these coins issued by earlier or contemporary dynasties, it is generally believed that the Vākāṭakas probably did not feel the necessity of issuing coins of their own in gold and silver. It is

[47] P. L. Gupta, 'Fabrication of Ancient Punch-Marked Coins', *Indian Numismatic Chronicle*, III, p. 133.

[48] V.S. Agrawala, 'Coin Data in Divyāvadāna', *Indian Numismatic Chronicle*, III, pp. 148-50.

[49] Cf. *VSH*, p. 146. Also see I. K. Sarma, *Coinage of the Sātavāhana Empire*, Delhi, 1980, pp. 37-38; Mala Dutta, *A Study of the Sātavāhana Coinage*, New Delhi, 1990, Chs.2 and 4; S. R. Goyal, *The Coinage of Ancient India*, Jodhpur, 1995, pp. 299-300, 310-14.

[50] *Ibid.*

[51] Cf. *Indian Archaeology—A Review*, 1972-73, p. 55.

[52] Bal Chandra Jain, *Inventory of the Hoards and Finds of Coins and Seals from Madhya Pradesh*, Varanasi, 1957, pp. 11-14; S. R. Goyal, *op. cit.*, p. 360.

[53] V. V. Mirashi, 'Dahigaon Hoard of Kshatrapa and Traikūṭaka Coins', *JNSI*, XXXV, pp. 118-22; idem, *Literary and Historical Studies in Indology*, Delhi, 1975, pp. 180-84.

also believed that they did not feel the need to issue coins in even cheap metals and the people of their kingdom depended for their day-to-day ordinary transactions on the coins of non-precious metals of the earlier and contemporary dynasties which they probably supplemented by the *cowrie*-currency as was done even in the Gupta empire. We know that the immediately preceding period was characterised by an extensive use of base metal coins for ordinary market transactions in the Deccan as in north India. We have the Sātavāhana base metal (copper, lead and potin) coins which have been found in thousands in the whole of the Deccan including the territory later occupied by the Vākāṭakas which has yielded enormous quantities of coins, especially in potin.[54] Further, the Kushāṇas and the Maghas as well as other ruling powers of northern India are known to have issued base metal specie on an extensive scale.[55] The Chinese traveller Fa-hien, who visited India during c.400-11 A.D., refers to heaps of *cowrie* shells in the markets of the cities of the Gupta empire.[56] Even if the Vākāṭakas had issued their own coins in cheap metals the coins of other dynasties in cheaper metals must also have been in circulation because the Vākāṭakas obviously did not issue a copious currency in cheaper metals either.

That the Vākāṭakas permitted the circulation of older or other contemporary currencies in their kingdom was conceded by A. M. Shastri. Writing the report on the coin finds from Pauni excavation in 1972 he had remarked, "It is likely that the Vākāṭakas, having no coins of their own, allowed the use of the coins issued by other contemporary dynasties such as the Western Kshatrapas, the Guptas and the Vishṇukuṇḍins."[57] In this context K. M. Shrimali argues that 'the archaeological evidence is against such a supposition', for 'Bhokardan, Arni, Pauni, Peddabankur, Dhulikatta, Ter, Malhar, Kahali, etc., have not yielded any noticeable evidence of the post-Sātavāhana settlements' and that there are no indications, at least in the present state of our knowledge, that the coins of the Sātavāhanas, Western Kshatrapas, Kushāṇas and Guptas, which have been reported from sites belonging to the Vākāṭaka territory, '*remained in circulation during the two centuries of the Vākāṭaka rule as well.*'[58] According to him, "a viable and meaningful explanation of this characteristic economic phenomenon of the reign of the Vākāṭakas, viz., the absence of money may

[54] *VSH*, p. 146; K. M. Shrimali, *op. cit.*, p.102; S. R. Goyal, *op. cit.*, pp. 299-300.

[55] *Ibid.*

[56] *Ibid.*

[57] In S.B. Deo and Jagatpati Joshi, *Pauni Excavations (1969-70)*, Nagpur, 1972, p. 34.

[58] Shrimali, *op. cit.*, p.103. Also see his 'Pattern of Settlements under the Vākāṭakas', *Proceedings of the Indian History Congress*, 44th Session, Burdwan, 1983, pp.101-12.

be sought in the large scale mechanism of land-grants, growth of small village settlements and relative non-urban economy."[59] Actually, these are very important conclusions of Shrimali drawn after a careful study of all the known Vākāṭaka inscriptions. But to argue for the total absence of money for such a dynasty, which ruled the Deccan and central India for about 250 years, does not seem reasonable. How could any dynasty function without currency ? Such a situation is not possible. Further, Shrimali himself recognises that earlier and other post-Sātavāhana powers 'have indeed left significant numismatic evidence of their regimes.'[60] Furthermore, the fact that the Vākāṭakas did not strike any coins is in itself a proof that earlier and other contemporary currencies were in circulation in their kingdom. His argument that there is no 'noticeable evidence' of the post-Sātavāhana settlements in some areas of the Vākāṭaka kingdom does not prove anything, for, as he himself believes, the territory under their jurisdiction 'comprised a vast land of over thirty districts of the present Madhya Pradesh, Maharashtra and Andhra Pradesh.'[61] Also, the list of the Vākāṭaka territories given by him is highly exaggerated and, going by the extant evidences, the Vākāṭakas had nothing to do with many of them.[62] However, as his inscriptional study suggests, there is no denying the fact that the Vākāṭaka rule in parts of central India and northern Deccan exhibits growth of small village settlements and relative decline of urban economy.[63] The genesis of this economic phenomenon may be sought in the large scale mechanism of land-grants of the Vākāṭakas most of which were given to the Brāhmaṇas.[64] While huge cash donations and gifts of cows, elephants, houses, etc., as well as donations of villages with privileges, are kown from the Sātavāhana inscriptions of the second century A.D.,[65] almost complete dissociation between money and land-grants that one notices in the Vākāṭaka inscriptions indicates the comparative paucity of coins during their rule. All the known Vākāṭaka grants which, 40/41 in number, record donations of at least 25 villages, of which

[59] *Ibid.*

[60] *Ibid.*

[61] *Ibid.*, p. 101.

[62] A. M. Shastri's 'Editorial Note' in Shrimali, *op. cit.*, p. 112, n. 4.

[63] For details cf.Shrimali, *op. cit.*, pp. 101-15; also see his *Agrarian Structure in Central India and the Northern Deccan (c. A.D. 300-500) : A Study of Vākāṭaka Inscriptions*, New Delhi, 1987, App. VII.

[64] *Ibid.*, p. 104; also Nandini Sinha Kapur, 'State Formation in Vidarbha : The Case of the Eastern Vākāṭakas', *The Indian Historical Review*, XXXII, 2, July 2005, pp. 21-25.

[65] Nasik cave inscriptions of Gautamīputra Sātakarṇi (years 18 and 24=c. 124 and c. 130 A.D. respectively); Karle cave inscription of Vāsishṭhīputra Puḷumāvi (year 7= c. 137 A.D.) and Nasik cave inscription of the same ruler (year 22= c.152 A.D.).

11 figure in the inscriptions of Pravarasena II (c.410/15 to 445/50) alone.[66] That many charters also record donations of land[67] which vary from 20 *nivartanas* to 8000 *nivartanas* by the royal measure[68] further suggest that the pressure on land was not much in the Vākāṭaka kingdom which resulted in the obvious growth of agriculture based rural settlements. This evidence is indicative of the fact that in the Vākāṭaka kingdom the growth of self-sufficient economic units precluded the use of coins by the rural peasantry making the use of money less important. It is against this economic background of the Vākāṭakas that the problem of their currency should be studied. Also, in the light of this economic condition the comparative paucity or the complete non-availability of their own currency may be understood. It is also possible to connect the paucity of coinage in the Vākāṭaka kingdom with the increasing feudal trends in the political and economic life of the country.

To sum up, the problem of the Vākāṭaka coins is passing through the same stage which was in the age of K. P. Jayaswal who attributed a coin to Pravarasena and raised the edifice of the Vākāṭaka coinage on its basis. For sometime his suggestion was widely discussed but ultimately it was proved that the particular coin belonged to Vīrasena, a non-Vākāṭaka ruler. In the same way, A. M. Shastri has attributed two copper coins to Narendrasena and one copper coin to Pṛthivīsheṇa and Prashant P. Kulkarni has attributed one copper coin to Pravarasena. God knows how much time will it take either to prove or disprove these assumptions. But the example of the coin of Vīrasena attributed by Jayaswal to Pravarasena shows how hazardous it

[66] Inscriptions of the main branch of the Vākāṭakas, which explicitly record donations of villages, include the following : Mandhal plates (year 5) of Rudrasena II; Pune plates (year 13) of Prabhāvatīguptā; Jamb plates (year 2), Belora charter (year 11), Mandhal plates (years 16 and 17), Chammak plates (year 18), Siwani plates (year 18), Miregaon charter (year20), Indore plates (year 23), Tirodi plates (year 23) and Balaghat plate all of Pravarasena II; Bamhani charter of the time of Narendrasena; and Mandhal plates (year 2), Mandhal plates (year 10) and Mahurjhari plates (year 17) of Pṛthivīsheṇa II. Among the inscriptions of the Vatsagulma branch of the Vākāṭakas, which mention donations of villages, are included: Washim plates (year 37) of Vindhyaśakti II; India Office plate and Bidar plates (year 5) of Devasena ; and Thalner grant (year 3) of Harisheṇa.

[67] Masod plates (year 19), Dudia plates (year 23), Wadgaon plates (year 25), Yawatmal plates (year 26), Pattan plates (year 27), Tigaon plates (year 29) and Pauni plates (year 32) of Pravarasena II and Thalner grant of Harisheṇa (year 3) record donations of land in different villages of the Vākāṭaka kingdom.

[68] One *nivartana* of land was about 3/4, 2, 2 1/4, 3 or 4 3/4 acres according to different authorities (*EI*, XXVIII, p. 245). It differed in different parts of the country and different periods of history.

is to hypothesize on the basis of the meagre evidence.

Thus, we observe that the question of the existence of the currency of an extensive kingdom, as the Vākāṭaka kingdom was, can not be decided by one or two copper coins. In fact no credence should be given to these coins unless they are obtained from regular archaeological excavations or unless their authenticity is proved by detailed investigation. Further, it is to be kept in mind that the coins of earlier and contemporary dynasties were in circulation in the Vākāṭaka kingdom. A study of their known inscriptions indicate the comparative paucity of coins resulting in the large scale mechanism of land-grants, growth of small village settlements and relatively declining urban economy.

FIVE

Revisiting the Inscriptions of Harsha

THREE COPPER PLATES OF HARSHA : SAṀVAT 22, 23 AND 25

As is well known, two copper plates of Harsha were discovered in the last quarter of the nineteenth century. The first was found in January 1888 from Madhuban, about 50 kms. north-east from Azamgarh in U.P.[1] It is dated in Saṁvat 25 (of Harsha) which corresponds to 631 A.D., measures 50x33 cms. and weighs 3.86 kgs. No seal was recovered with it.

The second copper plate was found in 1894 at Banskhera, a village about 40 kms. from Shahjahanpur.[2] It measures 40.5x32.5 cms. A seal was also shouldered to it but it was extremely blurred. The plate is dated in the year 22 (of the reign of Harsha), which corresponds to 628 A.D.[3]

More than a century after the discovery of Madhuban and Banskhera grants, in the year 1999 another copper plate grant of Harsha was found along with a seal from a place near Thanesar or Kurukshetra, the capital of Harsha. It saw its way to Jñāna-Pravāha, the Centre of Cultural Studies of Varanasi in February 2002. It may, therefore, be called Kurukshetra-Varanasi grant of Harsha. It was published in the *Jñāna-Pravāha*, Annual Bulletin, No. 5 (2001-02), of the aforesaid Centre by R.C. Sharma along with the text, translation and photographs of the copper plate and seal.[4] R.C. Sharma, K.K. Thaplyal,

[1] *EI*, I, pp. 65-75.

[2] *Ibid.*, IV, pp. 208-11.

[3] Cf. Shankar Goyal, 'Harsha ke Abhilekha : Kuchha Samasyayeṅ aur Sujhāva', in S.R. Dubey (ed.), *Ābhilekhika Adhyayana kī Pravidhi evaṁ Itihāsa-Lekhana*, Delhi, 2004, pp. 183-89.

[4] *Jñāna-Pravāha,* No. 5, 2001-02, pp. 223-32. We have also re-edited this inscription in 2004 and published it along with the text, translation and our comments (*PIHC*, 65th Session, Bareilly, pp. 178-89). It's revised version also appeared in *EI*, XLIII, i, pp. 40-51; also see my *Harsha Revisited : A Re-interpretation of Existing Data*, New Delhi, 2018, pp. 77-89.

T.P. Verma and Devendra Handa examined them to ensure their authenticity. For obvious reasons we shall discuss this copper plate in some detail.

Written in chaste Sanskrit and incised in the post-Gupta Brāhmī characters, the Kurukshetra-Varanasi copper plate of Harsha records the land grant given to Bhaṭṭa Ulūkhalasvāmin in 18 lines on a plate measuring 42.5 cm. in length and 31.5 cm. in width. The surface of the plate is rather uneven indicating rough handling at some stage. It weighs 3.80 kgs. The seal, which was originally shouldered to it but is now detached, is of mixed metal which is almost bronze. It appears that during the course of fixing of the seal with the plate the edges of the seal were twisted inside and, therefore, some letters in the beginning and end of lines have become blurred. Some portion of the seal being rubbed off is illegible, but its major part bears a sharp inscription in relief and can be read without much difficulty. It bears twelve lines which contain the genealogy of the Pushyabhūti dynasty from Naravardhana to Harshavardhana. The top of the seal illustrates a seated bull, Nandī, which symbolizes Harsha's faith in Śaivism also recorded in the epigraph. At the end of the inscription of the seal there are traces of rising sun with two half circles and rays radiating in two different directions.

The Kurukshetra-Varanasi grant was issued in the year 23 of Harsha (=629 A.D.).[5] Thus, it belongs to about the same general period to which his other two grants belong. The name of scribe in this case is missing, although in other copper plates their names are clearly mentioned. In the Madhuban grant he is called 'Gurjara' while the Banskhera plate gives the name of the scribe as 'Īśvara'.

The Madhuban and Banskhera plates record that land granted in each of them was given to two Brāhmaṇas but the Kurukshetra-Varanasi grant reveals that only one Brāhmaṇa namely Bhaṭṭa Ulūkhalasvāmin was its beneficiary. Both the earlier copper plates record the name of the *dūtaka* as Skandagupta, but in the case of the new find it is Kṛshṇagupta. Both these officers were of high rank and enjoyed the title of Mahārāja.

The Kurukshetra-Varanasi copper plate begins with *Om* and *Svasti.*

[5] There is some confusion in reading the date of the third copper plate of Harsha. But as the contents of all the three grants are almost identical we are certain that our reading is quite alright and all these copper plates belong to about the same general period of Harsha: Saṁvat 22 (Banskhera), 23 (Kurukshetra) and 25 (Madhuban). The reading of D.P. Dubey and A.K. Dubey ('Uttar Pradesh, Bihar and Uttarakhand' in *25 Years of Indian Epigraphy* (A Bird's Eye-view of the Progress of Epigraphy in Different States of the Country), ed. Shrinivas V. Padigar, Dharwad, 2016, pp. 301-02) that it is Saṁvat 33 instead of 23 in the Kurukshetra copper plate does not make much difference as far as the reconstruction of the history of the age of Harsha is concerned. But the readings of Saṁvat 8 or 53 are not at all convincing. We shall discuss this problem separately.

Om is in the symbolic form and can be explained as *Siddham* also.

The Madhuban copper plate does not contain the 'signature' of the king. But the Banskhera and the Kurukshetra-Varanasi grant claim to contain it. In the Kurukshetra-Varanasi grant the last line bearing the royal signature is preceded by the figure of a peacock with large stylized plumage and terminates with a floral motif flanked by two vertical lines. The letter *dhi* in centre of this line looks like a full vase (*pūrṇaghaṭa*) with foliage issuing from its brim.

There are a few omissions and alterations in the document due to the mistakes committed by the scribe. In line 1, last letter '*t*' in word *skandhāvārāt* is missing. In line 4, *na* was left out in word *bhuvana* but was later incised below. In line 7, vowel *ā* is missing in *prā*. In the same line, the last letter *yaḥ* is confusing in the word *satyānurodhena*. In line 8, in word *Bhaṭṭāraka*, letter *ra* was left out but marked later and it is very small and insignificant. In line 9, in word *Mahāsāmanta*, *ma* is missing after *sā*. In line 12, word *jyeshṭha* is incised as *jāshṭha*. In line 14, the last word is recorded as *sṭhānam* instead of *sthānam*. In line 15, *Lakshmyā* is misspelt as *Lyakshmyā*.

The perusal of the genealogical table of the three grants of Harsha suggests that the first three kings of the dynasty, i.e., Naravardhana, Rājyavardhana I and Ādityavardhana were simply Mahārājas and, therefore, must have been subordinate rulers. The next three kings, i.e., Prabhākara-vardhana, Rājyavardhana II and Harsha are, however, described as Paramabhaṭṭāraka Mahārājādhirāja. Similarly, the first three queens namely Vajriṇī, Apsaro and Mahāsenaguptā are mentioned simply as Devī but the last queen, viz., Yaśomatī, the mother of Rājyavardhana II and Harsha, has been honoured with the title Bhaṭṭārikā Mahādevī. However, the grants of Harsha do not show when did Prabhākaravardhana, the first Mahārājādhirāja, assumed this title. In our view Prabhākara was merely a Mahārāja till the marriage of Rājyaśrī with Grahavarman.[6]

The first king of the Pushyabhūti dynasty does not bear any religious epithet. However, the next three are called Paramādityabhaktas i.e. great devotees of the Sun. Rājyavardhana II is called a great devotee of Sugata i.e. Buddha, while Harshavardhana calls himself a great devotee of Maheśvara, that is Śiva.

IDENTIFICATION OF PLACE NAMES MENTIONED IN INSCRIPTIONS

The first copper plate of Harsha found from Madhuban was issued from the victorious military camp of Kapitthikā. Its object was to transfer Somakuṇḍakā village situated in the Kuṇḍadhānī *vishaya* of the Śrāvastī

[6] Shankar Goyal, *History and Historiography of the Age of Harsha*, Jodhpur, 1992, pp. 143-46; idem, *Harsha : A Multidisciplinary Political Study*, Jodhpur, 2006, Ch.4.

bhukti to two learned Brāhmaṇas, the Sāmavedī Bhaṭṭa Vātasvāmin of the Sāvarṇi gotra and the Ṛgvedī Bhaṭṭa Śivadevasvāmin of the Vishṇuvṛddha gotra, after taking it away from one Vāmarathya who had been enjoying it on the strength of a forged document (*śāsana*).[7] As the village granted by Harsha was situated in the Śrāvastī *bhukti*, it is evident that he had conquered this region by 631 A.D., the date of this inscription. Of the localities mentioned in the inscription, Kapitthikā apparently is Kie-pi-tha (Kapitha) of Yuan Chwang,[8] which, again, is the same as Sāṅkāśya, identified by the late Sir A. Cunningham[9] with modern Sankisa[10] on the Kālīnadī river about 40 miles north-west of Kanauj. Śrāvastī has been identified with modern Sahet-Mahet[11] on the south bank of Rāptī of the Gonda district of Uttar Pradesh,[12] while Kuṇḍadhānī and the village Somakuṇḍakā have yet to be identified.

The second grant of Harsha found from Banskhera was issued from the victorious military camp stationed at Śrī Vardhamānakoṭī. The village granted Markaṭasāgara lay in the Ahichchhatrā *bhukti*, and in the western *pathaka* of the Aṅgadīya *vishaya*. Of the localities mentioned in the inscription, Ahichchhatrā was capital of northern Pañchāla. It has been identified with modern Rāmanagar in the Bareilly district of Uttar Pradesh.[13] But it is not known which territory was meant by the place Aṅgadīya. Markaṭasāgara also could not be identified. The identification of Śrī Vardhamānakoṭī is also not certain. We know of a Vardhamāna in Kāṭhiāwāḍ which has been identified with modern Vaḍhvān.[14] There was a Vardhamāna *bhukti* in the Valabhi dominion.[15] Vardhamānakoṭī has also been identified with modern Burdwan[16] or Bardhanakoṭī of Dinajpur district of Bengal.[17] In the Mallasārul copper plate inscription of Vijayasena of the early sixth century we are informed of the existence of Vardhamāna *bhukti*.[18]

[7] The inscription proves that forgeries were known in ancient India. The Smṛtis prescribe punishments for the forgers of royal grants.

[8] S. Beal, *Si-Yü-Ki* or *Buddhist Records of the Western World*, Vol. I, Delhi, 1969, p. 202.

[9] *Archaeological Survey of India*, I, p. 271.

[10] Cf. the *Imperial Gazetteer of India*, 2nd edn., XII, p. 223.

[11] *Ibid.*, p. 126.

[12] V.A. Smith identifies the site of Śrāvastī in the district of Khajūrā in Nepal (*JRAS*, 1898, p. 527) but this view has no convincing argument.

[13] B.C. Law, *Historical Geography of Ancient India*, Paris, 1954, pp. 63 ff.

[14] *IA*, XII, pp. 190 ff.

[15] *JBBRAS*, XI, pp. 331 ff.

[16] B.P. Sinha, *The Decline of the Kingdom of Magadha*, Patna, 1954, p. 270.

[17] Nundo Lal Dey, *Geographical Dictionary of Ancient and Medieval India*, London, 1927, p. 25.

[18] *EI*, XXIII, pp. 155 ff.

It is also mentioned in the Irdā grant of the tenth century and the Naihati and Govindpur grants of the twelveth century.[19] There is a mention of Vardhamānapura in Malwa[20] in an inscription of the fifteenth century. It is probably the same Vardhamānapura which is mentioned in an inscription of the Paramāra king Jayavarmadeva.[21] But as Vardhamāna was the name of Mahāvīra, it is not impossible that several places were named after him. We think that Vardhamānakoṭī of the Banskhera inscription was situated somewhere in the western Uttar Pradesh.

The third and the last known charter of Harsha found from Kurukshetra was also issued from the victorious military camp of Śrī Vardhamānakoṭī. It refers to Paṇḍārāṭgāka village situated in the Saṁvarddha *vishaya* of the Jayaratha *bhukti.* We have seen that Śrī Vardhamānakoṭī has been recognized differently, and the other place names of this inscription have not been identified so far.

SOME OTHER PROBLEMS AND SUGGESTIONS

All the three grants of Harsha make a reference to Rājyavardhana II's victory over 'Devagupta and other wicked kings' and to his giving up his life in enemy's house in consequence of his adherence to his promise. This Devagupta is usually and rightly identified with Mālava ruler who, according to Bāṇa, was defeated by Rājyavardhana with 'ridiculous ease'. He was obviously some relation of Mahāsenagupta who had earlier succeeded in forcing the two sons of the latter— Kumāragupta and Mādhavagupta—to seek asylum in Thanesar.[22]

As regards the murder of Rājyavardhana, Harsha's inscriptions depose that Rājya gave up his life in enemy's house in order to adhere to his promise. This enemy is almost universally identified with Śaśāṅka of Gauḍa. But in recent years some scholars have opined, and rightly so, that though the murder of Rājya was certainly engineered by Śaśāṅka, yet there is some likelihood that Harsha himself was implicated in the conspiracy. R.C. Majumdar points out that Yuan Chwang has explicitly stated that Rājyavardhana was exposed to danger due to the 'fault' of Pushyabhūti ministers. One of these ministers might have been Bhaṇḍi who was a confidant of Harsha and was with Rājya at that time. Taking this testimony along with the fact that while Śaśāṅka and Harsha were Śaiva and Rājyavardhana a Buddhist, Majumdar posed the question : "Who knows that Rājyavardhana's death was not similarly encompassed by his ministers

[19] B.P. Sinha, *op.cit.*, pp. 270-71.

[20] *JASB*, LII, pp. 67 ff.

[21] *IA*, XIX, pp. 350 ff.

[22] Shankar Goyal, *op.cit.*, pp. 110-12.

with the help of Śaśāṅka who was known to be a great champion of orthodox faith?"[23]

In 1966, V.S. Pathak made the case against Harsha stronger by pointing out that the authors of the early medieval period, justified the violation of the right of the elder brother to the ancestral throne by the younger brother, their patron, by the use of several motifs (such as some divinity had sent their patron to become king, or that their father wanted his younger son to succeed him, or that the elder son was either incompetent or unwilling to rule).[24] As Bāṇa has used all these motifs, it logically follows that some need was felt to justify Harshavardhana's rise to power for which Bāṇa was asked to compose his *Harshacharita*.[25]

The suspicion of Harsha's complicity in the murder of Rājya was made stronger by Devahuti. "It is hard to escape the conclusion" she argued, "that the unusual twists in the story (of the *Harshacharita*), from the time of Prabhākara-vardhana's illness to the time of Rājya-vardhana's death, however cleverly manipulated, were rendered inevitable because of some episode uncomplimentary to the author's hero."[26]

The case against Harshavardhana was made almost airtight by S.R. Goyal.[27] Writing in 1986 he pointed out that Bāṇa not only uses the motifs to which Pathak has directed our attention but at one place has also mentioned that "Like the Lord of the Immortals (that is, Indra), he (that is, Harsha) appeared busy in wiping away the stain of his elder brother's slaughter" (*Amarapatirivāgrajabadhakalaṅkaprakshāla-nākulaḥ).*[28] Now, according to Indian mythology, Indra had committed the crime of killing Viśvarūpa, the three-headed son of Tvashṭṛ, who was in a sense his *agraja.* Therefore, it was said that Indra had committed the crime of killing his elder brother. Now, if according to Bāṇa Harsha was busy, like Indra, in wiping away the stain of his elder brother's murder then it can only mean that during the reign of Harsha rumours were afloat that he was implicated in the murder of Rājya. Thus, the theory proposed by R.C. Majumdar in 1943 that in some way the Pushyabhūti ministers belonging to the side of Harsha might

[23] R.C. Majumdar (ed.), *The History of Bengal*, Vol. I, Dacca, 1943, p. 76.

[24] For a detailed study of these motifs see V.S. Pathak, *Ancient Historians of India*, Bombay, 1966, pp. 18-21; Shankar Goyal, *op. cit.*, pp. 150-64.

[25] Cf. Shankar Goyal, 'The Rājyavardhana Murder Case', *Heritage of India : Past and Present* (Professor R.K. Sharma Felicitation Volume), ed. P.K. Mishra and S.K. Sullerey, Delhi, 1994, pp. 579-90; idem, *Harsha : A Multidisciplinary Political Study*, pp. 145 ff.

[26] D. Devahuti, *Harsha : A Political Study*, Delhi, 1983, p. 82.

[27] S.R. Goyal, *Harsha Śīlāditya*, Meerut, 1986, pp. 75-85.

[28] *Harshacharita*, trans. E.B. Cowell and F.W. Thomas, 2nd edn., Delhi, 1968, p. 204.

have collaborated with Śaśāṅka in the murder of Rājya has now become an almost airtight case, certainly much more than a merely *prima facie* case, against Harsha, the above-mentioned statement of Bāṇa, quoted by S.R. Goyal in 1986, providing clinching evidence for it.

The administrative structure of Harsha's empire was highly feudalized.[29] It seems that he himself began to make use of the titles of *mahāsāmanta, sāmanta,* etc. to honour some of the higher state employees, to bring them on a level with those who were previously autonomous feudatories. In the recently discovered grant Mahākshapaṭalā-dhikaraṇādhikṛta Sāmanta Mahārāja Kṛshṇagupta is mentioned as its Dūtaka. In the *Harshacharita* Skandagupta is the commander of elephant wing of the army but in the Banskhera plate he figures as Dūtaka Mahāpramātāra. In the *Harshacharita* he also advises Harsha. Mahāsāmantas or Sāmantas were somewhat of lower status than a Mahārāja.

Dūtaka brought the charter or king's order to the notice of the local officers. In the recent epigraph he is described as *Mahārāja, Mahāsāmanta* and *Mahākshapaṭaladhikaraṇādhikṛta* which probably meant the highest revenue officers and incharge of the revenue department. *Rājasthānīya* meant an officer dealing with the province as the local representative of the king. *Dussādhasādhanika* literally means an accomplisher of difficult task. *Pramātāra* (Pramātṛ) was a land surveyor. The words *bhaṭa* and *chāṭa* are to be explained probably as regular soldiers and as adhoc soldiers or new recruits respectively.

A designation that often appears in ancient records, including Harsha's grants, is that of *Kumārāmātya* which sometimes may have been a title of honour but more often than not appears to have carried some administrative responsibilities. Some of the *kumārāmātyas* figure as district or provincial functionaries, others as members of the central secretariat. Some of the highest government officers, such as the minister of interstate relations, were selected from among the *kumārāmātyas.*

Harsha's inscriptions mention the traditional *grāma* (village), *vishaya* and *bhukti* but not the *deśa* of the imperial Gupta epigraphs, although the division may have existed in his time. Anyway, in the Gupta period also *deśa* was more or less synonym for *bhukti.* The modern districts or commissioner's divisions and provinces may be considered modern counterparts respectively of the *vishaya* and *bhukti* with regard to size.[30]

[29] For the political culture of the age of Harsha and the feudalization of the administrative structure see Shankar Goyal, *The 'Medieval' Factor and the Age of Harsha : A Cultural Study*, Jodhpur, 2016, pp. 104-29.

[30] G.P. Sinha, *Post-Gupta Polity (500-750 A.D.)*, Calcutta, 1972, p. 72.

The governor of the *deśa* or *bhukti* was a nominee of the king. Sometimes he was designated *uparika* and could be honoured by titles such as *mahārāja* and *rājasthānīya*. *Rājasthānīya* literally meant viceroy (one who functions as a king in place of the latter).

Some designations mentioned in Harsha's grants apparently describe police duties. The *dussādhasādhanikas* were probably police officers who were expected to perform those duties which were regarded as difficult (such as arresting hardened criminals). *Chāṭas* and *bhaṭas* most likely performed police duties. The *Harshacharita* mentions *chara-bhaṭas* as soldiers in the vanguard of the infantry.

The *bhukti* and *vishaya* offices were called respectively *adhikaraṇa* and *adhishṭhāna* and were maintained by the keepers of records, the *pustapālas*. The legal aspects of the land transactions and possibly the revenue records concerning them were supervised by the *vishaya* and *grāmākshapaṭalas*. The latter were helped by *karaṇikas* (clerks). *Grāmāksha-paṭala* was probably the counterpart of modern *paṭavārī*. The *vishayapatis* worked in cooperation with representative bodies.

The land grants generally mention some taxes, which were exempted when the village was gifted away. *Udraṅga* was the main land tax.[31] *Uparikara* was an extra tax. The term *pratyāya* stands for all dues. The expression *sarvarājakulābhāvya pratyāya* means all dues or taxes, which were to be paid to the state. *Tulyameya* was a tax imposed on the articles of merchandise nature.[32] *Bhāga* was king's share of grain, *kara* a tax in kind (or simply a tax in general), *bhog* a periodical offerings,[33] *hiraṇya* a tax in cash and *bhaga-bhoga-kara*, sometimes written as a compound word, should mean a tax in shape of *bhāga* or *bhoga*.[34] The grants also mention *bhūmichchhidranyāya*, i.e., a piece of barren or jungle land brought under cultivation. It means that when the village was gifted, the donee enjoyed all the rights and could also exercise his authority on the nearby barren or unused land.

The last line of the Kurukshetra-Varanasi grant purports to contain

[31] C.V. Vaidya cites several epigraphic evidences in support of the view that *udraṅga* was land tax and *uparikara* was an extra tax (*History of Mediaeval Hindu India*, Vol. I, Poona, 1921, pp. 131-32). D.C. Sircar takes *udraṅga* to be the principal tax (*Indian Epigraphy*, Delhi, 1965, p. 360).

[32] G. Bühler takes *tulyameya* not as a tax but as adjective to the taxes that follow, and translates it as 'to be given according to the weight and according to measure' (*EI*, I, p. 75).

[33] D.C. Sircar suggests the possibility of *bhāga-bhoga-kara* being one compound meaning 'tax in the shape of *bhāga* and *bhoga*' (*Indian Epigraphy*, p. 394).

[34] G. Bühler translates *bhāga-bhoga* as 'share of the product enjoyed by the king' (*EI*, I, *op. cit.*).

the signature of Harsha. The Banskhera inscription also supposedly contains the signature of Harsha. According to V.A. Smith, in the Banskhera grant the name of Harsha was engraved following the form of his signature though the engraver used somewhat bigger than the usual size of the letters. But, as S.R. Goyal has pointed out, the form of the letters of Harsha's signature and those of the rest of the Banskhera grant are similar.[35] Therefore, as it cannot be even imagined that Harsha himself engraved the entire copper plate, it follows that the entire record, including its signature part, was engraved by Īśvara, the engraver of the grant. The statement of the last line that Harsha signed the record in his own hand probably only suggests what is meant by the phrase *baqalam khud* in modern parlance which only implies that only the original order was signed personally by the issuing authority. The phrase *svahasto mama* is found in Maitraka inscriptions; there also it probably suggests the same thing.[36] This argument of Goyal has been proved to be correct by the Kurukshetra-Varanasi grant because the script of its signature part is obviously different from the script of the signature part of the Banskhera record proving that none of them is in the handwriting of Harsha. Here it may also be pointed out that Harsha, who ruled for four decades, must have issued scores, even hundreds, of copper plate grants. That being so, it is difficult to assume that an emperor of his stature found time to personally engrave his signature on these plates, something quite different from putting one's signature on paper documents.

All the three known grants of Harsha were issued from the victorious military camp (*jayaskandhāvāra*) and not from the capital. This may perhaps suggest the celebration of important occasions of which one item was the donation of land or a village (*agrahāra*) to the learned Vedic Brāhmaṇas. The administrative and financial benefit of such gifts was availed of by the donee while the religious merit went to the king's parents and his elder brother as recorded in the epigraph.

[35] S.R. Goyal, *Maukhari-Pushyabhūti-Chālukyayugīna Abhilekha*, Meerut, 1987, p. 95.

[36] Shankar Goyal, in S.R. Dubey, *op. cit.*, p. 188.

APPENDIX

The Kurukshetra-Varanasi Grant of Harsha : Year 23

TEXT

1. ॐ स्वस्ति महानौहस्त्यश्वजयस्कन्धावारा(त्) श्रीवर्द्धमानकोटीवासक: महाराज श्री नरवर्द्धन: तस्य पुत्रस्तत्पादानुध्यात: श्रीवज्रिणीदेव्यामुत्पन्न: परमादित्यभक्तो महाराज श्री (राज्य-)
2. वर्द्धन: तस्य पुत्रस्तत्पादानुध्यात: श्रीमदप्सरोदेव्यामुत्पन्न: परमादित्यभक्तो महाराज श्रीमदादित्यवर्द्धन: तस्य पुत्रस्तत्पादानुध्यात: श्रीमहासेनगुप्तादेव्यामुत्पन: चतु: समु-
3. द्रातिक्क्रान्तकीर्ति: प्रतापानुरागोपनतान्यराजा वर्ण्णाश्रमव्यवस्थापनप्रवृत्त-चक्क्र एकचक्क्ररथ इ (व) प्रजानामार्तिहर: परमादित्यभक्त परमभट्टारक महाराजाधिराज
4. श्रीप्रभाकरवर्द्धन: तस्य पुत्रतत्पादानुध्यात: सितयशप्रतानविच्छुरित-सकलभुवनमण्डल: परिगृहीतधनदवरुणेन्द्रप्रभृति लोकपालतेजा-
5. सत्पथोपार्जितानेकद्रविणभूमिप्रदानसंप्रीणितार्थिहृदयो(ऽ*)तिशयितपूर्व्वराज-चरित: देव्याममलयशोमत्यां यशोमत्यामुत्पन्न ... (परम-)
6. सौगत: सुगत इव परहितैकरत: परमभट्टारक महाराजाधिराज श्रीराज्यवर्द्धन: राजानो युधि (दु)ष्टवाजिन इव श्रीदेवगुप्तादय: कृत्वा येन कशा-
7. प्रहारविमुखा: सर्वे समं संयता: उत्खाय द्विषतो विजित्यं वसुधां कृत्वा प्रजानां प्रियं प्र(ा)णानुज्झितवा (*)नरातिभवने सत्यानुरोधेन(य:)।[1] तस्यानुज-स्तत्पादानुध्यात: परममा-
8. हेश्वरो महेश्वर इव सर्व्वसत(त)वानुकम्पी परमभट्टारक महाराजाधिराज श्रीहर्ष: जयरतभुक्तविषयसंवर्द्धदुरित्ताणि परिभाष्यमाणा पण्डाराट्गाक ग्रामे स-
9. मुपगता महासा(म)न्त महाराजदुस्साधसाधनिकप्रमातारराजस्थानीय-(कु)मारमात्यो-परिकविषयपतिभटचाटसेवकादीन्प्रतिवासिजनपदांश्च
10. समाज्ञापयति विदितस्तुवो यथायमुपरिलिखितग्राम: स्वसीमा(प)र्यन्त: सोद्रङ्ग: सर्व्वराजकुलाभाव्य प्रत्यायसमेत: सर्व्वपरिहृतपरि-

11. हा(रो) विषयादुद्धृतपिण्ड(:) पुत्रपौत्रानुगश्चन्द्रार्कक्षितिसमकालीन: (भू)मिच्छिद्रन्यायेन मया पितु: परमभट्टार(क) महाराजाधिराज श्रीप्रभा-
12. करवर्द्धन देवस्य मातुश्च भट्टारिका महादेवी राज्ञी श्रीयशोमती देव्या: (ज्ये)ष्ठभ्रातृ परमभट्टारक महाराजाधिराज श्रीराज्यवर्द्धनदेवपादानां च
13. पुण्ययशोभिवर्द्धये भार्गवसगोत्रवहृवृच सब्रह्मचारी भट्टोलूखलस्वामिने प्रतिग्रहधर्मणाग्रहारत्वेन प्रतिपादित: विदित्वा भवद्भि: रस-
14. नुमन्तव्य: प्रतिवासिजनपदैरप्याज्ञाश्रवणविधेयैर्भूत्वा यथासमुचिततुल्यमेय-भागभोगकरहिरण्यादिप्रत्याया: अन्यैवोपनेया: सेवोपस्ठा(था)नं च
15. करणीयमित्यपि च। अस्मत्कुलक्रममुदारमुदाहरद्भिरन्यैश्च दानमिदमभ्यनुमोदनीयं। ल्य (ल) क्ष्म्यास्तडित्सलिलबुदबुदचंचलाया: दानंफलं पर-
16. यश: परिपालनं च।। [2] कर्मणा मनसा वाचा कर्त्तव्यं प्राणिने हितं हर्षेणैतत्समाख्यातं धर्म्मार्ज्जनमनुत्तमं।। [3] दूतकोत्र महाक्षपटलाधिकरणाधि-
17. कृत सामंतमहाराज कृष्णगुप्त: तदादेशाच्चोत्कीर्णं।।संव 20 (+)3
18. स्वहस्तेन मम महाराजाधिराज श्रीहर्षस्य [।।*]

TRANSLATION*

Om, Success. From the victorious military camp stationed at Śrī Vardhamānakoṭī, possessing large boats, elephants, and horses (this charter is issued). (There was) Śrī Mahārāja Naravardhana. His son, who meditated on his feet and who was born of Śrī Vajriṇīdevī, (was) Śrī Mahārāja Rājyavardhana(I), a great devotee of the Sun. His son, who meditated on his feet and who was born of Śrī Apsarodevī, (was) Mahārāja Śrī Ādityavardhana, a great devotee of the Sun. His son, who meditated on his feet and who was born of Śrī Mahāsenaguptādevī, (was) Paramabhaṭṭāraka Mahārājādhirāja Śrī Prabhākaravardhana, a great devotee of the Sun, whose fame had crossed the four oceans, who subjected other kings by means of his valour and love, whose power (that is, army) was used in regulating Varṇāśrama (the system of castes and stages), who like the *Ekachakraratha* (that is, the Sun) (having only one wheel in the form of the year) removed the sufferings of the subjects (or beings). His son, who meditated on his feet and who was born of Śrī Yaśomatīdevī having unsullied glory, (was) Paramabhaṭṭāraka Mahārājādhirāja Śrī Rājyavardhana (II), a great devotee of Sugata (i.e. Buddha) and who like Sugata was wholly given to doing good to others, who had covered the whole circle of the earth by the canopy of his pure fame, who contained in himself the essences of the (eight) guardians of the quarters—Kubera, Varuṇa, Indra, and others, who satisfied the

---

* Translation ours.

hearts of the supplicants by granting plenty of wealth and lands acquired righteously (and) who excelled the lives of the kings who preceded him.

Who, making all the kings, Devagupta and others, who had come united, to turn back like bad horses by striking with a whip and uprooting the enemies and conquering the earth and doing what was beneficial to the subjects, laid down his life in his insistence on truth, in the enemy's house. (v.1).

His younger brother, Paramabhaṭṭāraka Mahārājādhirāja Śrī Harsha, a great devotee of Maheśvara, who meditated on his feet, and who like Maheśvara showed compassion towards all beings, issued his commands to the Mahāsāmanta, Mahārāja Dussādhasādhanika, Pramātāra, Rājasthānīya, Kumārāmātya, Uparika, Vishayapati, Bhaṭas, Chāṭas, servants and others and the inhabitants those had assembled at Paṇḍārāṭgāka village situated in the Saṁvarddha vishaya in the Jayarata bhukti—

"Be it known to you, that, for the purpose of increasing the religious merit of (my) father, Paramabhaṭṭāraka Mahārājādhirāja Śrī Prabhākaravardhana, of (my) mother the queen Bhaṭṭārikā Mahādevī Śrī Yaśomatīdevī and of (my) revered elder brother Paramabhaṭṭāraka Mahārājādhirāja Śrī Rājyavardhana, there is granted by me the above-mentioned village, as far as its own boundaries and, as an *agrahāra* according to the rule of the 'complete gift' (*pratigraha*) and of *bhūmichchhidra*, to endure for the same time with the moon, the sun, (and) the earth, to be enjoyed (to be passed on to) by sons and son's sons and accompanied with the privileges of Udraṅga, to be free from all taxes from the royal family, and to be excused from all (other) taxes, to Brahmachārī Bhaṭṭa Ulūkhalasvāmin of Bhārgava *gotra* of Vahvṛcha (Ṛgvedī) śākhā, a righteously accepted *agrahāra*. Knowing this you should agree to this and the inhabitants with due obedience of (our) command should (henceforth pay) all taxes and fee like *tulyameya* (merchandise tax), *bhāga* (king's share), *bhoga* (periodical offerings), *hiraṇya* (cash or gold), other benefits due to royalty and service due to him.

This gift should be assented to by those who follow the noble course of our family and also by others. Charity and the protection of the glory of others (is the) reward of the goddess of wealth, fickle like the lightning or the bubble in water. (v.2).

Men (lit. creatures) should do what is beneficial by actions, by mind, and by speech. This unequalled (way of) the acquisition of Dharma is related by Harsha. (v.3)."

The Dūtaka here (is) Mahākshapaṭalādhikaraṇādhikṛta Sāmanta Mahārāja Kṛshṇagupta. This is engraved by his order. Saṁ 20+3. (This has been) signed personally by me Śrī Mahārājādhirāja Harsha.

INSCRIPTION ON THE SEAL*

Bull

1. (सिद्धम् महाराज) श्री नरवर्द्धन: तस्य पुत्रस्तत्पादानुध्यात: श्री वज्रिणी
2. (दे) व्या(मुत्पन्न:) परमादित्यभक्तो महाराज श्रीराज्यवर्द्धन: तस्य पुत्रस्त (त्)
3. (पादानुध्यात:) श्री अ (प्स)रोदेव्यामुत्पन्न: परमादित्यभक्तो महाराज श्रीमदादित्य-
4. (वर्द्धन: तस्य) पुत्रस्तत्पादानुध्यात: श्री महासेनगुप्तादेव्यामुत्पन्न: चतु: समु-
5. (द्राति)क्क्रान्त कीर्तिप्रतापानुरागोपनतान्यराजो वर्ण्णाश्रमव्यवस्थापनप्रवृ(त्त)-
6. चक्र एकचक्क्ररथ इव प्रजानामार्तिहर: परमादित्यभक्त: परमभट्टारक
7. महाराजाधिराज श्री प्रभाकरवर्द्धन: तस्य पुत्रस्तत्पादानुध्यात (अतिशयित)
8. पूर्व्वराजचरितो देव्याममलयशोमत्यां श्रीयशोमत्यामुत्पन्न: परमसौगत सु(ग-)
9. त इव परहितानुरत: परमभट्टारक महाराजाधिराज श्री राज्यवर्द्धन (स्त-)
10. (स्या) नुजस्तत्पादानुध्यात: परमभट्टारिका महादेवी श्री यशोमत्या (दे-)
11. (व्या) मेवोत्पन्न: परममाहेश्वर: महेश्वर इव सर्व्व (स-)
12. (त्वानु) कम्पक: परमभट्टारक महाराजाधिराज श्रीहर्ष (ष:)

Radiating Half Sun

* The seal furnishes the same genealogy of the Pushyabhūti family as is recorded in the copper plate; hence no separate translation is given.

SIX

The Plays Ascribed to Harsha and their Supposed Historical Importance

IMPORTANCE OF THE PLAYS FOR THE HISTORY OF HARSHA AND THE PROBLEM OF THEIR AUTHORSHIP

The authorship of the three plays, namely, *Ratnāvalī*, *Priyadarśikā* and *Nāgānanda* which ascribe themselves to Harsha and their place in the history of Sanskrit literature is a matter of great controversy. The subject-matter of the *Ratnāvalī* and the *Priyadarśikā* is the love affairs of Udayana, king of Vatsa. The *Ratnāvalī*, a *nāṭikā* of four Acts, describes the secret love of Udayana with Sāgarikā, an attendant of his queen Vāsavadattā. After many twists in the story the heroine turns out to be Ratnāvalī, the princess of Siṁhala, whom a shipwreck had brought to Udayana's court. The theme of the *Priyadarśikā*, also a *nāṭikā* of four Acts, is somewhat similar to that of the *Ratnāvalī*. In this work also the heroine, a princess of Aṅga, is admitted to the *antaḥpura* of Udayana under the name of Āraṇyikā and is made the maid-servant of the queen. The king falls in love with her. She is soon recognized as the princess of Aṅga and is saved by the king when a serpent bites her. The story ends with her happy presentation to the king by the queen herself. The story of the *Nāgānada*, a play of five Acts, concerns the love of Jīmūtavāhana, the Vidyādhara prince, for princess Malayavatī. In the first three Acts of the play, Jīmūtavāhana renounces his kingdom to serve his parents in the forest. In the Malaya mountains, he sees princess Malayavatī in a Gaurī temple, falls in love and marries her. If the *Nāgānanda* had ended with the first three acts, it would have passed for a short comedy of love like the *Priyadarśikā* and the *Ratnāvalī*. But in the last two Acts the story takes a new turn. After his marriage Jīmūtavāhana one day incidentally hears that Nāgarāja has made peace with Garuḍa and has stipulated to offer a serpent each day to the King of Birds. The prince is deeply moved and he saves that day's victim at the risk of his own life. In the end goddess Gaurī revives the prince and bestows the status of Chakravartin on him. According to the most orthodox Sanskritists, such as S.K. De and S. N. Dasgupta, these plays were not only composed by Harsha,[1] they are valuable for his history as well. V.S. Pathak, for instance, believes that Bāṇa wrote his *Harshacharita* on the model of the *Ratnāvalī.* He argues :

> The *Ratnāvalī*... describes the achievement of universal sovereignty by king Udayana... . The *Harshacharita*, likewise, aims at describing the achievement of universal sovereignty by Harsha. It is first indicated by the blessings of Lakshmī, the Goddess of Fortune, to Pushyabhūti that one of his descendants, Harshavardhana, would be a universal suzerain... . This is repeated by the royal astrologer at the time of Harsha's birth and by the king Prabhākara in his death-bed speech.
>
> Secondly, the supernatural factor in the form of blessings for the achievement of universal suzerainty is also common to both texts. It was prophesied by a sage of miraculous powers that Ratnāvalī would be the consort of a universal monarch, while in the *Harshacharita* Pushyabhūti received a boon from Lakshmī that he would be an ancestor of a universal ruler.
>
> In both cases, the universal sovereignty was connected with the king's meeting with a damsel—in the comedy, Udayana meets his betrothed consort Ratnāvalī and in the prose-narrative, Rājyaśrī was ultimately restored to her brother Harsha. Ratnāvalī, because of the prophecy of the *siddha*, and Rājyaśrī nominally as the word Rājya-śrī means 'the goddess of fortune manifested in sovereignty'—and also actually, because the throne of Kanauj was obtained by Harsha through his sister, the widowed queen of Kanauj, brought suzerainty respectively to Udayana and Harsha.
>
> As if not satisfied with the veiled allusion to the comedy, Bāṇa records the present of a *ratnāvalī* the jewelled (*ratna*) necklace (*ekāvalī*) by Divākara to Harsha after his meeting with Rājyaśrī. To make the allusion still clearer, he describes the jewelled necklace as 'a banner, which announces the coming of embodied Imperial power' and as 'a *svayaṁvara* garland of the goddess of universal fortune (*bhuvanaśrī*)'.[2]

According to Pathak, the basic philosophy of both the works is also the same.[3] In the *Ratnāvalī* the Sūtradhāra says —"Fate brings the loved one, and quickly restores him even from a different isle, or from the mid-ocean, nay even from the end of the quarters." This, according to Pathak, evidently alludes to the incident of the play in which the Siṁhala princess

[1] S.K. De, *History of Sanskrit Literature*, Calcutta, 1947, p. 258; S.N. Dasgupta, *A History of Sanskrit Literature*, Calcutta, 1975, p. 255.

[2] V.S. Pathak, *Ancient Historians of India*, Bombay, 1966, pp. 41-42.

[3] *Ibid.*, p. 42.

Ratnāvalī was separated from her relations because of the ship-wreck but was eventually rescued and restored to her betrothed lover. The initial action of fate which consists in the ship-wreck and the throwing of the princess into a sea of troubles is indicated in an *āryā* of the sixth chapter of the *Harshacharita.* "Like a (stormy) wind *upsetting a ship,* fate overwhelms even a man whose virtues are sung in distant isles and who has obtained the best of *a collection of jewels.*" This reference to the ship-wreck in the *āryā* leaves no doubt that Bāṇa is alluding to the *Ratnāvalī.*

> Moreover, sovereignty could be achieved through the mysterious workings of fate. Vāsavadattā, the chief consort of Udayana, was an impediment on the path of his attaining universal suzerainty through his marriage with Ratnāvalī. Likewise, Harsha could not become a king in the life-time of his brother Rājya. The ship-wreck which compelled Ratnāvalī to work as a maid and win the affection of the royal couple ultimately helped Yaugandharāyaṇa in his plan of uniting in marriage Udayana and Ratnāvalī. Similarly, the seemingly distressing circumstances in which Rājyavardhana and Grahavarman were killed, eventually paved the way for Harsha to become the ruler both of Thanesar and Kanauj.
>
> So similar are the themes and there are such parallels in their development that one can hardly escape the conclusion that Bāṇa wrote the life of Harsha on the model of his hero's comedy—the *Ratnāvalī.*[4]

The *Nāgānanda* of Harsha has been used by scholars for a different intent— it is cited as an argument in favour of the theory that Harsha had become a Buddhist in his later years. Its hero Vidyādhara prince Jīmūtavāhana in the last two Acts behaves like a bodhisattva. It has been argued that the play clearly advocates the ideal of peace and principle of non-violence. In the *nāndī ślokas* of the *Nāgānanda* a respectful reference is also made to Munīndra (Buddha), Bodhi and dhyāna (contemplation). R.S. Tripathi has described it as 'an almost Buddhistic play',[5] an opinion with which a number of other scholars including Dasharatha Sharma, L. M. Joshi, D. Devahuti and B. N. Sharma agree.[6] However, M. Winternitz opines that the *Nāgānanda* "can hardly be considered to be a Buddhist drama."[7] According to S. K. De also, "purely Buddhistic traits are not prominent" in

[4] *Ibid.*, p. 43.

[5] Rama Shankar Tripathi, *History of Kanauj to the Moslem Conquest*, Delhi, 1959, p. 181.

[6] Dasharatha Sharma, 'Harṣa : a Buddhist', *IHQ*, XXXII, Nos. 2 and 3, 1956, pp. 168-69; L.M. Joshi, *Studies in the Buddhist Culture of India*, Delhi, 1967, pp. 421-22; D. Devahuti, *Harsha : A Political Study*, New Delhi, 1970, Second edn. 1983, pp. 179-80; B.N. Sharma, *Harṣa and His Times*, Varanasi, 1970, p. 284.

[7] M. Winternitz, *A History of Indian Literature*, Volume III, Reprint, Delhi, 1963, p. 257.

the play.[8] This dissention has made it onerous to assess the value of the drama for the study of the religion of Harsha.

COMMON AUTHORSHIP OF THESE PLAYS

The problem of these plays has become more complicated because their ascription to Harsha is not beyond doubt. Let us examine this problem step by step. Firstly, this seems to be certain that these plays were composed by one and the same author. (a) The *Bharatavākya* of the *Priyadarśikā* is identical with the *Bharatavākya* of the *Ratnāvalī* except for very slight variations in the two closing lines. The *Bharatavākya* of the *Nāgānanda*, though a little different from those of the *Priyadarśikā* and the *Ratnāvalī*, also contains the same sense. (b) Some stanzas are identical or almost similar in the three plays.[9] (c) Numerous structural similarities, parallel situations and thought, and similarities of diction etc. also suggest that the author of these works was one and the same person. (d) And lastly, as seen above, the themes of the three plays betray common features. These similitudes prove that all these three plays were composed by one and the same author.

It may also be easily conceded that all these plays claim king Harshadeva as their author. In all the three plays in his introductory speech the Sūtradhāra says : "We have heard it by a series of rumours that our lord Śrī Harshadeva has composed a play called *Ratnāvalī* (or *Nāgānanda* or *Priyadarśikā*)." In another stanza also the Sūtradhāra tells us : "Śrī Harsha is a gifted master of poetry; this assembly is also an appreciator of merits; the stories of Bodhisattva (or Vatsarāja) catch the attraction of all; we, too, are skilled in the art of dramatic performance. Even each one of these facts would (by itself), be enough to produce the desired effect; but how much more than all this assemblage of excellences combined through the abundance of my good fortune." These passages distinctly show that these plays ascribe themselves to a king-poet named Harsha.

IDENTIFICATION OF KING HARSHADEVA WITH HARSHA OF THE PUSHYABHŪTI DYNASTY

The identification of king Harshadeva of these plays with Harsha of the Pushyabhūti dynasty is also almost certain. As generally pointed out by scholars, apart from Harsha of Kanauj three other kings named Harsha are known : (1) King Harsha of Kashmir, (2) Harsha, the father of Muñja Paramāra, and (3) Harsha-Vikramāditya of Ujjayinī mentioned in the *Rājataraṅgiṇī* of Kalhaṇa. As I-tsing (last quarter of the seventh century)

[8] S.K. De, *op.cit.*, p. 258.

[9] R.S. Tripathi, *op.cit.*, p. 181; B.N. Sharma, *op.cit.*, p. 284; A.B. Keith, *Sanskrit Drama*, Oxford, 1924, p. 170.

shows his acquaintance with the literary composition of Śīlāditya based on the story of Jīmūtavāhana, Māgha (8th cent. A.D.) refers to the *Nāgānanda*, and Dāmodaragupta (who lived under Jayāpīḍa of Kashmir from 779-810 A.D.) in the *Kuṭṭanīmata* mentions the *Ratnāvalī* as authored by a king, on chronological considerations Harshadeva, the author of the plays under discussion, can be identified neither with the father of Muñja Paramāra (10th cent. A.D.) and nor with Harsha, the tyrannical king of Kashmir (11th cent. A.D.). As regards Harsha-Vikramāditya of Ujjayinī, he is rather a shadowy figure; we are told nothing about him except that he was a patron of Mātṛgupta. The non-mention of the title Vikramāditya in the plays also makes his identification with their author doubtful. Therefore, probability is high that Harshadeva, who is claimed to have been the author of these plays, was no other than Harsha of the Pushyabhūti dynasty. The following facts may also be adduced in support of this conclusion : (a) Harsha Śīlāditya claimed some poetical skill for himself. It is indicated by the Sanskrit verses occurring in his Madhuban, Banskhera and Kurukshetra-Varanasi charters.[10] (b) According to Bāṇa, "in poetical contests he (that is, Harsha) poured out a nectar of his own which he had not received from any foreign source"[11] and that "his poetical skill finds words fail."[12] (c) Yuan Chwang claims that when Harsha met him for the first time, the latter uttered his (Yuan Chwang's) praise in "verses innumerable."[13] (d) The Jaina poet Svayambhū of the 8th century A.D. refers to Śrī Harsha as a poet 'well-versed' and Bāṇa as 'verbose'.[14] (e) In his *Udayanasundarīkathā* Soḍḍhala (11th cent. A.D.) enumerates Harsha, alongwith Vikramāditya, Muñja, Bhoja etc., among kings who were also Kavīndras (kings of poets). In the same work Harsha is referred to as one whose joy lay in diction (*gīr-harsha*). Jayadeva (12th century A.D.) calls king Harsha as the joy of the heart of 'lady-poetry' (*kavitākāminī*). The *Subhāshitaratna Bhāṇḍāgāra* includes Harsha's name in the list of well-known writers. The *Bhāvabodhinī* of

[10] *EI*, I, pp. 67-75; *EI*, IV, pp. 208-11; Shankar Goyal, 'The Recently Discovered Kurukshetra-Varanasi Grant of Harsha : Year 23', *Journal of the Epigraphical Society of India*, Vol. XXXI, 2005, pp. 136-46; idem, *Harsha : A Multidisciplinary Political Study*, Jodhpur, 2006, pp. 60-70; idem, *Harsha Revisited : A Re-interpretation of Existing Data*, New Delhi, 2018, pp. 69-76.

[11] *The Harṣa-carita of Bāṇa* (hereafter *HC*), trans. by E. B. Cowell and F.W. Thomas, 2nd edn., Delhi, 1968, p. 58.

[12] *Ibid.*, p. 65.

[13] S. Beal, *The Life of Hiuen-Tsiang*, Reprint, Delhi, 1973, p. 173; for details cf. Shankar Goyal, *Harsha : A Multidisciplinary Political Study*, pp. 305 ff.

[14] G.C. Choudhary, *Political History of North India from Jaina Sources*, Amritsar, 1954, p. 17.

Madhusūdana (17th cent. A.D.) describes Harsha as the patron of Bāṇa and Mayūra, and as the composer of the *Ratnāvalī*.

TRADITION THAT HARSHA PURCHASED THE AUTHORSHIP OF THE PLAYS FOR A PRICE

Nevertheless, the identification of Harshadeva, who is mentioned as the author of the dramas with Harsha Śīlāditya, does not necessarily mean that they were actually composed by him, for the tradition is also quite old that Harsha purchased their authorship from some other poet.[15] It is said in the *Kāvyaprakāśa* of Mammaṭa (11th cent. A.D.) that 'poetry redounds to fame and makes for wealth' (*kāvyaṁ yaśase arthakṛte*) and the author himself illustrates this statement by saying: "Fame—in case of Kālidāsa and others; wealth—as to Dhāvaka (variant reading, Bāṇa) and other poets, from Śrī Harsha and other kings—*Kālidāsād-ināmiva yaśaḥ Śrī Harshāder Dhāvakā* (variant reading *Bāṇā*) *dīnāmiva dhanaṁ*." The fact that enormous wealth was given by Harsha to Bāṇa is further recorded by Soḍḍhala (11th cent. A.D.) who says that "Harsha honoured Bāṇa with a gift of hundred crores of gold" (*yena rājñā sampūjitaḥ kanakakoṭi śatena Bāṇaḥ*). Similarly, Nāgojibhaṭṭa (17th cent. A.D.), in his commentary on the *Kāvyapradīpa* of Govinda, states that "Dhāvaka (variant reading, Bāṇa) was a poet, and having composed the *Ratnāvalī* in Śrī Harsha's name, obtained much wealth, that is the report" (*Dhāvakaḥ* [or *Bāṇa*] *kaviḥ sa hi Śrī Harsha-nāmnā Ratnāvalīṁ kṛtvā bahu dhanaṁ labdhavān, iti prasiddham*). Paramānanda, another scholiast, repeats a similar story that "a poet by name Dhāvaka having sold his own work, a play called *Ratnāvalī*, obtained much wealth from the king named Śrī Harsha, so it happened of old" (*Dhāvaka-nāmā kaviḥ svakṛtiṁ Ratnāvalīṁ nāma nāṭikāṁ vikrīya Śrī Harsha-nāmno rājñaḥ sakāśād bahudhanamāvapeti purāvṛttaṁ*). From this it has naturally been suggested that Bāṇa or Dhāvaka (according to the reading taken) was the real author of these plays and Harsha purchased their authorship from him for a price.[16]

[15] S.R. Goyal, *Harsha and Buddhism*, Meerut, 1986, pp. 106-07. On this, Romila Thapar makes a pointed remark : "What is significant is that", she writes, "now not only literary accomplishment but specific authorship had become associated with kings" (*The Penguin History of Early India*, Penguin Books, New Delhi, 2003, p. 289). This statement emphasizes the corrupt atmosphere of the court culture of the Pushyabhūtis.

[16] Cf. also R.S. Sharma who opines thus : "Harsha may have composed some pieces, but the proverb goes that royal authors are only half authors. In both ancient and medieval India, various achievements, including high literary attainments, were ascribed to a king in order to boost his image. The practice of praising the patron initiated by Harisheṇa in the time of Samudragupta became common and well established under Harsha. Evidently, the object in such cases was not only to win the

This incessant tradition cannot be disregarded easily.

In this connection it has been very logically argued that as Bāṇa himself has been accused of selling his works to Harsha, his statement regarding the poetical skill of the latter is of no value. Further, at one place he makes a reference to the poetical skill of Harsha in a very curious way (cf. *supra*): "in poetical contests he poured out a nectar of his own which he had not received from any foreign source." Why this emphasis on Harsha not having received the nectar of poetical skill from any foreign source ? The statement of Yuan Chwang that when Harsha met him for the first time the latter uttered innumerable verses in praise of the former is palpably wrong. For, whether or not Harsha was the author of these dramas it cannot be imagined that he could compose instantaneously innumerable verses in praise of a foreigner whom he had not even met earlier.[17]

PROBABILITY OF DHĀVAKA OR BĀṆA AS THE ACTUAL AUTHOR OF THE PLAYS

Some scholars wrongly give the emphasis on the fact that the Chinese pilgrim I-tsing who visited India within half a century of the death of Harsha refers to his composition on the life of the Bodhisattva Jīmūtavāhana, obviously the *Nāgānanda*. But this evidence of I-tsing or of any ancient Indian author who refers to these plays as the works of Harsha merely proves that they heard the tradition or read in these plays themselves that Harsha was their author; they do not explain how and why the rumour spread that Harsha purchased these plays from Bāṇa or Dhāvaka.[18] In view of these facts Brahme and Paranjpe, Wilson and Pischel attribute them to Dhāvaka while Bühler and Macdonell assign them to Bāṇa. Hall says that Bāṇa's claim is as good as Dhāvaka's. Some have assigned *Ratnāvalī* to Bāṇa and *Nāgānanda* to Dhāvaka. Weber also attributes *Ratnāvalī* to Bāṇa.[19] According to S. R. Goyal, "on the basis of elementary principles of textual criticism the reading 'Dhāvaka' should be regarded as correct because a well-known name like Bāṇa could be substituted by an ignorant later scribe for a lesser known name like Dhāvaka, and not the *vice-versa*. The fact that the language and style of the works of Bāṇa is altogether different from the language and style of the plays attributed to Harsha supports this conclusion. The argument that we know nothing of any poet named Dhāvaka does not cut much ice. There are a large number of ancient Indian poets who have survived in name only. Should we regard all of them as having

---

favour of the king but also to validate and exalt his position in the eyes of his rivals and subjects" (*India's Ancient Past*, Oxford, 2015, p. 263).

[17] S.R. Goyal, *op.cit.*, p. 107, n.1.

[18] Cf. Shankar Goyal, *op. cit.*, p. 48.

[19] All quoted by S.R. Goyal, *op. cit.*, p. 108.

been non-existent ?"[20] However, Goyal rightly acknowledges that the claim of Bāṇa for having been the actual author of these plays cannot be altogether ignored, specially if one is ready to concede that Bāṇa could and did deliberately adopt simpler language and style for these plays.[21] We find that there is a tradition that Bāṇa was a dramatist as well. A play named *Sarvacharita* is mentioned in his name. Śāradātanaya also refers to a play titled *Śāradachandrikā* composed by Bāṇa the plot of which was related to Chandrāpīḍa (*kalpitaṁ Bāṇabhaṭṭena yathā Śāradachandrikā—Bhāvaprakāśa*, G.O.S., 252). The fact that Bāṇa was given much wealth by Harsha has also been admitted by Bāṇa himself in his *Harshacharita.* He records that 'his gracious majesty (that is, Harsha)... shared with him in his wealth...and his state dignity'.[22] The kinsmen of Bāṇa also proudly point out that he occupied 'a cane-seat (*vetrāsana*)[23] beside our sovereign lord'.[24] But inquisitively Bāṇa does not divulge the nature of his work or achievement for which he was so rewarded. His silence becomes all the more meaningful and intriguing when it is studied against the background of his character and designs.

CONCLUSION

From this discussion two facts seem to be beyond doubt : (1) These plays were attributed to king Harsha even in the later half of the seventh century A.D.; and (2) their attribution to him will at all times remain questionable.

[20] *Ibid.*

[21] *Ibid.*

[22] *HC*, tr. E.B. Cowell and F.W. Thomas, p. 69.

[23] A chair made of cane, a *mūḍhā* in Hindi.

[24] *HC*, tr. E.B. Cowell and F.W. Thomas, p. 72.

Section II

Historiography

SEVEN

On the History of Emergence of Indian Coinage

I

The problem of the antiquity of coinage in India and the question whether coinage in India emerged indigenously or was the result of some foreign influence are intertwined with each other. Those scholars who believe that ancient Indian coinage was the result of the influence of some foreign country naturally carry back its antiquity only to that earliest period when India came into contact with the coinage of that country for the first time, irrespective of the testimony of indigenous sources. The very nature of such a supposition forces them to reject or explain away the evidence which might prove that coinage in India existed before this country came into contact with that foreign influence. On the other hand, those who believe that Indian coinage system emerged and developed indigenously have no such compulsion; they usually feel themselves free to make use of the testimony of the indigenous sources, sometimes even going beyond what their sources actually depose.

The historiography of the origin and antiquity of coinage in India has suffered from both these prejudices from the very beginning. As pointed out by S.R. Goyal, "During the days of the British rule in our country the tendency of the European scholars was to trace every achievement of our ancestors, including the evolution of coinage, to foreign influence. They usually suffered from their imperialist bias. The Indian historians, on the other hand, primarily as a reaction to the superiority complex of the European scholars, tried to prove indigenous origin and high antiquity for the various elements of our culture. The conflicting attitudes of Western and Indian historians on the question of the origin of Indian coinage is a good example of these tendencies."[1]

[1] S.R. Goyal, *The Coinage of Ancient India*, Jodhpur, 1995, p. 71.

II

A majority of the early scholars of the last century credited most innovations in Indian culture to the Greeks. Even Indian history was taken to begin with the invasion of Alexander in 327 B.C. It was, therefore, thought that the coinage was also introduced in India by the Greeks of Bactria. Wilson thought it likely that the currency in India consisted chiefly, if not exclusively, of lumps of gold and silver not bearing any impression, until the Hindus learnt the usefulness of money from their Bactrian neighbours and from their commerce, especially with Rome.[2] Prinsep also at first held the same view and doubted whether any native coins, properly so called, had circulation in India anterior to the invasion of Alexander the Great, though later on he modified his views and admitted that the Indians had an indigenous currency. But even then he continued to believe that the die-device was learnt by them from the Greeks.[3]

The Greek origin theory of Indian coinage was severely criticised by Altekar in 1953.[4] He pointed out that borrowing of one coin-type from another presupposes a sufficiently significant similarity in type, shape and metrology. But there is no such resemblance between Greek coins on the one hand and the punch-marked coins on the other, which represent the earliest coinage of ancient India. Secondly, the accounts of some of the historians of Alexander the Great clearly show that minted silver currency was already in existence in India prior to his invasion. Thus, in his *Life of Alexander* Quintus Curtius tells us that among the presents given by the king of Taxila to Alexander were included two hundred talents of *signati argenti*.[5] This expression can only refer to 'coined silver money' and not to silver bullion. Further, the larger Bhir Mound hoard of PMC, discovered at Taxila in 1924, also definitely proves that the silver PMC were in circulation in India at least a couple of centuries earlier than Alexander's invasion.[6] This hoard was found in the second stratum of Bhir Mound, which belonged to the 3rd or the 4th century B.C. It contained 1055 PMC of the usual type besides two coins of Alexander and one of Philip Aridaeus. The PMC from the hoard were very worn, indicating that they must have been in circulation for a considerable time, long before the advent of the coins of Aridaeus and Alexander in the hoard which were almost in mint condition.

[2] H.H. Wilson, *Ariana Antiqua*, repr., Delhi, 1971, p. 484.

[3] *JASB*, I,p. 394; J. Prinsep, *Essays on Indian Antiquities*, Vol. I, ed. E. Thomas, London, 1858, pp. 53-54.

[4] *JNSI*, XV, i, 1953, pp. 3-6.

[5] VIII. 12.42.

[6] *MASI*, No. 59, pp. 1-2.

III

Among early numismatists the theory of the Babylonian origin of PMC, the earliest coinage of India, was advanced by Kennedy.[7] He argued that the Babylonian shekels were marked with punches like the Indian punch-marked coins. Both bear no inscription and were flat in shape and both had standard weights but no standard size. Both used a small copper alloy. Further, the *Jātakas* prove that Indian merchants used to go to Babylon for trade. It is also almost certain that India imported silver from that quarter in the form of spreadout plates. One may, therefore, conclude that the Indian PMC were influenced by the Babylonian shekels. V.A. Smith's view was substantially the same.[8]

Kennedy's theory was criticised and rejected in 1953 by Altekar.[9] He argued that the weight system of the two currencies was different. The Babylonian shekel weighed 132 grains while the Indian PMC normally weighs 56 grains. The typical PMC originated probably in Madhyadeśa and it is very doubtful whether the Babylonian shekels were known to anybody in India except a few merchants of western India. The theory of the Babylonian origin of Indian coinage is, thus, untenable.

IV

In the early phase of numismatic studies J.A. Decourdemanches, a French scholar, advocated the theory of the Achaemenian origin of Indian coinage.[10] According to him, PMC, whether of silver or copper, constitute simply an Indian variety of the Achaemenian coinage. Just as Muslim rulers in later times issued some coins with Hindu symbols and inscriptions side by side with others with purely Arabic style and legends, the Achaemenian sovereigns struck punch-marked coins with Indian symbols side by side with their own Persian *sigloi.* Allan held more or less the same view. He opines, "It is very possible that the idea of a coinage came to India in the fifth or early fourth century B.C. from Achaemenid territory, being suggested by the sigloi although its character is entirely Indian."[11] But the hollowness of this theory was forcefully shown by Altekar. He argued that the Muslim sovereigns issued coins of the Hindu type because they were already current in the country. But why should Achaemenian rulers issue coins with Hindu symbols, when none such existed in the country before their advent? The shape, the size and symbols of the Persian *sigloi* are so totally different

[7] *JRAS,* 1898, pp. 279 ff.

[8] *IMC,* I, pp. 279 ff.

[9] *JNSI,* XV, i, pp. 7-8.

[10] *JA,* 1912, pp. 117-32.

[11] *BMC, AI,* London, 1936, p. lxxi.

from those of the punch-marked coins that they can never be regarded as the prototypes of the latter. The *sigloi* have nothing like a group of four or five punch-marked symbols; the punch-marked coins have nothing like the king as an archer half kneeling to right. The earliest punch-marked coins most probably originated in Madhyadeśa (modern U.P.) and the Achaemenian influence had never penetrated to that region in the 6th or 5th century B.C., when the punch-marked coins had become quite common in that province. The weight of a *sigloi* was about 86 grains; a normal punch-marked coin usually weighs only 56 grains; the two weight systems show no connection whatsoever.[12]

V

In the early phase of numismatic studies there were a number of numismatists, even among the Europeans, who did not subscribe to the theory of foreign origin of ancient Indian coinage. Rapson thought that the punch-marked coins were developed independently of any foreign influence.[13] The same was the opinion of Edward Thomas. He observed, "Designs, treatment and die-devices (of ancient Indian coins), evince independent thought. The Indian figures follow the ideal models of their own land and bear no trace of the conventionalities of the Greek art. The devices, though at times rising above mediocrity, effect only local associations and are as free from all symptoms of imitation of the favourite Greek subjects as their details are deficient in the boldness and freedom of classical dies."[14] Cunningham too did not believe in any foreign influence on the origin of Indian coinage.[15]

However, most early Western scholars, even if they subscribed to the theory of the indigenous origin of Indian coinage, did not assign a high antiquity to it. Allan, for example, did not think that the antiquity of the latter can go much further back than the 4th century B.C. While admitting that there is sufficient evidence to show that coins were known before the Mauryan period, he adds, "It is not impossible that the tradition of the great wealth of the Nandas owes its origin to their having been the first to issue coins on a large scale. In any case there is no evidence that coinage in India is older than the Nanda period and the earliest finds, Paila, Set Mahet, and Golakpur, may indicate the region in which punch-marked coins originated. The similarity in the constitution of the usual finds indicates that punch-marked coinage did not exist over a very long period; the fact that it had not

[12] *JNSI*, XV, i, p. 7.

[13] E.J. Rapson, *Indian Coins*, Strassburg, 1897, p. 2; *JRAS*, 1895, pp. 869 ff.

[14] *Prinsep's Essays*, I, p. 211.

[15] Cunningham, *Coins of Ancient India*, London, 1891, repr., Varanasi, 1971, p. 43.

been established is indicated by the rapidity with which the new coins with type and inscription struck from a single die ousted the punch-marked coins from the second century B.C. onwards."[16]

Other European scholars, however, placed the beginning of the Indian coinage slightly earlier. Kennedy thought that the punch-marked coins were copied from the Babylonian originals after the opening of the maritime trade with Western Asia in the 6th century B.C.[17] Smith's view was more or less the same. In his article on Numismatics contributed to the *Imperial Gazetteer* he wrote: "The introduction in India of the use of coins, that is to say, metallic pieces of definite weight authenticated as currency by marks recognised as guarantee of value, may be ascribed with much probability to the seventh century B.C., when foreign maritime trade seems to have begun. There is reason to believe that the necessities of commerce with foreign merchants were the immediate occasion for the adoption by the Indian people of a metallic currency, as well as alphabetical writing."[18] Later on, however, he slightly modified his view; for in his *Catalogue of the Coins in the Indian Museum*, he suggested that the earliest punch-marked coins, viz., the bent bar pieces, were not earlier than 500 or 600 B.C.[19] Cunningham's view on this question was more liberal. According to him, "PMC were certainly current in the time of the Buddha, i.e., in the 6th century B.C." But, he admits, "I see no difficulty in thinking that they might mount as high as 1000 B.C. They certainly belonged to the infancy of coinage."[20]

Among the Indian numismatists S.K. Chakrabortty was inclined to agree with the view of Cunningham. After making a review of the whole evidence, he concluded: "So it can be safely asserted that coinage in India was evolved at about 800 B.C. and if we fix the approximate date at 1000 B.C. and accept the view of Sir Alexander Cunningham, we are not likely to go wrong; at least the margin of error would be very small."[21]

D.R. Bhandarkar, however, placed the origin of coinage in India much earlier. After considering the available evidences, he came to the conclusion that the coined money was current in the Vedic period which according to him, in all probability extended from c. 2500 B.C. to 800 B.C. He argued that since coins like the *kṛshṇalas, suvarṇas, śatamānas* and *nishkas* are mentioned not only in the *Brāhmaṇas* but also in the *Saṁhitā* portion of the Vedas, the conclusion becomes irresistible that the art of coinage was known

[16] *BMC, AI*, Intro., p. lxxi.

[17] *JRAS*, 1898, pp. 279 ff..

[18] *Imperial Gazetteer*, II, p. 183.

[19] *Ibid.*

[20] *Coins of Ancient India*, p. 43.

[21] S.K. Chakrabortty, *A Study of Ancient Indian Numismatics*, Calcutta, 1931, p. 33.

to India when the Vedic Aryans composed the Vedic hymns, i.e. about the middle of the third millennium B.C.[22]

The theory of the antiquity of Indian coinage had been supported, even before D.R. Bhandarkar, by E. Thomas[23] and A.C. Das.[24] W. Elliot also took back the punch-marked coins to the third millennium B.C.[25] He pointed out how the punch-marked coins have been found among the ashes of men who introduced primitive tombs known as Pāṇḍukulīs in south India and are unearthed from the ruins of buried cities in excavating the head waters of the Ganges canal. But, as pointed out by Altekar, we have no idea whatsoever of the dates of the buried cities, and the punch-marked coins, if they were in circulation among the aboriginal tribes among whom the Pāṇḍukulī type of tombs prevailed, should have been found in several of them which have been opened by the archaeologists. But they have not been found in any such tomb except in the solitary instance recorded by Elliot, the date of which is uncertain.[26]

VI

After the discovery of the Indus Civilization some Indian scholars were tempted to stretch back the antiquity of Indian coinage to the Indus period. But no metallic pieces have been recovered from Indus sites which can be called coins. At Mohenjodaro in the DK area K.N. Dikshit recovered in 1926 from a wall of the Late Period, a silver casket, which contained jewellery alongwith twelve pieces of silver. Of these one square piece had a cuneiform inscription, showing that it was either imported from Babylonia or was inscribed in Sindh by somebody acquainted with the cuneiform script. Of the remaining pieces, three were silver ingots, weighing 34, 45 and 66.5 grains, obviously following no regular weight system. Of the other remaining pieces, four, which weigh about 45,90,91 and 94 grains, seem to follow a weight standard, but it is different from the Indus Valley weight system, of which the unit is of 13 grains. Only two other pieces weighing about 52 and 57 grains may be said to conform to this weight standard.[27] Two other pieces, which weigh 60.5 grains and 30.2 grains respectively, also do not follow the Indus weight system.[28]

[22] D.R. Bhandarkar, *Lectures on Ancient Indian Numismatics*, Calcutta, 1921, pp. 70-71.

[23] Cf. E. Thomas, *Ancient Indian Weights*, London, 1885, p. 34.

[24] A.C. Das, *Ṛigvedic India*, Vol. I, Calcutta, 1921, p. 140.

[25] W. Elliot, *Coins of South India*, London, 1886, p. 45; *JASB*, III, p. 44.

[26] *JNSI*, XV, i, p. 24.

[27] *JRAS*, 1937, pp. 7-26.

[28] *JNSI*, XV, i,pp. 14-15.

These are the only metallic pieces approaching the size and shape of coins. They bear no symbols or inscriptions (except the one which has a cuneiform inscription) and follow no recognised uniform weight standard. They probably show that bits of precious metal were beginning to be trimmed into definite sizes and weights, but no weight system was evolved as yet in their case, as was the case with stone weights. However, K.N. Dikshit considered all the pieces, square or rectangular, as following Babylonian weight standard and also as precursors of PMC. D.D. Kosambi, on the other hand, connected only three of them with a class of Indus weights and with the metrology of PMC. He accepted these three pieces to be as good coins as any. According to him, "There are two interpretations possible: that the pieces represent purchases of silver to an approximate weight; or that they were to be smoothed down at a later date to a precise weight, having had a little margin left and in fact as little margin as possible with fairly clumsy cutting tools. If the latter explanation is accepted, the conclusion must also be taken that we are already beginning to see bits of a precious metal trimmed to standard weight, hence the beginning of a coinage system. In any case the coinage that came later must have originated in some such way, if this be not its immediate origin."[29]

VII

Accepting that the earlier Taxila hoard was deposited in c. 317 B.C. (the last known date of Philip III Aridaeus), D.D. Kosambi constructed a chronology on the basis of a statistical analysis of the number of countermarks added to the punch-marked coins subsequently to their first issue.[30] He hypothesised that the countermarks were applied periodically and, therefore, the coins with more countermarks must show greater loss of weight due to circulation over a larger period. His analysis of the statistics demonstrated that such a hypothesis could be validated. A coin with five countermarks showed approximately 2% loss of metal, with ten countermarks 4% loss and with twenty countermarks 8%, etc. He then proposed on a hypothetical basis what he considered the period of time between each countermark might have been. His suggestion was 12 years or possibly 15. On the basis of this conjectural description of the significance of the marks on the coins, he suggested that the earliest coins in the hoard, i.e. those with 20 countermarks or more were made between 240-300 years before his estimated date of the deposit of the hoard — i.e. in c. 616-557 B.C.

[29] D.D. Kosambi, 'On the Origin and Development of Silver Coinage in India', *Current Science*, 10(9), pp. 395-400.

[30] *NIA*, 1941-42, pp. 1-35, 46-76.

D.D. Kosambi's mathematical calculation opened a new area of investigation for he undoubtedly demonstrated that there was a relationship between the number of countermarks on each coin and the loss of metal from it, but his conclusions have not been acceptable to others. Against Kosambi's suggestion Cribb argued (*infra*) that there is no basis for him to assume (a) that the hoard was deposited in c. 317 B.C., (b) that the countermarks were applied at fixed periods, (c) that the loss of metal was related to time in circulation, and (d) that coin wear proceeds at a rate of 1% per 30-40 years. Taking different hypothetical bases for examining the data, one could suggest that each time the coins were countermarked, metal was lost from them by the act of countermarking or by the friction caused during a check of fineness with a touch-stone, or that the coin of Philip III Aridaeus had been dug up previously by the depositor of the hoard decades after it was first made, then was kept as a lucky charm for a few more decades before he hid it again with the hoard. Furthermore, the rate of metal loss due to coin wear is impossible to be assessed and the probability of its being anything like that suggested by Kosambi does not accord with attested measurements of loss from wear in silver coins over known periods. According to Joe Cribb, "The weight loss measured in the earlier Taxila hoard could represent a period of as little as twenty years on the basis of published statistics even if it could be shown to represent loss by wear through use. Kosambi's deductions from the evidence of the weights of the coins in this hoard are virtually meaningless, yet it is now an accepted dictum that the punch-marked coins in this hoard were issued over a period of at least 100 years if not longer."[31]

VIII

The years immediately following the dawn of Independence in India witnessed an acute controversy over the śatamāna mentioned in literary texts, and its identification with the bent bar coins, the oldest available coins of India, found in the Gandhāra region. Among the prominent numismatists who figured in this controversy in early 1950s were included V.S. Agrawala, A.S. Altekar and D.C. Sircar. The controversy was relevant from the point of view of the historiography of the antiquity of Indian coinage because the beginning of silver coinage in India and the origin of Indian coinage (in the absence of any archaeological proof for the existence of a gold currency) should mean the same thing.

The name śatamāna literally means 'measuring a hundred' and the basis of the measurement has been supposed to be the *raktikā* or rattī usually regarded as weighing 1.83 grains. In his *Carmicael Lectures on Ancient Indian Numismatics* D.R. Bhandarkar had drawn the attention of scholars

[31] *JNSI*, XLV, p. 90.

to the mention of the coin called śatamāna in Kātyāyana's *Śrauta Sūtra*, Pāṇini's *Ashṭādhyāyī*, Kātyāyana's *Vārttika* on Pāṇini, *Śatapatha Brāhmaṇa*, *Taittirīya Brāhmaṇa* and *Vājasaneyī Saṁhitā*.[32] He also pointed out that Sāyaṇa in his commentary on the *Śatapatha* passages explains śatamāna as a round plate weighing one hundred *māna* and takes *māna* to indicate a rattī. Bhandarkar, therefore, assumed that śatamāna may have been of one hundred *mānas* or *guñja* berries (rattīs) in weight. In the *Cambridge History of India* A.B. Keith also spoke of the mention 'in the *Brāhmaṇas* of the śatamāna, a piece of gold in weight equivalent to a hundred Kṛishṇalas.'[33]

However, Bhandarkar understood śatamāna in the sense of a gold coin and not a silver one. He believed that gold coins called śatamāna were prevalent even in the early Vedic age. But A.S. Altekar rejected the theory of the existence of a gold currency in the Early Vedic age.[34] Though he conceded that a gold currency including the coins called śatamāna was prevalent in the age of the *Brāhmaṇas* and *Upanishads*, but he asserted that śatamāna as a gold coin went out of vogue in later times, and a silver śatamāna of 100 rattīs in weight came into vogue by c. 500 B.C. or 600 B.C. "The *Kātyāyana Śrauta Sūtra*", he pointed out, "while describing the Aśvamedha sacrifice in Chapter XVI, refers to a *dakshiṇā* of hundred gold Śatamānas... But later it again refers to a *dakshiṇā* in Śatamāna but adds that the Śatamāna was to be of silver in one case ... There is thus some literary evidence to show that at about 600 B.C., which is generally taken to be the time of the Śrauta Sūtras, a silver Śatamāna had come into vogue, weighing a hundred Rattis or 175 grains."[35]

Altekar identified the śatamāna of the Sūtra works and of the *Ashṭādhyāyī* of Pāṇini with the bent bar coins of Gandhāra which approximately weigh 100 rattīs. In his Presidential Address delivered at Nagpur before the Numismatic Society of India in December 1950 V.S. Agrawala had also expressed the same opinion.[36] In his paper titled 'Ancient Coins as Known to Pāṇini' also,[37] he emphasised that "Taking the literal meaning of śatamāna, of the weight of the 100 *mānas* or Kṛishṇalas as suggested in the *Vedic Index*, it would appear that the Takshaśilā bent bar coins (*śalākā*) represent the ancient śatamāna coins of silver."[38]

However, D.C. Sircar did not accept the interpretation of A.S. Altekar

[32] Bhandarkar, *op. cit.*, pp. 55 ff.

[33] A.B. Keith, in *The Cambridge History of India*, Vol. I, ed. E. J. Rapson, repr., Delhi, 1987, p. 137.

[34] *JNSI*, XV, i, pp. 10 ff.

[35] *Ibid.*, p. 21.

[36] *Ibid.*, XXII, ii, 1951, pp. 108 ff.

[37] V.S. Agrawala, *JNSI*, XV, i, pp. 30 ff.

[38] II. 152.

and V.S. Agrawala.[39] According to him, these scholars have adduced no evidence to prove that śatamāna weighed a hundred rattīs. In his view it actually weighed 10 dharaṇas or 320 rattīs or 100 mañjāḍīs. For this he has quoted the evidence of the *Smṛtis* of *Manu* [40] and *Yājñavalkya* [41] which explicity mention silver Śatamāna as equal to 10 dharaṇas or 320 rattīs. Sircar feels that the belief that the weight of the śatamāna was 100 rattīs is based on the name which literally means 'measuring 100', i.e. 'made up of 100 units of measurement', on the conjecture that this unit of measurement is no other than the well known rattī. But the evidence of the *Manu-smṛti* and *Yājñavalkya-smṛti* leaves hardly any doubt that the suggestion is absolutely unwarranted.

In his reply to the points raised by D.C. Sircar, Altekar argued that though there is no explicit statement that śatamāna weighed a hundred rattīs in the Vedic period, the probability is that that was its weight since earliest times.[42] The hundred it weighed should naturally be taken as referring to a tiny weight well known to the Saṁhitās and the Brāhmaṇas. Kṛshṇala or raktikā is referred to as such a weight in several passages of the *Taittirīya Saṁhitā*,[43] *Maitrāyaṇīya Saṁhitā*,[44] *Taittirīya Brāhmaṇa*,[45] etc. It is more likely that the hundred which the śatamāna weighed was this kṛshṇala or raktikā, so frequently referred to in the Saṁhitās and Brāhmaṇas, rather than mañjāḍī which is not mentioned in them at all. The śatamāna of 320 rattīs mentioned by Manu and Yājñavalkya seems rather to have been a currency of account books than of actual transactions. At any rate, we have so far discovered no silver coins weighing 320 rattīs.

From the above discussion it is obvious that Altekar and V.S. Agrawala were not able to meet squarely the objections of D.C. Sircar against their theory of the identification of the śatamāna of literature with the bent bar coins found in Gandhāra. But surprisingly the later scholars have generally preferred to go along with them rather than with D.C. Sircar.

IX

In 1953 the questions regarding the origin and antiquity of coinage in India were exhaustively discussed by A.S. Altekar.[46] In this article Altekar examined

[39] D.C. Sircar, 'The Śatamāna', *JNSI*, XV, ii, 1953, pp. 136-50.
[40] III. 135-37.
[41] I. 364-65.
[42] *JNSI*, XV, ii, pp. 146-47.
[43] II. 3.2.1.
[44] II.2.2.
[45] I. 3.6.7.
[46] A.S. Altekar, *JNSI*, XV, i, pp. 1-26.

all the earlier opinions in detail. He rejected all the theories advocating a foreign origin of Indian coinage. He was of the opinion that Indian coinage evolved indigenously but at the same time he did not subscribe to the view of D.R. Bhandarkar that there existed a gold currency in the early Vedic age. According to him, in the early Vedic age gold "was probably obtained in the form of gold dust from the Punjab rivers and was stored either in bags or *kalaśas* i.e. pots. For the convenience of use, gold dust was transformed into lumps of definite and well-known weights (*hiraṇyapiṇḍas*) of well recognised value; otherwise we cannot understand the gift of ten lumps of gold alongwith that of ten horses. Gold was also converted into several ornaments used on the different parts of the body. One of these, *nishka*, had also come to be of a definite and well known weight and of a universally recognised value. Hence, we find the kings described as giving the gift of ten or hundred *nishkas*. What prescisely was the weight of each *nishka* or *hiraṇyapiṇḍa*, we do not know." Though *hiraṇyapiṇḍa*, and *nishka* had become well known pieces of recognised weight and value, we can hardly describe them as gold coins in the modern sense of the term though the term *nishka* came later to be used for a coin denomination in gold. There is no evidence in the *Ṛgveda* that the *nishkas* were issued under the authority of the state or guilds and were stamped with crests, insignias, symbols or inscriptions, guaranteeing their contents and value.

The situation, according to Altekar, changed in the age of the Brāhmaṇas and Upanishads when something like a gold currency came into use. *Nishka*, *suvarṇa* and *śatamāna* were its main denominations. *Śatamāna* undoubtedly weighed 100 rattīs or 175 grains. In later times *suvarṇa* and *nishka* followed the weight standard of 80 and 320 rattīs respectively. The same may have been the case in this period also. Efforts were made to make the gold currency serviceable to the people by issuing smaller pieces, quarter the weight of the normal unit, which were known as *pādas*. *Pāda* was probably a quarter of the *suvarṇa* or *śatamāna*. However *nishkas*, *suvarṇas*, *śatamānas* and even *pādas* were used mainly at the time of the sacrifices of kings and marriages of rich persons, when gifts in gold were ragarded as particularly appropriate. They are nowhere mentioned in connection with the prices of any common article.

Gold currency became more common after 800 B.C. In the earlier ages, gold coins are mentioned only in connection with rich gifts from generous kings; now they begin to be mentioned in connection with ordinary economic transactions. *Śatamāna*, which was current as a gold coin in the earlier period, continued to be in use in this age also. It is, however, mentioned not by the *Tripiṭakas* or the *Jātakas*, but only by Pāṇini who observes that *śatamāna* denoted any object bought for a *śatamāna*. There is some literary evidence to show that at about 600 B.C., which is generally taken to be the time of the Śrauta Sūtras, a silver *śatamāna* had come into vogue, weighing hundred rattīs or 175 grains. Altekar accepts the suggestion of V.S. Agrawala that the bent bar coins in silver which have this weight, corresponded to the silver *śatamāna* ; especially since the archaeological evidence shows that they were in vogue as early as c. 400 B.C.

During this period, two types of silver coins were in use : one was *śatamāna* and the other was *kārshāpaṇa.* Of these, the former denomination was the earlier one.

The *Ashṭādhyāyī* of Pāṇini refers to the *kārshāpaṇa* which was the standard silver coin of the age, and to its several sub-divisions like *ardha-kārshāpaṇa, pāda-kārshāpaṇa,* one-eighth *kārshāpaṇa* (*dvimāshaka*), and a *māsha* or one-sixteenth *kārshāpaṇa. Kāhāpana* i.e. *kārshāpaṇa* is frequently referred to in the early portions of the Buddhist *Tripiṭakas.* Silver currency was thus quite well established in society earlier than the time of the Buddha and we may safely take its antiquity to c. 700 B.C. Cunningham's observation, 'I see no difficulty in thinking that they (i.e. silver punch-marked coins) may be as old as 1000 B.C.' was of course a mere conjecture; but it is quite possible to argue that if silver coins of about four or five different denominations were quite well established in c. 700 B.C., the antiquity of the silver currency may go back by three or four centuries earlier.

X

P.L. Gupta is one of the outstanding numismatists of India and PMC is his special field of study. Therefore, his views on the origin and antiquity of coinage in India need careful consideration.

P.L. Gupta has expressed his views on these problems, specially on the chronology of PMC, at several places.[47] In 1966 he presented a paper on 'The Chronology of Punch-Marked Coins' in the Seminar held on this subject by the Department of Ancient Indian History, Culture and Archaeology, Banaras Hindu University, Varanasi. In this paper and elsewhere also, he has argued that the contents of the Chaman Huzuri hoard show that the bent bars and a few other types of the 'Local' series of PMC were current long before the currency of the 'Imperial' series which is conspicuously absent in this hoard. Gupta, therefore, agrees with Durga Prasad in believing that the coins of the 'Local' series of PMC are older than the coins of the 'Imperial' series. The Local series represented the coinage of the janapadas and belonged to the period before the rise of the Magadhan empire. P.L. Gupta surmises that the Local series originated in the seventh if not in the eighth century B.C. In the conclusion of his discussion he suggests that PMC originated in c. 800 B.C. as

[47] E.g. in the *Punch-Marked Coins in the Andhra Pradesh Government Museum*, Hyderabad, 1960; *The Amarāvatī Hoard of Silver Punch-Marked Coins*, Hyderabad, 1963; *Coins*, New Delhi, 1969, etc.

the issues of various janapadas and that the coins of some janapadas were in circulation till the sixth century B.C. while those of others upto the fifth century. The coins of the Imperial series originated with the rise of the Magadhan empire some time in the sixth century B.C. This in brief is P.L. Gupta's view on the antiquity of coinage in India.[48]

One, however, wonders how and why P.L. Gupta puts the initial period of the Imperial series of Magadha in the sixth century B.C. when in that century, and even upto the emergence of the Nandas, Magadha was only one of the janapadas, and not an empire?

XI

In 1966 A.M. Shastri drew the attention of scholars to a śatamāna reference in the *Maitrāyiṇī Saṁhitā.*[49] Earlier Altekar had drawn the attention of scholars to the reference to the *śatamāna* of silver in the *Kātyāyana Śrauta Sūtra.*[50] V.S. Agrawala had pointed out a still earlier reference to the silver *ṣatamāna* in the *Śatapatha Brāhmaṇa.*[51] A.M. Shastri now traced, what he believed to be a much earlier reference to the *śatamānas* of silver in the *Maitrāyaṇī Saṁhitā* of *Yajurveda.*[52] Shastri agreed with Altekar and Agrawala in believing that like the gold *śatamānas* silver *śatamānas* must have also weighed 100 rattīs. "The so-called Long Bar or Bent Bar or single type coins, mostly hailing from the ancient province of Gandhāra", he observed, "and weighing in the proximity of 100 *rattis* of 175 grains are generally identified as the *śatamānas.* If this identification is correct and if the silver *śatamānas* mentioned in the above works are the same, the *Maitrāyaṇī Saṁhitā* reference noticed here for the first time tends to take back the antiquity of silver punch-marked coins to the Saṁhitā period which, even according to the most conservative estimate, came to a close not later than 1000 B.C. In the light of these facts it would appear that the observation of Cunningham, who had a rare insight into matters Indian, that the punch-marked coins might be as old as 1000 B.C. was not far wide off the mark." ..."About 1000 B.C. may, therefore, be taken to be the upper limit of the age of the punch-marked coins."[53]

[48] *SP, PMC,* Varanasi, 1966, pp. 5-6. For D.C. Sircar's criticism of P.L. Gupta's views see the same work, pp. 155 ff.

[49] A.M. Shastri, *SP, PMC,* p. 116; also see, Shankar Goyal, 'Ajay Mitra Shastri's Contribution to Ancient Indian Numismatics', *JNSI,* LXVI, 2004, pp. xl-xliii.

[50] XVI. 45.

[51] XIII, 42.10.

[52] II.2.2.

[53] For a criticism of A.M. Shastri's views vide Maheshwari Prasad, *SP, PMC,* pp. 161 ff.

XII

The historiography of the antiquity of coinage in India assumed archaeological dimension in the post-1947 era, for efforts are now being made to determine the chronology of PMC with the help of archaeological data.

The archaeologists generally fix the relative chronology of the excavated materials with the help of P.G. Ware (roughly 1000 B.C. to 600 B.C.), N.B.P. Ware (roughly 600 B.C. to 200 B.C.), etc. and with the help of C-14 dating applied to organic materials contained in the strata. The dating of the PMC is closely related to the dating of the N.B.P. ware since (1) the presence of the former has been reported from practically all the levels of the latter, specially at Atiranjikheda, Kauśāmbī, Rajghat, Rupar, Ahichchhatrā, Hastinapur, Besnagar, Rajgir, Hetimpur, etc., and (2) so far PMC have not been reported from P.G.W. levels, that is, the levels preceding the N.B.P. ware strata. In recent decades great progress has been made in C-14 method of dating. It is true that being objects of inorganic nature PMC can not respond to C-14 method of dating, but in various habitational deposits organic materials and samples of charcoal are found from N.B.P. and PMC bearing strata. The date of these strata may, therefore, be fixed with the C-14 method.

In the Seminar on the Chronology of the Punch-marked Coins held in the Banaras Hindu University, Varanasi, several scholars threw light on the archaeological evidence on the date of PMC. S.C. Ray read a paper on this subject.[54] Otherwise also he has published a monograph on the coins found in excavations.[55]

According to the chart given in the paper of S.P. Gupta, of the C-14 dates the major period of N.B.P. ware is bracketed between circa 500 B.C. and 105 A.D.; but it is only at Atiranjikheda that it is dated 530-85 B.C.[56] However, the evidence of a single date is never conclusive. The concentration of dates for N.B.P. is between circa 500 B.C. and 50 B.C. S.C. Ray has also pointed out that usually PMC are slightly later than the beginning of the N.B.P. At Hastinapur and Kauśāmbī PMC were slightly later than the initial stage of the N.B.P. One should, therefore, prefer the latter bracket and conclude that archaeologically the antiquity of coinage in India cannot be pushed back earlier than 500 B.C.

The composition of some hoards containing PMC confirm the theory that the circulation of these coins began only shortly before 500 B.C. In this

[54] *SP, PMC*, pp. 26-38.

[55] Cf. S.C. Ray, *Stratigraphic Evidence of Coins in Indian Excavations and Some Allied Issues*, Varanasi, 1959.

[56] *SP, PMC*, pp. 41-42.

connection the evidence of the following hoards is of special importance:

(i) Chaman Huzuri Hoard, 1933 : It contained 43 silver punch-marked coins together with Athenian and Achaemenian coins. Date of Burial : c. 4th century B.C.

(ii) Bhir Mound (Taxila) Hoard, No. 2, 1924 : It contained 33 bent bars, 1055 regular silver and 79 minute punch-marked coins with 2 coins of Alexander and 1 coin of Philip Aridaeus.

(iii) Bhir Mound (Taxila) Hoard, No. 1, 1912: It contained 176 silver PMC with a silver coin of Diodotus.

Of these the first two hoards suggest the existence of coined money before the invasion of Alexander which took place in c. 325 B.C. The pre-Alexandrian existence of PMC may be further assumed on the basis of their worn out condition implying a considerable period for their circulation, as against fresh mint condition of the coins of Alexander and Philip Aridaeus (last known date 317 B.C.).

The dating of PMC with the help of stratigraphic evidence and their association with datable objects appears to receive indirect support from the evidence of sculpture. The representation of coins, mainly square in shape, in the scene of Jetavana in the sculptures of Bharhut datable to the middle of second century B.C. and on the Mahābodhi Stūpa at Bodhgayā of about 100 B.C. is well known. The shape of coins depicted in these sculptures strongly suggests that they were intended to be punch-marked ones, and that they were in circulation, if not in the time of Buddha, at least in the period of the Śuṅgas. A sculpture from Amarāvatī also seems to depict coins, likely to be PMC, in the same context.

It may, however, be noted that some scholars do not accept the evidence of the coins found in excavations. For example, J. Cribb still dates the PMC to fourth century B.C. arguing that their association with the N.B.P. ware is chronologically uncertain.[57]

XIII

In 1973 Michael Mitchiner published his *The Origins of Indian Coinage* from London. He connects the beginnings of coinage in India with the second urbanisation. He argues : The date when urbanisation commenced in the Ganges valley is important because it provides an approximation to the earliest date when centralised economic structures evolved and hence the earliest date at which it is reasonable to infer that coinage could have commenced. By taking into consideration all the factors concerning the economic condition of the four major areas — Magadha, Kosala, Avanti

[57] J. Cribb, 'Dating India's Earliest Coins', *in South Asian Archaeology, 1983*, Naples, 1985, pp. 535-51.

and Gandhāra — he has come to the conclusion that one can place the commencement of the Taxila-Gandhāra and the Avanti coinage, like that of the two major Ganges Valley series, in the early sixth century B.C. On the antiquity of coins his views are broadly similar to P.L. Gupta's.[58]

XIV

In 1975 M. K. Dhavalikar sought to revive the theory of the Iranian impact on the origin of coinage in India.[59] He pointed out to the fact that the silver bent bar coins of Taxila conform to the weight standard of 175 grains. Therefore, V.S. Agrawala is justified in identifying them as the *śatamānas* of literature. A number of such bent bar coins have been found mostly in and around Taxila which was the ancient Gandhāra country. Allan had suggested that the coins of this type were struck on a Persian standard and that they represented double sigloi or staters. That the weight standard of the Indian *śatamāna* and the Persian double sigloi should be the same, cannot be taken as a mere coincidence. It, therefore, appears that the *śatamāna,* which was first a piece of gold of fixed weight and later of silver, both weighing 100 rattīs or 175 gr., was found by the Indian subjects of the Persian empire to conform to the standard of their overlords. The Persian silver coins which were already circulating in the adjoining region to the north-west appear to have been imitated by the Indians in Gandhāra (Punjab). This is now corroborated by the evidence from recent excavations in Iran.

In the excavation at Nush-i-Jan near Malayir was found a hoard of objects in a bronze bowl buried under the floor level of a structure which can be, according to A.D.H. Bivar, assigned on the basis of stratigraphical and other evidence, to the period of the Median kingdom during the seventh century B.C.[60] Among the contents of the hoard were a few bar ingots of silver of which only three were intact. Such bars have not so far been reported from any other site in the eastern Mediterranean region. These bars bear a striking resemblance to the earliest Indian coins which are known as bent bars. But the specimens from Nush-i-Jan hoard are simple bars; they do not bear any stamp or mark of the issuing authority in sharp contrast to the Indian bent bars which are usually stamped with the six-armed solar or wheel symbol. Such bent bars, twelve in number, were found in the Chaman Huzuri (Kabul) hoard in Afghanistan which has been dated to about 380 B.C.[61]

[58] M. Mitchiner, *The Origins of Indian Coinage*, London, 1973, Ch.1.

[59] M.K. Dhavalikar, 'The Beginning of Coinage in India', *World Archaeology*, Vol. 6,No. 3, London, 1975, pp. 330-38.

[60] A.D.H. Bivar, 'A Hoard of Ingot Currencey of the Median Period from Nush-i-Jan, Near Malayir', *Iran*, 9, London, 1971, pp. 97-111.

[61] Idem, 'The Chaman Huzuri Hoard : Counter-marked Greek Flans as the Prototypes of Indian Punch-marked Coins', *Numismatic Chronicle*, 15, pp. 163-72.

The typical Indian punch-marked coins were conspicuously absent in this hoard. It is significant that the bent bar coins have usually been found in those regions which once formed part of the Achaemenid empire.

Here, Dhavalikar juxtaposes the fact that the bent bars are the earliest coins and PMC begin to appear slightly later though not later than the fifth or fourth century B.C., as the evidence from excavations demonstrates. According to Bivar, the unstamped Median bar currency of the seventh century B.C. was replaced slightly later in the early fifth century B.C. by small oblong pieces of silver which obviously were cut off from the bar ingots. Gradually all the surviving 'bar ingots' in eastern Iran were also reduced to 'cut silver' and the latter in turn to smaller and smaller pieces. In course of time the cut silver currency became more widespread in the Achaemenian territory.

Dhavalikar feels that we may visualize a very similar process in India too, first in the north-western regions of the sub-continent where bent bar coins were current, and then in other parts. "The bar curencey must have been found to be not only cumbersome to handle but also difficult for smaller transactions. In India, therefore, pieces of silver cut off from such bars may have been issued by the authorities. It were these pieces of silver, either rectangular or oval or irregular in shape, which were stamped with symbols, and they are the true punch-marked coins of India. It appears that the bent bars were current only for a very brief period some time in the first half of the fifth century B.C. or even earlier, for they have been identified as the silver *śatamānas* of *100 rattīs* referred to in the Later Vedic literature. ...Soon after in the fifth century, the punch-marked coins appear and in a very short time become current almost all over north India, more particularly in the Gaṅgā Valley as the evidence from several excavated sites shows. Thereafter punch-marked coins begin to occur in eastern and central India and slightly later in western India as well."[62]

Dhavalikar also sees the impact of Iran in the word *kārshāpaṇa.* According to him, it is a reduplicated form in which the same idea is expressed twice, using two different words. The *karsha* was a Persian weight standard and *paṇa* the Indian weight standard. The early Indian copper coins which have been identified as of the *paṇa* class weigh *80* rattīs, or 146.4 gr. They, however, were current in those areas where silver currency was not in use. As Rapson observes, "We may gather both directly from the statement of the law books and more generally from the study of coins that in ancient India silver and copper coinages were often independent of each other and circulated in different districts. A copper currency was not necessarily regarded as merely auxiliary to the silver currency; but a copper

[62] Dhavalikar, *op. cit.*, p. 336.

standard prevailed in some districts just as a silver standard prevailed in others."[63]

XV

In his Presidential Address to the 68th Annual Conference of the Numismatic Society of India V.S. Pathak undertook a semantic and etymological study of some numismatic terms such as *mudrā, rūpa, sikkā, nishka, viśvarūpa, śatamāna, karsha, paṇa, āhata* and *ṭaṅka.*[64] As he claims, from his study a few interesting facts emerge which throw light on the origin of Indian coinage as well. According to Pathak's study, "In the second millennium B.C., there was a cultural intercourse between India and the Semitic countries as revealed by *mudrā-muzrā* and *nsc-nishka* series of words, and this contact was responsible for the introduction of the pre-numismatic stage when gold ornaments became the symbols of value and status.

"*Śatamāna* takes us to the next pre-numismatic phase when a well defined system of weights had come into existence. With *śatamāna* assuming a definite shape and weight, the stage was set for the appearance of *numisma.*

"A study of the root *paṇa*, to sell, indicates the development of mercantile economy which served as a catalytic agent for the induction of the numismatic age. Again *karsha* reveals India's contact with the Semitic countries. *Karsha* and *paṇa* envisage a new standard of weights. *Rūpya* emphasizes the growing popularity of silver. *Rūpa*, in its third stage of semantic development, had acquired the meaning of a design carrying the authoritative sanction. It heralded the appearance of *numisma* on the scene. Around this time or a little later, *siktā* seems to have migrated to Syria and in the course of development became a *sikkā.*

"*Āhata* indicates the continuity of the method of casting and *ṭaṅka* introduces a new method of coinage, to wit, punching, which subsequently developed into die-striking."[65]

XVI

An important contribution to the study of the antiquity and origin of Indian coinage was made by Joe Cribb in the form of his papers 'Investigating the Introduction of Coinage in India — A Review of Recent Research'[66] and 'Dating India's Earliest Coins'.[67] In these papers he has discussed historical

[63] *BMC, AWK*, London, 1908, p. clxxix.

[64] V. S. Pathak, *JNSI*, XLIII, i, 1981, pp. 1-18. On this, also see Shankar Goyal, 'Professor V.S. Pathak's Contribution to Numismatic Studies', *JNSI*, LXVIII, 2006, pp. 121-25.

[65] *Ibid.*, p. 17.

[66] *JNSI*, XLV, 1983, pp. 80-101.

[67] *South Asian Archaeology, 1983*, pp. 535-51.

methodology that has been used over the last few decades for establishing when and under what influence India's first coins came to be made and has also given his own views on the subject. He has classified the methods used for this purpose into three categories — literary, archaeological and numismatic.

According to Cribb, the conclusions one can draw from the use of literary sources are very meagre. Cribb feels that all these methods have not been properly used by scholars. That explains how they claim such widely differing dates for the origin of coinage in India. Archaeologists such as Ray[68] suggest c. 500 B.C. as the earliest date for Indian coins, scholars of literature such as Shastri[69] appear to find reference to coins in texts dated c. 1000 B.C. and numismatists such as P.L. Gupta[70] claim that coinage first appeared in the early 7th century or even 8th century B.C. Cribb points out that in order to make use of literary evidence in the attribution of particular coins to a particular date it is necessary to be certain that the objects being mentioned in the literature are coins and not uncoined metallic currency. It is also necessary to be certain of the date of the literary source and to be sure that it does not contain material added at a later period. Altekar and others have shown beyond doubt that the metallic currency referred to in the *Vedas* and many other early religious texts is not coinage, but either the metallic jewellery which was used for transferring or storing wealth or the weighed amounts of precious metal as a means of exchange etc. We should remember that when a coinage is based on the use of weighed pieces of metal and the names of the weights and of the coins are the same, the mention of a weight in a particular text by such a name cannot be used as evidence for coinage.

Only two Sanskrit texts of significant antiquity, Cribb points out, the *Arthaśāstra* of Kauṭilya and the *Ashṭādhyāyī* of Pāṇini, have been put forward with confidence and consensus as referring to the punch-marked coins. But Pāṇini's references to metallic currency do not contain any descriptions of coin production or management; they only indicate the value and purchasing power of certain units of gold and silver. Cribb argues that modern scholars are inclined to accept that Pāṇini was referring to coins in these cases because his earliest commentators showed the same inclination. Now, there can be no doubt that when Pāṇini's commentators wrote coins were already in use; his commentators, such as Patañjali (whom Cribb places in the first century A.D.), therefore, applied this terminology to the form of money they knew. Pāṇini makes the statement that a 'form' (*rūpa*) when 'stamped' (*āhata*) or when

[68] *SP, PMC*, p. 37.
[69] *Ibid.*, p. 116.
[70] *Ibid.*, p. 4.

'praise-worthy' (*praśaṁsa*) takes the ending *ya* (i.e. *rūpya).*[71] His commentators being familiar with coinage which was made by striking, immediately saw in this a reference to coinage they knew and stated that when a coin (*dīnāra*) was stamped (*āhata*) it could be called 'rūpya', i.e. 'formed', etc.[72] But when Pāṇini's statement is examined in its own context, only this much can be said that he was familiar with the fact that a 'form' could be made by striking — something known long before the invention of coinage in most parts of the world. Whether Pāṇini was familiar with coins or not, his *Ashṭādhyāyī* does not specifically states.

The *Arthaśāstra* of Kauṭilya, on the other hand, provides clear evidence of the manufacture, issue, etc. of early coins but, insists Cribb, there is no certainty as to when this evidence concerning coins was included in the text. Cribb reminds us that the traditional attribution of the *Arthaśāstra* to the Maurya period is much contested and it is possible, as Trautmann has shown,[73] that it contains later material (possibly even of several centuries later).

There are many references to coins in the Buddhist *Jātakas* also, but the anecdotal nature of these texts and the manner of their transmission by oral tradition prevents any chronological conclusions being drawn from such references, which did not assume their present form until a much later date.

The second method for determining the antiquity of Indian coinage is archaeological. Here, Cribb insists that chronological data derived from archaeolgical strata, associated artefacts and C-14 method should only be used for dating by application of the *terminus ante quem* thereby derived. Even though the evidence shows that coins were introduced at a date subsequent to c. 500 B.C., this is only a *terminus post quem* and does not show when the event happened. The earliest *terminus ante quem* derived from archaeological evidence obtained in this way is only c. 200 B.C. The other dating method available to archaeologists can only be used when a definitely datable object is found associated with punch-marked coins in such a way that one can be certain that they were deposited together. The only occasion when this has happened with punch-marked coins are the hoards from the north-west of the sub-continent which contain punch-marked coins deposited with datable Greek coins. The earliest of these hoards, the Chaman Huzuri hoard, is important as the earliest absolutely datable context for punch-marked coins. The hoard contained a number of 'bent bar' coins, a form of punch-marked coins local to the north-west of the sub-continent, particularly Gandhāra, together with a large group of Greek coins and another group of locally made copies of Greek coins. The

[71] V.2.120.

[72] *JNSI*, XV, i, pp. 27-41.

[73] T.R. Trautmann, *Kauṭilya and the Arthaśāstra*, Leiden, 1971, pp. 5-7.

hoard can be given a precise *terminus post quem* because it contained a barbarous copy based on an issue of Athenian coins which began in the 390s B.C. Recent opinion dates the striking of the barbarous copy in the hoard to the 360s B.C. on the basis of another example being found in a hoard of Babylonian coins deposited in the 340s B.C. The other hoards associate silver punch-marked coins with Greek coins issued in c. 317 B.C., c. 240 B.C. and c. 180 B.C. Thus, "the only chronological conclusions that can be drawn from the archaeological evidences are that coins probably existed in India by 360 B.C. and that the two literary sources (the *Ashṭādhyāyī* and the *Arthaśāstra*) pointing to the same conclusion are possibly accurate."

Numismatic evidence used in the dating of coins is of two kinds, internal and external. Unfortunately the designs of India's earliest coins provide no evidence of datable nature. Attempts have been made to link particular punch marks with the Mauryan emperors, Chandragupta and Aśoka, whose approximate dates are known, but these attributions are by their nature purely conjectural. Pioneers, such as Durga Prasad, and later P.L. Gupta and Mitchiner and many other numismatists, have been at work describing and classifying the punch-marked silver coins, so that it has been demonstrated beyond doubt that the punches were applied to the coins according to definite procedures.[74] Cribb points out that by utilising evidence, such as the association of coins with different punches in hoards, the examination of coin-wear within hoards, the identification of weight standards, the local nature of some issues, the development of punch types and flan manufacture, it is now possible to detect many previously unsuspected facts about the coins. Three phases of coinage may now be defined : (1) an early phase of local coinage; (2) a middle phase of a national coinage; and (3) a period of degeneration of the national coinage giving rise to some local issues. Within these phases development in weight standards, flan making technology and in the organisation of punch designs and application have been established so that the approximate position of any one coin within the period of issue of the punch-marked silver coinage can now be suggested with some confidence. This is a major advance on the form of classification available to those such as Durga Prasad and Allan who poineered these techniques.

Several scholars have applied external numismatic evidence by two different methodological approaches in an attempt to develop an absolute chronology from relative chronology.[75] The Chaman Huzuri hoard with a

[74] Durga Prasad, *JASB, NS,* 1934, XLV, No. 317, pp. 5-6; 1937, XLVII, No. 343, pp. 51-92; J. Allan, *op. cit.*

[75] E.g. P.L. Gupta, *The Amarāvatī Hoard of Silver Punch-Marked Coins,* Hyderabad, 1963; M. Mitchiner, *The Origins of Indian Coinage,* London, 1973; also *supra.*

terminus post quem of c. 360 B.C. contained punch-marked coins of only one type issued during the first phase of locally issued coins, as defined by the work on relative chronology. Two hoards found at the ancient site of Taxila in Pakistan contained coins of the middle phase of national coinage. The earlier of them has a *terminus post quem* of c. 323 B.C. as it contained a silver coin of the Greek king Philip III Aridaeus (323-317 B.C.; of the Babylon mint) and two earlier Greek coins. But these three hoards, although they give us clear *termini post quem* of their deposit, do not tell us how they were assembled or how long after those *termini* they were deposited.

Another method used to make absolute the relative chronology of the silver punch-marked coins which has now been constructed is to match it to the pattern of known historical events in ancient India. P.L. Gupta[76] and M. Mitchiner[77] are the foremost proponents of this approach. This method links together three separate techniques of dating.

The first technique is closely related to that used by Kosambi outlined above. The date c. 317 B.C. for the deposit of the earlier Taxila hoard is accepted without question and because the Indian coins in it show wear, it is presumed that they were issued prior to the date of the deposit of the hoard. It is also presumed that the least worn issues in the hoard were made in c. 317 B.C. and are, therefore, attributable to Chandragupta Maurya.

Using this as their starting point, a time-table for the whole silver punch-marked coinage has been worked out by the proponents of this method. It is argued that the national coinage which pre-dates the deposit of the earlier Taxila hoard should be apportioned to the rulers of the Magadhan empire named in Paurāṇika, Buddhists and Jaina texts and that the local coinages of the earliest phase should be attributed to the states which preceded the Magadhan empire on the basis of whichever states' territory they have been found in. In this way the earliest series of the national coinage is attributed by both Mitchiner and Gupta to the period of Ajātaśatru (c. 493-462 B.C.) and local coinages have been attributed to other states such as Kosala, Vatsa, Gandhāra, Kaliṅga, etc. before Ajātaśatru and his successors drew them into their empire, and to Magadha itself. Unfortunately, Cribb points out, there is no hard evidence to uphold these suggestions. Because a hypothetical explanation of historical events offers a logical framework, it does not follow that it must be the correct one. It cannot be presumed that changes in coin designs, weight standards and minting technology accompanied changes in the political situation. No sources either literary or inscriptional provide information about the political organisation of coinage production and distribution in ancient India. The assumption is that as Magadha drew the

[76] *SP, PMC,* pp. 1-18.

[77] Mitchiner, *op. cit.*

neighbouring states into its empire the national coinage was introduced to replace a pre-existing local coinage. But, he argues, there is no evidence at all that while they were carrying out this process, Ajātaśatru and his successors were issuing coins. Furthermore, present-day knowledge of the administrative organisation of the Magadhan empire does not provide any information on the regional administration of currency. An equally plausible hypothesis could be that the Magadhan emperors allowed their provincial administrators complete freedom in currency matters and coinage issue and that the local coins were issued as a result of this licence. Therefore, the evidence is not available for making any chronological conclusions about the local punch-marked coinages on the basis of such a methodology.

In the opinion of Cribb, the Gandhāra coins show all the features of the earliest phase of coinage in the Gangetic area. So it can be suggested that the features of all the Gangetic coins could have been derived from the Gandhāra coins. The reverse could also be suggested but that does not concur with the evidence. While the Gandhāra coins can themselves be shown to have been derived from another form of currency, known from the Chaman Huzuri hoard, in the Gangetic area no silver currency pre-dating the earliest phase of coinage is known. The weight standard used by the Gandhāra coiners was also derived from the local copies of Greek coins. The standard adopted for the Gandhāra coins for more than half of the copies was the Persian shekel of c. 12 grammes. The Nush-i-Jan find[78] has also shown that the use of unstamped bar shaped silver ingots was also peculiar to the Persian sphere of Central Asia. Dhavalikar[79] has already suggested that the bent bar coins were derived from this Iranian monetary practice. Allan[80] also pointed out that the bent bars were struck on the Iranian standard, as double the weight of the silver coins struck by the Persian empire. Furthermore, the discovery of contemporary forgeries of Gandhāra local coins at Kauśāmbī [81] provides confirmation that these coins were available as prototypes in the Gangetic area.

Thus, Cribb concludes, it is clear that the Gangetic local coinage could be derived from the Gandhāra local coinage, but it is not possible for the reverse to be postulated. It is possible to use this evidence to demonstrate a family tree of these coins which points to the Gandhāra local coins as the founder of the line and to indicate the founder's parentage in a marriage between Greek

[78] Bivar, 'A Hoard of Ingot Currency of the Median Period from Nush-i-Jan, Near Malayir', *Iran*, 9, pp. 97-111.

[79] Dhavalikar, *op.cit.*, pp. 330-38.

[80] Allan, *op. cit.*, p. 16.

[81] Dolly Mukherjee, 'Copper Bent Bar Coins in the Indian Museum, Calcutta', *JNSI*, XLI, i, pp. 1-8.

coinage and Iranian bar currency. The Chaman Huzuri hoard now gives some indication of the date when coinage was first made in India. The Greek coins in the hoard show that it could not have been deposited before the 390s B.C. and was probably deposited later than 360 B.C. The proportion of punch-marked coins in the hoard shows that they were probably current along with the Greek and local imitation coins at the time of the deposit of the hoard. The evidence of this hoard, therefore, shows that the punch-marked coinage of India had originated by the mid-4th century. The contents of the hoard do not give any indication of how long before this date the event took place. P.L. Gupta has suggested that because some of the Greek and Persian coins in the hoard might be 6th century issues, so may be the Gandhāra coins; but neither his attributions of the Greek and Persian coins, nor his disregard of the *terminus post quem* of the hoard is convincing. The only evidence of chronological value that we can deduce from the hoard is that which was already available to Quintus Curtius in the 1st century A.D. Rome, i.e. the Indians already had punch-marked silver coins when Alexander arrived in their territory.

The evidence of the Chaman Huzuri hoard for the date of the Gandhāra local coins and the finding of imitations of local Gandhāra coins in the Mauryan level at Kauśāmbī as dated by its association with Aśokan pillar also suggest a late 4th century B.C. date for the earliest Gangetic local coins struck in four denominations. Dhavalikar has expressed surprise over the fact that 'a fully fledged silver coinage was introduced suddenly into India', whereas all the ancient religious texts only refer to the monetary use of gold. According to Cribb, it is easy to explain this 'surprising' fact by showing that the whole concept of the monetary use of silver was introduced from Iran. Now one can easily say with John Allan, Joe Cribb concludes, that 'the idea of a coinage came to India in the ...fourth century B.C. from Achaemenid territory, being suggested by the *sigloi* (i.e, Graeco-Persian coins).'

XVII

In 1989 B.N. Mukherjee published a significant paper on the origin and antiqutiy of coinage in India in *JNSI*, LI.[82] Distinguishing between currency (represented by pieces of valuable metal of definite weight but without the mark of issuing authority) and money (such pieces with marks and/or legends of the issuing authority) he opines that the silver pieces of definite weight found at Mohenjodaro belonged to a metallic 'currency' system. They themselves cannot be considered as weights as their shapes were not conducive to their use as such. He points out that silver objects in substantial quantity have been found only at Mohenjodaro and Harappa. The data indicate that the chief (if

[82] B.N. Mukherjee, *JNSI*, LI, pp. 39-47.

not the only) source of supply of silver to Mohenjodaro or Harappa was somewhere outside the sub-continent. The above noted silver piece bearing cuneiform characters must have been imported from Mesopotamia, where the relevant script was in use and with which the Indus merchants had trade contacts.

Thus, it appears that in the last phase of the Indus civilization metallic currency was introduced in the sub-continent, probably inspired by a Mesopotamian system and with the help of imported silver, but the pieces of metallic currency were prepared following Indus weights and not, as apparently thought by K.N. Dikshit, any Babylonian weight system. Even if the piece bearing cuneiform characters was a piece of metallic currency following a non-Indian weight standard, it was certainly an import from outside and not a part of the Indus metallic currency system. Kosambi was also wrong in connecting only three pieces to a class of weights used in the Indus civilization.

Use of gold pieces struck on a definite weight standard is indicated by the texts of the Later Vedic period. The *Śatapatha Brāhmaṇa* refers to 'gold (pieces) of a hundred standard' (*śatamānāni hiraṇyāni*). Another passage of the same text may allude to silver as well as gold pieces 'of a hundred standard'. But there is no evidence that the pieces of metallic currency were used even in the Later Vedic age as coins.

The first indication of minting of coins in literary sources is provided by the *Ashṭādhyāyī* of Pāṇini, who may be placed between c. 600 B.C. and 325 B.C. with the probability of his living in the earlier half of this period. One shall have to admit the feasibility of the employment of the term *rūpya* as indicating 'a stamped coin' in his *Ashṭādhyāyī.* This evidence receives some support from the statement of Quintus Curtius according to whom Omphis, the King of Taxila, presented Alexander and his friends a gift 80 'talents of marked silver' (*signati argenti*). Further corroboration for this comes from archaeology, for the earliest strata yielding coins in excavations in the Indian sub-continent are datable to the period beginning from c. 600 B.C. This evidence cannot prove the existence of Indian coins in the 6th century B.C. But it certainly indicates that the date of the innovation of Indian coinage may not be placed earlier than c. 600 B.C.

Thus, literary and archaeological sources broadly agree in placing the innovative period of Indian coinage in the 6th-5th century B.C. (or between c. 600 and 325 B.C.?). We cannot be more precise on this point in the present state of our knowledge. Since the śatamāna seems to have been the most popular unit of weight followed by the pieces of metallic currency of the Vedic age, it would have been natural for the first coins to be struck on that standard. In fact, the Chaman Huzuri hoard, which is the earliest known treasure-trove including Indian coins, has yielded bent bar coins and some other circular(?) pieces which can be accepted as struck on the standard of śatamāna or one of its sub-multiples. Their manufacturing techniques (dropping blank, punching on cast metal, etc.), weight and the symbols punched on them, do not betray any fundamental influence from outside sources. This inference, however, does not deny the peripherical or superficial outside influence betrayed by the shape of the bar coins (popular in Gandhāra and nearby areas) or by the practice of striking or counterstriking a device on a substantial or the greater part of the reverse of some circular and saucer-shaped coins bearing a type on the greater part of the obverse. The shape of the bent bar coins might have felt the impact of the bar-shaped silver ingots current in Iran.

But neither the bar-shape nor the system of having two 'full' devices on both sides had any impact on the pre-Mauryan local series outside the north-west or on the earliest Indian coinage as a whole. The vast majority of the symbols on early Indian coins (including punch-marked pieces) can be traced to indigenous sources. Several of the symbols on the punch-marked pieces have been found even on Indus seals.[83]

Thus, concludes Mukherjee, 7th-6th century B.C. probably provided the first real and compelling opportunities for the emergence of coins in the Indian sub-continent. It did emerge in all probability by the next century (6th-5th century B.C.). If the Achaemenid empire had its bi-metallic currency by that time, it was merely coincidental. The currency system in the Achaemenid empire did not inspire the introduction of coinage in India, though peripheral influence from the 'west' on the Indian coinage in its very early stage cannot be ruled out.

XVIII

In 1994 S.R. Goyal published his *Indigenous Coins of Early India* from Jodhpur.[84] In its ch. IV he has discussed the problems of the origin and antiquity of coinage in India.[85] As regards the origin of the Indian coinage he believes that PMC, the earliest coins of India are Indian in origin and character and, therefore, he feels no necessity whatsoever to assume that Indian coinage came into existence as a result of foreign impact. But he is ready to admit that "some minor elements of Indian coinage were inspired by foreign influence. Of this only some vague indications are now available." For example, the term *karsha* (the first part of the term kārshāpaṇa) or *karshin* is used to denote a unit of weight in the Achaeminid records. In India also, Manu defines kārshāpaṇa as a paṇa of one karsha in weight. It is obvious,

[83] *JRAS*, 1935, p. 3051.

[84] Later reproduced in his *The Coinage of Ancient India*, Jodhpur, 1995.

[85] S.R. Goyal, *Indigenous Coins of Early India*, Jodhpur, 1994, pp. 52-76.

therefore, that the term 'karsha' was either a part of common Aryan heritage (of which there is no evidence) or was borrowed by Indians from Persians when north-west India was under Achaeminid rule (which is obviously likely). It is true that the weight of one karsha in India differed, but the fact that the terms *karsha* and *kārshāpaṇa* are unknown to the Vedic literature proves that the Iranian term '*karsha*' was affixed to the Indian term '*paṇa* ', a word known to the Brāhmaṇa literature as meaning 'to barter, purchase, buy' and probably having affinity with the term 'Paṇi' of the *Ṛgveda.*

Here, it may also be recalled that the word *māna*, used in the Vedic literature in the sense of a weight may be a descendant of the Babylonian term *mīnā* as it is undoubtebly the ancestor of the Hindi word *mana* (a weight equivalent to 40 sers). Actually, the possibility of some Babylonian influence on PMC cannot altogether be ruled out. Of course Kennedy's view that PMC owed its origin to the Babylonian shekel is untenable, for PMC are distinctly Indian in character, but it can hardly be denied that the Babylonian/Persian influence might have been one of the minor factors which helped Indian coinage to take a definite shape during its transition from 'the age of metallic pieces of well-known weight' to 'the age of coinage proper'.

In this connection Goyal also takes note of the evidence of the data provided by the Nush-i-Jan excavation in Iran. Here, he has followed Dhavalikar closely.

Goyal is also critical of those scholars who have tried to prove the existence of a gold currency in India in the Early Vedic age (D.R. Bhandarkar) or the Later Vedic age (A.S. Altekar). He argues that in this whole period our economy mainly depended on agriculture and local trade; hence it could not sustain and did not need a gold currency. So far as archaeological evidences go, the N.B.P. economy lacked the affluence of other contemporary cultures of the Middle-East and the Mediterranean regions. Gold appears to be quite scarce in India before the early centuries of the Christian era. The treasure-trove finds as well as excavated materials tend to show that gold, though not entirely unknown, was a scarce metal in the pre-Kushāṇa age. Most of the ancient gold objects found in India (gold coins, gold caskets, gold beads, gold ornaments, etc.) belong to the early centuries of the Christian era. These were more or less a new feature in Indian economic life and testify to the prosperity not experienced before. It was evidently the result of India's favourable trade with other countries. It is only at Taxila that gold objects of pre-Kushāṇa period are found in some appreciable numbers but they are almost entirely Greek or Graeco-Roman in character. The question of the existence of a gold currency in the Vedic age in particular and of the antiquity of gold coinage in India in general should be viewed against this background, Goyal insists.

Archaeologically, the oldest gold coins of India issued by indigenous rulers are those of the imperial Guptas, excluding a few rare gold PMC.[86] Before the Guptas the Kushāṇas issued copious gold coinage. Earlier still the Persians struck gold darics and three Bactrian Greek kings — Diodotus I, Diodotus II and Euthydemus I — and two Indo-Greek rulers Eucratides I and Menander are known to have issued gold coins; but as argued by S.C. Ray,[87] there is no evidence to show that they were ever meant for circulation in their Indian territories. None of these gold coins is bilingual and they are found only rarely; Taxila has yielded only one specimen. Probably these coins were issued for western trade of the people of the territories north of Hindukush. Here, it is interesting to note that according to Herodotus the Indian satrapy paid to the Achaemenids a tribute in gold dust (not in coins) and the king of Taxila paid Alexander 'coined silver' and not 'coined gold'. All these facts indicate the absence of gold currency in India in any period before the age of the Kushāṇas.

XIX

In the revised edition of her *Aśoka and the Decline of the Mauryas* published from Oxford in 1997, Romila Thapar wrote an 'Afterword' in which she has given her opinion on certain problems of the Maurya and pre-Maurya periods. Here, on the question of the beginning of coinage in India she observes : "General opinion however still adheres to the sixth century B.C. as the start of coinage. In any case they would have been in circulation prior to the Mauryas. The symbols on the coins are suggestive of an indigenous origin although the notion of coined metallic money was probably known from West Asian usage. Pre-Mauryan literary evidence, with the exception of Pāṇini, does not confirm the use of coins, but is familiar with using weights of gold and silver with a designated value. Punch-marked coins would have increased in number with the greater availability of silver and this may have required close connections with West Asia and Afghanistan, apart from the more sporadic mining in the sub-continent. ... The date should be determined by dated coinage in the Chaman Huzuri hoard and by the reference to Alexander receiving talents of marked silver. An examination of the symbols suggests that there were local issues of varying weight which are rare in northern India and national issues with a standard weight found all over the sub-continent. The coins were developed in the north-west and were imitated in the Ganges towns. However, the pre-Mauryan use of coins is suggested in other sources. The Nandas are said to have standardized weights

[86] One has been mentioned in *JNSI*, XXXIV, i, p. 101 and two in *ibid.*, ii, pp. 1 ff. One is also noted in Allan's *Catalogue.*

[87] *JNSI*, XXX, pp. 110 ff.

and this is likely to have included coins. Coins were a familiar item to Pāṇini, which would date them to at least the fifth century."[88]

XX

Thus, we observe that the historiography of the problems of the origin and antiquity of coinage in India has passed through several phases. As regards the antiquity of coinage in India now there is probably no scholar who would agree with D.R. Bhandarkar that coins were prevalent in India in the Early Vedic age (c. 2500 B.C.) though some, such as A.M. Shastri, have no hesitation in pushing back the antiquity of Indian coinage to c. 1000 B.C. and thus supporting what Cunningham had suggested long ago. Most numismatists now agree with the view that though metallic pieces of fixed weight might have been in circulation in the Later Vedic age, coinage proper originated in India in the sixth-fifth centuries B.C. (or a little earlier or a little later). Being supported by archaeologcial evidence most of them feel safer with a date in the vicinity of 500 B.C. Only Joe Cribb has argued for a date in the early fourth century B.C.

As regards the origin of Indian coinage, now most scholars subscribe to the theory of indigenous origin though some still believe that Babylonian/ Persian influence might have been one of the minor factors which helped Indian coinage to take a definite shape during its transition from the age of metallic pieces of definite weight to the age of coinage proper. Only Joe Cribb still gives full credit for this transformation to Iran.[89]

[88] Romila Thapar, *Aśoka and the Decline of the Mauryas*, Oxford, 1997, pp. 288-89.

[89] For the problems of the origin and antiquity of coinage in India, also see Shankar Goyal, *Ancient Indian Numismatics : A Historiographical Study*, Jodhpur, 1998, Ch. 1; idem, in *Studies in Indian Numismatics* (Special Centenary Volume), The Numismatic Society of India, Varanasi, 2009, pp. 53-88.

EIGHT

An Introduction to Gupta Numismatography

I

The study of Gupta coins started even earlier than that of the Gupta inscriptions.[1] The first hoard of Gupta gold coins, which probably consisted mostly of the issues of the later Gupta emperors, was discovered as early as 1783 at Kalighat,[2] ten miles from Calcutta, by a certain Mr. Nab Kishen who seems to have presented about 200 of its coins to Warren Hastings, the then Governor General under the East India Company. Hastings sent most of these coins to the Directors of the East India Company in London who presented 24 of them to the British Museum, a nearly equal number to the Museum of Mr. Hunter, and some pieces to the Ashmolean Museum, Oxford, and to the Public Library at Cambridge. The rest were eventually melted down. The coins of the British Museum, however, were examined by Mr. R. Payne Knight, a celebrated numismatist, in the early decades of the nineteenth century. He could not decipher the legends inscribed on these coins and treated them as just antiquities. He guessed that they were an imitation of Greek coins.[3] Marsden, however, in his *Numismata Orientalia*, published in 1823, successfully read the name Chandra and the title Śrī Vikrama.[4] Probably, he was helped by Charles Wilkins, who had attained partial success in deciphering an inscription of the Gupta period some years earlier, though his epigraphic studies were almost ignored at that time.[5] Marsden surmised that

[1] For the progress of Gupta numismatography, cf. my paper 'Historiography of Gupta Numismatics', *VIJ*, Vols. XXXI-XXXII, 1993-94, pp. 361-68; also see my *Ancient Indian Numismatics*, Jodhpur, 1998, pp. 152-75.

[2] J. Allan, *BMC, GD*, pp. cxxiv ff.

[3] Quoted by Richard Burn in *Bhārata Kaumudī, Studies in Indology in Honour of Dr. R.K. Mookerji*, p. 148.

[4] *Numismata Orientalia*, 1823, pp. 726 ff.

[5] S.R. Goyal, *A History of the Imperial Guptas* (henceforth *HIG*), Allahabad, 1967, p. 2.

these coins were issued about the fourth century A.D., though his reasoning was based on material which would now be rejected outrightly.[6]

In 1814, the Asiatic Society of Bengal laid the foundation of a museum where coins were also exhibited. In 1833, H.H. Wilson contributed a paper to the *Asiatic Researches*, Vol. XVII, on the coin-collection of the museum as it stood in that year. The plates which illustrate this paper were drawn by James Prinsep who was Wilson's assistant in the Calcutta mint. At that stage neither Prinsep and nor Wilson could make much of the Gupta coins. On the reverse of a Standard type coin of Samudragupta Wilson recognised *pa*, *ra* and *ka* but he could neither complete the word *parākramaḥ* and nor decipher any letter in the legend on the obverse. Similarly, on the reverse of a coin of Prakāśāditya he suggested *Śrī Praki* for *Śrī Prakā (śāditya)* and thought that the reading might be *Śrī Prakīrtti.* At that time nobody except Marsden had realized that the name of the king was written on the obverse in a perpendicular fashion. Within a few years, however, when the study of the Gupta inscriptions was resumed, the decipherment of the legends on the Gupta coins became easier. By 1835, Prinsep had made considerable progress in reading their marginal inscriptions and showed that the Gupta coins followed the pattern of the 'Indo-Scythic' coinage, but were purely Indian in execution.[7]

After the decipherment of the Gupta script, it became possible to connect the kings known from their coins with the kings mentioned in the Gupta records. It made the study of the Gupta coins immensely interesting and highly rewarding. But at that time Indian numismatics was in its infancy and scholars paid greater attention to the internal evidence of the coins, i.e., in the data provided by their types, symbols, inscriptions, fabric, metrology, etc. But they soon realized that the early Gupta emperors had modelled their coinage after the gold coinage of the Later Imperial Kushāṇas, though very soon the process of Indianization was at work and within a few decades the Gupta coinage had become almost thoroughly Indian in character. It led Allan to postulate the chronology of the early Gupta coins on the basis of gradual decrease in foreign influence on them. The hypothesis was basically sound, though too much emphasis on it led on occasions to quite erroneous conclusions.[8]

In the later half of the nineteenth century and in the early years of the twentieth, apart from stray pieces, a number of new hoards of the Gupta gold coins were found. Prominent among them were those which were found at Bharsar (1851), Jessore (1852), Allahabad (1864), Hugli (1883), Tanda

[6] *Ibid.*, p. 17.

[7] *Ibid.*

[8] *Ibid.*, pp. 102-10.

(1885), Kotwa (1886),[9] Basti (1887), Hajipur (1893) and Tekri Debra (1912). Their contents were intensively studied by the leading numismatists of the period and the results of these investigations were summed up by V.A. Smith in his *Catalogue of the Coins of Ancient India in the Indian Museum, Calcutta*, Vol. I : *The Early Foreign Dynasties and the Guptas* (1906)[10] and John Allan in his famous *Catalogue of the Coins of the Gupta Dynasties in the British Museum*, published in 1914. Allan's *Catalogue* remained the basic source book on Gupta coins for about half a century and is still a must for researchers on the subject.

Several other hoards came to light after the publication of Allan's work including those found at Kasarva (1912), Sakori (1914), Mithathal (1915), Bamnala (1940), Bayana (1946), Kusumbhi (1947), Khairatal (1948) and Kumarkhan (1952).

II

The Bayana hoard is the biggest hoard of the Gupta gold coins so far discovered. A.S. Altekar published a separate catalogue of its contents in 1954. (*The Gupta Gold Coins in the Bayana Hoard*, Bombay). By that time Allan's famous *Catalogue*, published in 1914, had long been out of print. Besides, numerous new types of Gupta coins had been brought to light during the intervening four decades and had been discussed in numismatic and other research journals. The Numismatic Society of India, therefore, planned a Corpus of Gupta Coins and entrusted the work to A.S. Altekar, who was well known for his researches in Indian numismatics. He set himself immediately to the task. The typescript of the volume was ready for the press as far back as 1946. But before its printing could be taken up, the unique hoard of Gupta gold coins at Bayana in the former Bharatpur State came to light and the task of cataloguing its coins was also entrusted to Altekar. On examining the hoard Altekar noticed that it contained several new types of the gold coins of the Guptas. He, therefore, decided to publish the catalogue of the Bayana hoard first. This was done in 1954. The preparation of *The Corpus of Gupta Coins*, which had been temporarily shelved, was next taken up and brought uptodate. The Numismatic Society published it as Volume IV of its series of the Corpuses of Indian Coins.

Altekar's *Catalogue of the Gupta Gold Coins in the Bayana Hoard* is a colossus which brought uptodate the material that had cropped up since

[9] Kotwa hoard is mentioned in *JRAS*, 1893, p. 47. However, it is not included in the list of the Gupta hoards given in the *BMC, GD*, pp. 18-19.

[10] Earlier in 1884 the *Catalogue of the Coins of Gupta Dynasty* was published by V.A. Smith (*JASB*, 1884, pp. 119 ff., with four plates). It was improved by the same author and appeared with additions in *JRAS*, 1889, pp. 1-159, with five plates.

the publication of Allan's *Catalogue.* It gives a description of 1821 coins found in the hoard and illustrates 459 of them, 188 more than illustrated by Allan. It disclosed a number of types and varieties that were unknown till then.

The *Bayana Hoard* is divided into two parts, viz., Introduction and the Coin Catalogue proper. After giving an account of the discovery of the hoard in section I of his introduction running in 158 pages, in section II Altekar describes other hoards of Gupta gold coins and the importance of the Bayana hoard. Section III deals with the history of the Gupta dynasty while section IV, in over 80 pages (xl-cxx), describes the coinage and coin types of the imperial Guptas. Here, the treatment is exhaustive and comparative. Not only the coin types of the hoard are described, but attention is also drawn to a few types and varieties that are not represented in it. The number of coins of each type in different museums is also stated and references are given to the corresponding varieties in Allan's *Catalogue.* Section V of the introduction deals with the metrology of each variety and type, section VI with the palaeography of the legends, sections VII with symbols and section VIII, written by Motichandra, discusses the data of Gupta gold coins for ascertaining the fashions of dress and ornaments and varieties of furnitures and weapons in the Gupta age. Then, follows the description of the coins of the Bayana hoard included in the *Catalogue* (pp. 1-308) followed by a brief description of the coin types of the successors of Kumāragupta I, not represented in the hoard, and eight appendices.

The Bayana hoard greatly advanced our knowledge about Gupta coinage. Of the 1821 recorded coins, Samudragupta's Standard type accounted for 143 specimens, Chandragupta II's Archer type for 798 (of which 757 were of Archer (Lotus reverse) type, and Kumāragupta I's Horseman type for 305 and Archer type for 183 specimens, thus confirming the fact that the above were the commonest types in Gupta mintage. These 5 types together accounted for 1429 specimens i.e. 79 percent of the total, and the remaining 25 types were restricted to 392 specimens. An analysis of the hoard shows that all the eight types of Samudragupta (if Chandragupta-Kumāradevī and Kācha coins are attributed to him) were included in it, viz. the Standard, Aśvamedha, Battle-axe, Archer, Lyrist, Tiger-slayer, Kācha and King-and-Queen types. Of Chandragupta II, the usual 6 types, viz. Archer (Throne reverse), Archer (Lotus reverse), Horseman, Chhatra, Lion-slayer and Couch types were found in the hoard. The two disputed types of this king, viz. King-and Queen-on-Couch and Standard types, are conspicuous by their absence. The unique specimen of Chakravikrama type, attributed to Chandragupta Vikramāditya, is the most significant type brought to light by the hoard. For Kumāragupta Mahendrāditya, all his previously known nine types occur in the hoard, a feature quite in consonance with that of the coins of his two illustrious predecessors. These nine types are : Archer, Swordsman, Horseman, Peacock, Tiger-slayer, Lion-slayer, Aśvamedha, Elephant-rider and Apratigha (the former Śrī-Pratāpa type). The Elephant-rider-Lion-slayer type, of which a single specimen was acquired by Hiranand Shastri, was represented by 4 new specimens. Then there were 4 quite new types contributed by this hoard, viz., Chhatra, Rhinoceros-slayer, Lyrist and King-and-Queen. The hoard was probably buried during the troubled days which preceded and followed the death of Kumāragupta I, for it contained no coins of his successors, except the solitary Chhatra type coin of Kramāditya, who has been identified with Skandagupta or Ghaṭotkachagupta by different scholars. The coins of the hoard also enabled the scholars to complete a number of legends that were not properly deciphered till then.[11]

Besides the problem of objective recording, these coins raise important historical and chronological problems. Take for example the attribution of the coins of the Chandragupta-Kumāradevī type. Altekar has examined in detail the various arguments advanced by Allan to prove that they were commemorative medals struck by Samudragupta in honour of his parents and has tried to show that these coins were jointly issued by Chandragupta I, the Gupta king, and Kumāradevī, the Lichchhavi princess. The attribution of Kācha coins raises another problem. Altekar changed his opinion on this question several times. In his Hindi book on the Gupta coins, of which the preface is dated 25.1.1954, he devoted six pages to prove the identity of Kācha with Rāmagupta and make the latter a full-fledged Gupta emperor who succeeded Samudragupta. In the *Bayana Hoard*, of which the preface is dated earlier (12.9.1953), Kācha and Rāmagupta are not identified and Kācha is taken as a predecessor of Samudragupta 'who successfully contested the throne and ruled for some time' (p.xvi), and Rāmagupta as a successor of Samudragupta who preceded Chandragupta II, probably because the discovery of the copper coins of Rāmagupta in Malwa had proved that "one and the same ruler could not have issued the coins with the name of Rāmagupta on copper coins and Kācha on gold ones, even if he had these two names." (p. xvi). However, in his *Coinage* published in 1957 Altekar placed Kācha after Samudragupta.

The Bayana hoard also helps us to revise the reading on the 'Two Queens type' coin of Kumāragupta, from *Śrī-Pratāpa* to *Apratigha* which is now undisputed. Its correct interpretation, however, is still a matter of controversy.

The numismatic sequence of the issues of Samudragupta as fixed by

[11] For a study of the legends on the Gupta gold coins in the light of the *Vishṇusahasranāma* cf. B.Ch. Chhabra, *JNSI*, IX, ii, pp. 137-45.

Allan on the basis of progressive Indianisation was as follows : I. Standard; II. Archer; III. Chandragupta-Kumāradevī; IV. Battle-axe; V. Kācha; VI. Tiger-slayer; VII. Lyrist; and VIII. Aśvamedha. Alteker has departed from this arrangement in favour of another, viz. I. King-and-Queen; II. Standard; III. Aśvamedha; IV. Battle-axe; V. Archer; VI. Lyrist; VII. Tiger-slayer; and VIII. Kācha.

A.S. Altekar summed up the knowledge of the Gupta gold coins to date in his *Coinage of Gupta Empire and Its Imitations* (Corpus of Indian Coins, Vol. IV), published in 1957 from Varanasi. It draws heavily on his *Bayana Hoard.* It is divided into twelve chapters. In its chapter I he has briefly dealt with the political history of the Gupta dynasty (pp. 1-11) while in chapter II he has given a general survey of the Gupta coinage. (pp. 12-25). Chapters III to X describe the coinage of the great Gupta emperors from Chandragupta I to Skandagupta. (pp. 26-261). Chapter XI deals with the coins of the successors of Skandagupta. (pp. 262-86). The silver and copper coins of the Guptas are also discussed and described at appropriate places. Symbols, metrology, palaeography and hoards are dealt with in chapter XII. (pp. 287-314). The work carries seven appendices of which appendix I (pp. 315-37) discusses the imitations of the Gupta coinage while appendix II (pp. 338-59) describes new discoveries which were made between 1953-57 when the book was in press.

The earlier publication of the *Bayana Hoard* did not render the publication of the *Coinage* superfluous because the Bayana hoard contained only gold coins of the Gupta kings. Their silver and copper coins were not included in it and though Altekar had described and discussed them in his Introduction to that volume, they were not illustrated. Besides, the Bayana hoard was apparently buried in the beginning of Skandagupta's reign as it did not contain any coins of the successors of Kumāragupta I except the solitary coin of Kramāditya. Though Altekar described them briefly in order to give the reader of the *Bayana Hoard* a fair idea of the coinage of the whole dynasty, the treatment of this matter was necessarily sketchy. The *Coinage* gives a detailed description of all these coins together with illustrative plates. It is, therefore, more comprehensive than the *Bayana Hoard.*

Guptakālīna Mudrāyeṁ (Coins of the Gupta Age) by Altekar (Patna, 1954) is also an authoritative treatise on Gupta coins written in Hindi. It contains twelve chapters dealing with Gupta history, coins and coin-types, coins of each emperor, a detailed description of all the coin-types issued in gold, silver and copper, including the coins of the later imperial Guptas, viz. Purugupta, Ghaṭotkachagupta, Narasiṁhagupta, Kumāragupta II, Budhagupta, Vishṇugupta, Vainyagupta and Prakāśāditya.

In his works, at several places Altekar states and discusses the views of other scholars on controverisal matters. But while stating his own views he is rarely dogmatic. He always keeps an open mind and is prepared to change his opinion when adequate evidence is put forward. For example, he changed his opinion on Kācha coins several times. Similarly, while describing the Chakravikrama type coins of Chandragupta II in chapter II, he at first stated that the god who is seen therein bestowing a gift on the king before him is Vishṇu himself (p. 23), but later, after weighing the evidence put forward by other scholars, he changed his opinion and admitted that the divine figrure is that of the Chakra Purusha aspect of Vishṇu. (pp. 147-48). It is now almost unanimously believed that the figure inside the Chakra represents Chakra Purusha who is shown bestowing on Chandragupta II three symbols of royal power, viz., *prabhu-śakti, utsāha-śakti* and *mantra-śakti*, i.e. the kingly virtues of authority, energy and counsel.[12] The symbology of this scene becomes clearer in the light of the data provided by the *Ahirbudhnya Saṁhitā*, a well known text of the Pāñcharātra Āgama, which 'on the basis of the internal evidence bearing on the religious conditions portrayed in it, should be assigned to Gupta period.'[13] From it we learn that Vishṇu, in the form of Chakra, was held as the ideal of worship for kings desirous of obtaining universal sovereignty. The *Ahirbudhnya Saṁhitā* clearly states that he who adores Lord Chakra Purusha becomes a Sārvabhauma or Universal Ruler in this world and also becomes a ruler in the other world. Anyone who does not pay homage to this deity cannot attain supreme kingship. As we have shown elsewhere, it is indeed a welcome addition to our knowledge of the political philosophy of the early imperial Guptas.[14]

The works of Altekar, described above, are indeed a landmark in the historiography of Gupta numismatics. For serious students and researchers of the Gupta coinage these are not only essential but shall remain a 'must' for decades to come.[15]

III

P.L. Gupta is one of the most renowned numismatists of India. He has written a number of research papers on Gupta numismatics though he has not come out with any monograph on the subject excepting a small work titled *Gupta*

[12] Shivaramamurti, *JNSI*, XIII, ii, pp. 180 ff.; V.S. Agrawala, *JNSI*, XVI, i, pp. 97 ff.

[13] Agrawala, *op. cit.*, p. 97.

[14] For details vide my paper titled 'Political Ideology of the Early Imperial Guptas', in *Reappraising Gupta History for S.R. Goyal*, eds. B.Ch. Chhabra, P.K. Agrawala, Ashvini Agrawal and Shankar Goyal, pp. 220-21.

[15] For Bayana hoard coins also see B.Ch. Chhabra, *Catalogue of the Gupta Gold Coins of the Bayana Hoard in the National Museum*, New Delhi, 1986; Shankar Goyal, 'A.S. Altekar and the Bayana Hoard', *JNSI*, LXVII, pp. 80-84.

Gold Coins in Bhārat Kalā Bhavan written in collaboration with Sarojini Srivastava (Kashi, 1981). In 1969 he published a general work on Indian numismatics titled *Coins* from New Delhi. Its second edition appeared in 1979. In its chapter VII (pp. 53-58) P. L. Gupta very briefly discusses coins and coin types of the Gupta emperors. But due to the nature of this work he gives only a survey of the subject. In 1970 he published his *Gupta Sāmrājya* in Hindi and in 1974 *The Imperial Guptas*, Vol. I, in English from Varanasi. In both of these works he deals with all the available sources at length. In his English work in the section on Gupta coins (pp. 69-112) he has given all the useful information on the subject.[16]

Among the major papers on Gupta coins written by P.L. Gupta are included those on the coins of Chandragupta-Kumāradevī type, coins of Kācha (whom he rightly identifies with Bhasma of *ĀMMK*), Kramāditya (known from a single specimen), Prakāśāditya and Kumāragupta Kramāditya. He rightly distinguishes between Kumāragupta Kramāditya II and another king with the same name and *biruda*. P.L. Gupta has also tried to show that Purugupta did not issue any coins.

In 1992 also P.L. Gupta presented some suggestions on Gupta numismatics some of which are quite illuminating.[17] One only wishes that a numismatist of his calibre had written a detailed monograph on the Gupta coinage.

IV

A small monograph titled *History and Coinage of Skandagupta Kramāditya* was published by Jai Prakash Singh in 1976 from Varanasi carrying a learned foreword by Lallanji Gopal. The work is divided into four chapters and five appendices. As the nomenclature of the book suggests, it is an addition to the literature on the coinage of the Gupta dynasty. Its Introductory chapter gives an outline of the reign of Kumāragupta I. Here, Singh rejects the arguments of S.R. Goyal who thinks that the discovery of Kumāragupta I's coins from Samand and Ellichpur, and the similarity of his silver coins of Class III with the Traikūṭaka coins prove that he may have expanded his kingdom in the southward direction. Singh also does not subscribe to the view that Kumāragupta's Tiger-slayer type coins are indicative of his conquest of the territory beyond the Narmadā. According to him, the suggestion of the conquest of a part of the south-western Deccan by

[16] For P.L. Gupta's contribution to the study of Gupta gold coins see my paper 'P.L. Gupta and Gold Coins of the Guptas' in *P.L. Gupta Felicitation Volume*, ed. Sarojini Kulashreshtha, Delhi, 1995, pp. 271-78.

[17] In *Political History in a Changing World*, eds. G.C. Pande, S.K. Gupta and Shankar Goyal, Jodhpur, 1992, pp. 177-92.

Kumāragupta on the basis of the discovery of his silver coins from there and his coins of the Tiger-slayer type is conjectural and fanciful. He observes that the coins may well have travelled to that region with merchants engaged in trade, and to think of a conquest of the region merely on the basis of these discoveries amounts to a misunderstanding of the numismatic evidence. "Had the coins been in active circulation in parts of Deccan, they must also have been found almost regularly from the area." (p. 8). On the suggestion of S.R. Goyal that "the horse-sacrifice, on the occasion of which the Aśvamedha coins of Kumāragupta I were issued, was performed to celebrate his southern adventure," Singh points out that, "Aśvamedha sacrifice in ancient India was performed by a king not necessarily after the successful completion of a campaign. Therefore, the issue of Kumāragupta's Aśvamedha coins cannot be connected with his so-called conquest of the south-western Deccan, or for that matter, with any other proposed victorious campaign." (pp. 7-8).

The last chapter of Singh's work describes the coinage of Skandagupta who is known to have struck coins only in gold and silver. But his coinage is rather scanty both in terms of numbers as well as types as compared to those of his predecessors probably because of "the troubled nature of his kingship due to his involvement in almost constant warfare with his enemies." (p. 75). Singh's description of the gold coinage of Skandagupta is quite interesting though not fully convincing. He includes the Archer, the King-and-Queen, the Horseman, the Chhatra and the Garuḍa types among the five gold coin-types of Skandagupta. But only the Archer and the King-and-Queen types are definitely attributable to him as they bear his name either on the obverse or on the reverse. However, such is not the case with the Chhatra and the Horseman type coins, both known from a single specimen each, which reveal only the *biruda* of the issuer (Kramāditya). Similar is the case with the Garuḍa type repousse coins.

On the controversy of the nomenclature of the King-and-Queen type Singh observes that "It is rather certain to suggest on the analogy of the King-and-Queen types of Chandragupta I, Chandragupta II and Kumāragupta I that this type of Skandagupta definitely belongs to this very class of Gupta coins." (pp. 79-80). According to him, the coin was in all probability struck in the beginning of the king's reign, sometime after his coronation. (p. 80).

Skandagupta was the second and the last Gupta emperor to issue silver coins of both the Western and Madhyadeśa types in fairly large quantity. His Western silver coinage is divisible into three classes : the Garuḍa, the Bull and the Altar types. Singh maintains that these coins were struck throughout the reign of the king and do not necessarily belong only to its early part as is often suggested, though some of them indeed belong to the early years of his reign. The Madhyadeśa coinage of Skandagupta is of a uniform type. Its reverse bears a fan-tailed peacock. The coins of this class are larger in size than the Western Indian issues and are certainly much better in execution. Singh thinks that this type of Skandagupta were also issued practically throughout his reign.

V

As is well known, the history of the Gupta age is the special area of interest of S.R. Goyal who appeared on the scene of Gupta studies with his doctoral dissertation *A History of the Imperial Guptas* published in 1967 from Allahabad. It was described by A.L. Basham as "the best analysis of the Gupta period which I have ever read." His *Guptakālīna Abhilekha* (Meerut, 1984) is also regarded as the most significant work on Gupta epigraphs after Fleet's *Corpus.* In the opening chapter of his *A History of the Imperial Guptas* (pp. 1-40), described by Eleanor Zelliot, as 'imaginative', 'well-written' and 'a model of historiography',[18] Goyal for the first time analysed the methods and techniques of studying various types of data, including numismatic evidence, for the reconstruction of Gupta history. While dealing with numismatic data of the period Goyal takes note of the work done by early numismatists (pp. 16-18), nature of numismatic evidence (pp. 18-19) and internal and external aspects of numismatic evidence. (pp. 19-23). He opines that the find-spots of a few coins, or even of a hoard, is by itself not always a reliable evidence on which to base conclusions regarding the location of the kingdom of the issuer. "But when coins of a particular class turn up year after year at an ancient site more certain conclusions can be drawn."[19] Similarly, when an area yields hoard after hoard, containing the coins of early rulers, that area may be regarded as the early centre of the activities of that royal family.[20] Unfortunately, earlier numismatists, and even a large number of recent historians, have paid sufficient attention neither to the composition nor to the provenance of the hoards of the Gupta gold coins and have not applied the age and area concept to the study of Gupta numismatics while a proper application of this principle is likely to yield very significant results.

Goyal also brought out a remarkable work on Gupta numismatics from Jodhpur in 1994, titled *An Introduction to Gupta Numismatics.* This work deals exhaustively with fundamental problems of Gupta numismatics. Divided into four chapters — Genral Features of the Gupta Coins, Gold Coin Types,

[18] In *Essays on Gupta Culture,* ed. Bardwell L. Smith, Delhi, 1983, p. 288. On this, also see S.R. Goyal, *The Imperial Guptas*, Jodhpur, 2005, Ch. 2.

[19] *HIG*, p. 22.

[20] *Ibid.*, pp. 22-23.

Silver and Copper Coins of the Guptas and Gupta Impact on post-Gupta Coins—the work also contains an exhaustive Bibiliography and numerous photographic illustrations and line-drawings. Goyal's work is somewhat unique because it seeks to make a comprehensive but compact study of almost all the aspects of Gupta coins in a scientific manner and includes the results of the latest discoveries and researches. On many numismatic problems it sheds new light and suggests new solutions.

On the attribution of Chandragupta-Kumāradevī coin-type Goyal has argued that these coins were issued either by Chandragupta I or by Samudragupta before he issued the Standard type coins. (pp. 41-46). According to him, the latter alternative seems to be the correct one. The Standard type coins were issued quite late in the reign of Samudragupta, for they bear long legends referring to his conquests indicating that they were not struck in the beginning of his reign; if Chandragupta I had issued the Chandragupta-Kumāradevī type coins it would be remarkable that Samudragupta did not immediately continue to issue gold coins. The assumption that Samudragupta issued Chandragupta-Kumāradevī type coins in the early period of his reign does not create such a difficulty.

The greatest hurdle in the suggestion that the Chandragupta-Kumāradevī type was issued by Samudragupta is the supposed absence of any clue to the identity of the commemorator.[21] To overcome this difficulty V.S. Agrawala argued that they were issued by the Lichchhavis who have been mentioned on the reverse of these coins,[22] while V.S. Pathak has suggested that the obverse legends *Chandraguptaḥ* and *Kumāradevī Śrī* and the device of the marriage-scene may together be taken as meaning *Chandraguptasya Kumāradevyāmutpannasya* while the reverse legend *Lichchhavayaḥ* may be construed as *Lichchhavinām-dauhitrasya.* Thus, legends and devices are subtle pointers to the identity of the commemorator, that is Samudragupta.[23] Sohoni[24] also opines that there is enough indication left by Samudragupta on Chandragupta-Kumāradevī type to indicate a reference to him, viz., names of his parents and of the community which had helped him. Goyal, however, feels that such a twist in the meaning of the legends is not altogether necessary. For, as pointed out by Jayaswal, no Hindu would ever think of celebrating the marriage of his father and mother.[25] It is, therefore, more reasonable to assume that Samudragupta issued these medals in the name of the Lichchhavis who were, after all, the

[21] Altekar, *Coinage*, pp. 28-29.

[22] *JNSI*, XVII, i, p. 119.

[23] *Ibid.*, XIX, ii, p. 141.

[24] *Ibid.*, p. 153.

[25] Jayaswal, *Hist. Ind.*, p. 91, fn. 1.

co-rulers of the empire. It is quite likely that when his accession was challenged by his rival brothers, he issued these medals in order to publicize the fact that he, being a *dvyāmushyāyaṇa* had a better title to rule over the amalgamated kingdom of the Guptas and the Lichchhavis which other princes, not connected with the Lichchhavis, did not have. It also explains why these coins are not found in Bihar, the region in which the Lichchhavi state was situated. For, if they were issued to publicize that he had a better title to rule over the amalgamated kingdom, it was only natural for him to circulate them in the region where the rebellious princes 'of equal birth' could hope to find some support. The Lichchhavi state must have been solidly behind him and, therefore, he did not feel the necessity of circulating such medallic pieces there.

On Śrī Vikrama coin of Samudragupta (pp. 103-06) Goyal has criticised the generally accepted opinion that the solitary coin giving the *biruda* '*Śrīvikrama*' to Samudragupta found in the Bamnala hoard was issued during the reign of Chandragupta II, when the obverse die of the Standard type coins of Samudragupta was inadvertently used with the reverse die of the Archer type of Chandragupta II. It is argued that as no Gupta king used two titles, it cannot be assumed that Samudragupta adopted both the titles *Parākrama* and *Vikrama*. However, Goyal has pointed out that Skandagupta assumed the titles *Kramāditya* and *Vikramāditya* both. Further, according to him, mertrology and other numismatic considerations are in favour of regarding this coin as the issue of Samudragupta.

Another theory of Goyal, which is worth-noting here, is concerned with the coins of Prakāśāditya. (pp. 96-101). In this he has given arguments to prove that Prakāśāditya ruled just after Bhānugupta (known date 510 A.D.). For this he has taken the help of the *Āryamañju-śrīmūlakalpa* which refers to 'Pra' initialled, that is Prakāśāditya as the rebellious son of 'Bha' initialled, that is Bhānugupta.

However, K.S. Shukla has tried to give a new turn to the problem of the identity of Prakāśāditya. He published another specimen of the Horseman-lion slayer type coin on which he has read thc circular legend on th obv. between II and IV o'clock as *Bhānugupta* and between VI and XII as *vijitya vasudhāṁ divaṁ jayati.*[26] His reading was accepted and hailed by the editor of the journal, T.P. Verma.[27] However, Verma rightly pointed out that K.S. Shukla's suggestion that the coin shows that Bhānugupta was the ruling emperor and Prkāśāditya his viceroy cannot be accepted. If Shukla's reading is correct, then Prakāśāditya should be regarded as the title of

[26] *JNSI*, XLII, pp. 120-22.

[27] *Ibid.*, Editorial Note.

Bhānugupta. P.L. Gupta and S.R. Goyal accept this obvious conclusion.[28] But lately the testimony of the coin itself has come to be regarded as suspect. Firstly, the original coin seen by Shukla in 1975 with a goldsmith at Nawal (Dist. Unnao, U.P.) has since disappeared and its present whereabouts are not known to anybody. Secondly, the photograph of the coin published in the *JNSI* is very poor and serves no useful purpose. Thirdly, it appears that Shukla's reading of the letters *Bhā, nu* and *gu* is not correct. Jagannath Agrawal rules out absolutely the reading *Bhānugupta* on it.[29] Fourthly, P.L. Gupta points out that in accordance with the norms of the circular legends on the Gupta coins, the coin should have the name of the king with or without his *biruda* just before the existing portion of the legend between V and VIII o'clock, and not between II and IV o'clock.[30]

Thus, the so-called new evidence on Prakāśāditya has proved to be a non-starter and we are back to the square one. After rejecting the testimony of this coin Ashvini Agrawal has reverted to the old theory of the identification of Prakāśāditya with Purugupta, while Goyal finds no reason to modify his original thesis on the subject according to which Prakāśāditya should be placed between Bhānugupta (known date 510 A.D.) and Narasiṁhagupta II, the contemporary of Mihirakula.

VI

Among recent publications on Gupta numismatics B.N. Mukherjee's *Coins and Currency System in Gupta Bengal* (New Delhi, 1992) deserves special mention. In this work a dependable attempt has been made to deal with the Gupta coins found from Bengal as well as with the currency system of this region on the basis of these coins, inscriptions and other material.

The work is divided into six chapters. Chapter I gives a brief idea of the extent and traditional divisions of Bengal and Gupta history and coins, especially those found in Bengal. Ch. II summarises the present state of our knowledge about the monetary systems of Bengal upto c. 1200 A.D. It contains some very interesting suggestions. In ch. III, dealing with the Gupta period, it is pointed out on the strength of epigraphic evidence that 15 Gupta *rūpakas* (silver coins) were equal to 1 *dīnāra* (gold coin) and the ratio in the value of gold and silver was 1:3.8. The find of an Aśvamedha type coin of Samudragupta and three Archer type gold pieces of Chandragupta II in a hoard with other antiquities found in an excavation at Mainamati in the Comilla district in a layer of eighth century A.D. may perhaps indicate the prevalence of the Imperial

[28] S.R. Goyal, *Gupta Sāmrājya kā Itihāsa*, Jodhpur, 1987, p. 339, n. 1.

[29] Quoted by Ashvini Agrawal, in *Numismatic Studies*, Vol. 2, p. 118, n. 32.

[30] In *Political History in a Changing World*, eds. G.C. Pande, S.K. Gupta and Shankar Goyal, Jodhpur, 1992, pp. 182-83.

Gupta gold coins in Bengal for about a couple of centuries after the end of the Gupta rule. No copper or lead coins of the Guptas have so far been reported from Bengal. These were apparently not in use in this region, their purpose being fulfilled by the uninscribed cast coins, Kushāṇa imitations and *cowries* for which archaeological and literary evidences are available. Ch. IV provides a description of the Gupta coin types reported from Bengal while ch. V discusses in brief the minting technique and style including artistic aspects of the Gupta coins. In this connection Mukherjee makes a few interesting suggestions including that the so-called *Apratigha* type symbolizes Kumāragupta's "resolve to lead an ascetic's life even while remaining on the throne." The monograph ends with ch. VI in which the conclusions drawn by the author are given.

B.N. Mukherjee's recent treatment of the history of the imperial Guptas in his 'Commentary' (pp. 764-94) on Raychaudhuri's *Political History of Ancient India* (New Delhi, 1997) in over thirty pages, however, has not much to commend itself. Here it might be worthwhile to discuss his analysis at some length, for it is also concerned with the numismatic sources and has direct bearing on the political history of the Gupta period as well. Mukherjee has claimed that his 'Commentary', printed after the end of the text of Raychaudhuri, has taken into account the discoveries and researches during the last four decades. He also claims that he has clearly indicated the new trends in research and also the impact of economic factors on the course of political hisotry. (p. xii). But to the great dismay of his readers in his treatment of the subject Mukherjee has failed to achieve these objectives. Unlike Raychaudhuri, whose work has been famous for its detailed references and the inclusion of the results of the recent-most researches, Mukherjee has not been able to utilize or even mention many of the significant works of the historians of the Gupta empire who wrote after the demise of Raychaudhuri in 1957 and before the publication of Mukherjee's 'Commentary' on his work. He has also been clearly unable to demonstrate the change from chronological reconstructions to socio-economic concerns in the study of the Gupta dynasty.

Among the most significant historians, whom Mukherjee should have cirtically discussed in his 'Commentary' is S.R. Goyal. As is shown by us elsewhere,[31] Goyal's doctoral dissertation, *A History of the Imperial Guptas* (Allahabad, 1967) forms a watershed in the historiography of the Gupta dynasty, for it treated Gupta history with a holistic approach, discussed various kinds of evidence, including numismatic, afresh and suggested new solutions to many a major problems of the history of the period. Between 1967 and 2015 Goyal published as many as ten monographs on Gupta age. But Mukherjee refers to none of Goyal's works; the only exception being latter's

[31] Shankar Goyal, *The Image of Classical India*, Jodhpur, 1997, pp. 37-91; idem, *The Classical Age : A Study in Feudalization*, New Delhi, 2022, Ch. 4.

doctoral dissertaion which has been included in the general Bibliography of the 'Commentary' but without making it a part of the discussion in the reconstruction of the Gupta history.[32]

VII

The monograph titled *Gupta Gold Coins with a Garuḍa-Banner* (Groningen, Egbert Forsten, 1994) is the doctoral dissertation of Ellen M. Raven presented and approved by the University of Leiden in 1991. It is indeed a stupendous and unique work dealing with the Garuḍa device found on the Gupta gold coins from all possible angles. It is only after going through her monumental work, which is in two volumes and covers cxxvii+490 pages and contains 113 tables, 59 plates, 2 maps and 139 line-drawing in 29 sheets, that one begins to wonder how did it happen that no one undertook a serious study of the Garuḍa-banner device earlier.

The work under discussion dwells upon only five gold coin types of the Guptas, for it is only on them that the Garuḍa-banner is depicted. Even the coins of Kācha and Ghaṭotkachagupta which bear Garuḍa-banner, have not been included in the study as the authoress could not examine them personally.

The first volume of the monograph is divided into five chapters. The first chapter explains the aims and scope of the book and reviews the work done by earlier scholars. The second chapter is devoted to the meaning of the Garuḍa-banner and to coin types featuring it. In chapter three the Garuḍa-banner design in its various forms has been presented and on that basis, applying 'the mint-idiom concept' a number of mints have been distinguished. The next chapter is devoted to the study of Garuḍa emblem in a variety of media—sculpture, terracotta, seals and coins of other dynasties of the pre-

[32] S. R. Goyal's works on Gupta history include :

1. *A History of the Imperial Guptas* (1967);
2. *Gupta evaṁ Samakālīna Rājavaṁśa* (1969);
3. *Guptakālīna Abhilekha* (1984);
4. *Samudragupta Parākramāṅka* (1987);
5. *Gupta Sāmrājya kā Itihāsa* (1987);
6. *Gupta aura Vākāṭaka Sāmrājyoṅ kā Yuga* (1988);
7. *An Introduction to Gupta Numismatics* (1994);
8. *Indian Art of the Gupta Age*, ed. (2000);
9. *The Imperial Guptas* (2005); and
10. *A History of the Vākāṭaka-Gupta Relations* (2006).

Here, mention may also be made of Goyal's Hindi monograph on the history of Lichchhavi period of Nepal which corresponded to the Gupta period of Indian history. (S.R. Goyal, *Prāchīna Nepāla kā Rājanītika aura Sāṁskṛtika Itihāsa*, Varanasi, 1973). Number 6 of this list is a thoroughly revised and updated version of No. 2.

Gupta and Gupta periods. The whole discussion of these four chapters is summarised in chapter five.

The sixth chapter, the first one of volume two, re-classifies the coins of five Gupta gold types containing the Garuḍa-banner device afresh and in detail king-wise. The seventh chapter (second and the last of the volume two) discusses weights, gold content and size of the coins under discussion. It is followed by two appendices.

Ellen has identified 14 basic images of Garuḍa and some 150 actual representations. She has also tried to find a pattern behind this variety and trace its chronological evolution. Though she is mainly concerned with gold coin types of the Guptas with Garuḍa-banner, she has also taken into consideration silver, copper and lead coins, including those of other dynasties on which this device occurs. The introduction of the concept of mint-idiom and the identification of five mints by her is highly interesting.

All in all, the work of Ellen is a masterpiece of numismatic research and can only be described as 'monumental' and 'stupendous'. It is only such researches that can give a new direction to numismatic studies.

VIII

According to the generally accepted view, the history of the silver coinage of the imperial Guptas started with Chandragupta II who issued them on the pattern of the silver coinage of the Western Kshatrapas. But in recent years evidence is accumulating to show that before Chandragupta II issued Śaka type silver money, his predecessors issued silver coins similar to their gold coins, though lighter in weight. Such coins of Chandragupta-Kumāradevī type and Lyrist and Standard types of Samudragupta have been published by various scholars. Whether these coins are genuine or fake is an interesting problem. According to S.R. Goyal, "now it appears better to assume that till the reign of Chadragupta II the imperial Guptas issued lighter weight coins in silver following their gold prototypes." (*The Coinage of Ancient India,* Jodhpur, 1995, p. 435). On the other hand, Ashvini Agrawal has very forcefully rejected all such coins as fakes. (*Oriental Numismatic Studies,* 1, New Delhi, 1996, p. 208). However, whether the silver coins mentioned above are genuine or not, the silver coins attributed to the first Gupta ruler by L.C. Gupta and S.J. Mangalam are certainly fakes.

Gupta and Mangalam have published a small monograph of 44 pages titled *Silver Coins of Śrī Gupta.* (Hyderabad, 1994). In this, they have published 106 silver pieces weighing between .7 and .83 gms which they have attributed to the first Gupta king. These coins contain on the obv. a crude portrait which Gupta and Mangalam have identified as that of Śrī Gupta because, according to them, the reverse legend on these coins reads *Śrī Gupta.* These coins are said to have been "picked up sporadically" from

Hajipur-Mirjapur region of Bihar. The authors of the monograph claim that the discovery of these coins from Bihar indicates "the veracity of the tradition and the historicity of Śrī Gupta's political career around Magadha." It is also contended that Śrī Gupta issued these coins as they were required for circulation during his region.

But the attribution of these coins to the first ruler of the Gupta dynasty has been rightly rejected by Ashvini Agrawal. (*op.cit.*). He points out that portrait on these coins resemble the one found on Indo-Sassanian coins of the post-Gupta period to which these coins really belong. The reverse motif has a degenerate fire-altar and the legend on this side of the coins cannot be read as *Śrī Gupta* by any stretch of imagination. So far all the finds of similar coins have been reported from Punjab; Bihar has yielded none except the ones under discussion. It is also to be noted that the Gupta dynasty originated in eastern U.P. and not in Magadha; S.R. Goyal has shown it almost conclusively.[33] Further, no dynasty of north India in the third and the first half of the fourth century A.D. issued silver coinage; they remained content with copper coins. It is, therefore, unrealistic to believe that a comparatively unknown ruler like Mahārāja Gupta issued a series in silver without any prototype, a series which was discontinued by his successors. In view of Ashvini Agrawal, therefore, the monograph deserves to be completely ignored by scholars. Such monographs tend to put young researchers and the study of numismatics both on the wrong track.

Among the books which dealt with miscellaneous aspects of Gupta numismatics, mention may also be made of S.K. Maity's *The Economic Life in Northern India in the Gupta Period* (Calcutta, 1957) and *Early Indian Coins and Currency System* (New Delhi, 1970) and some of his research papers which apply mathematical method to the study of ancient Indian numismatics, including Gupta numismatics. But he has laid too much stress on the principle that with the decline of the political fortunes of a dynasty the gold content of its coinage declined.[34] Maity has also utilised literary sources of the period for the study of the coin data. He opines that the silver kārshāpaṇa of Nārada and Bṛhaspati is not the same as rūpaka of inscriptions and that "the tables of Nārada and Bṛihaspati hardly correspond to the actual weights and denominations of the Gupta coinage."

In his *Aspects of Ancient Indian Technology* (Delhi, 1979) H.C.

[33] *HIG*, pp. 41-52.

[34] For a criticism of Maity's views on Chandragupta-Kumāradevī type see, S.R. Goyal, *HIG*, pp. 115-21; T.P. Verma, *JNSI*, XXXIII, i, p. 48; V.C. Pandey, *JNSI*, XXXVIII, pp. 25 ff.; also see T.P. Verma in *Reappraising Gupta History for S.R. Goyal*, eds. B.Ch. Chhabra, P.K. Agrawala, Ashvini Agrawal and Shankar Goyal, New Delhi, 1992, pp. 83-110. *Contra*, Ashvini Agrawal, *Rise and Fall of the Imperial Guptas*, Delhi, 1989, pp. 93-95; Ajay Mitra

Bhardwaj has made a scientific study of the four Gupta gold coins from Rajghat excavations. (pp. 127-28). He has not confined his analysis to specific gravity but also uses chemical, metallographic and hardness determinations as well which yield significant information about fabrication technique. According to Bhardwaj, from the macro- and micro-structures of the Gupta gold coins it may be concluded that the material has been either hot worked or cold worked followed by annealing above the recrytallization temperature, as is clear from the fine equiaxed grains. From this he infers that these coins are die-struck and not cast. He also opines that the occurrence of a clay mould of Archer type of Chandragupta II at Rajghat might be a forger's apparatus. However, some of Bhardwaj's observations and statements need revision. For example, he proposes a date bracket c. 260-540 A.D. for the Gupta coins (p. 23), though in any case they cannot be placed earlier than 319-20 A.D.

Another work, which also deals with the Gupta numismatics is *A Comprehensive History of India* (A.D. 300-985) edited by R.C. Majumdar and K.K. Dasgupta. (New Delhi, 1982). Its Volume Three, Part II, includes a chapter on the 'Coinage' by A.S. Altekar and B.N. Mukherjee. In it the section on the coinage of the imperial Guptas covers almost fifteen pages. (pp. 1369-1384). However, it has the disadvantage of being more a general introduction than an analytical assessment of the subject. In addition to this chapter Mukherjee has also written on the numismatic art of the period (c.A.D. 300-985) in the form of an appendix. (pp.1415-1433).

Among other miscellaneous works dealing with some aspects of Gupta numismatics mention may be made of Swati Chakroborty's *Socio-Religious and Cultural Study of the Ancient Indian Coins* (Delhi, 1986) in which she has discussed ancient Indian coins, including Gupta coins, from socio-religious and cultural points of view.

However, B.Ch. Chhabra's *Catalogue of the Gupta Gold Coins of the Bayana Hoard in the National Museum* (New Delhi, 1986), though quite excellent production-wise, does not suggest anything new.

The Coinage of Ancient India : A Numismatic, Archaeochemical and Metallurgical Study of Ancient Indian Coins by Satya Prakash and Rajendra Singh (New Delhi, 1986) also contains over forty pages on the coinage of the Gupta empire. But it hardly adds anything new to our knowledge of the subject.[35]

Among the recent monographs dealing with some problems of the Gupta coinage mention may be made of *Numismatics Studies*, 5 Vols., (New

---

Shastri, in *S.R. Goyal : His Multidimensional Historiography*, eds. Jagannath Agrawal and Shankar Goyal, New Delhi, 1992, p. 5.

[35] However, the Bibliography of this work offers some help in sorting out the hundreds of long and short articles on Gupta coins.

Delhi, 1991, 1992, 1993, 1996 and 1997). These volumes contain some notable papers on the coinage of the imperial Guptas from the pen of Ashvini Agrawal, Manmohan Kumar, S.V. Sohoni, etc.[36]

In his *Aspects of Ancient Indian Numismatics* (Delhi, 1996) Prashant Srivastava has discussed joint-issues of the imperial Guptas (pp. 133-76), their commemorative medallions (pp. 249-310) and victory medals. (pp. 332-43). But at many places his views are highly fanciful.

We have also discussed the history of ancient Indian numismatic studies from the late eighteenth century to the twentieth century in our *Ancient Indian Numismatics* (Jodhpur, 1998). We have also tried to find out along what lines the study of the coinages of various dynasties and periods has progressed.

Many scholars such as Jagannath Agrawal, S.V. Sohoni, K.K. Thaplyal, S.R. Goyal, T.P. Verma, Nisar Ahmad, P.N. Singh, Shankar Goyal,[37] etc., have written high class research papers on Gupta coins. It is difficult here even to enumerate such a large number of papers; to discuss their contents is an impossibility.

[36] Cf. Ashvini Agrawal, 'Some More Coins of Rāmagupta', *Numismatic Studies*, 1, pp. 99-101; idem, 'The Prakāśāditya Problem : A Reappraisal', *ibid.*, 2, pp. 107-18; idem, 'King and Queen Coin-Type of Skandagupta', *ibid.*, 3, pp. 57-63; Manmohan Kumar, 'Gupta Coin Moulds : Forgery or Trade Compulsions?', *ibid.*, 2, pp. 119-22 and S.V. Sohoni, 'A Note on Revanta Coin Type of Chandragupta II Vikramāditya and Kumāragupta I, etc.', *ibid.*, 3, pp. 55-56. Ashvini Agrawal also gives a reasonable but brief survey of the Gupta coins in his *Rise and Fall of the Imperial Guptas.* (pp. 15-33).

[37] For details, see T.S. Ravishankar, 'Shankar Goyal's Probings in Epigraphical and Numismatic Studies', in *Shanakar Goyal : Marching with History*, ed. Radhika Seshan, New Delhi, 2021, pp. 88-97.

NINE

S. R. Goyal's Contribution to Historical Studies

I

In recent decades the popularity of political history is declining very fast in India as well as in other countries. Therefore, in order to revitalize their discipline some political historians, both in India and the West, are pleading that the concept of political history itself should be modified.[1] They argue that now historians should cease to give emphasis only on the 'deeds' and 'dates' of the kings and should make a study of the political aspect of society their basic concern. In other words, they should give emphasis on 'how' and 'why' instead of only 'when' and 'what'. For this a study of the political events and institutions against various factors—religious, economic, social, etc.—is vital. This is what they call 'integral political history' or 'new political history'. It need not only be a study of the basic sources with a new angle but also a multidisciplinary approach to the political life of society and state. In India S.R. Goyal has been pleading for the adoption of this approach for several decades and now he is being supported by numerous others.[2] This chapter seeks to show what has he done to give a new definition and meaning to political history, specially of ancient India, and what has been his contribution to the discipline.

[1] For a detailed discussion and various references of Western and Indian scholars on the problem of the decline of political history in recent decades cf. Shankar Goyal, *Ancient India: A Mulidisciplinary Approach*, Jodhpur, 2006, pp. 1-26.

[2] S. R. Goyal, 'Need of a New Approach to the Writing of Political History of Ancient India', his lead-paper, in *Political History in a Changing World*, eds. G.C. Pande, S.K. Gupta and Shankar Goyal, Jodhpur, 1992, pp. 3-17 and reaction-papers on it by 53 eminent historians of India and other countries published therein, pp. 19-370. Also noticeable are S.R. Goyal's own numerous works some of which have been discussed in this chapter. On this approach, also see Romila Thapar, *The Penguin History of Early India from the Origins to AD 1300*, New Delhi, 2002, pp. xvii-xxx.

II

S.R. Goyal, former Professor and Head, Department of History, Jai Narain Vyas University, Jodhpur, has been described as 'one of the five best recent historians of ancient India' by David N. Lorenzen, the great Mexican Orientalist. Goyal combines all the qualities associated with scientific scholarship. He published more than fifty works, most of them quite voluminous, and over 175 research papers which cover so diverse fields as political history, religious history, literature, biographies, numismatics and epigraphy. He was honoured with the General Presidentship of the Silver Jubilee Congress of the Epigraphical Society of India held at Udupi in April, 1999 and was elected the Honorary Fellow of the Society. He also presided over the 90th Annual Conference of the Numismatic Society of India which was held at Santiniketan (West Bengal) on 1st to 3rd December, 2006. He was also invited to be the General President of the 2006 Annual Session of the Indian History and Culture Society held at Gwalior which he could not accept because of the clash of dates.

S.R. Goyal's doctoral thesis, *A History of the Imperial Guptas* (Allahabad, 1967), was acclaimed as 'the best analysis of the Gupta period which I have ever read' by A. L. Basham (National Professor of Australia) and as 'imaginative', 'well written' and 'a model of historiography' by Eleanor Zelliot (Minnesota, U.S.A.). The various theories propounded in it are described by R.C. Majumdar as 'deserving very careful consideration'. Among his other major works are included three 'corpus-like'volumes on ancient Indian inscriptions, a monograph on the recently found ancient Indian inscriptions, a three volume study on ancient Indian numismatics, two volumes respectively on Kauṭilya and Megasthenes, a volume on the literary chronology of ancient India, a volume on the birth and early growth of Indian society, two bulky volumes on ancient Indian religions, a three volume study on Indian Buddhism, a monograph on Śramaṇism, a three volume study on Hinduism, a volume on the Vākāṭaka-Gupta relations, a three volume study on ancient Indian history in about two thousand pages and four volumes on great rulers of ancient India.

S.R. Goyal has been honoured with many festschrifts, including *Reappraising Gupta History for S.R. Goyal* (eds. B.Ch. Chhabra et al) and *S.R. Goyal : His Multidimensional Historiography* (eds. Jagannath Agrawal and Shankar Goyal) published in 1992 sometime in his sixtieth year. A four volume festschrift in about two thousand pages in his honour entitled *Śrīrāmābhinandanam* (*Reconstructing Indian History for S.R. Goyal*) was published in 2003. Again, a two volume thematic felicitation volume entitled *Investigating Indian Society* and *Indian Society : The Regional Contours* was also brought out in his honour in 2013 on the completion of his eightieth year. It contains the articles of such eminent historians as G.C. Pande, R.S. Sharma, Romila Thapar, Irfan Habib, R. Champakalakshmi, Kumkum Roy and Kesavan Veluthat, undoubtedly some of the best minds of the Indological world. Yet another festschrift *Early India : Historical Probings* was published in his honour in 2015 on his 85th birthday containing articles from Romila Thapar, Irfan Habib, R. Champakalakshmi, Kumkum Roy, Samaresh Bandyopadhyay, D.N. Tripathi, U.P. Arora, J.M. Rai, and many others.

III

The position which S. R. Goyal enjoys in the Indian historical world today largely depends on his integral or holistic approach to history, specially political history, which he has been propagating for about half a century. When one goes through his writings explaining and elaborating his approach to history, one cannot but admire his courage and conviction—courage because he has sought to propagate an approach which is different from the approach of most established historians of the country and also from the approach of the Marxist historians who have emerged as the dominant group in the recent decades; and conviction because it developed gradually in course of his own academic journey and is based on sound reasoning and personal experiences as a historian with manifold interests. On many a problems he has come to conclusions which are radically at variance from the generally accepted views of other historians,[3] but he has always shown

[3] Such as 'in the Indus religion the supreme god was regarded as brother and husband both of the mother goddess'; 'the Paurāṇika date of the Bhārata War has become vitiated because these works have wrongly identified Janamejaya Pārikshita who flourished after the Dāśarājña with Janamejaya Pārikshita who flourished after the Bhārata War'; 'Rāma did not have any legitimate right over the ancestral throne'; 'the Brāhmī script was *invented* in the early Maurya period'; 'the pre-Aśokan society of India, barring the north-western regions, was largely illiterate'; 'Chāṇakya and Kauṭilya were two different persons, the former, a Jaina, was the *guru* and Prime Minister of Chandragupta Maurya while the latter, a Brāhmaṇa, who flourished in the third century A.D., was the author of the *Arthaśāstra*'; 'the personality of Heracles, as described by Megasthenes with reference to Mathurā, mainly includes the legends connected with Manu Vaivasvata of the Indian tradition'; 'when Megasthenes visited India, Paurāṇika king-lists existed in more or less the same form as they are found in the present-day Purāṇas'; 'the imperial Guptas belonged to the Brāhmaṇa order'; 'the original home of the Guptas was located in eastern U.P. with Prayāga as its early capital'; 'King Chandra of the Meharauli inscription was no other than Samudragupta'; 'there flourished two sets of kings named Narasiṁhagupta Bālāditya and Kumāragupta Kramāditya, the former set just after Skandagupta and the second in the post-Bhānugupta period'; 'the Mālava *janapada* of the Later Guptas was located in Rajasthan'; 'the Maukharis were a branch of the Mālavas and belonged to the Lunar race'; 'the testimony of Yuan Chwang regarding the *personal* faith of Harsha in Buddhism is not reliable, for Harsha remained a Śaiva throughout his

courage to put his suggestions before the historical world candidly though usually with such force of rigorous logic that even those who fail to agree with him frankly admit that he has put up a case which demands serious consideration.

IV

But here let me first discuss S.R. Goyal's approach to political history for which he has become well known throughout the Indological world. Goyal has been primarily involved with the study of political history of ancient India, but he has repeatedly expressed his dissatisfaction with the present state of the discipline of political history of ancient India. He has articulated his views on this question more than half a century ago in his celebrated thesis *A History of the Imperial Guptas* (Allahabad, 1967, ch.1), and also in several of his articles published in *Jijñāsā* (Vol.2, No.2, Jaipur, 1975, pp. 9-26), in *Indica* (Vol.14, No.2, Bombay, 1977, pp.85-98), in *Historical and Political Perspectives* (ed. D. Devahuti, New Delhi, 1982, pp. 93-101), in the foreword to S.K. Purohit's *Uttara Bhārata kā Prāchīna Rājanītika Itihāsa* (Jaipur, 1980, pp. ix-xx), in ch.1 of his own *Māgadha-Sātavāhana-Kushāṇa Sāmrājyoṅ kā Yuga* (Meerut, 1988), in his lead-paper entitled 'Need of a New Approach to the Writing of Political History of Ancient India' in *Political History in a Changing World* (eds. G.C. Pande, S.K. Gupta and Shankar Goyal, Jodhpur, 1992, pp.1-17) and in his ch. 'Rājanītika Itihāsa kī Vividha Avadhāraṇāyeṅ' published in *Prāchīna Bhārata kā Ādhunika Itihāsa-Lekhana* (ed. Shankar Goyal, Jodhpur, 2000, pp.1-10). It is also found reflected in his works on political history of ancient India, including *The Imperial Guptas : A Multidisciplinary Political Study* (Jodhpur, 2005).

Writing mainly with reference to ancient Indian political history, Goyal points out that for more than last hundred years or so historians are concerning themselves with the genealogy and chronology of kings and the

---

life'; 'the Jaina tradition has wrongly ascribed the elements of the personality of Nāgabhaṭa II Pratihāra *alias* Nāgāvaloka to Āma-Nāgāvaloka, the successor of Yaśovarman'; 'the Dīn-e-Ilāhi founded by Akbar was a new religion, and as such he did not remain a Muslim after its promulgation'; 'the unity in diversity of the Indian society is not the unity caused by the common elements in our cultural diversity, but the unity of the top of our social pyramid bound together by our religious tradition and the common bond of language—Sanskrit, Persian and English in different periods'; 'the adoption of adult franchise in our republican constitution has turned our social pyramid upside down, bringing the cultural elite bound by common language and religious tradition to the bottom and the masses at the top thus starting the process of deculturisation, at least temporarily', etc.

exploits of their armies, which very often they themselves led, and/or with coins, epigraphs and literary works produced under their direct patronage. He argues that political history of this kind is now losing ground to social, economic and cultural history. He stresses the need to come out the narrow and antiquated framework of the pioneering and distinguished scholars who were seriously handicapped by the paucity of sources and undeveloped methods and techniques of interpretation. He feels that many historians of ancient India have not kept up, in terms of sophistication of either their methodology or themes of research, with recent historians of modern India or with recent historians of ancient Europe and the Middle East. He finds monographs on two successive monarchs, describing the same political and administrative organisation made to look impressive with detailed footnotes, inane and boring. Merely paraphrasing material from literary chronicles or epigraphs is dubbed by him "pseudo-history".[4] Treatment of political history as unrelated to history of other aspects of life is, according to him, out-of-date. Thus, writing on the decline of Magadha in the fifth-tenth centuries A.D. without due stress on the phenomenon of feudalism or proper appreciation of the social, economic and religious *milieu* is regarded by him inadequate. Not identifying feudalism as the central theme of the early medieval Rajasthan polity is considered an avoidable lapse. He wishes political history to recover some of its old prestige as early as possible. He shows an awareness of advances made in the West and is firmly against Indian historians lagging behind much longer. To achieve this he suggests a substantial change in the content and character of the discipline. As shown above, he calls for a new style of political history of ancient India "devoted not only to the study of political events but also of structures, institutions, environment and power."[5] Political history, in his opinion, should now be viewed as the study of political activity in the total situational context. Forces and factors which profoundly influence people in society and condition events deserve adequate attention, and "why" and "how" should be considered no less important than "what" and "when" in any serious and worthwhile recounting of the past. As a corrective to the persisting malaise, he suggests that different aspects of history—political, social, economic, religious and cultural—should be studied as facets of an integrated reality and not in isolation from each other. The focus of study should shift from individuals to institutions, political structures, power and environment, and development in other branches of knowledge such as economics, demography, anthropology, sociology, etc., should be made use of to gain

[4] S. R. Goyal, 'Political History : A Reconsideration', *Jijñāsā*, A Journal of the History of Ideas and Culture, Jaipur, Vol. 2, No. 2, April 1975, pp. 25-26.

[5] *Ibid.*, p. 26.

insights and enrich perspectives for political history.

But Goyal does not neglect 'what happened' and 'when happened' aspects of political history altogether and to that extent he is in tune with the thinking of the traditional historians. But wherever possible he has shown how the writing of 'new political history' may be seriously attempted, at least in the case of some dynasties and some periods where our sources permit us to do so.

V

Let me now explain Goyal's attitude to the Marxist approach to history. History writing in modern India has passed through the spell of Marxist, generally called 'progressive', historiography. Marxist historians of India usually claim to be following and elaborating the thesis of D.D. Kosambi. In Kosambi's works history is defined as "the presentation in chronological order of successive changes in the means and relations of production"[6] and culture is defined as the "essential ways of life of the whole people."[7] He has asserted that culture is not "purely a matter of intellectual or spiritual values."[8] He discovers the characteristic expression of the Indian mind in the *Gītā*, the success of which he attributes to its teaching of the doctrine of Bhakti which "suited the feudal ideology perfectly."[9] As a supporter of integral view of history Goyal is naturally opposed to all such formulations and observes that "consciously or unconsciously most of the historians have come under the influence of Marxism. Marx looked upon politics as one of the superstructures of society and considered political history as a by-product of the history of production-relations. ... It is quite obvious that a concept leading to Marx's theory of the 'withering away of the state' can hardly increase the prestige of anything dealing with state and politics, including political history."[10]

Goyal is particularly critical of the Marxist concept of Indian feudalism. He is of the view that while some sort of 'feudalism' did exist in India in the early medieval period, neither it corresponded fully to European feudalism and nor was there any feudal age as such in Indian history. India did have her 'feudal' system and its impact on state and society, specially of the early medieval period, must be studied, but it should not be forgotten that Indian feudal system was as different from European feudalism as Indian

[6] D. D. Kosambi, *An Introduction to the Study of Indian History*, Bombay, 1956, p. 1.

[7] Idem, *The Culture and Civilisation of Ancient India in Historical Outline*, Eighth edn., New Delhi, 1982, p. 10.

[8] *Ibid.*

[9] *Ibid.*, p. 208.

[10] S. R. Goyal, 'Political History : A Reconsideration', *Jijñāsā*, *op.cit.*, p. 11.

caste system is different from the hierarchical social organisation of any other country.

However, Goyal is not against utilizing the models provided by the Marxists, and for that matter by anthropologists or sociologists. But he wants to be certain that the model concerned is in consonance with the data provided by our sources; and not try to bring our data in conformity with the model. The attempt of the Marxist historians, who first try to prove that Indian feudalism was more or less 'European' in character and then fit in even the *Gītā* in its general picture as a manual of feudal ideology, is an example where Goyal would differ with the Marxist approach.[11]

VI

Goyal gives emphasis on the use of original sources and also on new techniques for their interpretation. Though he believes that now archaeology, numismatics and epigraphy have emerged as distinct disciplines and it has become difficult for a historian to become an authority in the field of numismatics, epigraphy or archaeology, and *vice-versa*, but he also recognizes that in very exceptional cases a historian may be an epigraphist, archaeologist or numismatist as well. He, therefore, suggests that while a historian should stick primarily to his own discipline and should follow the expert opinion of archaeologists, numismatists and epigraphists on problems concerning their fields of specialization, a first rate historian may go through all the original sources personally, the knowledge of which is necessary for his researches. That explains why he has himself written so much on ancient Indian literature, coins and inscriptions. Significantly, he has written three volumes on ancient Indian political history entitled *Māgadha-Sātavāhana-Kushāṇa Sāmrājyoṅ kā Yuga*, *Gupta aura Vākāṭaka Sāmrājyoṅ kā Yuga* and *Maukhari-Pushyabhūti-Chālukya Yuga* which were published from Meerut in 1988 and each of these volumes is matched by a near 'corpus-like' volume on the epigraphs of the period covered by it—*Prāchīna Bhāratīya Abhilekha Saṁgraha — Prāk-Guptayugīna* (Jaipur, 1982), *Guptakālīna Abhilekha* (Meerut, 1984) and *Maukhari-Pushyabhūti-Chālukyayugīna Abhilekha* (Meerut, 1988). In this connection mention may be made of his Presidential Address delivered to the Silver Jubilee Session of the

[11] Cf. also Shankar Goyal, *Marxist Interpretation of Ancient Indian History*, Pune, 2000, pp. 85-86; idem, *The Classical Age : A Study in Feudalization*, New Delhi, 2022, pp. 1-17, 95-137. S. R. Goyal is deeply concerned with the gross misinterpretation and distortion of the Gupta golden age by D.N.Jha. For a detailed exposition of his views in this regard see my article 'A Critique of Professor D.N.Jha's Evaluation of the Classicism of the Gupta Age', in *Reappraising Gupta Histroy for S.R. Goyal*, eds. B.Ch. Chhabra, P.K. Agrawala, Ashvini Agrawal and Shankar Goyal, New Delhi, 1992, pp.60-72.

Epigraphical Society of India held at Udupi in April 1999 in which he took the discussion on the origin of the Brāhmī script to a new height by suggesting that it was *invented* in the reign of Aśoka even if some sort of writing did exist in the Vedic age.

Similarly, though not a professional or trained numismatist himself, Goyal has written not only some occasional papers on purely numismatic problems, but has also produced some remarkable works on ancient Indian numismatics titled *Indigenous Coins of Early India* (Jodhpur, 1994), *An Introduction to Gupta Numismatics* (Jodhpur, 1994) and *Dynastic Coins of Ancient India* (Jodhpur, 1995) which were also reproduced in the form of a single comprehensive volume titled *The Coinage of Ancient India* (Jodhpur, 1995). These deal exhaustively with some fundamental problems of ancient Indian numismatics.

One of the major contributions of S.R. Goyal in the field of numismatic studies has been his Presidential Address delivered to the 90th Annual Conference of the Numismatic Society of India which was held at Santiniketan (West Bengal) on December 1-3, 2006.[12] Here, contrary to the general belief he has opined that "India never saw an affluent gold coinage from the earliest times to the close of the early medieval period except in the age of the Kushāṇas and the Guptas" and that "even during the rule of these two dynasties our material prosperity was never very high, never comparable with the affluence of many other countries. It is indicated not only by a comparison of India's gold coinage with the coinage of other countries but also by the poor advancement shown by us in the construction of cities and in the fields of urban secular architecture and sculpture." Here, his views go against the prevalent general belief of our countrymen that ancient India was one of the most prosperous countries in the world.

The use of literary sources for the reconstruction of ancient Indian history depends upon the proper dating of our ancient texts. That is why Goyal gives utmost emphasis on the study of ancient literary chronology.[13] He argues that a proper stratification of the texts like the *Mahābhārata* and re-examination of their relative or absolute dates may create an altogether

[12] For a detailed study of S. R. Goyal's arguments see his Presidential Address 'The Myth of the Golden Bird (An Investigation into the Belief of Material Opulence of Ancient and Early Medieval India in the Light of Her Gold Coinage)' delivered to the 90th Annual Conference of the Numismatic Society of India, held at Santiniketan, West Bengal, on December 1-3, 2006 (*JNSI*, LXIX, i-ii, 2007, pp.1-24).

[13] For details see his *Literary Chronology of Ancient India*, Jodhpur, 2009; also vide, D. N. Bhargava, 'S.R. Goyal's Studies in Literary History and Chronology', in *S. R. Goyal: His Multidimensional Historiography*, eds. Jagannath Agrawal and Shankar Goyal, New Delhi, 1992, pp. 179-85.

different picture of our past. He even suggests new methods for determining the chronology of ancient Indian texts. In one of his more significant papers he shows how the changing meaning of the term *mahāmātra* may be utilized as a time-index for determining the general period of the texts in which it is used in a particular sense.[14] Further, he raises his voice against the indiscriminate use of the literary data without realizing the nature of the text from which it is taken. For example, he has argued that the *Arthaśāstra* of Kauṭilya is a normative work; therefore, even if it was written in the early Maurya period, which is itself a debatable point, it cannot and should not be presumed that the norms laid down in it were actually in force in that age.[15]

Goyal emphasises the need of greater specialized study of our sources and also explains the new techniques he has in mind to make them yield new information. He argues that history, especially ancient Indian history, is the final result of the labours of many specialists working in various related disciplines. Therefore, the historian must utilize what he may receive from competent archaeologists, numismatists or epigraphists, rather than trespass into their areas and mishandle things to the detriment of the quality of his own work. As regards new methodology, he finds the technique suggested by V.S. Pathak[16] for the study of the biographical literature useful and has successfully applied it to the study the *Rāmāyaṇa* of Vālmīki[17] and the historical dramas such as the *Devīchandraguptam* of Viśākhadeva.[18] He also believes that P.E. Shramm's principle of studying the symbolic material

[14] S. R. Goyal, 'The Varying Meaning of the Term Mahāmātra as an Index for Literary Chronology', *Journal of the Ganganatha Jha Kendriya Sanskrit Vidyapeetha*, Allahabad, L-LI, 1994-95, pp. 441-52.

[15] For a detailed discussion on the problem cf. S. R. Goyal, *The Kauṭilīya Arthaśāstra: Its Author, Date and Relevance for the Maurya Period*, Jodhpur, 2000, pp. 1-52, 69-72, and also his earlier works related to the Maurya age.

[16] For a detailed exposition of V.S. Pathak's technique also see Shankar Goyal, *History and Historiography of the Age of Harsha*, Jodhpur, 1992, pp. 15-29; idem, *Recent Historiography of Ancient India*, Jodhpur, 1997, pp. 347-62; idem, *Contemporary Interpreters of Ancient India*, Jaipur, 2003, pp. 67-73; idem, *Harsha : A Multidisciplinary Political Study*, Jodhpur, 2006, pp. 4-16.

[17] S. R. Goyal, 'Succession Problem in the Vālmīkīya *Rāmāyaṇa*', in *Professor D. N. Bhargava Felicitation Volume*, ed. Narendra Awasthi, Jodhpur, 1997, pp. 281-301; idem, *A Comprehensive History of Hinduism*, Jodhpur, 2018, pp. III. 61-90; also see my *Contemporary Interpreters of Ancient India*, pp. 79-80.

[18] S. R. Goyal, *A History of the Imperial Guptas*, Allahabad, 1967, pp. 223-27; idem, *The Imperial Guptas : A Multidisciplinary Political Study*, Jodhpur, 2005, pp. 261-74; also cf. P. K. Mitra, 'S.R. Goyal and Modern Historiography of the Gupta Age', in *Reappraising Gupta History for S.R. Goyal*, pp. 29-30; also see my *Contemporary Interpreters of Ancient India*, pp. 73-77.

is extremely valuable for writing a more meaningful political history of ancient India. He would like the 'new political history' to "abandon the presumption that only in the absence of written documents should it turn to non-written material", for, a careful study of ceremonials, symbols and motifs in their historical context is likely to shed more light on political institutions and ideologies of the ancient period.[19] To study the composition of the power-elite of a society he recommends the use of prosopography. He also suggests that political history can be enriched through an in-depth exploration of themes like the relationship of education to power, of religious and social groups to state structure and of geographical background, landed property and economic resources to wide-ranging political developments. These are only illustrative samples and do not exhaust the scope of greater possibilities. More themes and areas of research in political history may be identified by individual scholars on the basis of their expertise and specialization, range and depth of scholarship, vision, reflection and controlled imagination. With the help of examples from his own works and those of other historians Goyal shows how, through proper handling, the extant sources can be made to yield more data and add new meaning to political history. "If we stick to the current, or say traditional, concept of research in the political history of ancient India", he observes, "we are at the end of the road, for by now most of the materials for the reconstruction of political events of ancient Indian history are at our disposal."[20] Not that efforts have not been, and are not being made to change the situation. But these are either too feeble, or so limited that the results are not sufficient to put the old to rest. Everybody apparently accepts this but only a few like to come forward to disturb the staid position. Confrontation between the old and the new is not new in any academic field; it is an old phenomenon. But a time comes when it becomes so acute that a resolution cannot be postponed. Goyal feels that such a time has come.[21]

[19] S. R. Goyal, 'Political History : A Reconsideration', *Jijñāsā*, *op.cit.*, pp. 20-21.

[20] *Ibid.*, p. 26.

[21] Goyal's approach to political history and his vision of 'new political history' has been discussed in detail by a large number of scholars in *Political History in a Changing World* (eds. G.C. Pande, S.K. Gupta and Shankar Goyal, Jodhpur, 1992). "As far as I am able to see", writes J. Gonda, "it will indeed imply a new definition of political history. It will probably mean a turning-point in the study of Indian history." (p.370). A.K. Narain concurs with Goyal by stating that "one cannot agree more with Goyal that by and large history and historians in India have become stagnant." (p.23). A.K. Warder enthusiastically welcomes the prospect of the disappearance of Anglocentric or Eurocentric studies and its replacement by a new flowering of Indian tradition itself. (p.32). According to Alois Wurm, "Goyal's epoch-making contributions to scientific consciousness of history are not only an appropriate new definition of political history

VII

Though Goyal has decried the traditional type of political history as the record of the deeds and dates of kings, yet he does not altogether rule out the role of individual in history. He believes that there is some truth in the ancient maxim — *rājākālasyakāraṇam,* the king is the determinant of the time-spirit. He only emphasizes that a king is only one of the factors and quite often a very minor factor, not the sole factor, in determining the course of history of his own times. Goyal has written as many as four volumes on four separate rulers—*Priyadarśī Aśoka* (Meerut, 1988), *Chandragupta Maurya* (Meerut, 1987), *Samudragupta Parākramaṅka* (Meerut, 1987) and *Harsha Śilāditya* (Meerut, 1986) — and in all of them he has shown that though each of these rulers was the child of his age, to some extent his age was also influenced by his personality, thinking and initiative.

Goyal has evolved a specific criteria to assess and evaluate the achievements of a king. He has applied this criteria in the study of every major ruler. According to him, as the primary function of a ruler was to rule, to govern, therefore, he should primarily be judged as a king, not as a saint, a monk, a musician or a man of letters (if he tried to play such a role). Just as one does not evaluate a modern president or prime minister as a businessman or an actor or a poet (if he is so in his personal capacity) but assesses him with reference to his policies and their execution; similarly, one should judge the performance of a monarch only in his role as a ruler and nothing else. Now, in the context of ancient and medieval times a king may be viewed from four angles—as a conqueror, as an administrator, with reference to his activities for public welfare and as an individual. In his *Arthaśāstra* Kauṭilya states that

---

but also, and especially, a concerned appeal to all scholars to resurrect the phoenix of political historiology from the ashes of its suicidal self-complacence." (p.34). A.M. Shastri feels that "the need to widen and transform the outdated attitudes to history cannot be seriously disputed, and a historian cannot now afford to remain content with finding out only 'what happened'; he must also try in earnestness to find out 'why did it happen' wherever possible." (p.36). David N. Lorenzen opines that the call of S.R. Goyal, who in his view is one of the five best recent historians of ancient India, other four being A.K. Narain, Romila Thapar, P.L. Gupta and D.N. Jha, "for a new style of political history of ancient india deserves whole-hearted support from all historians engaged in this enterprize." (p.44). According to Vivekanand Jha, "Goyal deserves credit for stressing the need for change and improvement in ancient Indian political history and for his readiness to discard the stale and the puerile and to receive and welcome the best from both West and East, old and new." (p.63). Many other scholars such as K.D. Bajpai, B.P. Sinha, Lallanji Gopal, B.N. Mukherjee, J.P. Sharma, Sibesh Bhattacharya and S.D. Singh have, *mutatis mutandis,* expressed their agreement with the basic approach of Goyal.

the primary duty of a king is to establish *ekaiśvaryam*, sole sovereignty. Therefore, first of all, while making an estimate of a king we should compare the extent of the kingdom which was inherited by him from his predecessor with the extent of the kingdom left by him for his successor. The difference between the two will show his achievement, or otherwise, as a conqueror (subject of course to the length of his rule, resources at his command, difficulties which he had to face, and such other factors). Secondly, we should examine what did he do to make his kingdom secure and stable, that is whether or not he succeeded in establishing or strengthening an administrative structure which could impart stability to his kingdom. For, many a king, such as Yaśodharman and Harsha, were great conquerors but they failed to make their empires permanent. Thirdly, we should see whether or not the monarch under scrutiny did whatever he could for the welfare of his subjects. Kauṭilya also says that in the welfare and happiness of the people (*prajā*) lies the welfare and happiness of the king. After having evaluated him on these three counts we can judge him as a person—his qualities, character and personal achievements — whether or not he was of saintly temperament, a great musician, a man of letters, etc. But his personal qualities should not blind us to the far greater significance of the first three criteria. Akbar, for example, was personally quite illiterate, but he created conditions in which arts and letters flourished and the Mughal age became the second golden age of India, while Bhoja, though himself a great literary figure, as a king proved an utter failure for his policies led to almost complete collapse of the Paramāra empire.

Thus, Goyal has evolved a very scientific criteria for judging the place of a monarch in history. It is significant that this criteria relates the achievements of a king with the totality of the situation of his times.

VIII

From the view that political history should be studied in its total situational context it naturally follows that the history of other aspects of culture should also be viewed against the background of all the factors operating in society, including political. In other words, when we study the history of one aspect of society, that becomes the focal point of our study and other aspects throw light on it. And when we study the history of some other aspect, then that particular aspect occupies the centre of our attention and other aspects throw light on it. This is something entirely different from what we find in our present-day history books wherein the story of a particular period or of a king different chapters deal with different aspects of life, all of them, like the islands of a river, unconnected with each other. In Goyal's view of history, however, they are parts of one organic reality, each of them studied in its relation with others. For example, the identification of the social origins of the ancient ruling dynasties, that is the caste to which they belonged, is a favourite subject of the historians of ancient Indian political history. But usually they study it as an isolated topic having no bearing on the subsequent fortunes of the dynasty and the social class to which they belonged. In other words, discussions on the social origins of the ruling dynasties throw light neither on political and nor on social structure of the period. In his three volume study of ancient Indian political history (*Māgadha-Sātavāhana-Kushāṇa Sāmrājyoṅ kā Yuga, Gupta aura Vākāṭaka Sāmrājyoṅ kā Yuga* and *Maukhari-Pushyabhūti-Chālukya Yuga*) and in his *A History of the Imperial Guptas*, Goyal also discusses the caste origins of ancient dynasties and more often than not gives new suggestions. For example, he suggests that the Mauryas were Vrātya Kshatriyas, that the Guptas were Brāhmaṇas by caste, that the Maukharis were a branch of the Mālavas, that Yaśovarman was a Maukhari prince, that the Rajputs were of mixed origin, and so on. He also gives additional reasons to believe that the Pushyabhūtis were Vaiśyas and the Chālukyas were originally Brāhmaṇas. But Goyal does not only identify the caste of a dynasty, he also discusses its socio-religious *milieu* and correlates it with the attitude of its rulers and the policies followed by them. His treatment of the impact of the social origin of the Mauryas, and of their social background on their religious and other policies, of the Brāhmaṇical origin of the Śuṅgas on their policies and culture of the period, of the Brāhmaṇa origin of the imperial Guptas and their rise in a predominantly Brāhmaṇa culture-area on their political and religious policies, of the relationship of the Vaiśya origins of the Pushyabhūtis and the failure of Harsha in establishing a durable empire, etc., are some of the instances where Goyal has sought a correlation between political and social structures.

The works of Goyal on religious history of ancient India also reveal this approach emphatically. As has been pointed out by G.C. Pande, the renowned Buddhist scholar, in his foreword to Goyal's *A History of Indian Buddhism* (Meerut, 1987) the great merit of his work lies in the fact that "its point of view is that of a critical general historian who discusses the problems raised by the history of Indian Buddhism and its role in Indian culture" and that "he is interested in presenting and critically discussing the development of a major theme of Indian history in its social, cultural and intellectual aspects."[22] Goyal not only traces the pre-Buddha roots of Buddhist ideas in the ideologies current in the Vedic age but also in the factors of change in material culture and in the realm of ideas of the age of the Buddha. He also correlates the rise and growth of different phases of Buddhism and also its decline and revival in modern times with the changing

[22] G. C. Pande, his foreword in S. R. Goyal's *A History of Indian Buddhism*, Meerut, 1987, p. x.

pattern of culture in India. Goyal shows similar integrated approach in his *A Religious History of Ancient India*, in two volumes (Meerut, 1984 and 1986). Here, he treats religion in the context of social history. He delineates the story of Hindu religion against the background of the changes in society and correlates its fortunes with the changes in the social and political ideas and institutions. In the words of G. C. Pande, "He has certainly given the theme a rounded treatment which lifts it from the monotony of mere chronology or cataloguing of technical terms. Most writings on Indian religious history have suffered from an abstract and skeletal treatment and Professor Goyal deserves praise for his bold attempt as also for the caution which restrains him from losing religious history in any merely general or preconceived social history."[23] The same feature marks his a three volume study on Hinduism entitled *Pre-Paurāṇika Hinduism* (Jodhpur, 2008), *Fundamentals of Paurāṇika Hinduism* (Jodhpur, 2009) and *Paurāṇika Sects and Cults* (Jodhpur, 2017).

Goyal does not look upon the religious history of India as only a part of the 'superstructure' as the Marxist historians do; he believes that *sādhanā*, that is the pursuit of spiritual values embodied in the concept of *dharma* has remained the basic component of Indian culture through the ages and the Indian psyche has revealed itself through various modes of *sādhanā*, in different ages — *karma, jñāna, bhakti*, etc. That is why in the Indian context he gives greater emphasis on the role of ideas. Of course he concedes that material conditions did play a significant role in the determination of the pattern of Indian culture and seeks to understand and evaluate the Indian experience in the totality of its various aspects; he only insists that in India ideas played a greater and more significant role than material conditions. It makes his treatment of religious history of India different from other similar works which have appeared from time to time.

IX

Goyal believes in looking at history not only against the background of factors and forces operating in society but also in the total world context. That is why he has not only produced standard works on prehistory and ancient civilizations such as *Prāgaitihāsika Mānāva aura Saṁskṛtiyāṅ* (Gorakhpur, 1961) and *Viśva kī Prāchīna Sabhyatāyeṅ, upto 323 B.C.* (Gorakhpur, 1963) but has also studied political and religious history of ancient India in the light of the developments taking place in Central Asia, Iran, Western Asia, China, etc. Of course his increasing interest in political history, religious history, numismatics and epigraphy considerably decreased his zeal for world

[23] Cf. G.C. Pande's review in *The Indian Historical Review*, Vol. XI, Nos. 1-2, pp. 198-99.

history, but one must not deduce from this that he has lost his interest in it completely. His writings betray his passion for looking at Indian history in the total world context. While discussing the religious or political history of ancient India he discloses an all-pervasive vision extending deep both in time and space. He compares Aśoka with Ikhnaton, Samudragupta's Deccan campaigns with the similar campaigns of Alāuddīn Khalji, the place of Chandragupta II in Gupta history with that of Jahāngīr in Mughal history, and the nature of the organisation of Samudragupta's empire with that of Napoleon's. To discuss the place of Islam and Christianity in Indian history he delves deep in the history of these religions before they entered India. To explain the role of national ideal in modern Indian history he discusses its impact in European history. His vast intellectual horizon enables him to discuss the role of various languages in Indian history through the ages. To prove that pre-Aśokan Indians were largely an illiterate society despite the high level of culture in the Vedic age and the emergence of urban life in the post-Vedic period, he argues that though writing is usually found associated with urban life, it is not always necessary to presume the co-existence of the two. And to prove his point he gives the illustration of wheel which is regarded as the hub—an inaviodable component—of civilization. To illustrate the invention of Brāhmī during the reign of Aśoka he gives the example of Tibet where king Srong-tsan-gam-po got a script invented for the Tibetan language and used it, like Aśoka, for his inscriptions.[24] Thus, Goyal crosses the barriers of time and space and freely roams throughout the world to put his views in world perspective and give apt illustrations and facts to prove his point with telling effect. In this respect he is truly Nehruvian.

X

Goyal claims, and probably rightly, that his view of history is quite near to the ancient Indian definition of *itihāsa.*[25] *Itihāsa* literally means 'verily it so happened'. The early sources like the *Nirukta* and the *Bṛhaddevatā* give it the narrow meaning of *purāvṛtta* or 'ancient events'. But in the mature concept of it *itihāsa* included not only those compositions that may be called

[24] S. R. Goyal, 'Brāhmī Script — An Invention of the Early Maurya Period', his key-paper, in *The Origin of Brāhmī Script*, eds. S.P. Gupta and K. S. Ramachandran, New Delhi, 1979, pp. 1-53; also his Presidential Address delivered to the Silver Jubilee Congress of the Epigraphical Society of India, held at Udupi, Karnataka, in April, 1999, published in the *Journal of the Epigraphical Society of India*, Mysore, XXVI, 2000, pp. 1-19 and also his recent work *Brāhmī Script : An Invention of the Early Maurya Period*, Jodhpur, 2006.

[25] S. R. Goyal, *Māgadha-Sātavāhana- Kushāṇa Sāmrājyoṅ kā Yuga*, Meerut, 1988, p. 11.

political history, but also the history of moral and religious laws, social institutions and the science of economics and politics. In his *Arthaśāstra* Kauṭilya states:

> *Purāṇamitivṛttamākhyāyikodāharaṇaṁ dharmaśāstramartha-śāstraṁ chetītihāsaḥ.*

The same idea is expressed in an ancient verse quoted in Apte's *Sanskrit Dictionary*:

> *Dharmārtha-kāma-mokshāṇamupadeśa samanvitam/*
> *Pūrvavṛttaṁ kathāyuktamitihāsaṁ prachakshatee//.*

These quotations imply that history is that narrative of the past which exemplifies the fulfilment of the four ideals of life namely *dharma, artha, kāma* and *moksha.* Broadly speaking, *dharma* means a code of conduct, laws, duties and obligations, *artha* means economic welfare, *kāma* implies biological fulfilment and cultural well-being while *moksha* signifies liberation from transmigration. Thus, economic, social and cultural aspects of human life as well as ethical values are all included as legitimate parts of history. In this view naturally individual events of history serve as illustrations of the general evolution of society and the *Mahābhārata* becomes the ideal work of history since it seeks to convey the nature and diversity of human experience by illustrations. It is also to be noted that just as individual is not given much importance in the integral view of history, in ancient India also individual was not given much importance. In this view the dictum *rājākālasyakāraṇam* signifies not so much the primacy of the individual king as that of the state.[26]

[26] Shankar Goyal, *Prāchīna Bhārata : Itihāsa, Itihāsa-Lekhana aura Vichāradhārāyeṅ*, Varanasi, 2022, pp. 11 ff.

TEN

The Madras School of Ancient Indian Historians : A Critical Assessment

In this address I attempt to evaluate the history writing of the Madras school of ancient Indian historians. It has been inconceivable, in the time and space at my disposal, to deal with every majar historian or his work, and, consequently, I have confined myself to a few of the most important ones, and to their most valuable writings on the subject—S. Krishnaswami Aiyangar (1871-1946), K. A. Nilakanta Sastri (1892-1975) and T. V. Mahalingam (1907-1983), whose pioneering efforts definitely provided the much needed and reliable chronological framework to study south Indian history. Some other historians and their works are mentioned in passing, but as the Madras school of ancient Indian historians has produced so many luminaries, such as, V.R.R. Dikshitar, K.K. Pillay, C.S. Srinivasachariar, T.N. Ramachandran, K.V. Raman and P. Shanmugam, to name only a few, this address is not intended to investigate the whole field. I have also argued that now there is an immediate need to study the political history of south India from the holistic or integral point of view in which cultural and political aspects of life are treated as various aspects of an organic whole for the narrative part dominating in most of the recent works on political history treat it as if it has no relation with the socio-economic, religious and cultural changes.

I

S. Krishnaswami Aiyangar was born on April 15, 1871, in the village of Sakkottai (Shajikot), the ancient Raghunathapura, a suburb of Kumbhakonam. He was graduated from the Central College, Bangalore, and was awarded a degree in Physics. Since he did not get a distinction in that subject, he devoted himself to postgraduate studies in Mathematics, while working in a school in Bangalore itself. But after he was transferred to a teacher's post first at

Chikmagalur and then at Kolar, in the Mysore State, he had to give up the study of Mathematics for that of History and took his M.A. degree in it in 1899. Just when he was about to become the Headmaster of a High School, his M.A. thesis on the *History of Mysore under the Wodeyars* was published in the *Madras Review* of May 1900, and this enabled him to become a Lecturer in History in the Central College. His interest in ancient Indian history was due to his contacts with V. Venkayya and E. Hultzsch, both epigraphists, and interested in south Indian history. Instigated by their example, Aiyangar wrote two papers on Chola ascendancy and Chola administration which received encomium from Hultzsch who also suggested him to give real scope to his intelligence in interpreting the historical value of inscriptions.

When the University of Madras created a chair of Indian History and Archaeology in 1914, Aiyangar was appointed to that post. He held this post till 1929. But in between, in 1919, he was appointed Reader in the University of Calcutta and delivered some lectures on the contribution of south India to Indian culture. The University of Calcutta also conferred on him an Honorary Doctorate.

On assumption of the new office at the University of Madras, Aiyangar chalked out three lines of work. Firstly, he used to deliver every year a series of advanced lectures to the students of the honours classes on chosen topics of Indian history. The first of the advanced lectures was concerned with Vijayanagar and in the subsequent years practically the whole of the Hindu period down to the foundation of Vijayanagar was dealt with in these lectures. Secondly, he supervised university research students. During his fifteen years of office he successfully guided the work of four research students allotted to him. The works of these students included the following : *Sources of Vijayanagar History* by A. Rangaswami Saraswati, *History of the Nāyakas of Madura* by R. Sathianathaiyyar, *History of the Pallavas of Kāñchī* by R. Gopalan, and *Hindu Administrative Institutions* by V.R.R. Dikshitar.[1] Thirdly, Aiyangar was himself engaged in research work and published the results whenever ripe.

Aiyangar graced many posts of honour. He was elected a member of the Royal Asiatic Society in 1908 and was conferred a 'Diwan Bahadur' title in 1928. He was the Secretary of the All-India Oriental Conference for a number of years and presided over its Session in Mysore in 1935. He presided over the first section of the Indian History Congress in Allahabad in 1938 and was its General President in 1940 in Lahore. But the most signal honour was the

[1] Dikshitar was also his colleague in the Department of Indian History and Archaeology. He later on brought out several other works including *The Mauryan Polity* (Madras, 1932), *The Gupta Polity* (Madras, 1952) and *The Purāṇa Index*, 2 Vols. (Madras, 1951, 1952).

Campbell Gold Medal conferred on him by the Bombay Branch of the Royal Asiatic Society in 1940. He died in 1946 at the age of 76.[2]

Aiyangar has many works to his credit on a wide range of subjects. His *Ancient India and South Indian History and Culture* (Poona, 1941), his collected works, include most of his important papers on Indian history and culture from time to time. These papers are divided into two parts : papers on general Indian history upto 1300, both north and south, included in the first part which was published under the title *Ancient India*; and the other papers of the same useful character, but mainly relating to a later period of south Indian history and also some miscellaneous papers bearing upon topics of Indian culture forming another part in continuation, under the caption *South Indian History and Culture*. His *Ancient India*, being the first volume of his collected works, incorporates his lectures on ancient India, on such topics as the imperial Guptas,[3] the Hūṇa problem in Indian history, the Vākāṭakas and their place in Indian history, the Vākāṭaka-Gupta relations[4] and the Gurjara empire in north India. He was of the opinion that king 'Chandra' mentioned in the Meharauli iron pillar inscription was no other than Chandragupta I and, consequently, the first Gupta *Mahārājādhirāja* was the paramount ruler of almost the whole of India. His views on the early history of the Vākāṭakas were vitiated by this basic presumption.[5] With regard to his contribution to the history of north India, it may be stated that they incorporate all the latest researches upto 1941, the year of its publication.

Aiyangar's contributions to south Indian history and culture is tremendous. There is no field from the earliest times to the British period where his conclusions can be ignored even now. His *Some Contributions of South India to Indian Culture* (Calcutta, 1923) contain at one place his main contributions to the study of south Indian culture. According to him, south Indian culture has a character of its own despite the interaction between the north and the south. He points out that south India today presents Brāhmaṇa orthodoxy in its Vedic form, its chief features being performance of ritualistic sacrifices and cultivation of learning and its propagation; that modern Hinduism

[2] A reasonably good account of S. Krishnaswami Aiyangar's life and his contribution to south Indian history is given by G. S. Dikshit, in S. P. Sen (ed.), *Historians and Historiography in Modern India*, Calcutta, 1973, pp.60-68.

[3] S. K. Aiyangar's *Studies in Gupta History* (Madras, 1928) concentrates on the dynastic history of the Guptas.

[4] S. K. Aiyangar, *Ancient India and South Indian History and Culture*, Vol. I, pp. 91-92; idem, 'The Vākāṭakas and their Place in the History of India' in *ABORI*, V, pp. 31-54; idem, 'The Vākāṭakas in Gupta History', *QJMS*, XV, pp. 153-64.

[5] Shankar Goyal, *175 Years of Vākāṭaka History and Historiography*, Jodhpur, 2009, p. 5.

is the result of ritualistic Brāhmaṇism with the addition of theism which was originally northern but developed more fully in the south as the cult of *bhakti* ; that along with the notion of *bhakti* or devotion to a personal God is Tāntrism—worship offered by means of mystical signs and formulae, Andhra, instead of Tamilnadu, was probably responsible for this; that in the spread of Indian culture and the expansion of Indian commerce, the former in the east and the latter both in the east and west, the share of the south was considerable; that in administration, particularly local administration, which was fully developed under the Cholas and also in central administration, the south shows a distinctive character though the general notions were the same both in the north and in the south and these ideas continued right upto the British days in the south; and that the south has preserved Indian religions and learning better than the north. The conservation of both was due to the empire of Vijayanagar, the supersession of which empire by the Muhammadans was a short parenthesis in the history of the general development of religion and culture in south India. In the north, they were subject to great pressure and unavoidable modifications by the impact of Islam which came with the Muhammadan invasions.[6]

The chronology which Aiyangar has fixed for Tamil literature and history has been more or less accepted. He believes that Sangam literature is of a pre-Pallava character and, as such, referable to the early centuries of the Christian era; and the literature, the typical representatives of which are the *Tevāram* and *Tiruvāymoḷi* of the saints of the Śaivas and Vaishṇavas, belongs to the age of the Pallavas and is assignable to the period 300 to 900 A.D.[7] It was Aiyangar again who fixed the date of the Kaḷabhra interregnum in south Indian history from 300 A.D. onwards. The Kaḷabhras were active in south India upto700 A.D. or so. They were intruders from the north into the Tamil country and created an interregnum in Pāṇḍya rule. It is very likely that the Sangam order of society may have been destroyed by them.[8] Again, the credit for giving a more logical account of the origin of the Pallavas goes to Aiyangar. Earlier they were equated with the foreign Pahlavas. But, according to him, they were a dynasty of officers of the Sātavāhanas, probably related to them and they conquered the Kāñchī region. When the Sātavāhana dynasty broke

[6] S. K. Aiyangar, *Some Contributions of South India to Indian Culture*, pp. x-xvi; Dikshit, *op.cit.*, p. 62.

[7] *Ibid.*, pp. xvi-xvii; also see Shankar Goyal, 'The Nāyanārs and Āḷvārs and their Contribution to the Bhakti Movement in South India', his Presidential Address to the Cultural History Section of the South Indian History Congress, published in the *Proceedings of the Twenty-ninth Annual Session of the South Indian History Congress*, Tirunelveli, 2009, pp. 370-79.

[8] *Ancient India and South Indian History and Culture*, Vol. I,pp.464 ff.

up, they apparently set up independently and founded the new dynasty of the Pallavas, as distinct from the older chieftains, the Toṇḍamāns of the region. They promoted the religions, culture and language of the north, because they had imbibed them from the Sātavāhanas.[9] As regards the Cholas, Aiyangar's account of them in his collected works is still comprehensible; nobody has given a better description of the working of their self-governing local bodies. Though later researches have disproved some of his identifications of places in the Bengal expedition of Rajendra Chola Gangaikoṇḍa, he was the first Indian historian to describe the maritime relations, friendly and otherwise, between the Cholas and the Śailendra empire in Malaya and Sumatra.

Aiyangar's *South India and Her Muhammadan Invaders* (Oxford, 1921) covers the period from the decline of the Cholas and the Hoysalas to the rise of Vijayanagar. In it he emphasised the heroic efforts of the Hoysalas and the Kākatīyas and their feudatory chieftains to save south India from the effects of the Muslim invasions. His contribution to the history of Vijayanagar is significant. He is known for the new methods that he introduced in interpreting the history of Vijayanagar. If R. Sewell reconstructed *A Forgotten Empire* (London, 1924) with the help of the Persian and Portuguese and archaeological sources and H. Krishna Sastri added to them inscriptional sources, Aiyangar collected casual references to Vijayanagar history in non-historical literature in Sanskrit, Telugu and Kannada. It is with these sources that he was able to understand the character and significance of the emprie, about which he wrote eloquently at more than one place.[10] Not only has he fixed the character and significance of this empire, he has contributed to many aspects of its history. He holds that the founders were the officers of the Hoysalas,[11] he has contributed to the unravelling of the confusion caused by four monarchs who succeeded one another, all of them having almost similar names like Narasiṁha, Narasa and Vīra Narasiṁha.[12] It is in this work that we find the best account of the glorious reign of Kṛshṇadevarāya[13] and also of the battle of Talikota or Rakshasi-Tangadi.[14]

It is not only to political history that Aiyangar devoted his research. In

[9] *Ibid.*, pp. 498-500; also see Shankar Goyal, *Recent Historiography of Ancient India*, Jodhpur, 1997, p. 418. D. C. Sircar supports Aiyangar's theory in *The Classical Age*, in R. C. Majumdar, A. D. Pusalker and A. K. Majumdar (eds.), Bombay, 1962, Ch. XIII.

[10] The Madras University continued this work and produced three more volumes entitled *Further Sources of Vijayanagar History* (Madras, 1946) edited by K.A. Nilakanta Sastri and N. Venkataramanayya.

[11] *Vijayanagar Sixcentenary Commemoration Volume*, Dharwar, 1936, p. 10.

[12] *Ancient India and South Indian History and Culture*, Vol. I, Ch. II.

[13] *Ibid.*, Ch. III.

[14] *Ibid.*, Ch. IV.

the work titled *The Evolution of Hindu Administrative Institutions in South India* (Sir William Meyer Lectures that he delivered in 1930) he concluded that the Hindu monarchy, though autocratic in an emergency, "satisfied the exacting demands even of a pure and complete democracy not only in form but more completely in spirit." His *History of Tirupati* (in two volumes, Madras, 1940, 1941) is a model of its class.[15] It is an unprejudiced description of a shrine which at various stages came under the effect of the Jaina, Buddhist and Śaiva cults before it became and continues to be the most notable Śrīvaishṇava shrine equally popular with the rest of the Hindu community. In his Preface to the work Aiyangar wrote, "I have made use of all the sources of information with care that a work like this deserves and have adopted deliberately the method of letting the sources speak as far as they could, as in a controversial matter like this, it is much the best thing to set out the facts clearly and place them upon an indubitable footing, quite distinct from such inferences that one may have to deduce from these facts. ... The facts are there quite distinctly stated followed by such inferences I have been enabled to draw therefrom." Aiyangar studied Sanskrit language with great assiduity and care and attained a very high degree of proficiency in it. It is quite evident in his edited Sanskrit work, *Parama Saṁhitā of the Pāñcharatra*, with his Introduction and a English translation of the text. His other Introduction to *Maṇimekhalai in Its Historical Setting*, the work for which he received the Great Silver Medal by the Institut Historique et Heraldique, reveals a thorough knowledge of the various systems of Hindu philosophy, not the scrappy knowledge which most people get by reading incorrect translations of the original texts.

While delivering his Presidential Address (Section I) to the Allahabad Session of the Indian History Congress (1938), Aiyangar expresses his views on Aryanization of India or Indianization of the Aryans. "To melt all these various people into one uniform would have been a feat impossible of achievement," he writes. It was a long process, therefore, from this to go on assimilating various people that composed Indian society, and bringing them into the fold of a united Indian society, certainly not a united Aryan society in the narrower sense of the term. "The process must have been long and powerful", he says, "involving compromise of various kinds." The expansion of Aryans, according to him, was a process of Indianization, the Aryan Vedic organization expanded into the Indian caste system, an institution of gradual growth.

"History", according to Aiyangar, "should never serve the purpose of propaganda even for noble purpose." Elaborating his vision in his Presidential

[15] In one of his earlier works Aiyangar traced the early history of Vaishṇavism in south India (Madras, 1920).

Address to the Lahore Session of the Indian History Congress (1940), he says, "We have no right whatever to make history subserve our purposes, however noble they may be in themselves and the value of a study of history is lost completely for good and for evil by the slightest interference with the recording of its actual course." For one example, he explains, teachers of history have been admonished to teach history leaving out of it altogether all that would tend to promote sectarian fanaticism. An effort of abolishing what would promote religious bitterness is certainly a good thing and the way to teach it is not to remove from history the acts of fanaticism and fanatical personalities who played their part in history. The plainest way of teaching the youth to put an end to religious bigotry in their convictions and character is not to tell the lie that people were never fanatics in history and as such never committed any heinous act of promoting religious bitterness. On the other hand, without obscuring truth, the people have to be convinced of the consequences of evils resulting from fanatical acts of rulers which need be projected rather than quietly glossed over. The historian is, therefore, advised not to perpetuate lies in his pronouncements. Aiyangar also enjoined the historians to bear in mind the principle laid down by Lord Morley that "We have no right to expect from the past anything but that past in all its completeness, which means that a history of the past is intended to tell us what that past was, nothing more, nothing less." Our knowledge of history may not be quite accurate and absolutely correct in all its details from the imperfection of the material and even of the minds that go to work upon it, he observes, but we are bound in honour, may be even in common honesty, to tell the tale of what actually happened as accurately as we can get at that. It is then that history becomes a study of value as a record of actual human experience. Then only can it be made use of for studying progress in the past "to know what promoted real progress and what prevented it, thereby cultivating a critical judgement." That is the real teaching of history. We ought to recover from the past all that "we can possibly recover, and in true perspective. All narrowness in sentiment—sectional or local, and other kinds of patriotism must be kept aside."[16]

Aiyangar thought that the European savants could not understand our literature fully. He asserted that a specific study like that of the Vedas showed that while the European researches of it had undoubtedly made the meaning of words clear, an equivalent claim could not be advanced with truth in respect of the understanding of the ideas, the allusions and all that made it literature.[17]

Aiyangar also thought that our studies had reached a stage when an extensive reconstruction of history seemed called for and could be undertaken

[16] *PIHC*, Lahore Session, 1940, pp. 27 ff.

[17] *Ibid.*, p. 26.

with a chance of successful completion.[18] The Indian History Congress set up a body with Aiyangar as the Chairman of the Coordinating Committee to develop a comprehensive scheme of writing Indian history.[19]

Apart from being a member of the Mysore Education Service, Aiyangar also actively participated in public activities, such as, founding learned societies or being associated with them or editing journals. One of the earliest institutions, with the founding of which he was actively associated, was the Mythic Society of Bangalore. He was its first Secretary, and after continuing in that positon for some years, he worked as the Editor of its quarterly journal for five years. The best way to find out how active was he is to go through the various numbers of this journal. He delivered many lectures under its auspices, he presided over some, and when he was not doing either, he commented upon the lectures of others. His contributions in all these capacities are still worth perusal. The other journal with which he was involved was the *Indian Antiquary*. He was its Joint Editor for more than ten years along with Sir Richard Temple, S. M. Edwardes and E. A. W. Oldham. But it is as the Editor of the *Journal of Indian History* that he will be long remembered. Shafaat Ahmed Khan started it in 1921, but could not continue it after the third volume. Aiyangar took it up and struggled hard for five years and secured a recognised position for it, but its finances continued to cause anxiety. After a severe struggle each time, he continued the work, notwithstanding the great financial loss which it involved. The only reward which he recieved was the recognition from scholars and the ungrudging cooperation of his colleagues in the editorial staff, C. S. Srinivasachariar and V.R.R. Dikshitar,[20] until at last, he was able to persuade the University of Kerala, Trivandrum, to take it over and relieve him of this responsibility.

The books and many articles of Aiyangar deeply influened many historians of the country. G.S. Sardesai, for example, wrote, "When many years ago, I ploughed my lonely furrow trying to put into Marathi garb a connected story of India's past, I found myself entirely in the dark as regards any reliable data for the history of south India and the rich store of its past glory. ...My attention came to be drawn to the writings of this learned scholar and I must say that my whole view of the Maratha history was profoundly influenced by them. I then realised that we could not study the Marathas by themselves and neglect the pregnant issues offered by the indigenous Hindu civilization of peninsular India." Sardesai also admired Aiyangar's insistence

[18] *Ibid.*

[19] Aiyangar also contributed chapters to a similar scheme launched by the Bharatiya Vidya Bhavan, Bombay.

[20] Cf. *JIH*, XX, April 1941, pp. i-vii.

that Indian scholars should help themselves in the field of history as in other spheres of national regeneration. For Indians alone can study and accurately interpret the records and materials of ancient past. Many earlier histories of a number of distinguished western scholars had became obsolete, if not entirely misleading. Sardesai, therefore, recapitulated that "Aiyangar's career had been an inspiring example to many... and deserved to be cherished as such examples of devotion to scholarship were few and far between." Some of his close friends have described the reasons for his influence. Shafaat Ahmed Khan, for example, stated, "Upon everything he has written are stamped thoroughness and solidity. He has also shown in his person a rare devotion to learning and a singular capacity for making and retaining friends." Another contemporary of Aiyangar in the Central College, Bangalore, commented that he was "never in the way and never out of the way." All who knew him agreed that "he was essentially reasonable and had the gift of a quite persuasiveness which seldom failed to bring converts to the reasonable view."[21]

II

K. A. Nilakanta Sastri[22] belonged to the Madras school founded by S. Krishnaswami Aiyangar and was in a way the academic successor of the latter. He was born on Friday, August 12, 1892, in an economically modest but enlightened Telugu Niyogi Brāhmaṇa family of Tirunelveli, Tamilnadu, as the third and the last son of his parents. He was brought up in rural surroundings. He had his early education in George Secondary School, Kallidaikurichi, and in the Ambasamudram High School. His eldest brother A. Kuppuswami managed to get for him a Government Scholarship of the value of Rs. 14/- p.m. for his B.A. For M.A. he got the Thurso studentship which fetched about Rs. 20/- p.m. By sheer hard work he got not only a First Class in M.A. (1913) but also stood first in the Presidency.

After such a brilliant academic career, Nilakanta joined the Hindu College, Tirunelveli, as a Lecturer. He taught History there from 1913 to 1918. Then he served as Professor of History in the Benares Hindu University, from 1918 to 1920. In 1920 he joined Meenakshi College, Chidambaram, as Principal, and spent eight years in building up the college from an intermediate college of about 70 pupils in the beginning to the level of a university with 700 pupils on the rolls and magnificent new buildings and hostels at the end of 1928.

Nilakanta Sastri served as one of the most distinguished Professors of Ancient Indian History and Archaeology of Madras University from 1929 to

[21] Quoted by Dikshit, *op.cit.*, p. 67.

[22] For an account of K.A.N. Sastri's life and works vide S.P. Gupta (ed.), *Aspects of India's History and Culture*, New Delhi, 1973.

1947 when he retired on attaining superannuation at 55. But that was not the end of his academic career. He became Professor of Indology, Mysore University (1952-56) and Director, Institute of Traditional Culture (sponsored by the UNESCO), Madras (1957-71). For a year he was a Visiting Professor (1959) at the University of Chicago where he delivered a series of lectures on south Indian history.

Sastri graced numerous posts of honour. He was the General President of the Indian History Congress, Patna, in 1946 and the General President of the All-India Oriental Conference, Lucknow, in 1961. Also, he acted as Chairperson of many sessions of various seminars and conferences. He also served as the Honorary Member of l'Ecole Française d' Extreme Orient, Saigon, in Indo-China; the Royal Asiatic Society, Bombay, Ceylon and Malayan branches; the Hon. Fellow of the Royal Asiatic Society of Great Britain and Ireland; and the member of Central Advisory Board of Archaeology, New Delhi.

Even in his early years, K.A.N. Sastri was in the enlightened company of the cream of great scholars, like Professors Saranathan, Vaiyapuri Pillai, M. Raghava Iyengar and others. Dr. Rajendra Prasad was very friendly and kind to him even after becoming the President of India. Among his other academic friends and associates mention may be made of P. C. Bagchi, A.S. Altekar, R. C. Majumdar, N. P. Chakravarti, Tarachand, Bisheshwar Prasad, B.P. Saxena, H. C. Raychaudhuri, S. K. Chatterji and Nihar Ranjan Ray. Despite his being an orthodox Brāhmaṇa he could inculcate good relations with Father Heras, a Christian scholar. Among his students who made a mark in the field of politics and administration are included R. Venkataraman, the ex-President of India, S. Kameshwar Rao, and R. Tirumalai, retired officers of the Indian Administrative Service. Among his students who made a mark in the field of history, prominent are C. Minakshi, K. Gopalachari and A. Appadurai.

Sastri was not only a man of letters but also an exceptionally successful and inspiring teacher. He was an eloquent speaker. He knew the *Arthaśāstra* by heart. He was very strong in Sanskrit, Tamil, Telugu and English. He also learnt Dutch and French to study south-east Asian history. He knew many subjects besides history, knew the history of many countries besides India, and knew many branches of history besides political and dynastic. His independent scholarly pursuits continued till his incapacitation due to failing sight and deaf ears. He expired in 1975.

Nilakanta Sastri produced a considerable amount of historical literature. His works may be classified into five categories[23] according to their form and

[23] S. K. Mukhopadhyay, *Evolution of Historiography in Modern India : 1900-1960*, Calcutta, 1981, pp. 105 ff.

content :

A. His major works whose dominant trait is political : (i) *The Pāṇḍyan Kingdom* (1929), (ii) *Studies in Cōḷa History and Administration* (1932), (iii) *The Cōḷas*, I and II (1935, 1937, in one volume in 1955), (iv) *The Tamil Kingdoms of South India* (1948), (v) *Sir William Meyer Lectures on History of Śrīvijaya* (1949), (vi) *History of India* (three parts, 1950, revised edn. *Advanced History of India* (1970), (vii) *A History of South India* (1955), (viii) *The Culture and History of the Tamils* (1964), and (ix) *India — a Historical Survey* (1966), (revised edn. *Life and Culture of the Indian People*, 1974).

B. Works on cultural and social history : (i) *Gleanings on Social Life from the Avadānas* (1945), (ii) *South Indian Influences in the Far East* (1949), (iii) *Dravidian Literatures* (1949), (iv) *Cultural Expansion of India* (1959), (v) *Development of Religion in South India* (1963), (vi) *Cultural Contacts between Aryans and Dravidians* (1967), and (vii) *Sangam Literature — Its Cults and Cultures* (1972).

C. Edited works : (i) F. Max Müller's *India — What Can It Teach Us?* (1934), (ii) *Some Documents on the History of Cochin* (1939), (iii) *Foreign Notices of South India from Megasthenes to Huan* (1939), (iv) *Further Sources of Vijayanagar History*, 3 vols. (1946), (v) *Age of the Nandas and Mauryas* (1952), (vi) *A Comprehensive History of India* (Vol. II, 1957), (vii) *A Great Liberal: Speeches and Writings of Sir P. S. Sivaswami Aiyar* (1965), (viii) *India as Seen in the Bṛhat Saṁhitā of Varāhamihira*, and (ix) *B. C. Law Memorial Volume* (1946), Jt. Editor.

D. Works on methodology : (i) *Historical Method in Relation to Problems of South Indian History* (1941), (ii) *Lectures on Factors in Indian History* (1949), (iii) *Historical Method in Relation to Indian History* (1956), and (iv) *Sources of Indian History* (1961).

E. Some minor writings and stray historical articles : (i) *The Concept of a Secular State*, (ii) *Agastya*, (iii) *Alexander's Campaign against Porus*, (iv) *Nālandā*, (v) *Tirumala Naik, the Portuguese and the Dutch*, (vi) *Southern India, Arabia and Africa*, (vii) *South India*, and (viii) *South India and South-East Asia* — a collection of twenty-eight research articles. He also delivered some Presidential Addresses to the learned bodies.

The earliest work to come out from the pen of Sastri was *The Pāṇḍyan Kingdom*. It was an enlarged version of a series of lectures he delivered on this subject at the University of Madras in 1926. The Pāṇḍyas had at no stage any great influence on the main course of Indian history. Pāṇḍyan antiquities have also somehow failed to interest scholars. However, Sastri realized that a complete view of the story of south India cannot be obtained until the history of the Pāṇḍyas is fully worked out. Sastri himself began his work with the candid admission that his work makes no claim to be considered as "a full and satisfactory account of the Pāṇḍyan kingdom." But, as Father Heras pointed out in his review of this work, "Sastri was eminently successful in his enterprise" and by this book he "placed himself among the great professors and writers of the history of India."[24]

Studies in Cōḷa History and Administration may justly be called a spade work for his *magnum opus*, *The Cōḷas*. The history of the Cholas easily falls into five divisions, viz. : (i) the pre-Christian period, (ii) the literature of the Sangam age, (iii) the interval between the end of the Sangam period and the rise of the line of Vijayālaya, (iv) the period of the Vijayālaya line, and (v) the age of the Chālukya-Chola line of Kulottuṅga I. While giving details about various rulers of the dynasty Sastri also deals with the central and local governments, taxation and finance, population and society, agriculture and land tenure, industry and trade, education and learning and lastly religion and literature under the Cholas. A curious feature of *The Cōḷas* is that the Chola art does not find a place in it. Sastri considers the earlier phase of Indian history as its happier phase : "The history of the Cōḷa empire belongs, on the whole, to this earlier and happier phase of India's history."[25] In the opinion of A. L. Basham, "Despite the troubled times and the seething national unrest and aspiration of the late nineteen-twenties and thirties, much solid work was done along the lines laid down by Bhandarkar. H. C. Ray's monumental *Dynastic History of Northern India* (2 vols., 1931-36), and K. A. Nilakanta Sastri's very detailed study *The Cōḷas* (3 vols., 1935-37), are only two examples among many."[26]

The Tamil Kingdoms of South India and *The Culture and History of the Tamils* of Sastri give an excellent review of the government, socio-economic conditions, religion, literature and fine arts of the Chera, Chola and Pāṇḍyan kingdoms. *History of Śrīvijaya* or the *Sumātran Kingdom of the Śailendras* was the theme of Sir William Meyer Lectures Sastri delivered at the University of Madras in 1946-47. *Sangam Literature — Its Cults and Cultures* is another scholarly work of Sastri in which he made a successful attempt to bring into prominence the sober and realistic picture of the political, social, religious, and economic life that prevailed in the ancient Tamil country, with the help of the early Tamil classics. He depicts a vast panorama of life of the Sangam age. The language he employed here is rich, dignified and plainly direct.

K. A. N. Sastri's *The Cōḷas*, *Foreign Notices of South India*, *Further Sources of Vijayanagar History* and *South Indian Influences in the Far East*, etc., were great pioneer works in their respective fields of study. They are

[24] *JBHS*, September 1929, p. 278.

[25] K.A.N. Sastri, *The Cōḷas*, p. 446.

[26] A.L. Basham, in *Historians of India, Pakistan and Ceylon*, ed. C. H. Philips, London, 1961, pp. 285-86.

also the models of historical writing in which original sources, most of them unearthed by Sastri himself, have been critically examined and fully utilized.

Sastri wrote quite a few text books of south Indian history which are primarily based on published sources and works of earlier authors in the field. Of these *A History of South India* (from prehistoric times to the fall of Vijayanagar) is more than an ordinary text book. In fact it is by far the best work on south Indian history. In this work Sastri presented in a compact form a comprehensive account of the history of the whole of south India treated as a single geographical entity.[27] In it he has incorporated the results of his own researches, and has also brought together material previously scattered in many separate studies and presented it as a coherent narrative. Here, political history naturally occupies a predominant place, but an account is also given of social life, commerce, religion, philosophy, literature and the plastic arts. These subjects are treated in the course of the historical narrative and also in four separate chapters at the end of the book. The history of the Vākāṭakas is given in chapter VI. Both in respect of chronology and history he has broadly followed the outline of A.S. Altekar. For example, he believed that Rudrasena I was helped by Bhavanāga in his internal troubles, that the conquests of Samudragupta did not affect the Vākāṭakas, that the Guptas contracted matrimonial alliance with the Vākāṭakas to strengthen the Gupta position 'in execution of their plans against the Śakas', that Prabhāvatī gave considerable help to her father in the Śaka war, and so on.[28] The history of the Chālukyas of Badami,[29] Pallavas and Pāṇḍyas[30] are given in chapter VIII.

All in all, in his *A History of South India* Sastri takes the reader along with him amidst falling kingdoms and clash of arms. However, his work is not only the chronicle of kings or the wars they waged; it also includes a depiction of material conditions, social institutions, philosophy and religion and art and literature. Here, Sastri not only builds up the broad outlines of the history of peninsular India but has brought out the multicoloured and fascinating cultural life and cultural movements of the people of south India. His work reflects the true history of the life of the people and their cultural movements. Sastri's concept of history is so wide that it includes every aspect of the life of humanity.

[27] Shankar Goyal, *Recent Historiography of Ancient India*, p. 416.

[28] *Ibid.*, p. 408.

[29] K.A.N. Sastri also wrote two chapters on the Chālukyas of Badami and Veṅgī respectively for *The Early History of the Deccan* (London, 1960) edited by Ghulam Yazdani.

[30] In *A Comprehensive History of India*, edited by R.C. Majumdar and K. K. Dasgupta (1981), a chapter on the genealogy and chronology of the Pallavas has been written by S. K. Aiyangar and K. A. Nilakanta Sastri jointly and on the Pāṇḍyas and other dynasties by Sastri alone.

His scholarship and his intimate connection with the land and people give to his historical writings a distinct stamp of his own. This work established him as the foremost historian of south India. Commenting on this work B. K. Majumdar says, "the entire political history of ancient India has been covered by the valuable works of Dr. H.C. Raychaudhuri and Dr. H. C. Ray except perhaps the history of south India in its entirety which has been only presented to the public by Professor K. A. Nilakanta Sastri in his *A History of South India*, published in 1955."[31]

Sastri edited two very significant volumes entitled *Age of the Nandas and Mauryas* and *A Comprehensive History of India* (Vol. II)[32] sponsored respectively by the Indian History Congress and the Bhāratīya Itihāsa Parishad.[33] The first volume contains eleven chapters of which five are Sastri's contribution. Sastri's approach to the history of Aśoka was traditional in nature and his treatment of Maurya polity was based on the acceptance of the *Arthaśāstra* "as the authentic production of the Mauryan empire."[34] For him Maurya period was one of "great endeavour and noble achievement."[35] "Politically India became one, and the cultural unity in the midst of diversity that has always characterised her civilization became more marked than ever in this period."[36] "India was in the van of human progress," Sastri declares, "and one of her greatest emperors sent forth into the world the message of universal peace and love."[37] The second volume covers the history of the Mauryas and the Sātavāhanas (325 B.C. to 300 A.D.). In this work greater stress has been laid on cultural movements and social institutions.

Sastri also compiled and edited a few source books of south Indian history. Of these mention may be made of *Further Sources of Vijayanagar History*, 3 vols., *Some Documents on the History of Cochin* and *Foreign Notices of South India.* In the spirit of a genuine scholar Sastri has not only discovered and used new sources but has given them a systematic form for the benefit of future scholars in the field.

Now, we may discuss some of his minor works. His *Gleanings on Social Life from the Avadānas* is a collection of data on social life from two of the earliest known works of this class of the Buddhist literature—*Divyāvadāna* and *Avadānaśataka* (c. 100-150 A.D.). In *South Indian Influences in the Far*

[31] B.K. Majumdar, in *Historians and Historiography in Modern India*, ed. S. P. Sen, p. 102.

[32] Its chapter on Mauryan government, society and art was written by Sastri and P. C. Bagchi.

[33] Cf. Shankar Goyal, *op. cit.*, p. 120.

[34] K.A.N. Sastri (ed.), *Age of the Nandas and Mauryas*, p. 201.

[35] *Ibid.*, p. 8.

[36] *Ibid.*

[37] *Ibid.*

East he has studied the art and social life at the early stage of Hindu colonization of the east with a view to estimating the role of southern India in their evolution. In his view influences from other parts of India which flowed into the area were weaker and less persistent than those from south India. His *Cultural Expansion of India* [38] is an attempt to find out Indian elements in the cultural make-up of other countries, particularly those of Eastern Europe, Near East, Middle East, Central Asia, China, Indo-China and Indonesia. His *Sangam Literature — Its Cults and Cultures* is an account of the earliest Tamil literature known to us. It camprises more than two thousand poems which help create a pen-picture of polity, society and economy. *Dravidian Literatures* is a small booklet of only forty-eight pages giving general readers a short but compact outline of the chronology and content of the literatures in the principal languages (Tamil, Telugu, Kannada, and Malayalam) of south India. *Development of Religion in South India* contains the series of seven lectures Sastri delivered at the University of Chicago in 1959. From the integration of cults and the beginning of Hinduism to the present-day reform and modernization forms the theme of discussion. *Cultural Contacts between Aryans and Dravidians* is a course of four lectures which he delivered at the University of Patna in 1964. He is of the view that the Aryan-Dravidian contacts were friendly. The view put forward by some scholars that the Dravidians were pushed out of northern India has, Sastri believes, no real basis.

Nilakanta Sastri's two addresses, as Sectional President, 'Ancient India Section' and as General President, Indian History Congress, Calcutta, 1939 and Patna, 1946 respectively, provide an insight into his concept of history and political thinking. The Calcutta Address concentrating on 'the Conception of *Chakravartin*' is more a record of the attempts made by ancient Indian powers — the Mauryas and the Guptas in the north, and the Andhras, Pallavas and Cholas in the south to extend their political tentacles in India as also by the latter, particularly the Cholas, across the seas pursuing an active naval policy. This conception of *Chakravartin* might have led to an all-India State, and in the Mauryan empire this condition was nearly attained but the intense love of social and local autonomy on the part of the people forbade the rise of a centralized administration. In his words, "the pattern of peace-time life in ancient India was that of a number of closely-knit autonomous groups each contributing to a fairly rich and harmonious culture, richer and more harmonious perhaps than ever before or since but maintained on somewhat slender means."[39]

K. A. Nilakanta Sastri did not subscribe to any particular philosophy of

[38] Banikanta Kakati Memorial Lectures, University of Gauhati, 1956.

[39] Cf. B. N. Puri, *Ancient Indian Historiography*, Delhi, 1994, pp. 289-90.

history. He did not attempt to find out the forces behind the historical process or movement or identify the prime mover in history. He was also not concerned with such questions as : "What is the meaning of history ?" "What fundamental laws govern historical development and change ?" His view of history is quite simple. He regards history "as the entire record of men living in societies in their geographical and physical environment."[40] He sees the human race as a single society and looks at history in universal terms. In such a view India also becomes a part of universal history. "From the period of prehistory to the present age of atomic energy, India has been in close contact with almost every civilization of every age in the world. Well it may be said that India from time immemorial has been a part of universal history."[41]

In the nineteenth century, the main object of history was regarded as teaching of political events in their rigid chronological sequence. But Sastri had freed himself from this narrow perception. He believed that history is concerned not only with the political happenings, it is also concerned with the economic, social, cultural and religious aspects of life. Actually, his concept of history is so wide that it includes every aspect of the life of humanity. He does not negate the importance of chronology and political history but advocates the reconstruction of social and religious history also. "The stress on political history is not accidental or perverse and it does not proceed from a failure to realize the value or importance of social history. Any picture of social life, if it is to be of real significance, must have a firmly established framework of chronology to fit into. And this framework, which alone could support and hold together the reconstructions of social and religious history, cannot be built up except by fixing the details of political history. This is true in some measure of the history of all countries and is especially so, of our own."[42]

Sastri sees an intimate link between the past, present and future: "What we have been determines in a large measure what we are, and may well influence, if not decide, what we shall be."[43] He partly accepts Benedetto Croce's dictum that "All history is contemporary history." "It is in a sense true to say that the knowledge of the present is the key to the understanding of the past, that the knowledge of the past varies with the present, and insight into the past with the personality of the historian."[44]

Sastri believes in the uniqueness of historical situations. "No two historical situations are alike. It is often said that history repeats itself. It would

[40] Sastri, Presidential Address, in *PIHC*, Patna Session, 1946, p. 13.

[41] Sastri and Srinivasachari, *Life and Culture of the Indian People*, p. 6.

[42] S.P. Gupta (ed.), *op. cit.*, p. 9.

[43] Sastri, Presidential Address, *op. cit.*

[44] Sastri, *Historical Method in Relation to Problems of South Indian History*, p. 6.

be much truer to say that history never repeats itself."[45] The concept which arises out of the idea that history repeats itself denies the very idea of progress. Even the repetition of progress is not progress. Sastri was thus a great believer in the idea of progress.

According to Sastri, "History is a scientific discipline in which the student should be ready to go wherever his evidence leads him; but the conclusions of history will be viewed and understood by each generation according to its own lights."[46] To Sastri, "The historian, like a scientist, has to have a mind which is free from pre-occupation, which is free from theories and is ready to take in all the bits of evidence, and appraise, each such bit at its proper worth."[47] Further, "in the writing of the history of one's own country the temptation, to select some facts and suppress others that go against your thesis, or in your judgement do not redound to our credit, is strong, but must be resisted." He also emphasized : "It is the task of the historians of India to delineate impartially the successive phases of the country's development through the ages and enable the reader to arrive at just appraisal of the good and the bad, the strength and the weakness, that marked it at every stage."[48] According to Sastri, in search of truth the students of history should be ready to go wherever his evidence leads him. In his works he always tried to follow this principle and maintained all along a high standard of professional honesty. He knew it well that in a conflict between pre-conceived idea and historical documents, usually the former prevails with disastrous results for historical scholarship. He took care to avoid that danger and did not allow prevalent theories or formulations to influence his judgement.

Like other scholars he drew upon five categories of sources—literary evidence, archaeology, epigraphy, numismatics and accounts of foreign travellers. But he did not take his sources at face value. Rather, he verified the authenticity of his sources from different angles before using them in his history. He knew that the historian legitimately indulges in an act of creative imagination. But that is to be done within certain limits and in no case "the historian should allow the present to dominate the past and turn history into a handmaid of politics."[49] It is true that history is intrinsically far more complex than the more objective realms dealt with by the sciences. Still, the proper task of a historian, Sastri feels, is interpreting the past for the present not carrying the present into the past. Sastri himself tried to hold close to the texts and other categories of sources and interpreted them with impartiality and honesty.

[45] *Ibid.*, p. 7.

[46] Sastri, *Lectures on Factors in Indian History*, p. 2.

[47] Sastri, *Historical Method*, *op. cit.*, p. 8.

[48] Sastri, Presidential Address, *op. cit.*, p. 27.

[49] Sastri, *Historical Method*, *op. cit.*, p. 6.

In his Presidential Address to the Indian History Congress, Patna, in 1946, Sastri pointed out that the harm that results from one-sided history is immense, and when history is used as propaganda the consequences are likely to be deadly. He appreciates Kalhaṇa, 'the Father of Indian history', for having the ideal of truth and impartiality : "That noble-minded one is alone worthy of praise whose word, like that of a judge, keeps free from love or hatred in relating the facts of the past."[50] According to Sastri, we can have no better standard for the historian.

However, Sastri believed that historical truth is always many-sided, and there is always scope for differences of interpretation of the evidence at hand. The scope for such differences is particularly wide in our period in which almost all the sources bear a certain bias and offer divergent accounts of the same set of events.[51]

Sastri was ever willing to change his opinion or altering his conclusion, if newly discovered dependable data warranted such a change. For example, when new evidences came from the Chola inscriptions he unhesitatingly countermanded his earlier conclusions.

In his writings Sastri followed a simple, clear and lucid style by avoiding highly ornamental and complex sentences; his polished language and depth of feeling add charm and freshness to his writings. In the delineation of facts, Sastri had a rare combination of gifts — a mastery over all the varied and complicated sources and a balanced and accurate judgement. Therefore, whatever he wrote is always readable.

Though Sastri always maintained an all-India vision and approached Indian history from the standpoint of an Indian, his main contribution has naturally been to the history of south India. As V.A. Smith became the author of the first really complete history of India, to Sastri belongs the credit of writing a full-scale connected history of south India from prehistoric times to the fall of the Vijayanagar empire in the seventeenth century A.D. According to N. Subrahmanian, "K.A.N. Sastri's position as an Indologist is so central to the historiography of south India and especially Tamilnadu that it may be said that a greater part of the history of Tamilnadu has been settled by his efforts rather than anyone else's. Though S. K. Aiyangar was a pioneer and set the pace for Tamil historical studies, Sastri gave a nearly final shape to the picture."[52] In the words of S. K. Mukhopadhyay, "Sastri contributed more than anybody else towards the reconstruction of south Indian history and culture. He has not only built up the chronology of some of the important dynasties of south India, but has also uncovered the cultural and social history of the people. His aim

[50] Sastri, Presidential Address, *op. cit.*, p. 28.

[51] Sastri (ed.), *Age of the Nandas and Mauryas*, p. 4.

[52] N. Subrahmanian, *Tamilian Historiography*, Madurai, 1988, p. 143.

always had been to discover the rich cultural heritage of the south that lay hidden for a long time."[53]

According to Sastri, it is essential that each historian should accept the ideal of truth and impartiality, and refrain from deliberate suppression and distortion. But his own attempt at objectivity was a lamentable failure. Firstly, Sastri was a great Hinduphil which had great influence on his judgement of events and persons in the second volume of his *A Comprehensive History of India.* He has laid emphasis on the superiority of Hinduism and Indian culture. He sometimes betrays anti-Islamic bias also. He aimed to promote a sense of pride in his Hindu past, recollecting the glories of India for fifteen centuries, viz., between the risc of the Mauryan empire and the fall of the Cholas. According to him, though in the organisation of free government, ancient India must rank below some other lands and far below ancient Greece, but the continued vigour of the village institutions of the south mitigated for many centuries the evils of a weak central government. In all the other arts of civilized life south India was the peer of any other country. From the earliest times this part of India carried on and developed a maritime trade which linked her with the empires of Rome and of China. She gave Burma her earliest script and profoundly influenced the art and religion of distant Indo-China. Her social economy was securely built on the harmony of diverse groups, each free in its own sphere to pursue its proper methods and cherish its ideals. Its literature with its richness and power is the most precious treasure inherited from the past, vividly depicting the thoughts and lives of her saints, philosophers and kings, and providing moving and musical expression to the joys and sorrows of her people. He did not subscribe to the view held by many in the south that the people of the peninsula are the builders of the Indus civilization. He also rejected the view of some Tamilians, born out of narrow Tamil nationalism, that the people of the south are the original inhabitants of India. He was rather inclined to accept the view that the Dravidians, like the Aryans, came to India from outside, probably from central Asia and eastern mediterranean region. He also does not agree with the view that the Aryan penetration into the south was superficial and that it did not affect the life style of the people. On the contrary, he believes that Aryanisation of south India represented a happy blending of Aryan and Dravidian elements, a synthesis of two cultural traditions.

Though Sastri resents north-centred historical writing in modern India and argued that the south is not sufficiently represented in the works on Indian history, he has no bitter feeling against the north and never subscribed to the narrow regionalism of the south. He took care to avoid isolationism and chauvinism in his writings and had no sympathy for narrow Tamil nationalism.

Sastri had a very high opinion of the impact of Indian civilization in

[53] Mukhopadhyay, *op. cit.*, p. 115.

the countries of Asia and the world. He believes that there was a time "when Asia led the world in civilization and culture, and India led Asia."[54]

K.A. Nilakanta Sastri sees the colonization of south-east Asia also "as just a continuation of the process by which the Deccan and south India were Aryanised and Hinduised by the inflow of northern influences."[55] He had the insight of a social historian. He explains the social structure of the south in the days of the Cholas thus : "Caste was the basis of social organisation and each caste was more or less a hereditary occupational group with an active organisation for the regulation and protection of its economic and social interests; and the Indian society of those days is best conceived as a loose federation of strong self-regulating groups which shared a common background of social rights and obligations which made for mutual understanding and accommodation."[56] He is, however, silent on the problem of caste conflict or other social injustices like untouchability or unapproachability.

On the question of the Aryan penetration into the south, he observes : "The results of Aryan penetration into the south were more cultural than racial and the pre-Aryan inhabitants survived the 'conquest' in sufficient strength to retain their own language and many of their old habits and methods of life, with the consequence that the resulting culture was a real blend of the Aryan and Dravidian elements which shows several points of difference from the culture of the remaining parts of India which were more thoroughly Aryanised."[57]

In the same vain he describes the mission of the Hindu colonists thus: "Just as the Greek colonists carried to their new home fire from the hearth of the home city, so the Hindu colonists carried with them an organised culture basesd on four easily identifiable elements viz., a conception of royalty, Sanskrit as the means of literary expression, a mythology drawn from the Veda, Epics and Purāṇas, and a sociology based on the observance of the Dharmaśāstras, particularly the laws of Manu."[58]

Sastri gave a new perspective to Indian history by bringing the whole of south-east Asia within the orbit of the history of Indian culture. His vision has always been broad, as well as deep and penetrating, and did not leave a single known west Asian, Roman, Greek or any other source in order to explore the dimensions of India's contribution, as well as her debt, to world human thought and culture. His book *Cultural Expansion of India* is an

[54] Sastri, *Lectures on Factors in Indian History*, p. 1.
[55] Sastri, *South Indian Influcnces in the Far East*, p. 122.
[56] Sastri, *The Cōḷas*, Vol. II, p. 350.
[57] Sastri, *The Pāṇḍyan Kingdom*, p. 2.
[58] Sastri, *Cultural Expansion of India*, p. 68.

attempt to find out Indian elements in the cultural make-up of other countries, particularly those of Eastern Europe, Near East, Middle East, Central Asia, China, Indo-China and Indonesia. Sastri attempted to prove the widespread Indian influence in Asia and in different parts of the world. The term 'Greater India', which became widely current in historical circles at the time, was a sign of the growing national pride in the part India had played in the civilization of Asia while phrases such as "Indian colonies in south-east Asia", occurring time and again in many contexts, were indicative of the reactions of the historians to the political situation. According to Sastri, though the colonies had no politicial connection with the mother country, the new states were Hindu in every respect. Sastri compares Indian imperialism with Roman imperialism and British imperialism thus: "When an Indian empire was established, it made little difference to the lives of the people of its component parts, which went on as before. Yājñavalkya expressly states that when the conquest of a country was completed nothing in it was to be changed, and the king was to respect local customs and institutions as if they were those of his home country."[59] There should not be any consciousness of cultural superiority on the part of the conqueror and his followers over the conquered; and in a social milieu which exalted stability above change, the conqueror was strictly enjoined to maintain the status quo. Samudragupta's victorious march into the Deccan and Rajendra Chola's expansion to the Ganges are the most conspicuous examples of the sheer exhibition of *Parākrama* on the part of great rulers; they led to no permanent results; they were not meant to do so.

Sastri came from an orthodox Brāhmaṇa family, and his class prejudice and caste bias is evident from the following passage : "There is practically no evidence of ugly social conflicts and jealousies such as those between the right-hand and left-hand castes, or between Brahmins and non-Brahmins of more recent times. The general impression derived is one of social harmony, removed alike from the placid content which knows no ambition and the blind and ruthless pursuit of class-interests."[60] Sastri is silent on the problems of caste conflict or other social injustices like untouchability in the days of the Cholas in south India. This bias in the attitude of Sastri only shows how difficult it is for a historian to cut himself off from his social moorings.

Sastri has cautioned historians against certain common errors usually committed in the interpretation of the past such as the error of discovering in history the lessons which we wish to draw, the error of discovering all great and good things in the past of one's own country, taking sides in historical disputes and telling the tale almost exclusively from a particular point of view,

[59] Sastri, *The Conception of Empire in Ancient India*, in S. P. Gupta, *op.cit.*, p. 167.
[60] Sastri, *The Cōḷas*, Vol. II, p.350.

and making statements full of inaccuracies and factual mistakes. Sastri does not think that it is good and useful for a historian "to have preferences, leading ideas and superior conceptions."[61]

Sastri was the foremost historian of south India and one of the front rankers of modern India. He has contributed more than anybody else towards the reconstruction of south Indian history and culture. He not only built up the chronology of some of the important dynasties of south India, has also uncovered the cultural and social history of the people. His aim had always been to discover the rich cultural heritage of the south that lay hidden for a long time. In this self-imposed task he has been eminently successful. Well-equipped with history, archaeology, Sanskrit and languages of the south, he produced a large number of standard volumes on his subject. More than fifty years' study and research, combined methodology, a keen historical insight and, above all, the vast range of his specialized field, from the age of the Sangam to the Vijayanagar empire, combined to assure him a high place among the historians of modern India.

III

T.V. Mahalingam, one of the most eminent historians of south India, started his career as a Lecturer in the Madurai College, Madurai, and later served the Raja's College, Pudukkottai. He joined the University of Madras in 1947 and was appointed as Professor of Ancient History and Archaeology in the Department of Indian History and served there in that capacity till 1959. In that year the Department of Indian History was bifurcated and the Department of Ancient History and Archaeology was formed and Mahalingam was appointed its Professor and Head, the post he held till his retirement in 1971.

Besides contributing more than a hundred papers on history, historiography, epigraphy, numismatics, archaeology, art, architecture, religion and philosophy, Mahalingam also published over a dozen research monographs. These include *Administration and Social Life under Vijayanagar* (1940), *Economic Life in the Vijayanagar Empire* (1942), *Bāṇas in South Indian History* (1951), *South Indian Polity* (1955, 1968), *Nāgas in Indian History and Culture* (1965), *Nagesvarasvami Temple, Kumbakonam* (1967), *Early South Indian Palaeography* (1967), *Kāñcīpuram in Early South Indian History* (1969), *Studies in South Indian Temple Complex* (1970), *Mackenzie Manuscripts,* in two vols. (1972, 1976), and *Inscriptions of the Pallavas* (1984). For his work on social and administrative history of Vijayanagar he was awarded D. Litt. degree of the University of Madras. Mahalingam also conducted extensive explorations and a number of excavations in Tamilnadu.

[61] Sastri, *Historical Method, op. cit.*, p. 14.

He published the results of excavation of Tirukkampuliyur and Alagarai (*Report on the Excavations in the Lower Kavery Valley*, University of Madras, 1970). These excavations were conducted by him during 1962-1964. The two sites are located in the Tiruchirappalli district, Tamilnadu. It contains the details of material culture and antiquities unearthed in the above two sites. The different pottery types and graffiti found from these excavations broadly confirmed the cultural sequence arrived at other excavations conducted in Tamilnadu.

Mahalingam was the Sectional President (II) of the Indian History Congress, the Session held at Jaipur (Rajasthan) in 1951. He was also the President of the Nagpur Session of the Numismatic Society of India in 1970 and presided over the Third Annual Congress of the Epigraphical Society of India at Udupi (Karnataka) in 1977. In recognition of his services to the cause of history the Government of India honoured him by bestowing *Padma Shri* in 1969.

Mahalingam acquired reputation as a historian of south India quite early. The writing of south Indian history is full of problems. In his paper 'Problems of Historical Writing in India with Reference to the History of South India' published in the *Proceedings* of a Seminar held at the India International Centre, New Delhi, in 1963, Mahalingam discussed some of them in detail. Here, he pointed out that "So far as south India is concerned the geographical and travel accounts of Ptolemy the author of *Periplus* as also the historical and geographical writings of Livy, Pliny and other scholars of the Roman imperial age supply valuable information on our trade, situation of marts, etc. Fahien, Hieun Tsang and other Chinese travellers who had distant and vague peeps into our land have left some notes on what they observed and what they heard and in so far as these get local confirmaton are useful. In the medieval period Marco Polo was followed by a regular line of European travellers especially to the Vijayanagar empire whose testimony is quite valuable."[62] But this foreign evidence is supplemented only a little by local literature which has left us no connected history of the country while numismatics which along with archaeology speaks a limited and cryptic language is usually a supplementary evidence and never a leading or primary evidence on south Indian history.[63] In this situation the most formidable and probably the most useful source of historical information for early and medieval south Indian history is epigraphy. From the days of Aśoka to the days of dismembered Vijayanagar we get a plethora of lithic inscriptions and copper plate grants, but the collation of the material so gathered and the edition of the inscriptions (dynasty-wise or region-wise or arranged chronologically) or translations of these epigraphs have not

[62] T.V. Mahalingam, in *Problems of Historical Writing in India*, eds. S. Gopal, Romila Thapar et al, New Delhi, 1963, p. 32.

[63] *Ibid.*

been done in a systematic manner, though the subject needs almost immediate attention. Mahalingam, therefore, pleaded for an elaborate scheme for the complete and systematic edition of the innumerable epigraphs. He also emphasised the need for a detailed study of the records of the post-Vijayanagar period.

In this connection he drew special attention of the scholars to the manuscripts of the Mackenzie Collection. Of these manuscripts he catalogued 244 with their summaries in two volumes entitled *Mackenzie Manuscripts*, Vol. I (Tamil and Malayalam), and Vol. II (Telugu, Kannada and Marathi), and published them from the University of Madras, respectively in 1972 and 1976.

Colonel Colin Mackenzie came to India in 1783 and lived entirely in the Orient till his death in 1821. He was the first military engineer in Madras in the first two decades of the nineteenth century and later on the Surveyor-General of the East India Company at Calcutta. He collected during the period of his service in south India a good number of manuscripts in different languages of the region besides Sanskrit, Marathi and Arabic and arranged them with a view to preparing a history of south India from the early times to his own day. The manuscripts so collected by him are divisible into different groups, namely, local tracts (*kaifiats*), local history and biography, Purāṇic and legendary accounts of places and men, Jaina literature, works of purely literary nature like plays, tales and poems and works relating to astrology and astronomy. Among the historical manuscripts in the collection, a few are of some value to the historian of south India and among them are the *Karnataka Rajakkal Savistaracaritam* (detailed history of the Karnataka kings) and *Kongudesarajakkal* (kings of the Koṅgu country). These historical manuscripts cover a wide period and relate to the history of south India from the early times though the information they give about the early dynasties is not very reliable, for much of it is gossip and loose tradition. But they are of some value to the history of south India in the eighteenth century.[64]

The task of cataloguing the collection of these manuscripts was entrusted in 1930s to K. A. N. Sastri who along with N. Venkataramanayya used some of them pertaining to political history in *The Further Sources of Vijayanagar History* (3 Vols., Madras, 1946).

Of the records relating to political history, the accounts of the Pāḷayagārs are most useful for scholars interested in studying the nature of feudalism in south India. The *pāḷayam* was similar to the *jagir* of the Mughals while the *kāvali* lands were assigned to a few persons in a particular locality made responsible for the maintenance of law and order in the area, a purely police

[64] *Ibid.*, p. 34.

function. The accounts of the Pāḷayagārs provide valuable material for studying their interaction with the Nāyaks as well as the East India Company.[65]

The numerous *kaifiyats* or local registers, along with the *Aṭṭavaṇatantram* (an eighteenth-century administrative manual), constitute an invaluable source of the administrative history of the south from the sixteenth to the eighteenth century. The *kaifiyats* give an idea of the *ayagār* system which can be compared to and contrasted with the *jajmani* system.

The categories of land rights are discussed at several places, for instance in the *Aṭṭavaṇatantram* itself and when describing the agrarian set-up of the various districts. Villagers are said to be classified as cultivators, tax-payers through the labours of others and easy-goers (*khushbash*). Elsewhere there is reference to the renting of lands by contractors as apart from the fixed-rent lands.

The manuscripts relating to the social structure deal with the Koṅgu-Veḷḷāḷas (agriculturists), Kuṟumbas (shepherds), Maṟavas (cultivators) and Kaikkōlas (weavers) in some detail. The *Jātinūl* also records the mythological origins of the various castes.[66]

Mahalingam's *South Indian Polity* (Madras, 1968) is a comprehensive volume dealing with all aspects of polity, state, kingship, ministers, and other high officials and administration at different levels. It also deals with such interesting aspects of political life as emblems and royal *lāñchhanas*. Mahalingam assumes a decentralised polity as fundamental to feudalism and identifies locally powerful warriors as feudatories paying tribute to the Pallavas as token of their vassalage.[67] Obviously, it was in this sense that in 1928 Beni Prasad described the Gupta empire as a 'feudal-federal' organization.[68]

In 1969 Mahalingam brought out his *Kāñcīpuram in Early South Indian History* from Bombay. It discusses the history of Kāñchīpuram from its very beginning to the age of the later Pallava rulers of the tenth century. In its first chapter Mahalingam has delineated the early history of this city including its association with the Mauryas. Then, in the second chapter, is described the rise of the early Pallavas. Then, the history of the Pallava rulers is given in eleven chapters from Siṁhavarman to Aparājita. The last or the fourteenth chapter is devoted to the later Pallavas. The work is mainly concerned with the political aspect of the history of this dyansty.

T. V. Mahalingam's *Studies in the South Indian Temple Complex* was published from Dharwar in 1970. It contains three lectures delivered by him at the Kannada Research Institute in 1967. Its aim is to make a typological

[65] Vijaya Ramaswamy, in *IHR*, Vol. IV, No. 2, p. 475.
[66] *Ibid.*, p. 476.
[67] Shankar Goyal, *Recent Historiography of Ancient India*, p. 318.
[68] Beni Prasad, *The State in Ancient India*, Allahabad, 1928, p. 285.

study of the structural unit of a temple and the axial and peristylar adjuncts in the temple complex in south India, especially in the Tamil country. In lecture I, Mahalingam shows how, after the very first ritual in the construction being conceived as the *garbhādhāna*, the various parts of the structure are nomenclaturally equated with different limbs of the human body. It is followed by a discussion of references to building architecture in the Sangam literature. Early caves in Tamilnadu and Kerala, architectural terms in early Tamil literature, *vimāna*, different kinds of *śikharas*, *vimāna* above the cornice, *sāndhāra* and *nirandhāra* types of shrines, *vimānas* with more than one sanctum and influences on the shapes and types of *vimānas* are the other subjects covered by this lecture. In lecture II, Mahalingam deals with the structures aligned axially. The peristylar shrines including the *garbhagṛha* and the adjuncts around it, viz. the Devī shrines, the shrines for the *parivāra-devatās*, the Nāyanārs and Āḷvārs, besides other deities and saints of local importance glorified and sanctified in legends and *Sthalapurāṇas* are the subject of lecture III. Thus, within the limitations of a short monograph, Mahalingam has tackled all these topics with admirable clarity. But, as he himself says, each of the topics dealt with by him demands elaborate study.

The other important work of Mahalingam on the Pallavas is entitled *Inscriptions of the Pallavas* (New Delhi, 1984). It is described by many as a source book throwing light on many aspects of the early and early medieval south Indian history, polity, society, and economy. It is a rather bulky volume. It was the second in the series to be published after K. V. Ramesh's *Inscriptions of the Western Gaṅgas* (New Delhi, 1984) under the auspices of the ICHR. It contains 375 inscriptions found engraved on stone and copper plates. The volume brings together for the first time all the available Pallava inscriptions (known till 1976). Even though the Pallava dynasty in one form or the other ruled for nearly six centuries from the early fourth century to the end of the ninth century, there are not many inscriptions for the period upto 700 A.D. and so the bulk of the inscriptions belongs to the eighth and ninth centuries only. For about 300 inscriptions included in this volume both the texts and English abstracts are given and for the rest only the abstracts are provided.[69] Each inscription is provided with an Introduction as to the provenance, the references to earlier publications, language, script and the date. The text of the inscriptions given in this work are in Sanskrit, Prakrit, Tamil and early Kannada and are of considerable palaeographical and orthographical interest. Normally, the Pallava inscriptions refer only to the regnal years of the ruling king and so the addition of the equivalent date in Christian era has to be appreciated. The inscriptions are divided in six sections according to chronology; there are also two elaborate lists, topographical and king-wise, in

[69] Shankar Goyal, *op. cit.*, pp. 418-19.

the beginning to guide the reader. The Introduction carries a useful historiographical sketch and an outline of the Pallava history on the basis of the inscriptions. There is also a discussion on the significance of the inscriptions for the administrative and cultural history. In Section VI are included all the hero-stone inscriptions discovered and published by the Tamilnadu State Department of Archaeology till then. Mahalingam is hesitant to consider them as those of the Pallavas of Kāñchīpuram on the ground that the texts of those inscriptions depict a somewhat different linguistic and palaeographic tradition and they are confined to one particular fringe area. But, according to Y. Subbarayalu, a careful reading of those records leaves one in no doubt that they refer to the Pallava rulers of the main line only and that they supply some new information otherwise not found elsewhere.[70]

As Professor and Head of the Department of Ancient History and Archaeology, University of Madras, T.V. Mahalingam was actively associated with the Inscriptions Programme of the ICHR and prepared a series of ten volumes entitled *Topographical List of Inscriptions in the Tamil Nadu and Kerala States upto c. A.D. 1300.* Published from New Delhi between 1985 and 2000, obviously after his demise, it contains, on the whole, more than 15,000 inscriptions, lithic records as well as copper plates, listed and arranged according to the proforma mentioned in the Preface to the first volume. Each inscription gives its location, language, script, dynasty (king), approximate date and a brief summary of its contents. The significance of this series lies in the fact that it presents various facets of political, social, economic, religious and cultural life of the people in the districts of these regions covering all the villages in various *taluks* in the ancient and early medieval period of history. However, as the districts have been delimited recently the references given in these volumes should be taken as those of old division. But there is no doubt that the material can be fruitfully used for restructuring several unknown aspects of south Indian history and polity.

Another work executed but left unpublished was similar to the above. He, with B.R. Gopal (former Professor of History, Anantapur University, Anantapur), collected all the inscriptions of the Vijayanagar dynasty. They prepared summaries for all the inscriptions from all the four southern states and arranged them in topographical order. The type script was prepared but before it saw the publication, Mahalingam passed away. But the work of Mahalingam and Gopal is recorded by Noboru Karashima, who also died recently in 2015, in his work *Towards a New Formation : South Indian Society under Vijayanagar Rule* (Oxford, 1992, p. 39, fn. 11). Later on, inscriptions belonging to Karnataka and Andhra Pradesh states were published by the Government of Karnataka.

[70] Y. Subbarayalu, in *IHR*, Vol. XIII, Nos. 1-2, pp. 218 ff.

As the Sectional President (II) of the Indian History Congress, Jaipur Session (1951), Mahalingam highlighted the achievements and also the drawbacks of the period between 711-1200 A.D. Here, he also referred to the impact of the Arab and other Muslim invasions on Indian society and the special tax *Turushkadaṇḍa* imposed by the Gāhaḍavālas to meet foreign aggression. In the Deccan and south India the Muslims found conditions congenial for them, and friendly intercourse existed with the Muslim states of south-west Asia. Muslim saints like Nathadwali preached Islam in south India. He also refers to the growing influence of the *Āgamas* in temple rituals and worship and the bringing of priests from the north for the organization of such worship. There was a vigorous theistic devotional movement. On the philosophical side of the Hindu revivalist movement, Kumārila led a crusade against Buddhism and succeeded in reviving respect for the authority of the Vedas. Mahalingam, while appreciating the move for the revaluation of the history and culture of our country by Indian scholars, as well suggests that the "ideal history writer is one who is always fair-minded in his treatment and conclusions. If we are able to attain this ideal that would be the greatest service that we can render to our country and to Indian history."

In his Presidential Address to the Nagpur Session of the Numismatic Society of India (1970)[71] Mahalingam discussed the problems connected with the south Indian numismatics from Punch-marked coins onwards, including the Tamil-Brāhmī, Kalabhra, Pallava, Pāṇḍyan and Chola coins. Here, he has also taken into consideration the discovery of a large number of Roman and other foreign coins from different places in south India which adds a new dimension to south Indian numismatics. Though a number of such Roman coins belonging to the Kushāṇa and post-Kushāṇa period have been found at different sites in north-west and north India also, on account of the political and cultural exchange between the Kushāṇa and the Roman empires including north Africa, their provenance in the south is of great importance. They seem to have been in circulation or at least in use in places which had Roman contacts during the period from about the first century B.C. to the second century A.D. Roman contacts with south India during this and the succeeding periods are also borne out by archaeological evidence, such as Roman pottery, amphorae jars, dyeing watt etc. Excavations at places like Arikamedu, Uraiyur, Kāñchīpuram and Vasavasamudram in the Tamil area and Brahmagiri and Chandravalli in Mysore have established beyond doubt the cultural and trade contacts between south India and the Roman empire in the early centuries of the Christian era. Hence, the find of Roman coins as also other indications of the Roman contact bear out the extent to which and the period during which

[71] Cf. *Sixty Years of the Numismatic Society of India* (*1910-1971*), Numismatic Society of India, Varanasi, 1973, pp. 500-13.

Roman cultural traits found their way into the south Indian coastal and inland areas. According to Mahalingam, while considering the Roman coins in south India one is faced with problems like :

(1) Were the Roman *dinarii* accepted as regular currency or only as bullion weights as Wheeler thinks ?

(2) Did they influence the local currency ?

(3) Were the Punch-marked coins coeval with the Roman *dinarii.* If so, what was the relation between them ?

These are problems to which categorical answers may not be possible in our present state of knowledge. For an examination of such questions there is need for more reliable data about the coins with reference to their find spots, weights, legends, etc. and the provenance and nature of indigenous coins got from such places. But the questions like these emphasise the need for a proper study of the foreign coins in the country through the ages. The subject requires careful study. It may be of considerable interest that a few excavations in south India have yielded pottery of the Chinese origin. Also, a bilingual inscription in Tamil and Chinese has been found in China. In view of these facts Mahalingam observed, "I feel that there is great necessity for a comprehensive encyclopaedia on Indian numismatics providing detailed information on different types of coins, with particular reference to their denomination, value, metrology, legends, symbols and iconographic motifs on them. This can serve as an easy and useful reference book for the rising numismatists. The task is however difficult, and therefore it cannot be undertaken by one single scholar."[72]

In his Presidential Address to the Annual Session of the Epigraphical Society of India held at Udupi in 1977, Mahalingam emphasised the need of a close cooperation between historians, linguists and epigraphists. Epigraphy, which includes palaeography, he observed, has developed into a science by itself and one gets mastery over it with the necessary equipment, namely, in language and linguistics on the one side and the history on the other. With the growth of the corpus of epigraphical material there is growth in hair splitting discussion on its study and interpretation. Though epigraphy is an interesting subject by itself and one must acquire mastery over it for expanding one's knowledge of the history of our country, it is equally true that even for a proper understanding of the content of the inscriptions a fair knowledge of the history of the country is indispensable. It must be borne in mind that without a good grounding in our ancient lore and history, at least in outline, it is not easy to understand and interpret the inscriptions correctly. If one may say so, epigraphy is a means to an end and not an end in itself. The historian depends on the epigraphist for correct information and the epigraphist depends on the historian

[72] *Ibid.*, p. 513.

and linguist for proper interpretation. There is an acute need for cooperation among the three for the purposeful study of epigraphy. In this coordinated endeavour, Mahalingam asserts, the numismatist has also a share, for the legends on the coins have something to add to our knowledge of the palaeographical trends of a period.[73]

IV

Any attempt to discuss the nature of political history is likely to involve the definition and scope of history itself. A discipline may be defined in two ways: first, by a statement of its subject-matter, and second, by a statement of its aims and objectives with regard to that subject-matter. There are, of course, other criteria that may be used, but for the scholarly and scientific purposes these seem to be the most necessary of the usual requirements. As shown by us elsewhere,[74] the concept of integral or new political history maintains that political history is not merely the account of kings and important persons or of 'heroes' who are supposed to have made history; instead, it is primarily a study of the political aspect of society. Since the basic instrument for controlling the operation of all factors in the society since long has been the state, it is in the sphere of political history that the clearest manifestation of the interplay of all the determinants and the consequent changes in society is visible. As soon as this basic fact is accepted, political history would appear to encompass a much wider field, related with everything associated with man. It would thus seem that integral or new political history is closely related with a number of disciplines and other branches of knowledge such as archaeology, anthropology, political science, sociology and economics.

As a result of the close relationship of new political history with other disciplines it must be realized that events and movements should be studied against the background of various factors operating in society—social, political, economic, religious, ideological etc. Now the main question before the students of Indian political history should be 'why or how did it happen?' and not 'what and when did it happen?' In other words, the task before historians of earlier generations of India was to describe the past as it was; now, the task before the present generation is to delve into the causes, factors and consequences of events—in brief, to search for a pattern in the variegated panorama of our political past.

[73] Cf. *Presidential Addresses and Praśastis*, Epigraphical Society of India, Dharwad, 1985, p. 64.

[74] Shankar Goyal, *Ancient India : A Multidisciplinary Approach*, Jodhpur, 2006, Ch. 1; also see my Valedictory Address, 'Need of an Integral View to the Political History of South India', delivered at the University of Kerala, Thiruvananthapuram, *PSIHC*, 2002, pp. 515 ff.

Another aspect of new political history is that it has ceased to concern itself only with the elite class, viz., kings, nobles, priests, heroes etc., and has become the history of common people. But this broadening of historical canvas of the discipline does not mean that the importance of traditional type of political history has declined; instead, it is still the hard core of history. The state still remains the central point of historical investigation. Only, now the scope of politics is not confined to only kings and nobles; by becoming the history of the political life of society it has penetrated the vast masses of people. The rise and fall of dynasties, wars, chronology, battles of kings, their political relations, nature of the political organisation of their states, administration, causes of their success or failure in establishing a permanent imperial structure, impact of religious policies on their political activities, these and similar problems continue and will continue to occupy the attention of historians. Though political biographies and estimate of kings have ceased to be the focal point of historical research, they are still an important part of it and will continue to be related with and throw light on the political life of a society. That is why now we must give equal importance to the political history of the traditional type as well as to the new political history.

The persistence of the traditional attitude to the writing of political history of ancient north India and the inroads which the new approach is gradually making into it is best illustrated by the history of the Maurya and Gupta periods and the age of Harsha in which now 'how' and 'why' questions are being raised and events of these periods are being increasingly studied against the factors and forces operating in society. For example, S.R. Goyal has looked upon the history of the imperial Guptas not from the traditional 'what and when happened approach' but from the multidisciplinary standpoint in which main political developments and events are put in their proper context by an analysis of their determining influences—social, economic, religious, grographical, etc.— with the help of other branches of knowledge, of course without overlooking the need of reconsidering the 'what and when happened' problems afresh, wherever necessary.[75] I have myself exemplified my viewpoint with special reference to the political history of Harsha and his times and have tried to show that by the adoption of the new methodology and approach it should be quite possible to write a new political history of Harsha and his age devoted not only to his deeds, conquests and dates (as we find in the books so far written on him and other rulers), but to the political life of his period by correlating political institutions, policies and events and the personality of the monarch himself with socio-economic, religious and cultural

[75] Cf. S.R. Goyal, *A History of the Imperial Guptas*, Allahabad, 1967; idem, *The Imperial Guptas : A Multidisciplinary Political Study*, Jodhpur, 2005.

developments.[76] For other periods of Indian history this approach is still difficult to be pursued, mainly because of the paucity of data, but gradually the possibilities of treating the other periods and dynasties—specially the Sātavāhana, Kushāṇa, Vākāṭaka, Chālukya, Pallava and Chola—with this approach are increasing and one may hope that sooner or later, hopefully sooner, historians will be able to present an integral view of these dynastic periods based on their multidisciplinary study. Anyway, that should be the aim of the new generation of political historians of ancient India in the twenty-first century.

The periods of south Indian history of which an integral picture of political history may be attempted include those of the Chālukyas of Vātāpi, Pallavas, Cholas and the Vijayanagar empire. As shown in the preceding pages, some significant works dealing with their sources and various aspects of their history were published in the later half of the last century by S. Krishnaswami Aiyangar, K.A.N. Sastri and T.V. Mahalingam. Their contribution to the history of south India is well known. But as they were engrossed in the 'reconstruction' of political history and various aspects of cultural history, and rightly so, they did not find sufficient time to produce an integral view of political history. In his *A History of South India* (Oxford University Press, edn. 1966) Sastri presented in a compact form a comprehensive account of the history of the whole of south India from the prehistoric times to the fall of Vijayanagar treated as a single geographical entity. In it he has incorporated the results of his own researches and has also brought together material previously scattered in many separate studies and presented it as a coherent narrative. Here, political history naturally occupies a predominant place, though an account is also given of social life, commerce, religion, philosophy, literature and the plastic arts. However, these subjects are treated in four separate chapters at the end of the book. But highly illuminating and authoritative though their presentation is, it is not exactly in tune with the concept of intergral view of history suggested above in which cultural and political aspects of life are treated as various aspects of the organic whole. Similar is the nature of his other works including *The Cōḷas* (Madras, edn. 1975). The history of the Cholas falls into five divisions, viz.: the pre-Christian period, the age of the literature of the Sangam, the interval between the end of the Sangam period and the rise of the line of Vijayālaya, the period of the Vijayālaya line, and the age of the Chālukya-

[76] See, for example, Shankar Goyal, *History and Historiography of the Age of Harsha*, Jodhpur, 1992 ; idem, *Harsha : A Multidisciplinary Political Study*, Jodhpur, 2006. Recently for the first time I have studied the culture of the age of Harsha within the paradigm of Indian feudalism, cf. our works *The 'Medieval' Factor and the Age of Harsha : A Cultural Study*, Jodhpur, 2016; and also, *The Classical Age : A Study in Feudalization*, New Delhi, 2022.

Chola line of Kulottuṅga I. While giving details about various rulers of the dynasty Sastri also dealt with the central and local governments, taxation and finance, population and society, agriculture and land tenure, industry and trade, education and learning and lastly religion and literature under the Cholas. But nowhere did he study these aspects as various factors which influenced the course of their political history.

Similarly, as noted above, on the Pallavas an independent work entitled *Kāñcīpuram in Early South Indian History* (Bombay, 1969) was published by Mahalingam. It discussed the history of Kāñchīpuram from its very beginning to the age of the Later Pallava rulers of the tenth century. In its first chapter Mahalingam has delineated the early history of this city including its association with the Mauryas. Then, in the second chapter, is described the rise of the early Pallavas. The history of the Pallava rulers is given in eleven chapters from Siṁhavarman to Aparājita. The last or the fourteenth chapter is devoted to the Later Pallavas. The work is mainly concerned with the political aspect of the history of this dynasty. But Mahalingam also followed the traditional approach of earlier historians who wrote monographs on the history of India during the last hundred years or so.

I may further illustrate the point with the help of the history of the Chālukyas of Vātāpi. The Chālukya dynasty has been the subject of several independent works. R. S. Satyasraya has even discussed the origin of the dynasty in a separate monograph entitled *Origin of the Chālukyas* (Calcutta, 1937). The first full-length research monograph on the Chālukyas of Vātāpi entitled *Political History of the Chālukyas of Bādāmī* was produced by Durga Prasad Dikshit from New Delhi in 1980. But the monograph is written strictly on traditional lines though it brings at one place most of the material scattered in various journals and monographs. K.V. Ramesh, the author of another monograph on the subject entitled *Chalukyas of Vātāpi* (Delhi, 1984), is under the impression that "The time is not yet ripe for writing a comprehensive chronological-cum-political history of the Chalukya dynasty of Vātāpi or, for that matter, of any of the Indian ruling houses of the past", for he believes that "Inspite of nearly one hundred years of sustained epigraphical collection and research, there are many gaps which can be filled up only by conjectural arguments and assumptions."[77] Nevertheless, he wrote the present work because he felt that "even a critical re-examination of the already available Chalukya records and a study of their newly discovered inscriptions considerably improve our knowledge of their history."[78] But this justification may be given for writing a comprehensive chronological-cum-political history

[77] K.V. Ramesh, *Chalukyas of Vātāpi*, Delhi, 1984, Preface, p. vii.
[78] *Ibid.*

of many other dynasties. It seems that Ramesh is himself aware of such a possibility for he observes that "The information contained in the grant portions of the Chalukya records have been brought into greater use than in the previous histories of the family" though "no attempt has been made to study, in detail, their socio-economic implications."[79] Ramesh has not undertaken such a task "for reasons of lack of running information."[80]

Now, there is no denying the fact that being the pioneering efforts, the works of Aiyangar, Sastri and Mahalingam, and also of Ramesh, provided the much needed and reliable chronological framework to study south Indian history. But having said this, the fact remains that the period in which all of them worked on south Indian history, many other historians of the country were producing their works from altogether new angles—Marxist and integral. Had Sastri, Mahalingam and Ramesh taken up the history of south India from the integral standpoint, with their remarkable knowledge of the subject and grasp of source- materials, their works would have become trend-setters for the succeeding generation of historians.

What is more lamentable is the fact that although the traditional approach still survives in the more recent works on political history of south India, it is without the interpretative skill of Aiyangar and Sastri and the serious research of Mahalingam. Many of the works, published in recent decades, such as, K.K. Pillay's *History of Tamil Nadu—Her People and Culture* (in Tamil), (Madras, 1972), P.N. Chopra, T. K. Ravindran and N. Subramanian's *History of South India* (New Delhi, 1979), M. Rajamanickam's *History of Tamil Nadu* (Chennai, 1999), K. Rajayyan's *Tamil Nadu—A Real History* (Madurai, 2005) and Chithra Madhavan's *History and Culture of Tamil Nadu* (New Delhi, 2005), are not only cast in the same traditional mould but ceaselessly repeat what has been said earlier. The narrative part dominating in most of the recent works treats political history as if it has no relation to the socio-economic, religious and cultural changes. This reminds me of the remark made by R. Champakalakshmi that "History does not repeat itself, it is the historians who repeat one another."[81] But it is quite possible that the task is not as hopeless as it seems to be if we are determined to work in that direction.[82]

[79] *Ibid.*

[80] *Ibid.*

[81] R. Champakalakshmi, 'Historiography of South India—New Directions', her Presidential Address to the Historiography Section, *Proceedings of the South Indian History Congress*, VII Annual Session, Madras, 1987, p. 47.

[82] Cf., for example, S. R. Goyal, *Dakshiṇa Bhārata kā Itihāsa*, in Hindi, Jodhpur, 1995. In this work, quite often, Goyal has illustrated how the writing of new political history of the Deccan and south India may be seriously attempted, at least in the case of some dynasties and some periods where our sources permit us to do so.

ELEVEN

Problems of the Decline of Classical Political Theory and Political History

I

P. S. Bhati is a widely known political scientist. The main area of his study has been political theory (classical). Consequently, he is responsive to the problem of the decline of political theory. Now interestingly in the Western world the problem of the decline of political history is being solved by transforming the very concept of political history. The dictum of Jacques Pirenne that "the true aim of historical research is a knowledge of the factors that control men living in society"[1] will perhaps be acceptable, at least on a tentative basis, to the majority of present-day Western scholars for their investigations. This definition implies that the different aspects of history cannot be studied in isolation from one another but only as facets of an integrated reality. Benjamin Schwartz has this kind of political history in mind when he argues that a "political historian must welcome all the aid which economists, demographers, anthropologists and others can provide to help him to understand the situation in which political action takes place."[2] According to Le Goff also, the new kind of political history, the one that is concerned with 'long term structures', involves the study of the various semeiological systems belonging to the science of politics: vocabulary, rites, behaviour and mental attitudes. He feels that not only does the new science of politicology now contribute its concepts, vocabulary and methods, but geopolitics, political sociology and political anthropology all give political history nourishment and

[1] Jacques Pirenne, *The Tides of History*, quoted in *Problems of Historical Writing in India*, eds. S. Gopal and Romila Thapar, New Delhi, 1963, p. 56.

[2] Benjamin Schwartz, 'A Brief Defence of Political and Intellectual History—With Particular Reference to Non-Western Cultures', *Daedalus*, Cambridge, Mass., Winter 1971, p. 100.

support.[3] Thus it is apparent that political history in the West is staging a comeback by borrowing the methods, spirit, theoretical approach and materials of the very social sciences, such as political science, which are pushing it into the background.[4]

This is the essence of what is nowadays called the integral approach to political history. This approach is finding its adherents in India also. In recent decades in India it has been championed by S.R. Goyal[5] who does not support the view that political history is dead or dying; rather, he argues that political history is still the backbone of history and that it has now become the study of political activity in its situational context, of the functioning of the centres of political authority with a view to discovering the motivations of political life and recognising that components of political power have social, economic and religious bases.[6]

Similarly, P. S. Bhati also finds no problem when he supports the ideas of Michael Oakeshott, Leo Strauss, Hannah Arendt and some others who are trying to resurrect the traditional political theory. He is vehemently opposed to the idea that the traditional theory is dead. He has methodically exposed the drawbacks of the behavioural and post-behavioural ideologies of political science which appeared in the discipline not long ago. However, Bhati also asserts that today the need is to bring them together. The traditional theory,

[3] E. G. Goff, 'Is Politics Still the Backbone of History', *Daedalus, op.cit.*, p. 12.

[4] For the meaning and significance of integral political history, see Shankar Goyal, *Ancient India : A Multidisciplinary Approach*, Jodhpur, 2006, Ch.1.

[5] The problem of the decline of political history and the emergence of the integral approach in the discipline are interrelated issues. S.R. Goyal has repeatedly expressed his views on this question in his celebrated thesis *A History of the Imperial Guptas* (Allahabad, 1967, Ch.1), in several of his articles published in the *Jijñāsā* (Vol. 2, Jaipur, 1975, pp. 9-26), *Indica* (Vol.14, No. 2, Bombay, 1977, pp. 85-98), in *Historical and Political Perspectives* (ed. D. Devahuti, New Delhi, 1982, pp.93-101), in the foreword to S. K. Purohit's *Uttara Bhārata kā Prāchīna Rājanītika Itihāsa* (Jaipur, 1980, pp. ix-xx), in ch.1 of his own *Māgadha-Sātavāhana-Kushāṇa Sāmrājyoṅ ka Yuga* (Meerut, 1988), in his lead paper entitled 'Need of a New Approach to the Writing of Political History of Ancient India', in the *Political History in a Changing World* (eds. G.C. Pande, S. K. Gupta and Shankar Goyal, Jodhpur, 1992, pp. 1-17), and in his ch. 'Rājanītika Itihāsa kī Vividha Avadhāraṇāyeṅ', published in *Prāchīna Bhārata kā Ādhunika Itihāsa-Lekhana* (ed. Shankar Goyal, Jodhpur, 2000, pp. 1-10). It is also found reflected in his many works on ancient Indian history, including, *Harsha and Buddhism* (Meerut, 1986), *Prāchīna Bhārata kā Itihāsa*, in three volumes (Meerut, 1988), *Priyadarśī Aśoka* (Meerut, 1988), and *The Imperial Guptas : A Multidisciplinary Political Study* (Jodhpur, 2005).

[6] Our monograph *Ancient India : A Multidisciplinary Approach* has shown what S.R. Goyal has done to give a new definition and meaning to political history, specially of ancient India, and what more can be done in this field.

according to him, unsupported by the emperical theory would be faltering and imperfect, and emperical theory cut-off from the philosophical base would be ineffectual. For Bhati, a real political theory must be rooted in ethics, philosophy, history, economics and related disciplines. According to him, man is an associative animal and cannot live in isolation, and, therefore, political theory is worthless without ethical theory, because it depends fundamentally on the scheme of moral ideals and the thoughts of right and wrong. A political theory would be rootless without philosophy. Since philosophy goes straight to the heart of the truth, it would allow a student of political theory with a understanding of reason and necessity in everything unlike the illusory whirlwind of facts or emperical laws. It would build a politico-philosophical consciousness. Thus, Bhati emphasizes that the study of politics, neither can nor should be merely scientific. It is against this background that we have discussed the problem of the decline of traditional political theory afresh.

That P.S. Bhati is a great exponent of the value-laden political theory and has depicted remarkably well as to how the traditional political theory has been resurrected in the ideas of Leo Strauss, Hannah Arendt, Michael Oakeshott, etc., is evident. His book entitled *The Normative Traditions in Political Theory* (Jodhpur, 1998), his D. Litt. work, is a fitting reply to those who talk of the decline or demise of traditional political theory. Bhati has exposed the drawbacks of behaviouralism, and has cogently argued that normative theory is never dead; it is always alive.

The work of P.S. Bhati is divided into ten chapters : (I) The Normative Tradition in Political Theory ; (II) The Decline of Normative Political Theory and Its Revival; (III) The Behavioural Revolution: Its Utility and Its Limitations; (IV) Post-Behavioural Revolution in Contemporary Political Theory; (V) The Continuity of Normative Tradition in Political Theory; (VI) The Neo-Normative Thought of Michael Oakeshott; (VII) Hannah Arendt as a Neo-Normative Political Thinker; (VIII) Neo-Normative Ideas of Leo Strauss; (IX) The Old and the New in Contemporary Political Theory; and (X)The Relevance and Utility of Normative Political Theory. His principal contentions can be broadly summarised thus: (i) The central distortions and confusions in modern political theory result from the attempt to undermine the importance of normative theory by the behaviouralists. (ii) That this dichotomizing of political theory into two halves is dangerous and even fatal to the development of the discipline of political science. (iii) That the classical political tradition, effulgent in ideals and values, and capable of arousing impassion, should be resurrected. (iv) And that the real task in political theory lies in determining the existing and perceptive connections between the things human beings value most such as, moral autonomy, and the quest for a rational and philosophical order.

While discussing the relevance and utility of normative political theory in the last chapter of his work which, in a way, summarizes his thesis, Bhati points out that several old guards have discussed this point in detail though sometimes differently. For example, William T. Bluhm in his book *Theories of the Political System* (1971) discussed the relevance of normative political theory. His argument proceeds from the premise that modern political studies are already informed and sophisticated by the classics. The classical theories furnish the foundations of nearly all the work which is being done today in the field of politics. What is now required is synthesis, the building of bridges from theory to theory. He hopes that a comparative review of the classical theories in the context of this problem, and of the modern studies which build on them, may bring us some way on the road to such a goal. The famous political theorist Eugene J. Meehan in his work *The Foundations of Political Analysis : Empirical and Normative* (1971) starts with the idea of systematic inquiry as an operation which requires the use of various tools or instruments. These tools can be tested only in use. Explanations are such tools which provide people with the means of control over their environment. Another distinguished authority Andrew Hacker in his book *Political Theory: Philosophy, Ideology, Science* (1968) pleads for a close cooperation between the normative and empirical political theories.He enumerates the utility of both the traditional and contemporary concepts of political theory and says that there are few bridges between the two concepts of political theory. The views of Fred M. Frohock are also of great concern. In his book *The Nature of Political Inquiry* (1967), he discloses the tacit dimensions of political theory and weighs the stakes involved in choosing between the positivist and metaphysical epistemologies. A similar defence has been taken by Bernard Crick in *Political Theory and Practice* (1974), a worthwhile work on political theory. The provocative insights offered by Crick are philosophical and traditional. All these political thinkers, Bhati writes, are impressive because they see, or choose to see, that the task of reintegration, or the creation of a new political synthesis, is the main riddle confronting political theory today.

Thus, it could be prognosticated that the bases of a sound political theory cannot lie in the insipid tastes, indorous models and gibberish language. Normative theory properly serves to challenge the existing reality—organising principles. None being wholly acceptable, they constitute problems. Our problems, it should be clear, are posed not by an intractable reality, but rather by our constructs, definitions, and methods. Our organising principles pose a problem precisely to the extent that they fail to make reality yield. Therefore, the futurity of political theory will presumably lie in the study of values in its undefiled and virgin form. The ghosts of Plato, Hobbes, Hegel and Marx would continue to haunt the panquets that toast the future. The decorous normative tradition and chaste political values are central to the understanding of politics, and through it alone, one could hope to restrain the 'idiot masses' who have made over to the power elites and their 'crackpot realism' the final destiny of mankind. With the restoration of vestal and prude political values alone, the blessed moments would supervene and the heavenly days befall political theory.

II

P.S. Bhati has also been associated in writing a well-informative and useful text-book entitled *Political Theory and Organisation* with L. S. Rathore and S.A.H. Haqqi, much earlier. Published from Lucknow in the year 1989, it has been written in accordance with the contents of courses for the first year law students of five-year degree course. The book is unique on several grounds. Firstly, in it the political theories and principles of political organisation have been outlined in a clear and lucid style. Secondly, the topics like liberalism in India, the Hindu and Islamic conceptions of the State, and the Marxist thought in India, have been discussed quite explicitly and intelligently. The succulent presentation of the ideologies that have developed in modern India is an added attraction of this book. The work is undertaken from an objective perspective, presenting the various aspects of each ideology and concept, enabling a student to derive his own conclusions.

The contribution of Bhati in the preparation of the work is indeed immense. As Rathore in his 'preface' candidly acknowledges, "most of the chapters relating to political theory were initially written by Bhati who has done a commendable job and without whose cooperation it was wellnigh impossible for us to complete the present project in time."

III

The year 1980 saw the publication of P.S. Bhati's research article entitled 'Political Ideas of Michael Oakeshott' jointly with L.S. Rathore (*IJPS*, Vol. 3, No. 2 and Vol. 4, No. 1, January, 1980, pp. 254-64). One of the foremost and a leading political thinker of our times who not only continues to support the traditional-philosophical political theory but is sincere and impressive in his criticism of the empirical-analytical approaches is Michael Oakeshott. He stands out in the history of modern normative philosophy as the creator of a system. He has come to exert a great influence in recent political theory. Appealing to individual's aesthetic sense, Oakeshott has been able to build an original, stirring, and convincing case for the renewed study of the works of political philosophy. His major contribution has been to recover political theory as a tradition of enquiry and regain for political science the possibility of a critical, theoretical analysis. He treats philosophy and science as basically two different kinds of activities and believes that it would not be correct to transfer the methods and concerns of the one to the other.

Oakeshott's *Rationalism in Politics* is a wonderful work that rejects the idea that political philosophy is dead. A collection of ten seminal essays, first published in 1962, it has become a sort of 'underground classic'[7], for it embodies the mature reflections on diverse themes of a brilliant, highly sensitive, and genuinely philosophical mind.

Another important work by Michael Oakeshott in the field of political philosophy is *On Human Conduct* (Oxford, 1975). It gives a sustained reflection on the nature of political activity in general, and on the major concepts that have been generated in the western tradition for the purpose of such reflection. It provides to a general reader the benefit of Oakeshott's suggestions on Plato, Aristotle, Montesquieu and Hegel, and their specific relation to his own ideas in a fashion more direct than is to be found in any of his earlier writings.

Some scholars have tried to underrate the significance of Oakeshott's writings and have styled him as 'arrogantly conservative'. They have argued that the reason of his success lay in writing beautiful and charming English prose.They have tried to dismiss him as a 'literary essayist'. They have even characterized that his writings lack erudite scholarship or profound philosophy. They have tried to expose the weaknesses of his traditionalism. They have exposed the limitations of his epistemology. But whatever may be the criticism levelled against Oakeshott the fact remains that as an annihilator of scientific method and as a destroyer of the politics of rationalism, he is always superb. According to L.S. Rathore and Bhati, "the style with which he has exposed and unproductiveness of quantitativism and infertility of modern rationalism is unrivalled elsewhere. He not only dismantles and overthrows empiricism and rationalism but regenerates and reanimates a normative edifice based on the historical and philosophical study of political science."

IV

In his another learned article entitled 'Rise and Decline of Behavioural Revolution in Political Science' (*IJPS*, Vol. 8, July,1984, pp. 106-21) P.S. Bhati categorizes the behavioural revolution[8] in political science into three phases. It emerged a little before the First World War and reached its final form when the Second World War was in progress. During this period there was an increasing use of empirical and quantitative methods.[9] But the traditional and normative rules in political science were also maintained. New methods

[7] Cf. Randhir Singh, *Reason, Revolution and Political Theory*, New Delhi, 1967, p. 4.

[8] This modern political analysis rests upon four basic principles : (a) search for more comprehensive scope; (b) search for realism; (c) search for precision; and (d) search for intellectual order. In brief, political behaviour theories are nothing more than the application of precise scientific methods to the study of politics.

[9] Paul F. Lazarsfeld and Morris Rosenberg (eds.), *The Language of Social Research*, Glencoe Free Press, 1955, p. 4.

were used to enable a somewhat more precise description and analysis of the prevailing paradigms of political science. But in the post-Second World War period the real empirical and quantitative emphasis began. In the sixties, however, the growth of mathematical techniques, multivariate analysis and quantitative strategies were developed to such an extent that the theoretical equipment was more or less given up. The decade of sixties was the peak of the growth of the behavioural revolution. In the seventies the decline of this revolution began.

Nowadays there is more criticism of behaviouralism than support to it. The traditional political scientists have always criticized this tendency. According to them, the behaviouralism and the post-behaviouralism[10] have not been successful in establishing explanatory laws, as compared to the older and the well known generalizations arrived at in the traditional political theory. Of course, there are supporters of behaviouralism nowadays as well. There is a conflict between tradition and modernity. The present-day necessity is to reconcile them. The traditional theory, unsupported by the empirical theory would be inarticulate and fragmentary, and empirical theory cut-off from the philosopical base would be feckless, soon to dodder and evanesce. What is needed, is a new creative political theory, based on 'precision without criticism', meaning thereby, flourishing within the genial range of normative and empirical fields.[11]

V

Again, in 1986, P.S. Bhati published another significant paper entitled 'Post-Behavioural Revolution in Contemporary Political Theory' (*IJPS*, Vol. 10, December, 1986, pp. 102-09) which examines the post-behavioural ideology in political science quite in detail. As is apparent, the progress of behavioural thought in political science was a factor of supreme importance for decades.[12] It is indubitable that it rocked the discipline of political science and tried to cramp and crumble political theory.[13] Its adherents have been unerringly critical of traditional metaphysical speculation about values. It was identified with

[10] The essence of post-behavioural revolution is that it arose out of a deep dissatisfaction with behavioural research. It is both a movement, that is, an aggregate of people, and an intellectual tendency. For the tenets of the post-behavioural approach, see David Easton, 'The New Revolution in Political Science', Presidential Address, 65th American Political Science Conference, New York, September, 1969, in Michael Hass and Henry S. Kariel (eds.), *Approaches to the Study of Political Science*, Pennsylvania, 1970, pp. 512-13.

[11] Cf. also, L. S. Rathore, 'Political Theory : A Quest for Reconciliation', *The Indian Journal of Political Science*, Vol. XXXVIII, No. 1, January-May, 1977, p. 7.

[12] Evron Kirkpatrick, 'From Past to Present', in Donald M. Freeman (ed.), *Foundations of Political Science: Research Methods and Scope*, New York, 1977, p. 29.

[13] L. S. Rathore, *In Defence of Political Theory*, New Delhi, 1986, p. 59.

new tools, for example, survey research, computer analysis, and mathematical applications that have a great importance for any subject involved in the study of mass aggregates. The movement also produced concepts, methods, goals, and results that were relevant to the purpose of political science. As a result, the behavioural movement enjoyed conspicuous success for over two decades.[14]

However, towards the end of the sixties a powerful attack was launched on it by David Easton who had been a prominent supporter of behaviouralism. It arose out of deep dissatisfaction with the kind of political search and teaching which was attempting to change the study of politics into a more strict scientific discipline based on the methodology of the natural sciences. The behaviouralists, now turned to the post-behaviouralists, admitted that too much time had been spent by them on insignificant and very often irrelevant research. While they were engaged in building up of various paradigms, conceptual frameworks, models, theories and metatheories, the world was facing more and more acute social, economic and cultural crises, of which they appeared to be totally ignorant. Fear of the nuclear bomb and mounting internal cleavages were conditions which political science, neither behavioural nor traditional, had predicted. "What kind of research was that, argue the post-behaviouralists, which did not take note of these acute social maladies and problems ? What was the use of developing high technical adequacy and sophisticated research tools, asked the post-behaviouralist, if the political scientist was not able to comprehend contemporary social and political problems and make his own contribution towards resolving them ?"[15] Post-behaviouralism is, therefore, both a movement, that is, an aggregate of people, and also an intellectual tendency. It tries to push political science in new directions. Similarly, behaviouralism in the fifties, by adopting a new technology, sought to add to rather then to deny our heritage. This new development is then a real revolution, not a reaction; a becoming, not a preservation; a reform, not a counter-reformation. Therefore, post-behaviouralism stands as the most recent contribution to our collective heritage. Because of it, as an intellectual tendency it is not the threat and danger that intellectuals appear to be afraid of. Rather, in the broad historical perspectives of our subject, the post-behavioural upheaval represents an opportunity for necessary change.[16]

Like behaviouralism, it is not full and correct as regards to study of political science. This thought current is a syndrome of a peculiar type, depicting adequately competent signs of indigene and impecuniosity. Limited in

[14] Kirkpatrick, *op.cit.*, pp. 33-34.

[15] S. P. Varma, *Modern Political Theory*, New Delhi, 1976, pp. 97-98.

[16] Easton, *op.cit.*, p. 528.

observation, untrained in making accurate deductions, intolerant towards traditional values with vision atrophied, most of us have yet to find out the infirmities that gird the post-behavioural thought. Although its supporters claim to have discovered a 'new voice' but perhaps like the 'dying swan's song that provides the semblance of being the most beautiful, its voice has lost its capacity to survive, and more so in these difficult times. A variegated ideological theme could be true neither to the classical heritage nor to the scientific curiosity.[17]

VI

P.S. Bhati's article entitled 'The NormativeTradition in Political Theory' (*IJPS*, Vol. 12, December, 1988, pp. 79-106) is a quality article and a substantial contribution to the discipline of political science. In it Bhati seeks to study the development of normative tradition from the classical days to the age of Karl Marx. As is well known, the normative political theory has a long tradition. Its history is more than 2400 years old. It originated in the political thought of the classical period in Greece. The names most intimately associated with the classical normative political theory are those of Socrates, Plato and Aristotle. The word "political" also comes from the Greek word "polis". Greece, in fact, furnished us the main outline of the discipline of political science. The greatest contribution of ancient Greece to the modern world is philosophy. Since philosophy goes straight to the heart of truth, and since the nature of political reality "makes philosophy particularly suitable to its study",[18] it gives a student of political science a knowledge of reason and necessity in everything. When we describe the political philosophy of Plato (428-348 B.C.) and Aristotle (384-322 B.C.) as classical political philosophy we presume that it is the classic form of political philosophy.[19] Plato was the first well-known political theorist who expressed the classical political theory with "the greatest clarity and imaginative beauty".[20] He laid down his political philosophy in a series of famous dialogues, namely, *Apology*, *Crito*, *Phaedo*, *Republic*, etc. He concerned himself with the fundamental normative questions, such as,the meaning of justice and the relations between the man and the state.[21] Aristotle, the most famous pupil of Plato, in his *Politics*, relies upon the wisdom of experience and bases his views upon a close analysis of what he found around him. His conviction that a political theory must combine a knowledge of political good and of political mechanics, played a significant role in the development

[17] Rathore, *op. cit.*, pp. 64-65.

[18] Alex N. Dragnich and John C. Wahlke, *Government and Politics : An Introduction to Political Science*, New York, 1966, p. 16.

[19] Leo Strauss, 'What is Political Philosophy', in James A. Gould and Vincent V. Thursby (eds.), *Contemporary Political Thought*, New York, 1969, p. 58.

[20] John Bowle, *Western Political Thought*, London, 1954, p. 49.

[21] F. W. Coker, *Readings in Political Philosophy*, New York, 1962, p. 2.

of political science.[22]

A very significant school of thought which came into existence after the death of Aristotle was that of the Stoics. It was through Stoicism that much of the Greek philosophy came to western Europe in the early centuries B.C. Stoicism flourished for a period of about five hundred years, from the time of its founder, Zeno(340-265 B.C.), to the death of Marcus Aurelius (121-180 A.D.) who was one of the last and the most famous of its exponents. The Stoic philosophy enjoys an important position in the history of political thought. It set forth very clearly the idea of the equality of men. It established the concept of the law of nature which later on became the foundation of Roman law. The belief in universal brotherhood of men, and world government are definitely the legacy of Stoics.[23]

The normative theory during the Roman period was remarkable not for the 'originality of its conceptions', but for its educative power. Polybius (204-122 B.C.), who was taken as a prisoner from Greece to Rome, produced some pantoscopic normative ideas that have had a lasting importance. He wrote his *History of Rome* to show her greatness and to find out and enunciate its cause. The political ideas of Polybius relating to the 'mixed constitutions' and the doctrine of 'checks and balances' were most widely read by the subsequent political thinkers. Cicero (106-43 B.C.) was a principal philosopher of the Roman age. He was the only Roman native who wrote widely on the problems of political theory. In the history of political thought he occupies a prominent place. Cicero was a very prolific writer and he wrote on different branches of knowledge. His normative political theory was legalistic. He viewed the state 'as a moral community', a group of persons who in common possess the state and its law.

The downfall of the Roman empire was concommitant with the rise of Christianity. Christianity taught that man is the creature of God and that essentially he is a spiritual being. It is believed that beyond the kingdom of man there is the kingdom of God and if an individual is to enter that kingdom he must surrender his will to God and put an end to his rebellion. Thus, there is introduced into life a duality unknown in the Greek world—man is not only a citizen of the world (the kingdom of man) but he is also, at least potentially, a member of the kingdom of God. Man is faced for the first time with a dual loyalty—a loyalty to Caesar and a loyalty to God.

One of the greatest figures of the early Christian thought was St. Augustine (354-430 A.D.). He was probably the 'greatest of the Fathers of the Church'. His concept of justice occupies an axial place in the normative

[22] George Catlin, *A History of Political Philosophers*, London, 1950, p. 102.

[23] George H. Sabine and Thomas L. Thorson, *A History of Political Theory*, New Delhi, 1963, p. 133.

philosophy. He believed that the essence of justice is the relation between man and God from which right relations between man and man will automatically follow. Therefore, his political theory sees the state in terms of moral purpose rather than formal authority, having the monopoly to use force or sovereignty.

But the medieval thought found its greatest exponent in St. Thomas Aquinas (1225-1274 A.D.). He represents the totality of medieval thought. His normative theory is best found in two of his works, *On Kingship* and the *Sun of Theology*. In the realm of political philosophy St. Thomas accepted Aristotle's ideas concerning the origin, nature and function of the state but argued that the state could never be self-sufficient and its aims must always be secondary to the higher end of spiritual salvation for individuals whose final destiny does not belong to this world. St. Thomas' treatment of law and justice exhibits well the salient characteristics of his normative philosophy. Of the thinkers who propounded rich normative doctrines from the standpoint of the imperial interest was Dante Alighieri (1265-1321 A.D.). His chief political work was *De Monarchia*. It was written in Latin for the purpose of making an argument for a universal empire.[24] In such an empire there would be no place for the Papacy exercising secular power, for the emperor would derive his power directly from God without the intervention of Pope. Marsiglio of Padua (1275-1343 A.D.) was perhaps the greatest political thinker in Europe after the death of Aristotle.[25] Though a medieval thinker, Marsiglio was modern in many ways. His advocacy of the separation of Church from the state led to the development of modern secularism. Also, his plea for the representative government and belief in the sovereignty of people brought him in line with many modern political thinkers.

The Conciliar Movement marked the end of an old and the beginning of a new age in political theory. It also marked the end of the Middle Ages and the birth of the modern age in world history with its reassertion of the humanistic and scientific outlook. It was during Renaissance that the human mind shook itself free from the bonds of Medievalism and sought inspiration in the great works of ancient Greeks and Romans.[26] The political theory of the early Renaissance is probably best seen in the writing of Niccolo Machiavelli (1469-1527 A.D.). The work by which he is best known is *The Prince*. Modern political thought actually begins with him.[27] Despite the fact that he is hardly a

[24] C. S. Maxey, *Political Philosophies*, New York, 1956, p. 123.

[25] R.H. Murray, *The History of Political Science from Plato to the Present*, London, 1926, p. 81.

[26] Maxey, *op. cit.*, p. 125.

[27] For the political thought of Machiavelli, vide Shankar Goyal, 'Politics and Ethics in Kauṭilya and Machiavelli', in our *History and Politics*, Jodhpur, 2015, pp. 74-81.

political theorist, he is regarded as the father of modern political theory. He makes the first decisive break with the thought of the Middle Ages on political problems. For Machiavelli the state is a natural unit. It comes out from and exists in the midst of a play of natural forces which the ruler must understand and make use of.

The modern tradition of Natural Law begins with Jean Bodin, a French political thinker of the sixteenth century. Though Bodin's sovereign is 'unrestrained by law' still he maintains that 'sovereign is bound by the law of God and of nature'. Hugo Grotius (1533-1645), a Dutch lawyer, could be styled as the founder of modern Natural Law. Here, Natural Law is no longer considered in the context of theology, but is equated with natural reason. Another exponent of Natural Law, who followed the traditions of Grotius, was Richard Hooker. According to him, there are various kinds of law : eternal law, Natural Law, law of reason and human law. The eternal law is the law of God's own nature. The modern theory of Natural Law is best explained by Thomas Hobbes (1583-1679) and John Locke (1632-1704), both great English political thinkers. Hobbes developed an entire edifice of law by rational deduction from an imaginary 'state of nature' in which men lived according to the dictates of nature. Hobbes made a distinction between Natural Right and Natural Law. Natural Right, according to him, is the freedom possessed by every individual to do what seems best for his preservation while Natural Law is a rule based on reason. For Hobbes the state of nature is "a state of enmity, malice, violence and mutual destruction", for Locke it is "a state of peace, goodwill, mutual help and preservation". J.J. Rousseau's (1712-1778) thoughts are different from Hobbes and Locke. His theory of Natural Law is full of paradoxes and his ideas about it are vague and inconsistent. Thus, the doctrine of Natural Law, in one form or the other, played a significant role in western political thought from the days of Stoics up to the end of the seventeenth century.

Late in the medieval period two important principles made their appearance. They helped in making the transition to the enlightenment. One was that the ruler or monarch was a representative of the people with a constitutionally defined or limited sphere of power. The other was that the political community consisted not of the private rights of all individuals but of the rights of a representative assembly. People were represented not in their private capacities, but as citizens.[28] John Locke, mentioned earlier, and David Hume, another British philosopher, also contributed to this new concern which was the anti-thesis to both the medieval spirit and autocracy.

The Marxian tradition emanates from the assumption that philosophers

[28] F. W. Maitland, *Political Theories of the Middle Age*, Cambridge, 1927, pp. 62-63.

all along have interpreted the world, the necessity however, is to change it. The most powerful exponent of this view was Karl Marx (1818-1883). He was probably the greatest socialist writer and thinker and, obviously, 'the first scientific socialist thinker'. He not only outlined the ideal of socialism but also suggested coherent means and methods to achieve it.

Thus, it is obvious that the normative political theory has a complicated arrangement, sensitive frontiers and includes qualitative ideas, which can be best understood by studying the many ways that its recognized masters have practised it. No philosopher and no historical age may be regarded to have defined it conclusively. For the student of history, normative theory provides "an indispensable key", for the student of contemporary public affairs and the inquirer who wishes to peep into the future, it provides an "equally valuable guide". To modern behavioural thinkers, it is necessary to remember that history may not repeat itself, but, in every age there is a large carry-over of the past political thinking and a heavy seeding of ideas that bear fruit in years to come.[29]

VII

The year 1989 saw the publication of a very scholarly article of Bhati entitled 'The Decline of Normative Political Theory and Its Revival' (*IJPS*, Vol. 13, December, 1989, pp. 66-82). As is well known, the philosophically oriented or the normative political theory is as old as an organised political society. In the scholarly world it is defined by many as a systematic thinking about the purpose of government.[30] Contrary to some political scientists, we believe that it would continue to occupy a significant place in political inquiry and analysis despite the vigorous efforts made by many contemporary empirical theorists to build up a value-free political science. Bhati enumerates the factors that have contributed to the notion that political theory is "dead". According to him, the so-called "decline" has been attributed to several causes : (i) The first reason for the decline of political theory is the very success of political science itself, by which it meant that formidable growth in the volume of behavioural studies and the improvement in the techniques they employ.[31] (ii) The second reason, argue the critics, is inherent in the imperfections of traditional political theory and its mode of inquiry. (iii) Thirdly, as emphasised by David Easton and others, "the historical approach" "a form of historical analysis" "historical interpretation" has "managed to crush the life out of

[29] Cf. also, Rathore, *op.cit.*, p. 112.

[30] John Plamenatz, 'The Use of Political Theory', in *Political Philosophy*, ed. Anthony Quinton, Oxford, 1967, p. 19.

[31] H.R.G. Greaves, 'Political Theory Today', *Political Science Quarterly*, Vol. LXXV, March, 1960, p. 3.

value theory" and has resulted not only in "the decline of interest in creative values and the growth of moral relativism" but also in an "indifference to casual theory".[32] (iv) And, lastly, the apathy for political theory is the result of technological revolution around the end of World War II, although traces of it were evident much earlier.

However, imperfections not withstanding, political theory is not dead, it is up again with rejuvenation and renewed vigour. There is a "renewed interest taken by theorists in the prescriptive discussion of social and political issues."[33] Political theory is "alive again" because of its inner dynamism which provides "a free play to every man's natural creativity and creative impulses."[34] Political theory is up again or has revived, meaning thereby the increased interest taken by contemporary political theorists in : (i) a critical, theoretical analysis of politics; (ii) combining the realms of fact-finding systematic knowledge and theory-building on the one hand, and the sphere of social policy, political problems and ideological issues on the other; and (iii) the reassessment of key political concepts. On the whole, political theory cannot hope to develop in the absence of a philosophic framework and that the most important dividing line between political theories running along the value committed. Value-free axis seems to be a passing fad.

VIII

While numerous approaches to political science have been advocated from time to time, they might be broadly divided into two groups : the scientific-behavioural (modern) on the one side, and, thc normative-philosophical (traditional) on the other. Further, each of these two approaches may be mainly differentiated by the emphasis they lay on values as against facts or on facts as against values.[35] P.S. Bhati is the traditional political scientist who believes that the study of politics neither can nor should be purely scientific.[36] Therefore, in his very thoughtful and emotional paper entitled 'The Old and New in

[32] David Easton, 'Classical Theory', in *Approaches to the Study of Political Science*, eds. Michael Hass and Henry S. Kariel, p. 52.

[33] Peter Laslett and W.G. Runciman (eds.), *Philosophy, Politics and Society*, Oxford, 1967, p. 1.

[34] Bertrand Russell, *Political Ideas*, London, 1963, p. 12.

[35] Two opposing positions are taken up in this respect by those who have been described by Robert A. Dahl as Empirical Theorists and Trans-empirical Theorists. The Empirical Theorists believe that an empirical science of politics based on facts alone is possible, whereas the Trans-empirical Theorists are of the opinion that the study of politics should not be purely scientific. See, his *Modern Political Analysis*, Englewood Cliffs, N. J., Prentice Hall, 1953, p. 101.

[36] Vide also, Varma, *op.cit.*, p. 22.

Contemporary Political Theory' (*IJPS*, Vol. 14, December, 1990, pp. 44-58), he argues that the most probable way out for the political theory ought to be to conserve its reflexive, appreciative or traditional character, rooted in prescriptive values, stimulative convictions and macro-generalizations, arrived at by historical observations. A real political theory, therefore, we feel, must be rooted in ethics, philosophy, history, economics and related fields. Man is an associative animal and can not live in isolation and, therefore, political theory is idle without ethical theory, because it depends fundamentally on the scheme of moral ideals and the thoughts of right and wrong.[37] A political theory would be rootless without philosophy. As has been mentioned, philosophy goes straight to the heart of the truth, it would provide a student of political theory with a understanding of reason and necessity in every thing unlike the illusory whirlwind of facts or empirical laws. It would create a politico-philosophical consciousness. Similarly, political theory owes much to history. It is through history that political theory can be used to recreate life, to understand the political phenomenon, to show the creative manifestations and reveal the movements of political life. Croce's dictum that "all history is contemporary history" and Will Durant's observation that "the present is the past rolled up for action and the past is the present unrolled for understanding", are worth bearing in mind by a student of political theory. To neglect the study of history is to neglect the real source of knowledge relevant to the study of political ideas and institutions.[38] History, therefore, continues to occupy its place, or at least a proper place, in the fructification of political theory.[39]

Thus, it is doubtless that political theory remains unproductive without being conjoined with the study of history, philosophy and economics in depth. The induction of mathematics and statistics are of no avail because these subjects are more to the point to the study of physical and biological sciences than political science. Mathematics and mechanics are insufficient to political research and not capable of containing the rich, moving, living current of political life. It is through postulatory, critical and interpretative norms that one can look into the mysteries of political society and touchy human relations much clearly than those who have invented, for a good or evil, the new scientific theories for understanding political society. It is in the interpretative or appreciative enterprise and not in behavioural and quantitative models, that the core of political theory remains.

[37] In this regard, Ivor Brown's dictum that "politics is but ethics writ large" is still true and relevant. For further details, cf. his *English Political Theory*, London, 1929.

[38] G. R. Elton, *Political History : Principles and Practice*, London, 1970, p. 160.

[39] Nagendra Singh Bhati, 'Shankar Goyal on the Problems of the Decline of Political Theory and History', in *Shankar Goyal : Marching with History*, ed. Radhika Seshan, New Delhi, 2021, Ch. 9.

Political theory, therefore, ought to be rooted in value premises, and factual knowledge ought to supplement its dimensions. The values ought to be at the centre and the factual knowledge or engineering ought to stay at the boundary. Like light and shadow, they may mix and overlap each other, mingle and intermingle. A value-fact confluence model, where values are pivotal would, perhaps, be a more relevant style in political theory towards the building of a same society.

Section III
History

TWELVE

The Rājyavardhana Murder Case

In history very few princes have been as unfortunate as Rājyavardhana II was.[1] He was not only murdered but also became a victim of the deliberate misrepresentation of facts about him in the *Harshacharita.*[2] Bāṇa mentions him with every respect, but he also deliberately tries to create the impression that it was Harsha not Rājyavardhana, who was born to succeed Prabhākara-vardhana. Gods, providence and Prabhākara himself, all wished for the succession of Harsha. Actually, it seems to have been the main purpose of Bāṇa to impress on his readers that Harsha was born to rule the earth as a chakravartin. This is clearly seen in the motif of the boon granted by goddess Lakshmī to king Pushyabhūti that in his family there "shall arise an emperor named Harṣa, governor like Hariśchandra of all the continents, world-conquering like a second Māndhātṛi, whose chowrie this hand, spontaneously abandoning the lotus, shall grasp."[3]

Bāṇa's partiality for Harsha is quite obvious. He noted the birth of Rājya briefly but grows eloquent on the birth of Harsha. He tells us that when Yaśomatī was pregnant with Harsha she behaved and thought like the mother of a chakravartin. Nothing like that is claimed when she is said to have been pregnant with Rājya.

> As pregnancy (with Harsha) came on, her cup-like bosoms grew dark in their tender nipples, as if stamped for an emperor to drain... In her dreams all the four sky-elephants seemed to consecrate her,... Even in play she would suffer no violation of her will. Moreover a wish grew upon her to bathe even in the united waters of the four great oceans.[4]

[1] S. R. Goyal, *Harsha Śīlāditya*, Meerut, 1986, Ch. 4; idem, *Maukhari-Pushyabhūti-Chālukya Yuga*, Meerut, 1988, p. 147.

[2] Shankar Goyal, *Harsha : A Multidisciplinary Political Study*, Jodhpur, 2006, pp. 145 ff.

[3] E.B. Cowell and F.W. Thomas, *The Harṣa-charita of Bāṇa* (hereafter referred to as *HC*, Eng. tr.), Second edn., Delhi, 1968, p. 97.

[4] *HC*, Eng. tr., pp. 108-09.

Similarly, when Harsha was born a Maga astrologer named Tāraka told Prabhākaravardhana that at that time "all the planets were at their apexes." Therefore, "he shall be coryphaeus of the Seven Emperors (*chakravartins*), Seven Imperial Signs, and the Great Jewels, Lord of the Seven Oceans,"[5] etc. No such prophecy is made at the time of the birth of Rājya. That according to Bāṇa Harsha's birth was celebrated with much greater enthusiasm than was shown when Rājya was born has already been noted.

BĀṆA'S TREATMENT OF THE HISTORY OF RĀJYAVARDHANA

From the time of the fatal illness of Prabhākara Bāṇa gradually but tenaciously seeks to prepare the psychology of his readers for the succession of Harsha in preference to Rājyavardhana by using subtle, and sometimes not so subtle, literary devices and skilful portrayal of the main characters and by omitting to mention some significant facts known to us from other sources which went against his avowed purpose and by 'introducing' or 'creating' such 'facts' which are palpably false or impossible but carry his story in the desired direction. Viewed in this light the fact that Rājya was murdered in suspicious circumstances becomes more significant and the questions arise 'why has Bāṇa given a twist to the history of Rājya and the accession of Harsha ?' and 'did Harsha in some way maneuvere to gain the ancestral throne for himself?' The answer to the second question has been given in affirmative by several scholars. Long way back in 1943 R. C. Majumdar wrote : "Who knows that Rājyavardhana's death was not similarly encompassed by his ministers with the help of Śaśāṅka who was known to be a great champion of orthodox faith?"[6] Similarly, in 1966 V. S. Pathak interpreted the literary devices used in the *Harshacharita* to show that the avowed purpose of Bāṇa was to whitewash the violation of the law of primogeniture by his patron.[7] Therefore, Devahuti, who also believes that in some way Harsha connived at gaining the throne, was wrong when, in 1970, she wrote that we must examine our sources more closely 'as the doubt has never been raised before' in this regard.[8] In 1986 S. R. Goyal also made almost a legalistic case to prove the connivance of Harsha in the murder of Rājya.[9] We also do not agree with Devahuti when she opines that this 'question is of minor importance'.[10] It is indeed a vital question, for the murder of Rājya sealed

[5] *Ibid.*, p. 110.

[6] R.C. Majumdar, *The History of Bengal*, I, Dacca, 1943, p. 76.

[7] V.S. Pathak, *Ancient Historians of India*, Bombay, 1966, pp. 45 ff.; also see, Romila Thapar, *Early India*, New Delhi, 2002, p. 288.

[8] D. Devahuti, *Harsha : A Political Study*, New Delhi, Second edn., 1983, p. 80; 1st edn., Oxford, 1970.

[9] S.R. Goyal, *op.cit.*, Ch. 4.

[10] Devahuti, *op. cit.*

his fate and changed the course of the history of seventh century north India. Further, the question is also vital for the study of Harsha himself because it is concerned with his character and the political values he cherished.

NO MENTION OF THE ACCESSION OF RĀJYA BY BĀṆA

According to Harsha's inscriptions, Yuan Chwang's account and the *Mañjuśrīmūlakalpa*, Rājyavardhana succeeded Prabhākaravardhana, but the fact remains unsupported by the *Harshacharita*. Bāṇa does not make even a reference to Rājya's being a Crown Prince or to his coronation for this post.[11] After his return from the Hūṇa War, in 'the morning' Rājyavardhana made the pledge not to ascend the throne. At that very time Saṁvādaka suddenly (*sahasaiva*) brought the sad news of the murder of Grahavarman and Rājyavardhana resolved to leave the same day (*adyaiva*) for Kanauj where he was killed. This course of events leaves no time for his coronation and rule.

PRABHĀKARA'S SUPPOSED PREDILECTION FOR HARSHA

Bāṇa begins to prepare his readers earnestly for the succession of Harsha as soon as Harsha returns to the capital. He had already told his readers that Harsha was sent by gods to rule as a chakravartin. He had also shown that even in the womb of her mother the imperial status of the would-be child was indicated by the behaviour of his mother. Now Bāṇa uses other devices at his command for this purpose. One of the devices was the supposed predilection of Prabhākara for Harsha. According to Bāṇa, Harsha met Prabhākara twice before the latter's death and on both the occasions Prabhākara pleaded with him to wear the crown after him. In both the speeches mention of Rājyavardhana as the heir-apparent is conspicuous by its absence. Prabhākara expresses no regrets at his absence, makes no inquiries after him of Harsha who had been the last to see his brother and gives no advice to the younger son to serve the elder loyally on the latter's accession to the throne. On the other hand, the ailing king is said to have bequeathed his sovereignty to Harsha. On the first occasion he said :

> Upon you my happiness, my sovereignty, my succession, and my life are set, and as mine, so those of all my people. ... You are the fruit of stainless deeds stored up in many another life. You bear marks declaring the sovereignty of the four oceans, one and all, to be almost in your grasp. ...[12]

On the second occasion Bāṇa makes him say :

> To say you are the lamp of our line were almost depreciation of one whose brilliance compares with the god of day. To call you a lion among heroes is

[11] For the coronation of the Crown Prince vide the Haraha record of the Maukharis and the *Kādambarī* which mention respectively the coronation of Īśānavarman and Chandrāpīḍa as the Crown Princes of their respective fathers.

[12] *HC*, Eng. tr., p. 142.

> like a reproach to one whose prowess is seconded by penetrating insight. To declare this earth yours is almost a vain repetition, when your bodily marks proclaim an universal emperor's dignity. To bid you take to yourself glory is almost contradictory, when glory has herself adopted you. 'Succeed to this world' is a command too mean for an intending conqueror of both worlds. 'Appropriate my treasury' is a grant of little service to one whose sole craving is for the accumulation of fame spotless as moonlight. 'Make prize of the feudatory kings' is almost meaningless, when your virtues have made prize of all beings. 'Support the burden of royalty' is an injunction misbecoming one accustomed to support the burden of the three worlds. 'Protect the people' is but reiteration, when the sky has your long arm for its bar. ...[13]

These speeches of Prabhākara are, to say the least, highly unusual and, if one can say, impossible. For we must remember that at that time Harsha was hardly 15 or 16 years old and his ability as a prince was yet to be tested. When only a short while later Rājyavardhana goes to punish the wicked lord of Mālava, Harsha pleads to let him accompany him saying :

> If I am regarded as a boy, then I should all the more not be abandoned; if as needing protection, the cage of your arms is an asylum; if incompetent, where have I been tried ?[14]

On the other hand, Rājyavardhana was not only elder, he was a warlike prince with military skill and heroism. That is why he was selected for the campaign against the Hūṇas. Therefore, there is apparently no reason due to which Prabhākara would had wanted to suppress his claim to the throne.

RĀJYAVARDHANA'S SUPPOSED AVERSION TO RULE

However, the impression created by the unusual desire of Prabhākara, which could not have been a fact, is sought to be confirmed by Bāṇa by later descriptions. It starts with Harsha's fears regarding his brother's aversion to the throne, expressed by Bāṇa in the following words :

> Pray heaven my brother, when he learns of our father's death, a type of the world's dissolution, may not after a bath of tears assume two robes of bark ! or seek (194) a hermitage as a royal sage ! or, man-lion as he is, enter a mountain cave ! Though his lotus eyes brim with a flood of tears, may he yet look upon the lordless earth ! Tormented by the poisonous pangs of a first loss, may the best of men yet remember himself ! Never may indifference due to the transitoriness of things lead him to slight the advances of sovereign glory ! All aflame with the fire of direful pain, may he have recourse to the coronation bath ! Once arrived here may he not, when pressed by the kings, display a contrary mind ! [15]

[13] *Ibid.*, pp. 155-56.

[14] *Ibid.*, p. 175.

[15] *Ibid.*, pp. 162-63.

The account reaches its logical culmination and Harsha's fears prove true. On return, 'all the kings being admitted' Rājyavardhana thus spoke to Harsha :

> ... It is some native cowardice or womanishness which has rendered me subject to the flame of filial grief. ... My mind seeks to avoid a glory, which, as if belonging to outcasts, if of no noble sort, banner-borne, crimson of hue, turbaned with many shrouds of the dead. Like the house sparrow, I cannot endure to abide even a moment in a home which has become a hell. I desire therefore in a hermitage to purge with the pure waters of pellucid streams that run from mountain tops this fond defilement which clings to my mind as to a garment. Therefore do you receive from my hands the cares of soverignty, a gift not high esteemed indeed and reft of the joy of youth, like old age, which Pūru welcomed at his father's will. Dismissing all the sports of youth, deliver your bosom like Viṣṇu to the embraces of Glory. I have abandoned the sword.[16]

Thus, instead of the motif of the 'inability or incompetence of the elder brother to rule', Bāṇa uses the motif of 'elder brother's desire not to rule'. But he finds it difficult to make this trait appear natural in the character of Rājya. For Rājya was, as we have seen, a brave fighter, a hero. He willingly went to fight against the Hūṇas. Even when he was renouncing the throne, his sorrow and the world-renouncing trait of his character at once evaporated when the news of the murder of Grahavarman was received and like a true fighter he at once, indeed the same day, proceeded to avenge the murder of his brother-in-law. He immediately abandoned the decision to retire, and declared his resolve to avenge the family honour. 'This task, my noble brother', he said to Harsha, 'is my royal house, this my kin, my court, my land, my people... this and no other is my assumption of the bark dress... Let all the kings and elephants stay with you. Only Bhaṇḍi here must follow me with some ten thousand horses.'[17] Obviously, therefore, Bāṇa's depiction of him as man of world-renouncing temperament is not correct.

It is also quite inexplicable why Harsha did not oppose his father's desire to make him his successor when his elder brother was alive and why did he not protest against his brother's unusual decision if he was really grieved by it. It seems significant that on both the occasions Bāṇa depicts Harsha as suffering great mental torture but only in silence, which in the circumstances could have actually been taken for a tacit acceptance of the offer. Harsha, who had listened in silence to his elder brother's earlier declaration regarding his giving up the succession, is shown protesting loud on this occasion at not being allowed to join the campaign. Rājyavardhana, thereupon, consoled him by saying :

[16] *Ibid.*, p. 170.
[17] *Ibid.*, p. 175.

> Why thus, dear brother, by putting forth too great an effort add importance to a foe too slight for our power ? A concourse of lions in the matter of a deer is too degrading. ... Moreover for the province of your prowess you have already the earth with her amulet wreath of eighteen continents. ... Only, in the unbearable hunger which has been aroused in me for our enemies' death, forgive this one unshared morsel of wrath.[18]

Having said this Rājya, on the same day (*tasminnevavāsare*), 'set out to seek the foe'.[19]

RĀJYAVARDHANA'S VICTORY OVER THE MĀLAVA KING AND HIS MURDER BY THE GAUḌA KING ŚAŚĀṄKA

After this we get only one more information about Rājyavardhana from the *Harshacharita*, and that concerns his facile victory over the Mālava king and his subsequent murder by the Gauḍa ruler. Actually, we have more than one version of this sad episode which essentially convey the same information but differ in details. In the *Harshacharita* we are told that 'many days having elapsed' (*atikrānteshubahushuvāsa-reshu*)[20] after the departure of Rājyavardhana for Kanauj, Harsha, who was having ominous dreams and evil portents 'announcing the death of no mean king', was brought the sad news by Kuntala, a chief officer of cavalry, that :

> his brother, though he had routed the Mālwa army with ridiculous ease, had been allured to confidence by false civilities on the part of the King of Gauḍa, and then weaponless, confiding, and alone, despatched in his own quarters.[21]

Bāṇa does not give the names of the Mālava and Gauḍa kings; even their friendship is not explicitly mentioned by him. But the fact that Rājyavardhana was murdered by the Gauḍa ruler immediately after the defeat of the Mālava king becomes explicable only on the assumption that both of them were friends and had invaded Kanauj jointly, through at the time of the defeat of the Mālava king, his Gauḍa ally was busy elsewhere and could come only when the Mālava king had been routed. Śaṅkara, the commentator of the *Harshacharita*, though by no means wholly reliable, for he was writing long after these events took place, gives us some additional details about this episode. He explains that :

[18] *Ibid.*, p. 176.

[19] *Ibid.*

[20] *Ibid.* According to Bühler, it means 'some months' (*EI*, I, p. 70, n. 12).

[21] *Ibid.*, p. 178. The word *svabhavana* (own quarters) is generally taken to mean the quarters of the Gauḍa rulcr. V.S. Agrawala, however, takes it to mean 'the quarters of Rājyavardhana himself ' (*Harshacharita : Eka Sāṁskṛtika Adhyayana*, Patna, 1953, p. 126). But the records of Harsha specifically state that Rājyavardhana was killed in the mansion of his foe.

> Śaśāṅka enticed Rājya-vardhana through a spy by the offer of his daughter's hand, and while the unlucky king with his retinue was participating in a dinner in his enemy's camp, he was killed by the Gauḍa king in disguise.[22]

The identity of the Mālava king is indicated by the copper plate inscriptions of Harsha which in an identical verse state :

> By whom, plying his whip in battle, the kings Devagupta and others—who resembled wicked horses—were all subdued with averted faces; who, after uprooting his enemies, after conquering the earth, and doing what was agreeable to his subjects, in consequence of his adherence to his promise gave up his life in the mansion of his foe.[23]

As suggested by Raychaudhuri, king Devagupta of these inscriptions should be identified with the Mālava ruler who, according to Bāṇa, was defeated by Rājyavardhana with 'ridiculous ease'. He was obviously some relation of Mahāsenagupta who had earlier succeeded in forcing the sons of Mahāsenagupta to seek asylum in Thanesar.

Another source on the murder of Rājyavardhana is Yuan Chwang. While referring to the dynasty of Harsha (which he wrongly places in Kanauj, probably because Kanauj was the capital of Harsha at the time of his visit), he says :

> During two generations there have been three kings. (*The king's*) father was called Po-lo-kie-lo-fa-t'an-na (Prabhākaravardhana); his elder brother's name was Rājyavardhana (Ho-lo-she fa-t'an-na).
>
> Rājyavardhana came to the throne as the elder brother, and ruled with virtue. At this time the king of Karṇasuvarṇa (Kie-lo-na-su-fa-la-na),—a kingdom of Eastern India—whose name was Śaśāṅgka (She-shang-kia), frequently addressed his ministers in these words : "If a frontier country has a virtuous ruler, this is the unhappiness of the (*mother*) kingdom." On this they asked the king to a conference and murdered him.[24]

A little later Yuan Chwang adds :

> The accumulated merit and the conspicuous virtue of the former king were so illustrious as to cause his kingdom to be most happily governed. When he was followed by Rājyavardhana we thought he would end his years (*as king*); but owing to the fault of his ministers, he was led to subject his person to the hand of his enemy, and the kingdom has suffered a great affliction; but it is the fault of your ministers.[25]

St. Julien's translation of this vital passage runs as follows :

> But by the incapacity of his (Rājyavardhana's) ministers he has gone and fallen under the sword of his enemy; that has been a great disgrace to the realm. It is we who are to blame.[26]

[22] Quoted in *The Classical Age*, Bombay, 1954, p. 122.

[23] *EI*, I, p. 74.

[24] S. Beal, *Si-Yü-Ki* or *Buddhist Records of the Western World*, I, Delhi, 1969, p. 210.

[25] *Ibid.*, p. 211.

[26] Quoted in Majumdar, R. C., *The History of Bengal*, I, p. 72, n. 3.

According to Devahuti, the phrase 'owing to the fault of his ministers' may also be interpreted as 'owing to a lack of virtue on the part of the ministers'.[27] If this meaning is accepted then we get the hint that Rājyavardhana's ministers had shown some dishonesty. In the *Life* the episode is narrated thus :

> At that time (*when Rājyavardhana was on the throne*) the king of Karṇa-suvarṇa, in Eastern India, whose name was Śaśāṅkarāja, hating the superior military talents of his king, made a plot and murdered him.[28]

The identity of the king who murdered Rājya with Śaśāṅka is probably indicated by Bāṇa also in the phrase suggestive of the rise of Śaśāṅka: "In the firmanent the rising clear-flecked moon shone like the pointed hump of Śiva's tame bull"[29] (*prakaṭakalaṅkudayamānaṁ.. akāśatākāśe śaśāṅka maṇḍalam*). Śaṅkara, the commentator of the *Harshacharita*, also says that Rājyavardhana was killed by Śaśāṅka, the king of Gauḍa (*Śaśāṅka nāmā Gauḍādhipaḥ*).[30]

From all these sources it is obvious that Rājyavardhana succeeded in defeating the Mālava king (Devagupta) but was himself murdered by the Gauḍa ruler (Śaśāṅka) treacherously. This basic assumption does not go against any of our sources. But when we examine 'The Rājyavardhana Murder Case' in depth, several problems arise and intriguing questions pose themselves.

QUESTION OF THE TREACHERY OF ŚAŚĀṄKA

Let us first take up the question of the treachery of Śaśāṅka. On the basis of the above accounts, historians are generally and rightly agreed that Śaśāṅka treacherously murdered Rājyavardhana. R. P.Chanda[31] was the first to challenge the accuracy of this view. He tried to give some reasons for the theory that Rājyavardhana was either defeated and taken prisoner by or surrendered to Śaśāṅka. R. D. Banerji and Majumdar[32] also supported Chanda. This view was, however, opposed by R.G. Basak[33] and D.C. Ganguli[34] who reiterated the theory of Śaśāṅka's treachery. R.C. Majumdar has specially laboured to prove that Śaśāṅka did not kill Rājyavardhana treacherously. He makes much of the minor discrepancies in the different accounts. According

[27] Devahuti, *op. cit.*, p. 84, n. 4.

[28] S. Beal, *The Life of Hiuen-Tsiang*, New Delhi, 1973, p. 83.

[29] *Ibid.*, p. 168. According to Bühler, in one manuscript of the *Harshacharita* the name of the Gauḍa ruler is given as Narendragupta (*EI*, I, p. 70). According to the *Āryamañjuśrīmūlakalpa*, Rājyavardhana was killed by a king of the Nagna caste. Both these statements are unsupported by contemporary evidence.

[30] *Gauḍarājamālā*, pp. 8 ff.

[31] Quoted by R.C. Majumdar in *The History of Bengal*, I, p. 73.

[32] Cf. *The History of Bengal*, I, pp. 71-76.

[33] R.G. Basak, *History of North-Eastern India*, Calcutta, 1934, p. 144.

[34] *IHQ*, XII, pp. 462 ff.

to him Bāṇa, Yuan Chwang and the epigraphs of Harsha, all present the side of Rājyavardhana and were hostile to Śaśāṅka. This attitude of scepticism while evaluating our ancient sources is praiseworthy, but to discard the evidence of several authorities which basically state the same thing, cannot be regarded as justified. Actually, our sources are not contradictory, rather they supplement or elaborate each other. The elements of discrepancy in them are of very insignificant nature. Even the testimony of Śaṅkara does not go against other sources; contrary to what Majumdar says neither there is anything 'impossible' in his version of the story nor is it inconsistent with other sources. We should remember that none of our sources suggest a 'war' between Rājya and Śaśāṅka. On the other hand Bāṇa, at another place, alludes to the treachery of Śaśāṅka. There he makes Harsha say :

> Except the Gauḍa king what man would by such a murder, abhorred by all the world, lay such a great soul low...when...he had laid his sword aside... With what design did this mean remorseless being bring my lord to his death, working his way like a worm into a sandal pillar capable of delighting a whole world ?[35]

At one other place also Bāṇa makes a veiled reference to Śaśāṅka's villainy by warning Harsha through his army commandant against the dangers of being too trustful.[36] Actually, the attempt of R. C. Majumdar and his supporters to justify the conduct of Śaśāṅka is unnecessary. For, as pointed out by Devahuti, "there is nothing particularly unusual or abhorrent, by standards accepted then as now, in plotting an enemy's death in war. Śaśāṅka appears to have been a practical, hard-headed man and may have felt that Rājya-vardhana, being the brother-in-law of the murdered king (that is, of Grahavarman), should be removed from the scene surreptitiously rather than in open combat, for almost certainly the Kanauj forces would have rallied round the Vardhana on the battlefield."[37]

HARSHA'S INVOLVEMENT IN THE MURDER OF RĀJYA

'The Rājyavardhana Murder Case' has another dimension as well. Despite the indubitable fact that Śaśāṅka was directly responsible for his murder, very strong indications are also available suggesting that Harsha was in some way implicated in it (or at least it was then believed that he was implicated in the conspiracy which led to the end of Rājyavardhana's life). The first scholar to make such a hint was R. C. Majumdar who, as early as 1943, in his anxiety to absolve Śaśāṅka of the charge of murdering the Pushyabhūti king treacherously, raised the finger of suspicion in the direction of Harsha's

[35] *HC*, Eng. tr., pp. 179-80.
[36] *Ibid.*, p. 192.
[37] Devahuti, *op. cit.*, p. 85.

ministers by pointing out that Yuan Chwang has explicitly stated that Rājyavardhana was exposed to danger due to the 'fault' of Pushyabhūti ministers. Taking this testimony along with the fact that while Śaśāṅka and Harsha were Śaiva and Rājyavardhana a Buddhist, Majumdar posed the question: "who knows that Rājyavardhana's death was not similarly encompassed by his ministers with the help of Śaśāṅka who was known to be a great champion of orthodox faith ?"[38]

Then, in 1966, V. S. Pathak made the case against Harsha stronger by pointing out that the authors of the early medieval period, when confronted with the task of justifying the violation of the right of the elder brother to the ancestral throne by their patron kings, usually pleaded that (i) their patron was sent on the earth by some god to rule over the earth as a chakravartin; (ii) the father of their patron wished to give the ancestral throne to the younger son because he was abler and worthier; and (iii) the elder brother was not competent (or was disinclined) to rule. Now, as Rājyavardhana was killed in suspicious circumstances and as Bāṇa has used all these motifs, it logically follows that some need was felt to justify Harsha's rise to power for which Bāṇa was asked to compose his *Harshacharita*.

The suspicion of Harsha's complicity in the murder of Rājya was made stronger by Devahuti who, writing in 1970, thus observed on the *Harshacharita* of Bāṇa :

> It is hard to escape the conclusion that the unusual twists in the story, from the time of Prabhākara-vardhana's illness to the time of Rājya-vardhana's death, however cleverly manipulated, were rendered inevitable because of some episode uncomplimentary to the author's hero. In spite of the speech attributed to Prabhākara-vardhana virtually bidding Harsha to succeed him, it is difficult to see why the king would want to suppress the rightful claim of his eldest son to the throne.[39]

Devahuti also raised some pertinent, but from the point of view of Harsha, awkward questions : Why did not Harsha make known to Rājya-vardhana, and to all witnesses present, his great mental anguish at being offered the throne which should fittingly have been occupied by his brother ? Why did he not reject the proposal even once, in an effort to persuade Rājya-vardhana to act in the traditional way ? On the other hand, why did he choose to speak out and protest at being left behind when his brother wished to set out for Kanauj with Bhaṇḍi and ten thousand cavalry to take revenge on the king of Mālava ? Did Harsha depend on the support of the key man Bhaṇḍi, whom he had been able to win over to his side after the king's death and before the return of his brother to the capital ? Was it the pressure of such a

[38] *The History of Bengal*, I, p. 76.

[39] Devahuti, *op. cit.*, p. 82.

situation that forced Rājya-vardhana to offer the throne to Harsha, perhaps with a view to seizing power for himself later ? Did Rājya-vardhana reckon that the sudden Kanauj episode provided him with an opportunity to change the situation in his own favour ? Was the decision to conduct the campaign on his own, and to take Bhaṇḍi and a body of picked soldiers with him, guided by such a motive ? It is not possible to answer these questions, but the fact that Bāṇa's narrative gives rise to them proves that a complex situation existed even if it remains obscure. In any case the problem was easily and summarily solved by Rājya-vardhana's early death in the Kanauj campaign. ... The suspicion, if warranted, attached to the circumstances in which he became king was both covered up and forgotten by several aiding factors, for instance the crowding of many events into a very short period, culminating in the speedy removal from the scene of the rival successor, in the most natural circumstances. For Hsüan-tsang, or the much later author of the *Mañju-śrī-mūla-kalpa*, no undignified situation may even have existed, so regular Harsha's succession seemed after the death of Rājya-vardhana,...[40]

The case against Harshavardhana has been made almost airtight by S. R. Goyal.[41] Writing in 1986 he pointed out that Bāṇa not only uses the above-mentioned motifs to which Pathak has directed our attention, but from several other motifs used by him it seems that his avowed purpose was to show that it was Harsha not Rājya who was born to rule as a chakravartin. That is why (1) he tells us that the behaviour of Yaśomatī, when she was pregnant with Harsha, showed that the child in her womb was destined to be a chakravartin ruler. (2) On the birth of Harsha he makes an astrologer tell Prabhākara that the child shall be a coryphaeus of the Seven Emperors and bearer of Seven Imperial Signs. (3) He does not mention that Rājya was ever made the Crown Prince. (4) He also omits to mention that Rājya ascended the throne though Yuan Chwang, the inscriptions of Harsha and the *Āryamañjuśrīmūlakalpa* testify to it. On the contrary he describes the events in such a way which leaves no time at all for the coronation of Rājyavardhana. (5) Harsha is shown as keeping silence when on two occasions Prabhākara asked him to ascend the throne. According to Bāṇa, at that time Harsha felt great mental anguish but did not say a single word. Similarly, he did not say a single word when Rājya asked him to accept the family sovereignty though he is said to have suffered great mental anguish at that time also. The question arises how did Bāṇa, who wrote his *Harshacharita* after a gap of more than 15 years at least, know what Harsha was thinking on these occasions, S. R. Goyal pertinently asks. If these scenes

[40] *Ibid.*, pp. 82-83.
[41] S.R. Goyal, *Harsha Śīlāditya*, Ch. 4.

represent the factual situation, then to the courtiers and to all those present it would had appeared that Harsha had been offered the crown by both Prabhākara and, Rājya and he had accepted their offers, atleast tacitly. (6) Subsequently also, Bāṇa tries to prove that Harsha was born to be a chakravartin. In ancient India, Goyal points out, the symbols of a chakravartin included *ekāvalī* (one-string necklace), an umbrella, a *mudrā*, etc. The motif of *ekāvalī* is brought in by Bāṇa when the Buddhist sage Divākaramitra presented the pearl-wreath Mandākinī to Harshavardhana which had earlier been with king Sātavāhana, the Lord of the Three Oceans. The motif of umbrella is introduced when Bhāskaravarman, the king of Kāmarūpa, is said to have sent to Harshavardhana the umbrella named Abhoga, which originally belonged to Varuṇa and was a symbol of universal sovereignty. But it is nothing more than a piece of Bāṇa's poetical fancy for, as pointed out by S. R. Goyal for the first time, Kalhaṇa informs us that Abhoga had returned to Kashmir in remote antiquity and from there Varuṇa had taken it back to his abode.[42] The motif of *mudrā* comes into the picture when at the beginning of his military campaign Harsha happened to drop the newly-made golden seal with the symbol of bull, the letters of which became distinctly marked on the dry soft earth as if to signify that the earth shall be stamped with the single seal of his sole command.[43] The use of all these motifs by Bāṇa tends to support the thesis of V.S. Pathak that the avowed purpose of Bāṇa was to justify the accession of Harsha.

BĀṆA'S EXPLICIT REFERENCE TO HARSHA'S COMPLICITY IN THE MURDER OF HIS ELDER BROTHER

S. R. Goyal has also produced an extremely significant piece of evidence from the *Harshacharita* which indubitably proves that Harsha was accused, in his own days, of complicity in the murder of Rājya. In the Seventh Chapter of his *Harshacharita* Bāṇa casually mentions that "Like the Lord of the Immortals, he (that is, Harsha) appeared busy in wiping away the stain of his elder brother's slaughter" (*Amarapatirivāgrajaba-dhakalaṅkaprakshā-lanākulaḥ*).[44] Now, it is a very important statement, for according to Indian mythology Indra had committed the crime of killing Viśvarūpa, the three-headed son of Tvashṭṛ, who was in a sense his *agraja*. Therefore, it was said that Indra had committed the crime of killing his elder brother. Now, if according to Bāṇa Harsha was busy, like Indra, in wiping away the stain of his elder brother's murder then it can only mean that during the reign of Harsha rumours were afloat that he was implicated in the murder of Rājya. Thus, the theory adumberated by Majumdar

42 *Rājataraṅgiṇī*, III. 49-62.

43 *HC*, p. 198.

44 *Ibid.*, p. 204.

in 1943 that in some way the ministers of the Pushyabhūti dynasty belonging to the side of Harsha might have collaborated with Śaśāṅka in the murder of Rājya has now become an almost airtight case, certainly much more than a merely *prima facie* case, against Harsha, the above-mentioned statement of Bāṇa quoted by S. R. Goyal providing clinching evidence for it.

Of course in the present state of our knowledge it is impossible to identify the connecting link between the murder conspiracy and Harsha. But it may be hazarded that probably Bhaṇḍi was such a link. Obviously Harsha depended upon him quite heavily. It was probably the reason why Rājyavardhana, wishing to keep him before his own eyes, forced him to accompany him in the Mālava campaign. Bhaṇḍi, therefore, was most likely one of those ministers to whose 'fault' (or lack of virtue, or lack of honesty) Yuan Chwang has pointed out. It is quite significant that Harsha did not even rebuke Bhaṇḍi for his incompetence when the latter described the events leading to Rājyavardhana's death. In this connection it may also be noted that no fight at all is known to have taken place between Śaśāṅka and Harsha for a long while. No change in the political scenerio will be needed if one assumes that Bāṇa's denunciation of Śaśāṅka was for the sake of appearances only. Otherwise Harsha's revenge on Śaśāṅka should have formed the most important chapter of his *Harshacharita*.[45]

[45] It is also possible that Bāṇa did not have any first hand information about the murder of Rājya. He heard the rumours about it like others to counteract which he was asked to compose his work. What was he told by Harsha is anybody's guess. But it is obvious that Harsha himself could have hardly confessed his guilt to Bāṇa.

THIRTEEN

Yuan Chwang's India and Harsha's Empire

THE PROBLEM

The general description of India and its parts as provided by the Chinese pilgrim Yuan Chwang is obviously related to the question of the extent of the empire of Harsha. As a result, we feel, an analysis of both these issues seems to be inevitable. As is well known, in the beginning of the Indological studies historians generally believed that the empire of Harsha included almost the whole of north India. When the study of Indian history was in its infancy, and people were not critical of the meagre contemporary data available on ancient Indian history, scholars readily accepted the vague statements of Yuan Chwang and Bāṇa regarding the extent of Harsha's empire and also his mention as Sakalottarāpatheśvara, and pictured him as a great monarch and the last great empire-builder of Hindu India. According to V.A. Smith, in the later years of his reign Harsha ruled "over the whole of the basin of the Ganges (including Nepāl), from the Himalaya to the Narmadā."[1] His hold over Mālwā, Gujarat and Saurāshṭra "was undisputed", and "even the king of distant Assam (Kāmarūpa) in the east obeyed the orders of his suzerain (Harsha) whose son-in-law, the king of Valabhī in the extreme west attended in the imperial train."[2] Smith was supported by K.M. Panikkar[3] and M. L. Ettinghausen.[4] R. K. Mookerji took a cautious stand on this question and opined that Harsha's sphere of authority was, of course, "less extensive than the sphere of influence or suzerainty."[5] He was conscious of the difference in his treatment between sphere of

[1] V. A. Smith, *The Early History of India*, 4th edn., Oxford, 1924, p. 354.
[2] *Ibid.*
[3] K. M. Panikkar, *Śrī Harsha of Kanauj*, Bombay, 1922, p. 22.
[4] M. L. Ettinghausen, *Harṣa Vardhana, Empereur et Poète, etc.*, London, 1906.
[5] R. K. Mookerji, *Harsha*, London, 1926, p. 37.

authority and sphere of influence saying that in the records of the times, direct rule is sometimes confused with the power and authority indirectly exercised. He ends his survey of Harsha's empire with a conclusion that "it was undoubtedly much larger than that of any other individual state of the times in northern India", that "it comprised practically the whole of the United Provinces (present Uttar Pradesh and Uttaranchal), a larger part of Bihar and Bengal (with the exception of only Karṇasuvarṇa), Orissa, and such parts of the Punjāb, Rājpūtānā, central and western India, for which Yuan Chwang does not mention any other rulers"[6] and that "Harṣa achieved the proud position of being the paramount sovereign of the whole of northern India." He tried to find support for his view from references to Harsha in south Indian inscriptions as "the Lord of the Whole Uttarāpatha". He accepted this as Harsha's estimate in the 'public opinion' of that time. According to C. V. Vaidya also, Harsha's empire, "included probably the whole of northern India exclusive of Sind, the Punjab and Kashmir," over which he could establish only nominal suzerainty.[7] N. R. Ray also opined that Harsha's political supremacy extended over almost the whole of northern India, upto Jālandhara in the north-west and touched the Brahmaputra valley in the east. In the south it extended from the kingdom of Valabhī to Ganjam district in Orissa.[8] The view that Harsha was the lord of almost the whole of north India is held even now by several scholars. For example, after his survey of the conquests of Harsha, B.N. Sharma concludes that "I find that Harṣa was certainly the paramount ruler of the entire north who ruled over the greatest empire of his times. His empire included the territories of Kashmīr and Nepāl in the north, and it touched the Narmadā as its southern border. In the north-west it touched major portions of Punjab and Sindh and in the west it touched the Bharoach coast and the Arabian sea. In the north-east his suzerainty was acknowledged as far as the Brahmaputra valley and in the east his empire included Bengal. In the south-east the whole of Orissa was within the limits of his domain and it touched the Bay of Bengal. And thus his claim to the status of an emperor having sway over the entire northern India appears well-founded."[9] D. Devahuti is not so liberal in her estimate of the extent of the empire of Harsha but she also believes that in it were included the regions to the east of the Indus and the Satluj, to the north of Narmadā, to the south of the Himalayas and that it also comprised Bengal and Orissa. Kāmarūpa, Kashmir, Gujarat and Malwa were included within the sphere of his influence the degree of which varied

[6] *Ibid.*
[7] C. V. Vaidya, *History of Mediaeval Hindu India*, Vol. I, Poona, 1921, p. 11.
[8] *IHQ*, 1927, pp. 769-93.
[9] B. N. Sharma, *Harṣa and His Times*, Varanasi, 1970, p. 236.

in different regions.[10] According to R. S. Sharma, "his authority was limited to north India except Kashmir, Rajasthan, Punjab, Uttar Pradesh, Bihar and Orissa were under his direct control, but his sphere of influence spread over a much wider area. It seems that the peripheral states acknowledged his sovereignty."[11] Romila Thapar has also commented on this problem in her recent work stating that "in the course of the forty-one years that Harsha ruled, he included among his tributary rulers those of Jalandhar (in the Punjab), Kashmir, Nepal and Valabhi. Shashanka, ruling in the east, was hostile to him and Harsha was unable to extend his power into the Deccan."[12]

Here it may be recalled that N. R. Ray and some other scholars believe that Harsha also carried his victorious arms to the far south.

The view that Harsha ruled over almost the whole of north India was probably first opposed by R. C. Majumdar. As early as 1923[13] he opined that Harsha was the master of a much smaller empire which included only U.P., portions of eastern Punjab and Magadha. According to this view, "Harsha's domains were bounded by the Himalayas, the western Punjab, Rajputana, central India and Bengal."[14] As regards Orissa he, at that time, held that Harsha no doubt proceeded as far as Koṅgoda or Ganjam district, "but that does not mean that he conquered it permanently." Here Majumdar quoted Smith approvingly who also did not include Koṅgoda in the empire of Harsha.[15] In *The Classical Age*, however, he has included Orissa in the empire of Harsha.[16]

R. S. Tripathi dealt with this problem at great length in his *History of Kanauj*. In this work he advises that "it is high time to give up all the exaggerated notions of Harṣa's sovereignty or political jurisdiction extending upto Kashmir and Sindh, Gujarat and even the far south, Kāmarūpa (Assam) and Nepal."[17] The empire of Harsha in his view consisted of "portions of eastern Punjab, almost the whole of the present United Provinces (Uttar Pradesh excepting Mathurā and Matipura), Bihar, Bengal and Orissa including Koṅgoda or the Ganjam region."[18] Chatterjee also holds a similar

[10] D. Devahuti, *Harsha : A Political Study*, 2nd edn., New Delhi, 1983, Ch. 4 and the map given at the end of her work.

[11] R. S. Sharma, *Ancient India*, 5th repr., New Delhi, 1995, p. 171.

[12] Romila Thapar, *The Penguin History of Early India*, New Delhi, 2003, p. 289.

[13] *JBORS*, IX, Pts. iii and iv, reprinted in the *Readings in Political History of India*, ed. S. P. Gupta, Delhi, 1976, pp. 127-37.

[14] *Ibid.*, p. 133.

[15] *Ibid.*, p. 129.

[16] R. C. Majumdar, in *The Classical Age*, eds. R. C. Majumdar and A. D. Pusalker, Bombay, 1954, p. 112.

[17] R. S. Tripathi, *Hisory of Kanauj to the Moslem Conquest*, Delhi, 1959, p. 119.

[18] *Ibid.*, pp. 118-19.

view but adds that Harsha had his sway over Valabhī, eastern Mālava, western Mālava and Sindh also.[19]

SOME METHODOLOGICAL CONSIDERATIONS FOR DETERMINING THE EXTENT OF HARSHA'S EMPIRE

While discussing the extent of the empire of Harsha certain points should be kept in mind. Firstly, one should differentiate between the areas directly ruled by an emperor, areas rull led by kings who accepted his suzerainty (real or nominal), areas which were under his sphere of influence, areas which were independent but the rulers of which thought it prudent to maintain friendly relations with the emperor, and areas which were independent but were considered 'natural prey' to the ambition of the emperor. Most earlier scholars donot make such differentiation though, as noted, some historians have tried to distinguish between areas under Harsha's direct control and areas within the sphere of his influence. We, however, believe that in the age of feudal-federal polity the relationship of the imperial authority with the various regions was not only of two types—directly controlled regions and regions within the sphere of influence—it could be of several types, the quantum of hold exercised by the imperial authority on them differing from state to state. Secondly, we should remember that the nature of the relationship between the imperial authority and a particular state could undergo a subtle change without any formal recognition being accorded to that change. Initially, for example, two states could contract an alliance on the basis of equality but in course of time one of them could emerge as stronger, the other adjusting itself to the changed situation by making a show of respect to its former ally in a suitable manner (as happened with Harsha and Bhāskaravarman). Sometimes the changed relationship was accorded a formal recognition; sometimes no such recognition was deemed necessary. Such changes in the relationship of two powers could take place several times in long course of their relationship. Sometimes a small state, though formally independent, tolerated the arrogance and even plunder of its border areas by the more powerful neighbour without making any fuss over it (as Kashmir did in the tooth-relic incident). Such weaker states, quite independent for all practical purposes, may be included neither among the subordinate states and nor within the sphere of influence of the more powerful neighbour. S.R. Goyal calls them 'natural prey' of the more powerful neighbour.[20]

Here it may also be emphasised that we should not draw any specific

[19] G. S. Chatterji, *Harshavardhana*, 2nd edn., Allahabad, 1950, p. 169.

[20] S. R. Goyal, *Maukhari-Pushyabhūti-Chālukya Yuga*, Meerut, 1988, p. 241.

conclusion about the extent of empire of any ruler from such conventional phrases as "Sakalottarāpatheśvara", "Lord of the Four Oceans", "Trisamudrādhipati" (Lord of the Three Oceans), etc. For example, the description of Śaśāṅka as 'the lord of the entire earth bound by the four oceans' does not mean anything so far as the extent of his empire is concerned. Similarly, Harsha has been described as the lord of the entire Uttarāpatha not because he ruled over the entire north India but simply because the authors of the Chālukya records wanted to enhance the glory of Pulakeśin by claiming that he defeated even the lord of entire Uttarāpatha which in their eyes might have been a justifiable exaggeration because Harsha in fact was the most powerful ruler of the north. In the same category we can place the description of Harsha by Yuan Chwang as the "Lord of the Five Indies" because whether this term is taken in its wider sense or in the narrower sense Yuan Chwang has used it loosely. The evidences of such sources as the verse of Mayūra are too vague and hyperbolic to merit any serious consideration.

The meaning of the term 'five Indies' used by Yuan Chwang in connection with Harsha's conquests is somewhat problematical. In the general description of India he applies it to the whole sub-continent saying that "The countries embraced under this term of India are generally spoken of as the five Indies. ... on three sides it is bordered by the great sea; on the north it is backed by the Snowy Mountains."[21] As noted by T. Watters, other Chinese travellers too state that India had five main divisions, north, east, west, central, and south.[22] The indigenous sources, such as, the *Bhuvanakosha* section of the Purāṇas, divide the country into *madhyadeśa*, *udīchya*, *prāchya*, *dakshiṇāpatha*, and *aparānta*, sometimes adding to the list the Himalayan and Vindhyan regions also.[23] Therefore, the use of the term 'five Indies' by Yuan Chwang to denote the whole country was justified. But the pilgrim uses the term in a limited sense also. With reference to his account of Kanauj and Maharashtra he uses it to mean only the territory under Harsha's rule. In his description of Harsha's exploits as the king of Kanauj he states that after six years of warfare he subjugated the 'five Indies', and in describing the conflict between Harsha and Pulakeśin II of Maharashtra, he mentions that the former gathered troops from the 'five Indies'. According to Chatterji, one Chinese text has the variant 'five Gauḍas' for 'five Indias'.[24] Devahuti feels that "this reading fits the context perfectly.

[21] Samuel Beal, *Si-Yü-Ki* or *Buddhist Records of the Western World*, Book I, Delhi, 1969, p. 70.

[22] Thomas Watters, *On Yuan Chwang's Travels in India* (A.D. 629-646), Vol. I, Delhi, 1961, p. 140.

[23] D. C. Sircar, *Geography of Ancient and Medieval India*, Delhi, 1960, p. 73.

[24] Chatterji, *op.cit.*, p. 104.

There is both literary and epigraphic evidence to show that Gauḍa was used to denote *uttarā-patha*, the north, just as Draviḍa was used as a generic term for *dakshiṇā-patha*, the south, the Vindhyas dividing the two regions. The *Śabda-kalpa-druma* quotes stanzas from the *Skanda-Purāṇa* giving the five divisons of the south- and north-Indian brāhmaṇas, grouped respectively as *pañcha-Draviḍa* and *pañcha-Gauḍa*."[25] However, S. R. Goyal does not feel satisfied with this interpretation because at the time Yuan Chwang wrote that Harsha collected troops from the 'five Indias', he had not become the ruler of Orissa, one of the 'five Gauḍas'. He, therefore, believes that the Chinese pilgrim had used the term 'five Indias' and not 'five Gauḍas' and that too figuratively, depicting Harsha as a *chakravartin*. Yuan Chwang was too well aware of what it implied to have credited Harsha with actual dominion over the whole sub-continent. His statement about Harsha's rule over the 'five Indias' should be regarded as symbolic as Bāṇa's description of his patron as the "Lord of the Four Oceans" or of the "Four Quarters".[26]

But instead of depending on such vague references we should rely on the description by Yuan Chwang of the political condition of India as he found it in the last decades of Harsha's reign. But here also we should not be rigid in our interpretation. It is generally believed that those kingdoms whose rulers have not been mentioned by Yuan Chwang were included in the empire of Harshavardhana and those, whose rulers have been mentioned by him, were independent. But this criterion cannot be applied everywhere. For example, the pilgrim mentions the rulers of Mu-t'o-lo (Mathurā) and Mo-ti-pu-lo (Matipura, near Bijnor) though these could not have been independent kingdoms as they were situated in the vicinity of Kanauj. Actually Yuan Chwang describes the kingdoms of India not only by referring or not referring to their kings. Sometimes he mentions a kingdom and its ruler by name along with his dependencies, sometimes he gives the names of the dependencies but not of the king, sometimes he mentions the name of the kingdom along with the number of dependencies but does not give their names. As a matter of fact we should realise that he was not writing a political gazetteer of India following fixed rules for making entries in it; he was trying to give a general description of the country and has recorded the information which appeared to him interesting due to whatsoever reason. It may also be remembered that he could describe a dependent state in greater detail because it could be larger, more important and stronger than its neighbouring independent but much smaller and politically insignificant state.

[25] Devahuti, *op.cit.*, pp. 97-98.

[26] S.R. Goyal, *op.cit.*, p. 188; Shankar Goyal, *The Classical Age : A Study in Feudalization*, New Delhi, 2022, pp. 248-49.

GENERAL DESCRIPTION OF INDIA IN YUAN CHWANG

Let us now make a region-wise survey of the data provided by Yuan Chwang about the nature of Harsha's political relations with various states keeping in mind also his wars and conquests.[27] Here we should remember that, according to Yuan Chwang, the people of Yin-tu (the Chinese name for India) use local appellations for their respective countries, and he himself understands this to mean that the natives of India had only designations of their own states, such as, Magadha and Kauśāmbī, and that they were without a general name under which these could be included.[28] Yuan Chwang, of course, must have known that the people had a name for the whole country, such as, Jambudvīpa or Āryāvarta,[29] but he has obviously in mind the common people : that they had no sense of belonging to a country and so no need to use a name for it.[30]

KINGDOMS SITUATED TO THE NORTH-WEST OF MATHURĀ

Now let us move on to Yuan Chwang's description of India. He reached Kia-pi-shi (Kapiśā) in May 630. At that time Kapiśā was a strong and independent kingdom situated between the Hindukush and the Indus. It was then ruled by a Buddhist king of Kshatriya caste who every year made a silver figure of the Buddha eighteen feet high and convoked Mahāmoksha-parishad in which alms were given to the poor. His power extended over more than ten of the neighbouring lands.[31] Lan-po (Lamghan), Na-kie-lo-ho (Nagarahāra or Jalalabad), Kien-t'o-lo (Gandhāra) and Fa-la-na (Varana, identifiable with Bannu ?, Bolor ?) were also his dependencies.[32] Apparently, Kapiśā had nothing to do with Harsha. Similarly, the kingdom of U-chang-na (Udyāna) also, situated to the west of the Indus, had no political dealings with Kanauj.[33]

To the east of the Indus Kia-shi-mi-lo (Kashmir) was the first

[27] The following analysis about the nature of Harsha's political relations with various states is based on known facts as well as conclusions arrived at and suggestions made in our work *Harsha : A Multidisciplinary Political Study*, Jodhpur, 2006, Ch. 6. On this, also see Shankar Goyal, *The Significance of Yuan Chwang in the Context of the Seventh Century : A Critical Assessment*, New Delhi, 2018, pp. 14-20.

[28] *Travels*, I, pp. 131-32.

[29] Yuan Chwang himself mentions that the 'Brāhmaṇa' country (obviously a rendering of 'Brahmavarta') was a popular name for India (*Records*, I, p. 69; *Travels*, I, p. 140).

[30] J. S. Grewal, 'Hiuen Tsiang's India', in *India—Studies in the History of an Idea*, ed. Irfan Habib, New Delhi, 2005, p. 62.

[31] *Records*, I, pp. 54 ff.

[32] *Ibid.*, pp. 90-91, 98; II, p. 281.

[33] *Ibid.*, p. 119.

important kingdom. It had Ta-ch'a-shi-lo (Takshaśilā), Sang-ha-pu-lo (Siṁhapura), Wu-la-shi (Urasa, modern Hazara), Pun-nu-ts'o (Punch) and Ho-lo-she-pu-lo (Rājapurī or Rajori) as its dependencies.[34] It was an independent kingdom but weaker than that of Harsha, and was, therefore, his 'natural prey'.

In the Punjab, Tsch-ka or Cheh-ka (Ṭakka) was the largest kingdom situated between the Indus and the Beas with its capital near Śākala.[35] It had two dependencies—Mou-lo-san-pu (Multan ?) and Po-fa-ta (Parvata).[36] It was outside the pale of Harsha's authority.

Yuan Chwang mentions four kingdoms of the eastern Punjab and the hilly region situated to its north-east. They were Chi-na-po-ti (Chīnapati), She-lan-to-lo (Jālandhara), K'iu-lu-to (Kulūta) and She-to-t'u-lo (Śatadru).[37] He does not say anything about their political status. However, about Jālandhara he says that it was 'formerly' ruled by a Buddhist convert who was rewarded by the king of Mid India with the important office of the 'sole inspector of the affairs of religion (*the three gems*) throughout the five Indies'. This 'former king' may be identified with Wu-ti or Udita of Jālandhara, who was charged by a king of Mid India (identifiable with Harsha) to escort Yuan Chwang to the borders of India.[38] According to Devahuti, by his phrase 'former king' the pilgrim means that Wu-ti, at the time of his visit a royal official for the affairs of religion for the 'five Indias', had at one time been the independent king of Jālandhara.[39] And if Jālandhara had come under the suzerainty of Harsha, then the other three kingdoms might also have been forced to do so. But we cannot be certain of that.

Between Jālandhara and Mathurā were situated the kingdoms of Sa-t'a-ni-ssu-fa-lo (Sthāṇvīśvara) and Su-lo-k'in-na (Śrughna).[40] Yuan Chwang does not say anything about their rulers, though we know that Sthāṇvīśvara was the ancestral kingdom of Harsha. The hilly kingdoms of Po-lo-hih-mo-pu-lo (Brahmapura, in Kumaon-Garhwal region), Su-fa-la-na-kiu-ta-lo (Suvarṇagotra, to the north of Brahmapura) and Kiu-pi-shwang-na (Goviśaṇa, corresponding to Kashipur, Rampur and Pilibhit districts)[41] were neighbours of Śrughna. Yuan Chwang does not say anything about their rulers except about Suvarṇagotra which he describes as "the eastern

[34] *Ibid.*, pp. 136, 143, 147, 148, 163.
[35] *Ibid.*, p. 165.
[36] *Ibid.*, II, pp. 274-75.
[37] *Ibid.*, I, pp. 172, 175, 177, 178.
[38] S. Beal, *The Life of Hiuen-Tsiang*, New Delhi, 1973, pp. 189-90.
[39] Devahuti, *op.cit.*, p. 104.
[40] *Records*, I, pp. 183, 186.
[41] *Ibid.*, pp. 198, 199.

women's country" where husband of the queen was called a king but did not administer the government. The suzerainty of Harsha over these states, though quite likely, cannot be definitely proved.

U.P., BIHAR AND NEPAL

Now let us consider the kingdoms situated roughly in the present Uttar Pradesh (excluding Uttaranchal) and Bihar. They were Mu-t'o-lo (Mathurā), Mo-ti-pu-lo (Matipura, modern Madawar Near Bijnor in western Rohilkhand), O-hi-chi-ta-lo (Ahichchhatrā, Ramnagar in Bareilly district), Pi-lo-sha-na (Vīraśāṇa ?, identified with Atranjikhera, near Kanauj), Kie-pi-ta (Kapitha or Sānkāśya, modern Sankisa), Kie-jo-kio-she-kwo (Kanauj), O-yu-t'o (Ayodhyā), O-ye-mu-khie (Hayamukha, modern Daunḍiakhera on the banks of the Gaṅgā), Po-lo-ye-kia (Prayāga), Kiao-shang-mi (Kauśāmbī), Pi-so-kia (Viśoka or Vaiśaka, not yet identified), Shi-lo-fu-shi-ti (Śrāvastī), Kie-pi-lo-fa-su-tu (Kapilavastu), Lan-mo (Rāma or Rāmagrāma), Kie-shi-na-kie-lo (Kuśīnagara), P'o-lo-ni-sse (Vārāṇasī), Chen-chu (not yet identified, but possibly Ghazipur), Fei-she-li (Vaiśālī), Fo-li-shi (Vṛjji)[42] and Mo-kie-t'o (Magadha).[43] In the north of Uttar Pradesh and Bihar was the kingdom of Ni-po-lo (Nepal).[44] Yuan Chwang does not mention the rulers of these kingdoms except those of Matipura, Mathurā, Kānyakubja, Kapilavastu, Magadha and Nepal. The king of Matipura was a Śūdra by caste who did not believe in Buddhism and worshipped the *devas* (i.e., the Hindu deities). Mathurā is said to have been governed by a Buddhist king who, with his ministers, applied himself to religious duties with zeal. The kings of Matipura and Mathurā, because of the close proximity of their kingdoms to Sthāṇvīśvara and Kanauj, must have been the feudatories of Harsha. Kanauj was the capital of Harsha himself. In Kapilavastu there was no sovereign, each city had its own chief. As regards Nepal and Magadha we find that Harsha had no jurisdiction over Nepal while Magadha was conquered by him shortly before 637 A.D.

BENGAL, ASSAM AND ORISSA

In the eastern direction, between Magadha and Assam, Yuan Chwang places the kingdoms of I-lan-na-po-fa-to (Hiraṇyaparvata, identified with modern Munghyr), Chen-po (Champā, modern Bhagalpur), Kie-chu-hoh-khi-lo or Kiu-chu-wen (Kajaṅgala or Kajughira, modern Rajmahal), Pun-na-fa-t'an-na (Puṇḍravardhana, modern Pabna), San-mo-ta-th'a (Samataṭa), Tan-mo-li-ti (Tāmralipti, modern Tamluk) and Kie-lo-na-su-fa-la-na (Karṇasuvarṇa,

[42] *Ibid.*, I, pp. 179-240; II, pp. 1-80.

[43] *Ibid.*, II, pp. 82-185.

[44] *Ibid.*, pp. 80-82.

corresponding to Burdwan, Birbhum and Murshidabad).[45] To their east was situated the kingdom of Kia-mo-lu-pọ (Kāmarūpa) ruled byKumārarāja. About Hiraṇyaparvata the pilgrim informs us that "in recent times the king of a neighbouring state had deposed its ruler and given the capital to the Buddhist brethren." This king of the neighbouring state might have been Harsha. No king of Champā is mentioned by Yuan Chwang and about Kajaṅgala he tells us that the native dynasty had been extinguished centuries before his arrival and the capital was deserted. So, king Śīlāditya, during his progress to 'East India', held his court there in temporary grass huts which were burnt when he left the place. As regards Puṇḍravardhana, Samataṭa, Tāmralipti and Karṇasuvarṇa the pilgrim reports that shortly before his visit they were ruled by Śaśāṅka. But after his death, sometime between 619 and 637, these regions came under the suzerainty of Harsha and Bhāskara; probably they divided the Bengal regions of Śaśāṅka's empire among themselves as they were won as a result of their joint campaign. The occupation of Karṇasuvarṇa by Bhāskara evidenced by his Nidhanpur plates could have taken place only after the fall of Śaśāṅka while there is no reason to presume that it took place after the death of Harsha. The fact that when Bhāskara came with Yuan Chwang to meet Harsha he brought a large force with him, including twenty thousand elephants and thirty thousand ships, also tends to suggest that Bhāskara was in control of large tracts of Bengal.

To the south of modern Bengal were situated the kingdoms of U-ch'a or Wu-t'u (Oḍra) and Kung-yü-t'o (Koṅgoda, modern Ganjam).[46] Yuan Chwang is silent about the governments of both but he testifies that Harsha conquered them towards the close of his reign, between 639 and 642.

MAHARASHTRA, GUJARAT AND CENTRAL INDIA

The strongest kingdom to the south-west of Kanauj was Mo-ha-la-ch'a or Maharashtra. It was ruled by Pulakeśin II. According to Yuan Chwang, Harsha had made vigorous efforts to conquer it but had not succeeded till 641 A.D.[47]

[45] *Ibid.*, II, pp. 186, 191, 193, 194, 199, 200, 201.

[46] *Ibid.*, II, pp. 204, 206.

[47] We believe that Harsha-Pulakeśin tussle was a long drawn affair. So far scholars have been assuming that Pulakeśin II had fought and defeated Harsha either between 610 and 612 or some time before 634, the date of the Aihole record. *But the struggle between these two great monarchs was going on even in 640 when Yuan Chwang visited Maharashtra.* His testimony proves that (1) the Harsha-Pulakeśin conflict recorded in the Aihole inscription was not decisive. (2) This struggle was a protracted one and was going on in 640, for in his record of the journey made in 640 Yuan Chwang explicitly says that at the time of his visit Harsha had 'not yet conquered' Pulakeśin. It, therefore, follows that the conflict which took place before 634 was only one of

On the western coast was the kingdom of Po-lu-kie-ch'o-po (Bhṛgukachchha or Bharuch), identifiable with the Gurjara kingdom of Lāṭa (south Gujarat) whose king Dadda II gave shelter to the king of Valabhī when the latter was invaded by Harsha. Therefore, there is no question of Lāṭa having been under Harsha's subordination. As regards Fa-li-pi (Valabhī), Yuan Chwang tells us that the reigning king T'u-lo-p'o-po-t'a (Dhruvabhaṭa or Dhruvapaṭa) was the nephew of Śīlāditya, the former king of Mālava, and the son-in-law of Śīlāditya of Kanauj. He participated in the religious assembly of Kanauj and quinquennial ceremony of Prayāga. Taking this information along with the evidence of the Gurjara records, we believe that Dhruvabhaṭa (Dhruvasena II of Valabhī records) was invaded by Harsha. He took shelter with Dadda II but later on thought it more prudent to accept the overlordship of Harsha. Harsha won him over by giving his daughter in marriage. Dhruvabhaṭa's status was not equal to that of Bhāskara, as he was not a Mahārājādhirāja and had to taste the might of Harsha, but being the ruler of a big and powerful kingdom and the son-in-law of the emperor his status could not have been very much low either. The fact that his successor Dharasena IV assumed imperial titles in 645-46 A. D., even when Harsha was alive, also shows that Harsha's influence on Valabhī was only nominal.

According to Nogāvā grants of Dhruvasena II, he was ruling over Mālavaka in 639-40. But in the same year Yuan Chwang describes Mo-la-p'o (identified with western Malwa) as an independent kingdom with some dependencies of its own. Probably a tussle for power was going on in that region in c. 640 A.D.

In central India, north of Narmadā, Yuan Chwang also describes three other kingdoms—Wu-shê-yen-na (Ujjain), Chi-ki-t'o or Chih-chi-t'o (Jijhauti ?[48] in Bundelkhand) and Mo-hi-ssu-fa-lo-pu-lo (Maheśvarapura, the region around Gwalior).[49] The rulers of these kingdoms were

---

the numerous battles fought by them. It is, thus, quite possible that the conflict between the two also occurred before the battle recorded in the Aihole *praśasti* of 634, for which no evidence is now available. This analysis renders the question of the date of the Harsha-Pulakeśin war mentioned in the Aihole *praśasti* quite irrelevant. We can safely say that the conflict recorded in the Aihole *praśasti* was in the nature of a battle, not of a war. That is, the Aihole *praśasti* records only one phase of the long-drawn war between Pulakeśin and Harsha, and not the whole war (Shankar Goyal, *Harsha : A Multidisciplinary Political Study*, pp. 203-08).

[48] As the name *Jijhauti* or *Jejākabhukti* probably came into existence in the post-Harsha period, this identification may not be correct. But this much is certain that Chih-chi-t'o was situated in the Bundelkhand region.

[49] *Records*, II, p. 271.

Brāhmaṇas—those of Ujjain and Maheśvarapura being non-Buddhists and that of Chih-chi-t'o a staunch Buddhist.

SINDH AND RAJASTHAN

Beyond Valabhī to its north was the kingdom of Sin-tu (Sindhu). According to Yuan Chwang, its king, who was of Śūdra caste, was a believer in Buddhism. He had under him three dependencies. The pilgrim does not give any indication of Harsha's suzerainty over it. As regards Bāṇa's statement that Harsha appropriated the fortune of its monarch, it probably refers to some clash in which Harsha's troops plundered the border areas of Sindh.

Now remains the region presently called Rajasthan situated to the north of Gujarat and Malwa, east of Sindh, west of U.P. and south of the Punjab. Yuan Chwang refers to only two kingdoms of this region—Kiu-che-lo[50] (Gurjara) ruled by a Buddhist king of Kshatriya caste and Po-li-ye-to-lo (Pāriyātra, identified with Bairat).[51] It was ruled by a Vaiśya king. He is described as brave, impetuous and warlike. In the *Harshacharita* Pāriyātra is mentioned as a kingdom which Harsha's feudatories wished to conquer. The Gurjara kingdom is generally identified with the Pratihāra kingdom of Mandor. But the Pratihāras of Mandor were Brāhmaṇas and they nowhere call themselves Gurjaras. S. R. Goyal has, therefore, identified the Kiu-che-lo of Yuan Chwang with the Chāpa kingdom of Bhinmal.[52]

FEUDAL NATURE OF POLITY MAKES THE DETERMINATION OF THE EXTENT OF HARSHA'S EMPIRE DIFFICULT

Now we are in a position to determine the extent of the empire of Harsha and the sphere of his influence by taking together the testimony of Yuan Chwang and other sources. First of all let us reiterate that we cannot proceed with the assumption that we should regard Harsha as the ruler of only those countries which are specifically mentioned by Yuan Chwang as under his suzerainty. If the description of Yuan Chwang is taken literally one must conclude, as Majumdar[53] has pointed out, that "Harshavardhana was merely the king of Kanauj", for the Chinese pilgrim does not name even one kingdom except Kanauj as subject to the Pushyabhūti authority. But such a conclusion will be against the known facts of Harsha's conquests as known from inscriptions and Yuan Chwang himself. According to Tripathi, therefore, it may be assumed that those territories of north India were included within the empire of Kanauj about the governments of which Yuan

[50] *Ibid.*, p. 269.
[51] *Ibid.*, I, p. 179.
[52] S.R. Goyal, *op.cit.*, p. 240.
[53] *JBORS*, 1923, p. 318.

Chwang maintains silence.[54] But this line of approach also creates difficulties, for Yuan Chwang mentions the kings of Mathurā (Mu-t'o-lo) and Matipura (Mo-ti-pu-lo) also who, if one follows the reasoning of Tripathi, must be placed beyond the sphere of Harsha's influence. But that is impossible. How could Harsha, the ruler of Thanesar and Kanauj, who carried his victorious arms in Orissa and Gujarat, leave Mathurā and Matipura, both situated in U.P. between Kanauj and Thanesar, as separate independent entities ? The testimony of Yuan Chwang, therefore, should not be analysed in this fashion. It must be kept in mind that he was not writing a political gazetteer. It must be realised that about various states he mentions only those facts which he thought were interesting or significant. But he has certainly not followed a set formula. Further, it must be remembered that in that age of feudal polity in which an emperor had his subordinate kings who in turn had their own feudatories, a feudatory of the emperor could be more important than an independent king. Yuan Chwang, therefore, could mention a feudatory king and omit to mention a minor ruler of an independent state. Hence we should determine the nature of Harsha's relations with any particular state by taking into consideration all the known facts about it.

CONCLUSION

Viewed thus the states of the age of Harsha as narrated by Yuan Chwang may be divided into the following categories :

(1) Those kingdoms about the rulers or administration of which Yuan Chwang is silent or we know from the other sources that they were included in Harsha's empire. They were: Thanesar, Śrughna, Brahmapura, Goviśaṇa, Ahichchhatrā, Vīraśāṇa, Sankisa, Kanauj, Ayodhyā, Daunḍiakhera, Prayāga, Kauśāmbī, Viśoka, Śrāvastī, Rāmagrāma, Kuśīnagara, Vārāṇasī, Vṛjji, Magadha, Hiraṇyaparvata, Champā, Kajaṅgala, Orissa and Ganjam. Among these may also be included Chīnapati, Śatadru and Kulūta, though there remains some element of doubt about their being under the suzerainty of Harsha. Many of the kingdoms of this category were conquered by Harsha quite late in his life.

(2) Jālandhara, Mathurā and Matipura, whose kings have been mentioned by Yuan Chwang, may have been under Harsha's control.

(3) Suvarṇagotra and Kapilavastu may have been independent, but it is more probable that they were under Harsha's suzerainty.

(4) Puṇḍravardhana, Samataṭa, Karṇasuvarṇa and Tāmralipti were conquered jointly by Harsha and Bhāskara from Śaśāṅka. Whether they were occupied by Bhāskara or Harsha is not definitely known. Probably the regions east of Gaṅgā were occupied by Bhāskara.

[54] Tripathi, *op.cit.*, p. 115.

(5) Ujjain, Mo-la-p'o, Chih-chi-t'o and Maheśvarapura, whose rulers are mentioned, might have been under some sort of Harsha's influence. It is only then that Harsha's war with Pulakeśin II on the banks of the Narmadā and Bāṇa's statement that Harsha's commands were obeyed in the Vindhya region, may become explicable. Even then Bāṇa's statement cannot be regarded as reflecting the situation prevailing in 606 A.D.

(6) Valabhī was practically independent but nominally under Harsha's suzerainty from the date of his Valabhī invasion till Dharasena IV assumed imperial titles in c. 645 A.D.

(7) King of Kāmarūpa was a friend of Harsha and fully independent though, in his later years, he must have become aware that he was not as powerful as the Kanauj monarch was.

(8) Sindh and Kashmir were independent but 'a natural prey' for Harsha.

(9) There is no evidence whatever that Nepal in the north and the Lāṭa kingdom of the south-west (Bhṛgukachchha) were under Harsha's suzerainty.

(10) Surrounded as it was by Malwa, Gujarat, Sindh, Punjab and Kanauj, Rajasthan, at least parts of it, must have been under some sort of influence of Harsha. The prevalence of the Harsha era in Rajasthan gives additional weight to this view.[55]

(11) Harsha tried to conquer Pulakeśin II but did not succeed.

(12) There is no evidence that Harsha carried his arms into the deep south.

Accordingly we can include in the empire of Harsha only Punjab (of the Indian Union), Haryana and U.P.[56] The kingdoms of Jālandhara, Matipura and Mathurā probably enjoyed more autonomy than other regions. Suvarṇagotra and Kapilavastu were also probably only under his nominal suzerainty. Magadha, parts of Bengal and Orissa were conquered by him in the last ten to fifteen years of his reign; among these Orissa was quite a late addition. In the east whether trans-Gaṅgā regions were occupied by him or by Bhāskara is difficult to say. Kāmarūpa was never under his suzerainty. The kingdoms of Rajasthan and the region between Yamunā and Narmadā were under his influence. Valabhī accepted his suzerainty but quite late in his reign and renounced it before his death. Kashmir and Sindh were his 'natural prey' but no more. He tried to conquer Maharashtra but did not

[55] D. C. Sircar, *The Guhilas of Kiṣkindhā*, Calcutta, 1965, p. 47. Sircar has prepared a list of sixteen inscriptions the dates of which may be referred to the Harsha era (excluding the charters of Harsha himself). Of them as many as nine belong to Rajasthan.

[56] Shankar Goyal, *The Classical Age*, p. 189.

succeed and the view that he invaded far south is baseless. These conclusions are significantly different from the conclusions of other scholars and we realize that in the case of several regions we have not been able to form a definite opinion. But in the present state of knowledge, we believe, this is the best one can do and a greater precision in our conclusions is not warranted by our sources.

FOURTEEN

On the Harsha-Pulakeśin II Struggle

One of the most important military adventures of Harshavardhana (606-46 A.D.) was against Pulakeśin II, the Chālukya emperor of Vātāpi. Pulakeśin II inherited the Chālukya kingdom in c. 610 A.D. after securing victory in a civil war against his uncle Maṅgaleśa. The civil war brought in its wake confusion and anarchy. But Pulakeśin soon mastered the situation and effectively established his power in the home provinces. Thereafter, he set out to conquer new territories. We learn from his Aihole inscription of 634 A.D. that in the south he succeeded in reducing the kingdoms of the Kadambas, the Gaṅgas, the Āḷūpas and the Mauryas, while further north he subdued the Lāṭas, the Mālavas, and the Gurjaras. These latter exploits brought him into conflict with Harsha. According to his Aihole *praśasti*:

> envious because his troops of mighty elephants were slain in war, Harsha, whose lotuses, which were his feet, were covered with the rays of jewels of the chiefs that were nourished by his immeasurable power... was caused by him (Pulakeśin) to have his (Harsha's) *harsha* (joy) melted away by fear.[1]

Also, according to the Nirpan,[2] Karnul,[3] and Togarchedu[4] grants of Pulakeśin's successors, their illustrious ancestor acquired the title *Parameśvara* after defeating Harsha, the lord of "the whole region of the north" (*Sakalottarāpatheśvara*).[5] The Chinese pilgrim has also left a record of this struggle. Writing about Maharashtra, which he visited in c. 640 A.D., and its ruler Pulakeśin II and his army, he says:

[1] *Epigraphia Indica*, VI, text of the Aihole *praśasti*, v. 23.
[2] *Indian Antiquary*, IX, pp. 124-25.
[3] *Ibid.*, XI, p. 66.
[4] *Ibid.*, VI, pp. 85 ff.
[5] *Uttarāpathādhipati* in the Nirpan grant.

> The king, in consequence of his possessing these men and elephants, treats his neighbours with contempt. He is of the Kshattriya caste, and his name is Pulakeśi (Pu-lo-ki-she). His plans and undertakings are wide-spread, and his beneficent actions are felt over a great distance. His subjects obey him with perfect submission.[6]

Then describing the attack of Harsha on Pulakeśin he records:

> At the present time Śīlāditya Mahārāja has conquered the nations from east to west, and carried his arms to remote districts, but the people of this country alone have not submitted to him. He has gathered troops from the five Indies, and summoned the best leaders from all countries, and himself gone at the head of his army to punish and subdue these people, but he has not yet conquered their troops.[7]

As regards the cause of the Harsha-Pulakeśin war, it is obvious that as both these monarchs were ambitious, sooner or later they were bound to come into conflict. Further, their interests clashed in Orissa, Central India and Gujarat. According to the Aihole inscription, Pulakeśin made the kings of Lāṭa, Mālava and Gurjara his feudatories[8] and Yuan Chwang says that before invading Pulakeśin Harsha conquered the eastern (Orissan) and western (obviously Gujarat) regions. Probably he wanted to make himself safe both on the eastern and western sides. But when he invaded the Maitrakas, Dadda II, the Gurjara king of Lāṭa, gave shelter to the Valabhī monarch. Later Harsha succeeded in contracting a matrimonial alliance with Dhruvasena II and in weaning him away from the Chālukya orbit. It is usually believed that the kings of Lāṭa, Mālava and Gurjara, who had been threatened by Prabhākaravardhana now made common cause against Harsha and sought the protection of Pulakeśin to thwart Pushyabhūti ambitions. Pulakeśin gave a willing ear to their appeal for succour,[9] leading to utter discomfiture of the Kanauj emperor.

The battle between Harsha and Pulakeśin recorded in the Aihole inscription seems to have been fought mainly with the help of their respective elephant forces. Yuan Chwang informs us that Pulakeśin possessed an excellent elephant-corps, and that the beasts were made drunk before being launched into the battlefield. On the other hand, we gather from Bāṇa that the elephant-corps was the strongest division of Harsha's army as well. The Aihole inscription also refers to Harsha's mighty elephants. This battle, therefore, may well have been one of the most memorable from the point

[6] Samuel Beal, *Si-Yü-Ki* or *Buddhist Records of the Western World*, II, reprinted, Delhi, 1969, p. 256.

[7] *Ibid.*, pp. 256-57.

[8] Cf. R.C. Majumdar, ed., *The Classical Age*, Bombay, 1954, pp. 104-09; R.S. Tripathi, *History of Kanauj*, Banaraas, 1937, pp. 111-12.

[9] *Epigraphia Indica*, VI, pp. 9-10.

of view of the display of tactics in elephant warfare.[10] Most likely the battle took place somewhere on the banks of the Narmadā, for after narrating the defeat of Harsha in verse 22 of his inscription, in the verse 23 its author Ravikīrtti describes the sandy banks of the Narmadā and the Vindhya region. Here it may be noted that Bāṇa makes it clear that the whole of the Vindhya ranges were in atleast indirect possession of Harsha. We learn from the *Harshacharita* that when Harsha reached the Vindhyas in search of his sister Rājyaśrī, Nirghāta told him : "According to your command everyday a search is carried on by diligent messengers." This shows that Harsha's commands were carried out quite faithfully and loyally in the Vindhya region. Therefore, this region must have been within the sphere of Harsha's influence. (Incidentally it also shows that Rājyaśrī was recovered from the Vindhya region quite a while after 606 because in that year Harsha could have no authority there).

Be that as it may, Pulakeśin may well have encountered Harsha's armies on the banks of the Narmadā, but, as Vincent Smith says, 'The king of the Deccan guarded the passes on the Narmadā so effectually that Harsha was constrained to retire discomfited, and to accept that river as his frontier'.[11] Thus, in this particular battle Harsha was defeated. Pulakeśin's vast resources and military strength, the hazards of fighting on enemy soil in unfamiliar surroundings, and geographical factors such as the formidable Chālukya boundary of hilly forests and a wide river were probably the factors which led to Harsha's defeat.

The date of the Harsha-Pulakeśin struggle has been an issue of acute controversy. According to some scholars, including J.F. Fleet, R.K. Mookerji, K. C. Chattopadhyaya and K. V. Ramesh,[12] the battle recorded in the Aihole inscription was fought between 610 and 612. They argue that Pulakeśin II's Hyderabad grant of 612 A.D. informs us that he acquired the title of 'Parameśvara' 'by defeating hostile kings who had applied themselves (or, a hostile king who had applied himself) to the contest of a hundred battles' while the records of his successors state that he assumed this title after defeating Sakalottarāpatheśvara Harsha. It proves that Pulakeśin defeated Harsha before 612, the date of the Hyderabad grant. Secondly, they point out that, according to Yuan Chwang, after becoming king Harsha fought incessantly for six years and then reigned in peace for thirty years.

[10] D. Devahuti, *Harsha : A Political Study*, 2nd edn., Oxford, 1983, p. 109.

[11] V.A. Smith, *Early History of India*, 4th edn., Oxford, 1924, p. 353.

[12] J.F. Fleet, *Dynasties of the Kanarese Districts*, p. 351, n. 4; R.K. Mookerji, *Harsha*, London, 1926, p. 36; K.C. Chattopadhyaya, in *Proceedings of the Indian History Congress*, III, pp. 586 ff.; K.V. Ramesh, *Chālukyas of Vātāpi*, Delhi, 1984, pp. 74-75.

Therefore, he must have defeated Pulakeśin II before the end of his sixth year, that is 612 A.D.

But A.S. Altekar, R. S. Tripathi, G.S. Chatterji and D. Devahuti[13] place the Harsha-Pulakeśin war, *mutatis mutandis*, between 630 and 634. They argue that (1) if Pulakeśin had defeated Harsha before the Hyderabad grant was issued in 612 this fact would had been mentioned in this record. (2) It is impossible to believe that in that age of anarchical conditions and feudal polity Harsha could have reigned peacefully continuously for thirty years (612-642 A.D.). Chinese sources specifically mention that between 618 and 627 Śīlāditya fought wars on unprecedented scale. His Valabhī invasion also occurred during the reign of Dadda II, who began to rule in 629 A.D. (3) Harsha was not in a position to invade Pulakeśin before 612 A.D. He was himself occupied in making his position secure and establishing his authority in the recently acquired Maukhari domains (if he had indeed acquired them by that year). Similarly, Pulakeśin II, who ascended the throne in 610-11, could not defeat Harsha before 612. (4) The Harsha-Pulakeśin war was the result of the clash of their interests mainly in Gujarat and Malwa. Therefore, unless Harsha could subdue the Maitrakas of Valabhī he could not have thought of invading Maharashtra. (5) Pulakeśin's Lohner grant of 630 A.D. does not refer to his victory over Harsha. (6) It is possible that Pulakeśin adopted the title 'Parameśvara' after defeating his enemies like Ḡovinda and Āppāyika (mentioned in the Aihole *praśasti*) before 612, but his successors, wishing to attach it greater significance, claimed that he adopted it after defeating Harsha, the Lord Paramount of the Whole of North India. Their claims regarding Pulakeśin's adoption of the title 'Parameśvara' and the defeat of Harsha at the hands of Pulakeśin are both correct; only their causal relationship and chronological sequence are incorrect.

Many of these arguments of those who place the Harsha-Pulakeśin war between 630 and 634 may easily be explained away, separately. One can, for example, maintain that the non-mention of the defeat of Harsha in the Hyderabad grant, and also in the Lohner grant, does not prove anything; it is *argumentum ex-silentio.* It may also be argued that before 612 Harsha was not such a mighty ruler as to have deserved a specific mention in the Hyderabad grant. But taken together these arguments are quite strong and need serious consideration.

However, we can look at the problem of the date of the Harsha-

[13] A.S. Altekar, in *Annals of the Bhandarkar Oriental Research Institute*, XIII, pp. 300-06; R.S. Tripathi, *op.cit.*, pp. 124-29; G.S. Chatterji, *Harshavardhana* (in Hindi), 2nd edn., Allahabad, 1950, pp. 76-80; D.C. Sircar, in *The Classical Age, op.cit.*, p. 237; D. Devahuti, *op.cit.*, pp. 107-08.

Pulakeśin war from a different angle.[14] We believe that the Harsha-Pulakeśin tussle was a long drawn affair.[15] So far scholars have been assuming that Pulakeśin II had fought and defeated Harsha either between 610 and 612 or some time before 634, the date of the Aihole record.[16] *But the struggle between these two great monarchs was going on even in 640 when Yuan Chwang visited Maharashtra.* His testimony proves that (1) the Harsha-Pulakeśin conflict recorded in the Aihole inscription was not decisive. (2) This struggle was a protracted one and was going on in 640, for in his record of the journey made in 640 Yuan Chwang explicitly says that at the time of his visit Harsha had 'not yet conquered' Pulakeśin. It, therefore, follows that the conflict which took place before 634 was only one of the numerous battles fought by them. It is, thus, quite possible that the conflict between the two also occurred before the battle recorded in the Aihole *praśasti* of 634, for which no evidence is now available. This analysis renders the question of the date of the Harsha-Pulakeśin war mentioned in the Aihole *praśasti* quite irrelevant. We can safely say that the conflict recorded in the Aihole *praśasti* was in the nature of a battle, not of a war. That is, the Aihole *praśasti* records only one phase of the long-drawn war between Pulakeśin and Harsha, and not the whole war.

Here it may also be pointed out that the *Harshacharita* of Bāṇa does not mention the Harsha-Pulakeśin II struggle. It is consonant with our view that the *Harshacharita* was composed in c. 620 A.D. and that the Harsha-Pulakeśin tussle began after c. 620 and that it was a long drawn affair.[17]

[14] S.R. Goyal, *Harsha Śīlāditya*, Meerut, 1986, pp. 144 ff.

[15] Cf. Shankar Goyal, 'Harsha's Relations with Deccan and the Far South : Some Problems and Suggestions', in *Proceedings of the South Indian History Congress*, Twenty-Second Annual Session, Thiruvananthapuram, 2002, pp. 135-37; idem, *Harsha Revisited : A Re-interpretation of Existing Data*, New Delhi, 2018, Ch. 1; idem, *The Classical Age : A Study in Feudalization*, New Delhi, 2022, pp. 186-89.

[16] *Contra*, for example, Ranabir Chakravarti, *Exploring Early India*, New Delhi, 2017, pp. 319-20.

[17] Regarding the suggestion that the *Harshacharita* was composed in c. 620 A.D., see Shankar Goyal, *History and Historiography of the Age of Harsha*, Jodhpur, 1992, pp. 61-67; idem, *Harsha : A Multidisciplinary Political Study*, Jodhpur, 2006, pp. 41-47; S.R. Goyal, *op.cit.*, Ch.1; idem, *Harsha and Buddhism*, Meerut, 1986, App.1, pp. 143-49; also see, Romila Thapar, *The Past Before Us : Historical Traditions of Early North India*, New Delhi, 2013, pp. 479 ff.

FIFTEEN

Harsha's Place in History

WAS HARSHA THE LAST GREAT EMPEROR OF HINDU INDIA ?

The question of Harsha's place in history is extremely controversial. It is usually believed that he was the first great conqueror to establish a large empire in the post-Gupta period and was the last great emperor of Hindu India. According to Devahuti, "Harsha had the difficult task of building up another empire almost a century after the beginning of the decline of the previous one."[1] From this statement it seems that no empire was established in the period which intervened the decline of the Guptas and the rise of Harsha. But this view completely overlooks the empire-building achievements of the Aulikaras of Daśapura who ruled from the Arabian Sea in the west to the river Lauhitya in the east and from Kashmir in the north to the Mt. Mahendra in the south-east. The argument that their empire was a shortlived one would be irrelevant here, because it would also apply to the empire of Harsha which proved to be equally ephemeral. Then, there were the imperial Maukharis who dominated the north Indian political scene for over half a century. They fought the Āndhras of the south, the Gauḍas of the east, the Himalayan tribes in the north and the Hūṇas in the north-west. Actually Harsha, who somehow succeeded in acquiring the Kanauj throne after the murder of Grahavarman, was their political successor just as Chandragupta Maurya was the political heir of the Nandas and Pushyamitra Śuṅga was that of the Mauryas.

Equally untenable is the view that Harsha was the last great emperor of Hindu India. As pointed out by R.C. Majumdar long ago,[2] the empires of Lalitāditya Muktāpīḍa, Yaśovarman of Kanauj, Pāla emperors Dharmapāla

[1] D. Devahuti, *Harsha : A Political Study*, New Delhi, edn. 1983, p. 268.

[2] *JBORS*, IX, Pts. iii and iv and *IHQ*, V, June 1929, both reprinted in S. P. Gupta ed., *Readings in Political History of India*, Delhi, 1976, pp. 127-42.

and Devapāla, Pratihāra emperors Mihirabhoja and Mahendrapāla, etc. were much more extensive and some of them much more stable. From the testimony of Kalhaṇa it is evident that Lalitāditya conquered more territories than Harsha. Yaśovarman also ruled over a much larger empire than was enjoyed by Harsha. Dharmapāla's empire as described in the verse 12 of the Khalimpur plates was also no less extensive than that of Harsha. The boundaries of the empire of Mahendrapāla, according to the most reliable evidences of epigraphs, were formed by Kathiawar, Karnal and northern Bengal. Besides, whereas Harsha's empire rose and fell with him, the Pratihāra empire continued for several generations. The achievements of Harsha look bigger because we have more detailed sources for him the study of which creates a false impression about his importance.

FACTORS AND FORCES IN THE FAILURE OF HARSHA IN IMPARTING STABILITY TO HIS EMPIRE

Harsha ruled for forty years or slightly more (from 606 to 646 or 647 A.D.). In this period he expanded his paternal kingdom into a respectable empire which earned him the title *Sakalottarāpatheśvara* even from his rivals. But with his death his empire collapsed like a house of cards. Pt. K. C. Chattopadhyaya has opined that as Harsha died a 'premature' death he could not provide stability to his empire. But if a king dies after ruling for more than forty years his death cannot be called 'premature' by any standard. He apparently had sufficient time to evolve an administrative structure which could sustain the stresses and strains of adverse circumstances. But he did not or could not do so. After initial years of his reign he had no internal problems, did not have to contend with any political rival after the death of Śaśāṅka and did not have to deal with foreign invasions from the north-west or from the south (his war against Pulakeśin II was of his own seeking). Therefore, his failure to evolve an infrastructure which could provide permanency to his imperial edifice is rather strange. No scholar, except S.R. Goyal,[3] has raised this problem and tried to solve it.

Harsha probably died without leaving a son; atleast our records do not refer to any son of his; rather by referring to A-lo-na-shun, one of his ministers or courtiers as his successor, they indicate that Harsha might have left no male issue. Further, even if he did leave a male issue in 646 A.D. he could not have been more than twenty years old for Harsha himself was a celibate till c. 625 A.D. But if an empire collapses because its ruler dies without leaving a male heir, then the political system of the empire will have to be regarded as faulty. It is true that in such a situation problems do arise.

[3] S. R. Goyal, *Maukhari-Pushyabhūti-Chālukya Yuga*, Meerut, 1988, pp. 365-72.

But a good political structure is expected to sustain the shock of such problems. When Alexander died there was no effective male issue in his line. But his empire did not collapse with his death; his commanders became his successors. Alexander's policy of founding Hellenic cities, establishing Greek colonies in Asiatic provinces, encouraging marriages between Greeks and non-Greeks and his satrapal system proved quite effective in keeping his Asiatic empire almost intact. Harsha is not known to have evolved devices of any kind to make the foundations of his empire strong.

The early medieval Indian kingdoms were usually tribal in character. The kingdoms of the Chālukyas, Guhilas, etc. drew sustenance from their respective tribes. But Harsha did not belong to a tribe; he belonged to a *varṇa*, and that too Vaiśya *varṇa*, which had no political experience, ambitions and future. Therefore, even if Harsha left any brother or cousin whose accession was contested by his other relations or by his ministers like Aruṇāśva, that successor must have found to his dismay that he did not have any tribal base to fall back upon.

Then, Harsha was born and brought up in the atmosphere of the Chakravartin ideal based on the concept of *dharmavijaya.* It encouraged feudalization of the state apparatus. But Harsha did not have the foresight of a Samudragupta to follow this policy only sparingly in distant provinces, keeping the central regions under his direct control. He left even Matipura and Mathurā, situated near Kaṇauj itself, under almost independent kings. The threat of Bhāskara to Śīlabhadra that he would 'trample to the very dust that monastery of Nālandā' when Harsha was at the height of his glory, shows that even on Magadha his hold was not very firm.

Harsha rarely lived in his capital city, that is Kanauj. He used to roam from one region to another either to wage wars or on some other business. Both Yuan Chwang and Bāṇa refer to his tours and temporary pavilions made of grass for his stay. Apart from Thanesar (his original capital) and Kanauj (his later capital) he is known to have gone to the Aṭavi region of the Vindhyas (in search of Rājyaśrī), on military expeditions against Sindh and 'snow bound hilly region', Maṇitāra (on the banks of Ajirāvatī, where Bāṇa met him), Kapitthika (from where Madhuban charter was issued), Vardhamānakoṭi (from where Banskhera charter was issued), Gauḍa (where he defeated Śaśāṅka), Gujarat (when he invaded the king of Valabhī), the frontier of Kashmir (where he appropriated the tooth-relic), Orissa (to conquer which he went personally), Kajaṅgala (where he first met Yuan Chwang), the border of Maharashtra (where he went at least twice in his effort to defeat Pulakeśin), Magadha (where he got vihāras and statues constructed), and Prayāga (where he went at least six times for his quinquennial assemblies of charities). And these are only his known journeys; he must have visited numerous other places during his long reign of forty years. As, according to Bāṇa, his army covered eight *krośas* (about nine miles) in one day and, according to Yuan Chwang, he took 90 days to reach Kanauj from Kajaṅgala, and as on many occasions he stayed for some months at some places (for example, he stayed at least for 75 days at Prayāga during his sixth quinquennial assembly), and as his military campaigns must also have been time-consuming, it must be conceded that he used to remain outside the capital for the greater part of the year. No wonder if his administration became slack.

Harsha's empire could never become economically viable. In his age charity (*dāna*) was regarded as a great virtue, but Harsha carried it to the extreme. According to Yuan Chwang, the personal income of the king was mostly used in charities, religious activities and in giving help to the meritorious and religious institutions. The same must have been the case with the state income. Harsha gave immense wealth to the Brāhmaṇas and Buddhist monasteries and spent a lot on construction work in temples and vihāras. The climax of his charities was of course *sarvasvamahādāna* at Prayāga which took place every fifth year. It is well to remember that all this was unproductive investment and Harsha is not known to have done anything for increasing agricultural or industrial productivity of his realm or helping the peasants, merchants, traders, etc. His charities must have increased the burden of the people enormously because what he spent on them from his treasury must have been replenished by additional taxes. How much careless he was to the cause of the peasants even during the march of his army has been vividly described by Bāṇa.

The military organisation of Harsha was feudal. He is said to have had a very large army but he had, if at all, only a small militia of his own; the rest of the army was composed of the feudal levies which must have been basically loyal to their respective lords. Therefore, the successor of Harsha (whosoever he was) must have found to his dismay that he had a very small army on which he could depend. If one compares the description of the gigantic army of Harsha which was in existence at least till 643 A.D., with the complete absence of any defensive system at the time of the invasion of Wang Hiuen-ts'e (who could boast to have conquered the successor of Harsha with only 7,000 Nepalese cavalry and 1,000 or 1,200 Tibetan infantry), he can describe the situation as only amazingly pathetic and can explain it only on the hypothesis that most of the units of the feudal militia which composed the army of Harsha, were taken back by their respective masters after the death of the emperor. If Harsha could not visualize such an eventuality, the fault was certainly his.

Then, there was no discipline in the army of Harsha. Its feudal atmosphere—*harems* of the emperor, vassal kings and feudal lords (which accompanied them to the battle front), their kitchens with every facility of tasty and rich food and the arrangement of all the articles needed for their luxurious living and the battery of servants and maid-servants which accompanied them—greatly hampered its mobility and marred its discipline.

Harsha did not take interest in the construction of forts also which were a must in that feudal age. Psychologically speaking, an emperor who lived in grass huts when on tours could hardly think of constructing forts at strategic points for the defence of the empire.

Harsha's short-sightedness is evident also from the fact that he hardly had any north-western or Himalayan policy worth its name. He made no attempts to increase his influence in the Indus region—the direction from which India was constantly invaded in the past. Appropriating the *lakshmī* (wealth) of the king of Sindh was a poor substitute for a scientific north-western policy. In the Himalayan region this was the age of kings Aṁśuvarman in Nepal and of Sroṅ-tsan-gam-po in Tibet who were introducing far-reaching changes in these countries. Even distant China was taking interest in them, the fruits of which were reaped by Wang Hiuen-ts'e. But Harsha, their immediate neighbour, did not take any cognizance of the developments taking place in these kingdoms.

HOW MUCH WAS HARSHA A SUCCESSFUL MONARCH ?

An accurate assessment of the achievements of a king is a difficult preposition. Scholars declare a king great sometimes for his military achievements but sometimes they give more weight to his literary or artistic attainments, religious policy, contribution to public welfare, his high moral character, etc. However, the office of a king is essentially political and, therefore, he should be evaluated as a political person first. S.R. Goyal[4] has suggested four tests for evaluating the achievements of a monarch :

1. What did he do to expand his kingdom ? (Keeping in mind his assets and difficulties both).

2. What did he do for the stability and consolidation of his kingdom ? (Here one should investigate whether he evolved or strengthened an administrative structure which could impart durability to his political edifice).

3. What did he do for the welfare of his subjects ?

4. And lastly, what were his personal attainments ? (This is the least important of these tests because if a king passes in the first three tests, he will be regarded as successful; otherwise his personal accomplishments of

[4] *Ibid.*, pp. 359 ff.; also see Shankar Goyal, *Recent Historiography of Ancient India*, Jodhpur, 1997, pp. 386-88; idem, 'S.R. Goyal's Appraisal of the History and Sources of the Gupta and post-Gupta Periods', in *Reconstructing Indian History for S.R. Goyal*, Vol. I, ed. Shankar Goyal, Jaipur, 2003, pp. 403-05.

even highest merit would be of no use for the state and society. Akbar, for example, though illiterate, should be declared successful from this angle because he created conditions in which arts and literature flourished while Bhoja Paramāra, himself a literary giant, would be regarded a failure as a king because his policies resulted in the loss of whatever he had inherited from his predecessors).

Now, let us assess the achievements of Harshavardhana on the basis of these four tests.[5] From the point of view of the first test Harsha was a great success, for he inherited a kingdom which was confined to the Śrīkaṇṭha *janapada*, with some influence over the neighbouring states. At the time of his accession he was over-burdened with difficulties, both internal as well as external. But in the four decades of his reign he made himself the greatest monarch of north India so much so that he could be described by the rival Chālukyas as *Sakalottarāpatheśvara*. By any standard it was no mean achievement. But from the point of view of the second test, he was an utter failure because he could not evolve an administrative structure which could impart even a semblance of stability to the imperial edifice he erected in his life time. With his death his empire immediately collapsed, like a house of cards—probably at a more swift pace. So far as the third test is concerned, Harsha is not known to have taken any pains for the welfare of his subjects, excepting of course giving regular charities, opening *puṇyaśālās* and the like. He must be praised for these activities but at the same time it must also be pointed out that he is not known to have taken any steps for the betterment of the condition of the peasantry, or for the improvement of trade, commerce, etc. On the other hand, his wars and religious policy proved to be a great burden on the people. His addiction to charities was an extremely poor substitute for the public welfare measures which he could but did not undertake.

That Harsha's personal accomplishments—our fourth test—were great, can hardly be doubted. Both Bāṇa and Yuan Chwang praise his personal qualities. Bāṇa virtually makes him an abode of all the qualities which our ancients sought in an ideal king and in an ideal hero of an epic. It may also be easily conceded that, according to our sources, he was not given to those vices which, according to the epigraphic records of Yaśodharman and the Maukharis, were commonly found in the monarchs of that age. His interest in performing arts is reflected by a reference to his *vīṇā*-playing in the *Harshacharita* and it is said that he authored three Sanskrit plays. I-tsing relates that Harsha versified his play *Nāgānanda* and had it set

[5] Shankar Goyal, *Harsha : A Multidisciplinary Political Study*, Jodhpur, 2006, pp. 321-23; idem, *The Classical Age : A Study in Feudalization*, New Delhi, 2022, Ch. 8.

to music and had it performed. Probably he is the earliest royal author whose works have survived to this day (though it it also likely that they were composed by some ghost-writer, probably Bāṇa). Though he did not succeed in establishing an administrative organisation which could make his empire stable, but in his own way he did take deep interest in the administrative affairs of his realm. But from his activities it is also clear that he suffered from over-ambition; one may even say that he was power-hungry (as is indicated by his possible complicity in the murder of Rājya). He could also take undue advantage of his military superiority (as is evidenced by the Kashmir tooth-relic incident and by the fact that he forced Bhāskara to send the Chinese pilgrim to him), could enlist the support of writers like Bāṇa and/or Mayūra for propaganda on his behalf, and was greatly enamoured by foreign (Chinese) scholars. But these are all ordinary human failings.

Thus, the achievements of Harsha were mainly his personal achievements. He was undoubtedly an ambitious ruler. But he was only 'the child of his age' which was the age of transition dominated by feudal atmosphere; he had no capacity to change the direction of the tendencies of the period. Even Mohammad Tughluq, that crazy emperor of the Sultanate period, made several bold experiments in revenue system, coinage, location of the capital, etc. But Harsha was interested only in wars and charities, not in evolving a stable political structure or introducing innovative changes in economic and military organisation. The result was complete collapse of his empire as soon as he died. Instances of such complete collapse are not wholly unknown but they are not too many either. Harsha, therefore, cannot be regarded as a great monarch of India. He was, however, more fortunate than other rulers, for we have two detailed sources of information about him—Bāṇa and Yuan Chwang—which create a false impression in the minds of modern researchers that he himself was a great ruler—in the opinion of several historians the last great emperor of Hindu India. But actually in Indian history he cannot be put in the category of Mahāpadmananda, Chandragupta Maurya and Samudragupta. He was an important ruler only in comparison with the lesser monarchs of our country, such as Khāravela of Kaliṅga and Yaśodharman-Vishṇuvardhana of Malwa.

SIXTEEN

The Problem of Harsha Era

From the account of the Wang Hiuen-ts'e embassy,. however, it becomes certain that Harsha's death took place in or shortly before 648 A.D. (more likely in 646 or 647 A.D.). As he ascended the throne in 606 A.D., the initial year of the Harsha era, he ruled for forty years or a little more. But R. C. Majumdar[1] has doubted the almost unanimous view of scholars that Harsha founded an era the initial year of which was 606 A.D. D. C. Sircar,[2] D. Devahuti[3] and S.R. Goyal[4] have answered the doubts expressed by Majumdar. Here we propose to give a résumé of the arguments of both sides.

The view that Harsha founded an era the initial year of which was 606 A.D. rests on the testimony of Alberuni. Writing about India in the eleventh century Alberuni (Abū Raihān) states :

> ...people...have adopted...the eras of
> 1. Śrī Harsha
> 2. Vikramāditya
> 3. Śaka
> 4. Valabha and
> 5. Gupta
>
> ...His (i.e. Śrī Harsha's) era is used in Mathurā and the country of Kanoj. Between Śrī Harsha and Vikramāditya there is an interval of 400 years, as I have been told by the inhabitants of that region. However, in the Kashmirian calendar I have read that Śrī Harsha was 664 years later than Vikramāditya. In face of this discrepancy I am in perfect uncertainty. ...[5]

[1] R.C. Majumdar, in *IHQ*, XXVII, pp. 183 ff.; XXVIII, pp. 280 ff.

[2] D.C. Sircar, *IHQ*, XXVII, pp. 321 ff.; XXIX, pp. 72 ff.

[3] D. Devahuti, *Harsha : A Political Study*, edn. 1983, New Delhi, pp. 269-71.

[4] S.R. Goyal, *Maukhari-Pushyabhūti-Chālukya Yuga*, Meerut, 1988, pp. 338-44.

[5] *Alberuni's India*, trans. E.C. Sachau, II, London, 1888, p. 5.

Thus, relying on the Mathurā and Kanauj tradition, Alberuni places the commencement of the Harsha era 400 years before Vikramāditya, i.e. in 457 B.C. But he also notes that according to the Kashmir calendar, Harsha being '664 years later than Vikramāditya', the Harsha era should be placed in 606-07. A.D. Devahuti believes that "it was this era which was prevalent in al-Bīrūnī's time in Mathurā and Kanauj. It seems that the inhabitants of the region deliberately misguided the Muslim scholar in order to impress him with the antiquity of the era they used. ... His critical pen, however, has preserved for us the valuable information he got from the Kashmir Calendar that 'Śrī Harsha was 664 years later than Vikramāditya'."[6]

Apart from Alberuni's testimony there are some other evidences regarding the start of Harsha's era as also of his reign from 606 A.D. Firstly, there is a large number of inscriptions which are found in various regions between Bihar in the east and Rajasthan and the Punjab in the west and bear dates in an era starting from an epoch about the beginning of the seventh century A.D. There is no satisfactory way of explaining the origin of this era except by supposing that its reckoning started from the accession of Harsha who held sway over the same area during that period. In this connection D.C. Sircar has referred to the following records : (1) Kot (old Bharatpur State) inscription of the year 48; (2) Dungarpur (Rajasthan) plates of Bhāvihita, dated year 48; (3) Shahpur (Patna District, Bihar) image inscription of the time of Ādityasena, dated year 66; (4) Dhulev (old Udaipur State) plate of Bhetti, dated year 73; (5) Dungarpur (Rajasthan) plates of Bābhaṭa, dated year 83; (6) Und (near Attock in West Pakistan) inscription of the year 158; (7) Tasai (former Alwar State, Rajasthan) inscription of the year 182; (8) Punjab inscription of the year 184; (9) Kaman (old Bharatpur State) inscription bearing dates ranging between the years 180 and 279; (10) Khandela (old Jaipur State) inscription of the year 201; (11) Udaipur Museum inscription of the year 207; (12) Khajuraho (old Chhatarpur State, Bundelkhand) inscription of the year 218; (13) Ahar (Bulandshahr District, U.P.) inscription containing dates ranging between the years 258 and 298; (14) Kaman (old Bharatpur State, Rajasthan) inscription of the year 263; (15) Pehoa (Karnal District, East Punjab) inscription of the year 276; and (16) Pinjaur (old Patiala State) inscription of the year 583. It may be noted that the prevalence of the era in the Punjab till the 12th century A.D. explains its appearance in the Kashmirian calendar about 1030 A.D. when Alberuni wrote his aforesaid work.[7]

Secondly, the fact that Harsha ascended the throne in 606 A.D. is also proved by the Chinese evidence. In the *Records* of Yuan Chwang it is

[6] D. Devahuti, *op. cit.*, p. 270.

[7] D.C. Sircar, *The Guhilas of Kiṣkindhā*, Calcutta, 1965, p. 47.

stated that "After six years he (Harsha) had subdued (or repulsed) the Five Indies. Having thus enlarged his territory, he increased his forces;... After thirty years his arms reposed,... ."[8] Now, Yuan Chwang has made this statement with the year 643 A.D. as his review-point of Harsha's career—the year when he took leave of Harsha. Thus, the determinant date at the other end of Harsha's career was obviously 606-07, the addition of 36 years to which would bring his history up to 643. Some scholars argue that according to the Chinese annals the death of Harsha took place in or shortly before 648 A.D. Therefore, it must be assumed that Harsha's accession took place in 648–36=612 A.D. It is further pointed out that in the *Life* Harsha is said to have told the Chinese pilgrim in 642 A.D. that he had been the lord of India for 'thirty years and more'.[9] It also suggests that he ascended the throne in 612 A.D. In order to reconcile this discrepancy (between the testimony of Alberuni suggesting 606 as the date of Harsha's accession and the Chinese testimony indicating 612 for this event) it is said that Harsha became the lord paramount of Kanauj in 612; it was in that year that he founded his era. But he counted it from 606 A.D. when he had ascended his paternal throne of Thanesar. But to us it seems that Yuan Chwang himself did not know the date of Harsha's death when he submitted his *Records* to the Chinese emperor in 648 A.D. He was using 643 A.D. as the review-point of Harsha's career and, therefore, there is no need for us to hypothesize that Harsha founded his era in 612 but counted it from 606 A.D. As regards the statement of Harsha made in 642 about the length of his reign, it may be noted that he gave Yuan Chwang the round figure 'thirty years and more', not an exact one. Even now people refer to such figures (say 34, 35, 36, etc.) in this fashion ('thirty years and more'—*tīsa se kuchha adhika sāla*).

Lastly, astronomical data provided by the *Harshacharita* helps us to determine the date of Harsha's birth in 590 A.D. All the circumstances of that period, which we have already discussed in detail, support the view that Harsha ascended the throne at an early age.[10] The Harsha era, beginning in 606 A.D., when Harsha would be only 16, is in accordance with this fact.

[8] S. Beal, *Si-Yü-Ki* or *Buddhist Records of the Western World*, II, Delhi, 1969, p. 213.

[9] S. Beal, *The Life of Hiuen-Tsiang*, New Delhi, 1973, p. 183.

[10] Vide, Shankar Goyal, *Harsha : A Multidisciplinary Political Study*, Jodhpur, 2006, pp. 161-62.

SEVENTEEN

Need of an Integral Approach to the Writing of Political History of South India

Since the beginning of the Indological studies in modern times history writing of ancient India proceeded on two tracks—first, the discovery, study and interpretation of the original sources and, second, the changing attitudes of the historians. From the point of view of their attitudes it is convenient to divide the historians who wrote before India became independent into two broad categories—those who directly or indirectly supported the British interests and those who opposed those interests. However, in recent years the Marxist view of history has also increasingly become popular in India and many works of singular importance have been produced on ancient Indian history by eminent Marxist historians. They have undoubtedly tended to enlarge the vision of our traditionalist historians. The Marxist approach to Indian history, however, often implies the application of modern criteria to ancient India. Though it has served as a corrective for the over-sentimentalized and over-spiritualized accounts of ancient India but, it is feared, it is tending to err in the opposite direction. D.D. Kosambi, a great Marxist historian, had himself protested that some of the so-called Marxists conveniently forget that Marxism is not a substitute for thinking but is a methodology of analysis and that their application of dialectical materialism to the interpretation of the history of India is grossly mechanical rather than critically discerning.[1]

However, restricting myself to the writing of political history in India one finds that till the 1960s it was dominated largely by the deeds and dates of kings with the result that in the age of mass democracy, in which we are living, it tended to loose its popularity. Actually, the most damaging criticism

[1] D.D. Kosambi, *An Introduction to the Study of Indian History*, Bombay, 1956, pp. 1-16.

levelled against the traditional form of political history in the West also has been that it is elitist in content, that it lays too much emphasis on kings and heroes, and that it pays too much attention to political events, military conquests and chronology. This criticism obviously could be levelled even with greater force against modern writings on ancient Indian political history, for these dealt with, till recently, nothing except chronology, wars and conquests of great kings and even now this tendency is quite dominant. But by the middle of the twentieth century voices began to be raised against this type of political history writing in India also. Among them those who raised their voices were not only Marxists but such scholars as well who gave emphasis on an integral view of history. Both of them realized the need of formulating a new approach to political history though their idea about this approach differed. The Seminar on the 'Problems of Historical Writing in India' organised by the India International Centre, New Delhi, in 1963, was one of the early attempts in this direction. In this Seminar many scholars of Marxist and non-Marxist persuation participated, though by that time the Marxist school had not acquired much popularity. Most of the participants in that Seminar, including Nurul Hasan, A.K. Narain, Romila Thapar, V.S. Pathak and T.V. Mahalingam, felt that political history should no longer be regarded as primarily chronological history of political events. Instead, it should be the history of the functioning of the centres of political authority with a view to discovering the motivations of political life, and recognising that the components of political power have social, economic and religious bases.

The emphasis on a new type of political history soon attracted the attention of some younger scholars. Among them was included my esteemed father S. R. Goyal who was then a young teacher in the University of Gorakhpur. There he worked under the supervision of V. S. Pathak for his Doctoral dissertation on the political history of the imperial Guptas. Pathak suggested to him that instead of devoting his attention on the questions 'who', 'when' and 'what', that is genealogy, chronology, wars and conquests, etc. of the Gupta rulers he should work on 'why' and 'how' problems analysing the factors and forces which conditioned the nature and shape of political events, and that was what he did. The result was his thesis, *A History of the Imperial Guptas* (Allahabad, 1967), which soon acquired recognition and admiration of scholars as a model of 'New Political History'. It immediately earned for him a place among the chief interpreters of the Gupta age. Now, a number of scholars concede that a study of the political events of the Gupta age in their situational context is not only possible, but desirable also. The method and approach to the political history of the Guptas advocated in this work was articulated by him in several of his papers and was followed in his subsequent works on political history of various other periods of ancient India. Meanwhile, the integral view of political history was becoming increasingly popular in the Indian historical world. After all Goyal was probably one of the many who had adopted this approach. In 1992 from Jodhpur was published *Political History in a Changing World.* It was an edited work (its eds. being G.C. Pande, S. K. Gupta and myself) containing a lead-paper entitled 'Need of a New Approach to the Writing of Political History of Ancient India' by my father along with reaction-papers of over 50 scholars of India and other countries, including A. K. Narain, G. C. Pande, A. K. Warder, David N. Lorenzen, G.M. Bongard-Levin, Alois Wurm, P.K. Mitra, Mubarak Ali, V. S. Pathak, B. N. Mukherjee, Sibesh Bhattacharya, A. M. Shastri, Lallanji Gopal, K.V. Raman, A.V. Narasimha Murthy, etc. It provided a rich food for thought to all those who were concerned with the discipline of political history and wanted this discipline to regain its popularity, vitality and relevance.

I also made some humble contributions in this field. In 1992 I published my research work (not Doctoral dissertation) entitled *History and Historiography of the Age of Harsha.* Probably it was the first work on the age of Harsha which was mainly concerned with 'how' and 'why' questions. Then in 2001 I brought out a monograph entitled *An Integral Approach to the Political History of Ancient India* in which the application of this approach to the various periods of ancient Indian history has been highlighted. The work also sought to show what S.R. Goyal has done to give a new definition and meaning to the political history, specially of ancient India, and what more can be done in this field. Again in 2006 I published my D. Litt. work entitled *Harsha : A Multidisciplinary Political Study* in which I have tried to look upon the political history of the age of Harsha as an integral study of political life and institutions with a multidisciplinary approach. This work is virtually an exercise in putting into practice the concept of 'integral' or 'new political history'. The National Seminar on the 'Need and Scope for Integrated Multidisciplinary Approach in the Study of Regional History and Heritage' organised in the Department of Ancient Indian History, Culture and Archaeology of the University of Bhagalpur on 21st February 2003, in which I delivered a lecture entitled 'Political History as an Integral Study of Political Life and Institutions' in the Address Session of the Seminar, is also an indication to the fact that gradually Indian historians are awakening more and more to the need of adopting an integral approach to the study of Indian history.

I am sorry for having taken a lot of time in giving what may appear to be mainly personal account of our forays—my father's and mine — in the field of multidimentional integral view of history. But as it throws some light on the growing popularity of this approach, I feel that your time is not entirely wasted.

Now to return to the nature of integral view of history. When in the Western world scholars became aware of their own dissatisfaction with the traditional political history dealing mainly with 'when', 'who' and 'what' questions they sought to transform the very concept of political history[2]—their dissatisfaction was a clear case of their discipline becoming aware of itself, acquiring self-consciousness.[3] Be that as it may, the dictum of Jacques Pirenne that "the true aim of historical research is a knowledge of the factors that control men living in society"[4] seems to have become acceptable, at least on a tentative basis, to the majority of them for their investigations. This definition implies that the different aspects of history cannot be studied in isolation from one another but only as facets of an integrated reality, and that the focal point of history is not an individual, however great he may be, but society. If this view is correct, they pleaded, political history can be regarded neither as a mere chronicle of events nor only as an account of kings and emperors; it should be regarded as basically the study of the political aspect of social life. Actually, both of them are woven into a variegated texture by various elements which in the pattern are inextricably joined. In such a view of political history, as Herbert Butterfield argues, society "is not merely a picture of still life or a kind of background to the story that is being told—a massive piece of scenery to be described in an introductory chapter or mentioned on occasion in parenthesis. It is an active collaborator in the work of history-making; and for that very reason it turns out to be at all times an important source of historical explanation."[5] In such a view political history becomes the study of political activity in its situational context, of the functioning of the centres of political authority with a view to discovering the motivations of political life and recognizing that components

[2] E.G. Goff, 'Is Politics Still the Backbone of History?' *Daedalus*, Cambridge, Mass., Winter 1971, pp. 1-19; Benjamin Schwartz, 'A Brief Defence of Political and Intellectual History—With Particular Reference to Non-Western Cultures', *ibid.*, pp. 98-112; Gordon Craig, 'Political History', *ibid.*, Spring 1971, pp. 323-38; also see S.T. Bindoff, 'Political History', in *Approaches to History*, ed. by H.P.R. Finberg, London, 1962, pp. 1 ff.

[3] For a full discussion on how 'integral' or 'new political history' in India has entered the state of self-consciousness cf. Shankar Goyal, 'Political History : The Loss of Innocence', in *Political History in a Changing World*, eds. G. C. Pande, S. K. Gupta and Shankar Goyal, Jodhpur, 1992, pp. 290-99.

[4] Jacques Pirenne, *The Tides of History*, quoted in *Problems of Historical Writing in India*, eds. S. Gopal and R. Thapar, New Delhi, 1963, p. 56.

[5] Herbert Butterfield, *George III and the Historians*, quoted in *Problems of Historical Writing in India*, p. 58.

of political power have social, economic and religious bases. Benjamin Schwartz had this kind of political history in mind when he argued that "a political historian must welcome all the aid which economists, demographers, anthropologists and others can provide to help him to understand the situation in which political action takes place."[6] That is why he believes that political history involves "conscious activity set within the frame-work of all the problems, pressures and constraints imposed by the objective situation."[7] According to Le Goff also, the new kind of political history, the one that is concerned with 'long term structures', involves the study of the various semiological systems belonging to the science of politics : vocabulary, rites, behaviour and mental attitudes. He feels that not only does the new science of politicology now contribute its concepts, vocabulary and methods, but geo-politics, political sociology and political anthropology all give political history nourishment and support.[8]

Thus, political history in the West is staging a comeback by borrowing the methods, spirit, theoretical approach and materials of the very social sciences, such as political science, which are pushing it into the background. It is shifting its focal point from kings to society and making the notion of power and the institutions connected with it its central theme.[9] For while the term 'politics' suggests the idea of surface and the superficial, the word 'power' evokes centre and depth. Surface history having lost its relevance and charm, political history is becoming history in depth by becoming the history of power.[10]

How political history of ancient India can be revolutionized with the help of other branches of knowledge may be illustrated by a few examples. There was a time, for instance, when archaeology was regarded as nothing but a handmaid of history, as if its sole aim was not more than to provide raw material for the historian. That view is now a thing of the past; now archaeology enjoys a status of its own as one of the important disciplines contributing its share to the unearthing of the story of man.[11] History and archaeology cannot afford to ignore each other, and yet flourish. For

[6] Schwartz, *op.cit.*, p. 100.

[7] *Ibid.*, pp. 99-100.

[8] Goff, *op.cit.*, p. 12.

[9] For a detailed analysis of the Western approach to political history cf. S. R. Goyal, 'Political History : A Reconsideration', *Jijñāsā*, A Journal of the History of Ideas and Culture, Jaipur, Vol. 2, No. 2, April 1975, pp. 9-26.

[10] Cf. L.S. Rathore, 'Politics, History and Philosophy', in *Political History in a Changing World*, pp. 219-27.

[11] For a new awareness in the discipline of archaeology cf. Shankar Goyal, 'New Archaeology', *Prāchya Pratibhā*, Bhopal, Vol. XI, 1983, pp. 59-64.

example, today pottery has lost its importance in our life because vessels of copper, bronze, stainless steel, plastic, etc. have replaced earthen household pots. But for the ancient period pottery forms the ABC of archaeological interpretation. It has proved to be the best of the indices of cultural changes in a society. Pottery has its own 'styles' which have been changing from age to age. Its material, shape, colour, texture, decoration, moulding, burning and treatment—to be short, its 'feel', have as many variations as the styles of an art object; and for a historian, trained in field-archaeology, it is not difficult to single out pottery of one period from another. Thus, a graph of Indian pottery through the ages can be very revealing and helpful in determining political chronology. By a careful study of a detailed graph or a series of graphs and correlating this information with other data, changes in the social and economic fabric of a society may be traced and they in turn may be related with political changes.

It is also necessary for political historians to correlate the literary sources through cross-checking with archaeological evidence. Archaeology can provide the historian with more precise data which may result in a better comprehension of the material provided by literary sources on the forms of socio-economic institutions, which in turn are known to have influenced the course of political life.[12] This would, however, require the working out of a common model for historians and archaeologists so that such questions may be asked by both which may relate to a common set of problems.

Similar is the case of education, which in the Indian context appears so much unrelated with and separate from political history. But education is power and also an instrument of power. Therefore, a study of the power-elite of a society must include in its ambit a study of the educated class and its impact on political life. In ancient India, at least in the age of the Buddha and that of Harsha, and probably those of the Guptas and the Rajputs also, it is possible to collect bio-data of a large number of educated people of the greater part of the country and classify them into regional, caste and religious groups. Further, in some cases their association with the ruling class may also be determined. Thus, some idea of the role of the educated class and its impact on society and state may be worked out. In Europe this branch of historical investigation, called prosopography or collective biography, has been developed during the last four decades or so into one of the most valuable techniques for historical investigation especially after the researches of Charles Beard, A.P. Newton, R.K. Merton and Lewis Namier. It is used as a tool to attack two of the most

[12] For a general assessment of the possible ways in which archaeological data may provide evidence for social and economic history see Romila Thapar, 'The Historian and Archaeological Data', in her *Ancient Indian Social History*, Hyderabad, 1978, pp. 193-210.

basic problems of history.[13] The first is concerned with the roots of political action : the uncovering of the deeper interests that are thought to lie beneath the rhetoric of politics, the analysis of social and economic affiliations of political groupings, the exposure of the working of a political machine and the identification of those who pull the levers. The second is concerned with social structure and social mobility.[14] Unfortunately, historians neither of ancient India, nor probably even of medieval and modern India, are thinking in this direction.

Another important branch of knowledge which may be utilized to impart new vigour and relevance to political history is the history of religion. It is generally assumed that the rulers of ancient India by and large followed the policy of religious toleration. With this basic assumption our historians keep themselves satisfied with citing instances which prove that a particular king employed the followers of various religions and sects as his ministers, commanders, etc. But religious toleration has several connotations. On the one hand, it may mean total indifference to all religions and religious rituals and, on the other, it may imply active patronage of a particular sect mixed with a feeling of hostility towards other sects without actually persecuting their followers. Further, the impact of religion on the state could be felt in many ways and through many institutions. For example, it operated through the caste system which determined the nature of the caste composition of state armies, place of priests in the hierarchy of officials, extent and nature of the royal patronage to religious establishments, and also through a king's willingness to follow the advice of a saint such as the Buddha. In any case, religion had much to do with state structure. But this line of enquiry has not been properly pursued except by a few—such as P.V. Kane, U.N. Ghoshal and A.S. Altekar. Even the results of their researches have not been integrated with the general framework of ancient Indian political history.

In ancient India a shift in the centre of political power sometimes took place in terms of social groups. Thus, we read in the *Śatapatha Brāhmaṇa* : "To the king (Rājan) doubtless belongs the Rājasūya; for, by offering Rājasūya he becomes the king, and unsuited for the kingship is Brāhmaṇa."[15] But in the centuries following the disintegration of the Maurya empire there took place a great reaction against the supremacy of the Kshatriyas, so much so that Manu, as if in retort to the author of the *Śatapatha Brāhmaṇa*, declared : "a Brāhmaṇa who knows the Veda deserves to be made a king, a commander-in-chief, the wielder of the power of

[13] Cf. Lawrence Stone, 'Prosopography', *Daedalus*, Winter 1971, pp. 46-79.
[14] *Ibid.*, pp. 46-47.
[15] Eggling, *Śatapatha Brāhmaṇa*, III, p. 4.

punishment."[16] That this new principle was concomitant with an actual change in the nature of kingship becomes clear from the fact that almost all the important dynasties of the post-Mauryan period belonged to the Brāhmaṇa order. Pushyamitra, the founder of the Śuṅga dynasty, Vasudeva, the Kaṇva ruler, Simuka, the first of the Sātavāhanas and many others—the Kadambas, the Vākāṭakas and probably the imperial Guptas as well—were Brāhmaṇas by caste.

The dominance of the Brāhmaṇas in this period is evidenced at various other levels of state structure also. Next to the kingship, the army was the important organ of the state. Generally speaking, in ancient India the right to bear arms was regarded as an exclusive privilege of the Kshatriyas. But Manu extended this privilege to the Brāhmaṇas.[17] Kāmandaka also states that the priest, minister and nobles are the principal leaders of the army.[18] That the Brāhmaṇas used to occupy the important position of *senāpati* is rendered clear by the epic example of Droṇa and historical example of Pushyamitra. As regards the office of minister, Kātyāyana insists that he should be recruited from the Brāhmaṇa order.[19] Vasudeva, the minister of Devabhūti, was a Brāhmaṇa. So was Pṛthivīsheṇa, the minister of Chandragupta II. Many other examples may easily be collected. The psychology of the militant Brāhmaṇas, who aspired to political power, is best exemplified by Mayūraśarman, the founder of the Kadamba dynasty, who according to the Talagunda inscription, was enraged at the insulting behaviour of a mounted guard and decided to give up the sacrificial ladle for weapons of war.[20]

Thus, we find that a study of the social centres of political power and an analysis of various social components of the state structure in ancient India may lead to very significant conclusions. But it gives rise to new questions also. It may make one worder how and why a shift in the social centre of political power took place in the age of Harsha when an imperial dynasty of Vaiśya caste came into existence. But, unfortunately, little has been done in this field. Most of our researchers have been busy writing papers for determining the caste of this or that dynasty, instead of correlating the various levels of political structure with the changing pattern of the political prestige of the various sections of society. This cannot be done unless the student of political history is ready to take help from the sister branch of social history.

[16] *Manusmṛti*, XII, 100.

[17] *Ibid.*, VIII, 348.

[18] *Nītisāra*, XV. 20.

[19] Cf. R.S. Sharma, *Aspects of Political Ideas and Institutions in Ancient India*, Delhi, 1959, p. 190.

[20] D.C. Sircar, *Select Inscriptions*, Calcutta, 1965, pp. 451 ff.

The political history of ancient India can also be enriched by a study of political events against their geographical and economic background. For example, "there seems to be an intrinsic connection between the proprietary right over land and the form of government. The land system in the republican states differed materially from the one found in the monarchical states."[21] Therefore, the expansion of the Magadhan empire and the eventual decline and disappearance of ancient Indian republics cannot be properly understood unless we appreciate the inner contradictions in the economy of the latter. Similarly, the weakness of the tribal republics of the third century A.D. (such as the Lichchhavis and the Mālavas) was apparantly caused by their growing attraction to the monarchical form of government without giving up the facade of republicanism. Further, the fact that the Gaṅgā basin was the heartland of several great north Indian empires, including that of Harsha, was the result of its geographical homogeneity and economic resources. The role of geographical and economic factors is also apparent in the attitude of the north Indian conquerors towards Peninsular India, for while they found it difficult, as Harsha did, to overcome the geographical difficulties involved in the conquest of the trans-Vindhyan region, the wealth of the Deccan, accumulated because of its natural resources, pearl industry and sea-borne trade, lured them to make attempts in that direction. The operation of these twin factors usually resulted in a policy of carrying out military raids instead of making a bid for outright conquest.

The economic factor also conditioned the policy of the northern empire-builders towards western India, the land of Bhṛgukachchha (Bharuch) and Śūrapāraka (Sopārā) which were the main centres of India's trade with the West, and also towards Bengal, the land of Tāmralipti, India's 'Window to the East'. Therefore, without projecting Samudragupta's conquest of the Deccan and Bengal, Chandragupta II's conquest of western India and Harsha's conquests both in the East and the West against the geographical and economic factors, one can hardly assess their actual significance. But so far most of our historians have been content with discussions on the identification of the kings defeated by Samudragupta, fixing the date of Chandragupta's conquest of western India and such other problems, while an attempt towards correlating ancient Indian political history with the fruits of the researches in economic history might lead to a tremendous transformation of the former.

This concept of new political history—dedicated not only to the study of political events but also to the study of structures, institutions, environment and power, against the background of factors operating in society—is

[21] Jaimal Rai, *The Rural-Urban Economy and Social Changes in Ancient India*, Varanasi, 1974, pp. 30 ff.

obviously vastly different, though much more difficult than the traditional type of political history which refuses to lift itself from the level of events and great men. Lucien Febvre was not very wide off the mark when he said that pseudo-history, that is the current type of political history, indeed makes "few demands. Very few. Too few."[22]

Another aspect of new political history is that it ceases to concern itself only with the elite class, viz., kings, nobles, priests, heroes, etc. and becomes the history of common people. But this broadening of historical canvas of the discipline does not mean that the importance of political history has declined; instead, it is still the hard core of history. The state still remains the central point of historical investigation. Only, now the scope of politics does not remain confined to kings and nobles; by becoming the history of the political life of society it penetrates the vast masses of people. The rise and fall of dynasties, wars, chronology, battles of kings, their political relations, nature of the political organisation of their states, administration, causes of their success or failure in establishing a permanent imperial structure, impact of religious policies on their political activities, these and similar problems continue and will continue to occupy the attention of historians. Though political biographies and deeds of kings have ceased to be the focal point of historical research, they are still an important part of it and will continue to be related with and throw light on the political life of a society. We should not forget that the biography of an Aśoka or a Harsha provides as if a paved road which may help the student of history enter and explore the dense jungle of the data concerning their respective ages. That is why, now we must give equal importance to the political history of the traditional type as well as to the new political history.

Thus, the adoption of the integral vision of political history does not at all mean that now historians need not make any efforts to reconstruct the outline of the deeds and dates of the kings and of the sequence and nature of political events. It only means that now we must also study political events against the background of various factors operating in society. It may be that even now a causal relationship between political events and social, economic, religious and other factors may not be established in every case, but at least the events may be viewed in the factorial perspective. This is something entirely different from what we generally find in the researches of Marxist historians wherein only blatant materialistic interpretation of ancient India dominates.[23] I, therefore, think that the adoption of the integral

[22] Quoted in *Daedalus,* Winter 1971, p. 12.

[23] For a detailed exposition of the Marxist approach see Shankar Goyal, *Marxist Interpretation of Ancient Indian History*, Pune, 2000; also see my *Contemporary Interpreters of Ancient India*, Jaipur, 2003, pp. 183-273.

vision of political history will make our study much more meaningful and interesting and will also make it more relevant from the point of view of the present-day problems of our society.

The integral or holistic view does not also imply giving up the study of the original sources, for the study of original sources is and shall always remain a must for historical reconstruction. However, now ancient Indian numismatics, epigraphy and archaeology have become independent disciplines. Therefore, it is not possible for a general historian to be an expert in epigraphy, numismatics and archaeology. On the other hand, the scholars of these disciplines are not usually good historians. Therefore, now it should be realized that only in exceptional cases a historian of India's political past can hope to be an expert in one or more disciplines concerning historical source-material. It is no reflection on the capabilities of our historians; it is only an expression of the realization of their limitations which the expanding frontiers of knowledge are imposing. After all, if it may be conceded without any hesitation that a social historian may not be a good student of art or archaeology, why should one hesitate to accept that a historian may not be a good numismatist, epigraphist or archaeologist ? Now, he can hardly hope to emulate the A.S. Altekars, T.V. Mahalingams, K.A.N. Sastris, R.C. Majumdars and S.R. Goyals who were great historians and at the same time were good Sanskritists, epigraphists and in many cases expert numismatists. Nowadays only in some rare and exceptional cases a historian is found to be a good scholar of some discipline concerning source-material of ancient Indian history. This is an imporant aspect of the study of ancient Indian political history which the students of integral or new political history must keep in mind.

The persistence of the traditional attitude to the writing of political history of ancient north India and the inroads which the new approach is gradually making into it is best illustrated by the history of the Maurya and Gupta periods and the age of Harsha in which now 'how' and 'why' questions are being raised and events of these periods are being increasingly studied against the factors and forces operating in society. As has been noted earlier, S.R. Goyal has looked upon the history of the imperial Guptas not from the traditional 'what and when happened approach' but from the multidisciplinary standpoint in which main political developments and events are put in their proper context by an analysis of their determining influences—social, economic, religious, grographical, etc.— with the help of other branches of knowledge, of course without overlooking the need of reconsidering the 'what and when happened' problems afresh, wherever necessary.[24] I have myself exemplified my viewpoint with special reference

[24] Cf. S.R. Goyal, *A History of the Imperial Guptas*, Allahabad, 1967; idem, *The Imperial Guptas : A Multidisciplinary Political Study*, Jodhpur, 2005.

to the political history of Harsha and his times and have tried to show that by the adoption of the new methodology and approach it should be quite possible to write a new political history of Harsha and his age devoted not only to his deeds, conquests and dates (as we find in the books so far written on him and other rulers), but to the political life of his period by correlating political institutions, policies and events and the personality of the monarch himself with socio-economic, religious and cultural developments.[25] For other periods of Indian history this approach is still difficult to be pursued, mainly because of the paucity of data, but gradually the possibilities of treating the other periods and dynasties—specially the Sātavāhana, Kushāṇa, Vākāṭaka, Chālukya, Pallava and Choḷa—with this approach are increasing and one may hope that sooner or later, hopefully sooner, historians will be able to present an integral view of these dynastic periods based on their multidisciplinary study. Anyway, that should be the aim of the new generation of political historians of ancient India in the twenty-first century.

The periods of south Indian history of which an integral picture of political history may be attempted include those of the Chālukyas of Vātāpi, Pallavas and Choḷas. Some significant works dealing with their sources and various aspects of their history were published in the later half of the last century. The names of some of the luminaries who come to our mind in this connection include K.A.N. Sastri (1892-1975) and T.V. Mahalingam (1907-1983).[26] Their contribution to the history of south India is well known. But as they were engrossed in the 'reconstruction' of political history and various aspects of cultural history (and rightly so), they did not find sufficient time to produce an integral view of political history. In his *A History of South India* (Oxford University Press, edn. 1966) K.A.N. Sastri presented in a compact form a comprehensive account of the history of the whole of south India from the prehistoric times to the fall of Vijayanagar treated as a single geographical entity.[27] In it he has incorporated the results of his own researches and has also brought together material previously scattered in many separate studies and presented it as a coherent narrative. Here, political

[25] See Shankar Goyal, *History and Historiography of the Age of Harsha*, Jodhpur, 1992 ; idem, *Harsha : A Multidisciplinary Political Study*, Jodhpur, 2006; idem, *Harsha Revisited : A Re-interpretation of Existing Data*, New Delhi, 2018; idem, *The Classical Age : A Study in Feudalization*, New Delhi, 2022.

[26] For a critical assessment of K.A.N. Sastri's contribution to the south Indian history vide Shankar Goyal, 'Historiography of Professor K.A.N. Sastri', *Journal of Indian History and Culture*, XII, Chennai, 2005, pp. 36-50; idem, 'Professor K.A.N. Sastri's Approach to History', *Proceedings of the South Indian History Congress*, XXV Annual Session, Madurai, 2005,pp. 694-99.

[27] Vide Shankar Goyal, *Recent Historiography of Ancient India*, Jodhpur, 1997,p. 416.

history naturally occupies a predominant place, though an account is also given of social life, commerce, religion, philosophy, literature and the plastic arts. However, these subjects are treated in four separate chapters at the end of the book. But highly illuminating and authoritative though their presentation is, it is not exactly in tune with the concept of intergral view of history suggested above in which cultural and political aspects of life are treated as various aspects of the organic whole. Similar is the nature of his other works including *The Cōḷas* (Madras, edn. 1975). The history of the Choḷas easily falls into five divisions, viz.: (i) the pre-Christian period, (ii) the age of the literature of the Sangam, (iii) the interval between the end of the Sangam period and the rise of the line of Vijayālaya, (iv) the period of the Vijayālaya line, and (v) the age of the Chālukya-Choḷa line of Kulottuṅga I. While giving details about various rulers of the dynasty Sastri also dealt with the central and local governments, taxation and finance, population and society, agriculture and land tenure, industry and trade, education and learning and lastly religion and literature under the Choḷas. But nowhere did he study these aspects as various factors which influenced the course of their political history.

Similarly, on the Pallavas an independent work entitled *Kāñcīpuram in Early South Indian History* (Bombay, 1969) was published by T.V. Mahalingam. It discussed the history of Kāñchīpuram from its very beginning to the age of the Later Pallava rulers of the tenth century. In its first chapter Mahalingam has delineated the early history of this city including its association with the Mauryas. Then, in the second chapter, is described the rise of the early Pallavas. The history of the Pallava rulers is given in eleven chapters from Siṁhavarman to Aparājita. The last or the fourteenth chapter is devoted to the Later Pallavas. The work is mainly concerned with the political aspect of the history of this dynasty. But Mahalingam also followed the traditional approach of earlier historians who wrote monographs on the history of India during the last hundred years or so.

The point may be further illustrated with the help of the history of the Chālukyas of Vātāpi. The Chālukya dynasty has been the subject of several independent works. R. S. Satyasraya has even discussed the origin of the dynasty in a separate monograph entitled *Origin of the Chālukyas* (Calcutta, 1937). The first full-length research monograph on the Chālukyas of Vātāpi entitled *Political History of the Chālukyas of Bādāmī* was produced by Durga Prasad Dikshit from New Delhi in 1980. But the monograph is written strictly on traditional lines though it brings at one place most of the material scattered in various journals and monographs.[28] K.V. Ramesh,

[28] *Ibid.*, p. 417.

the author of another monograph on the subject entitled *Chalukyas of Vātāpi* (Delhi, 1984), is under the impression that "The time is not yet ripe for writing a comprehensive chronological-cum-political history of the Chalukya dynasty of Vātāpi or, for that matter, of any of the Indian ruling houses of the past", for he believes that "Inspite of nearly one hundred years of sustained epigraphical collection and research, there are many gaps which can be filled up only by conjectural arguments and assumptions."[29] Nevertheless, he wrote the present work because he felt that "even a critical re-examination of the already available Chalukya records and a study of their newly discovered inscriptions considerably improve our knowledge of their history."[30] But this justification may be given for writing a comprehensive chronological-cum-political history of many other dynasties. It seems that K. V. Ramesh is himself aware of such a possibility for he observes that "The information contained in the grant portions of the Chalukya records have been brought into greater use than in the previous histories of the family" though "no attempt has been made to study, in detail, their socio-economic implications."[31] Ramesh has not undertaken such a task "for reasons of lack of running information."[32]

Now, there is no denying the fact that being the pioneering efforts, the works of Sastri and Mahalingam, and also of Ramesh, provided the much needed and reliable chronological framework to study south Indian history. But having said this, the fact remains that the period in which all of them worked on south Indian history, many other historians of the country were producing their works from altogether new angles — Marxist and integral. Had Sastri, Mahalingam and Ramesh taken up the history of south India from the integral standpoint, with their remarkable knowledge of the subject and grasp of source- materials, their works would have become trend-setters for the succeeding generation of historians.

What is more lamentable is the fact that although the traditional approach still survives in the more recent works on political history of south India, it is without the interpretative skill of Aiyangar and Sastri and the serious research of Mahalingam. Many of the works, published in recent decades, such as, K.K. Pillay's *History of Tamil Nadu—Her People and Culture* (in Tamil), (Madras, 1972), P.N. Chopra, T.K. Ravindran and N. Subramanian's *History of South India* (New Delhi, 1979), M. Rajamanickam's *History of Tamil Nadu* (Chennai, 1999), K. Rajayyan's *Tamil Nadu—A Real History* (Madurai, 2005) and Chithra Madhavan's *History and Culture of Tamil Nadu*

[29] K.V. Ramesh, *Chalukyas of Vātāpi*, Delhi, 1984, Preface, p. vii.

[30] *Ibid.*

[31] *Ibid.*

[32] *Ibid.*

(New Delhi, 2005), are not only cast in the same traditional mould but ceaselessly repeat what has been said earlier. The narrative part dominating in most of the recent works treats political history as if it has no relation to the socio-economic, religious and cultural changes. This reminds me of the remark made by R. Champakalakshmi that "History does not repeat itself, it is the historians who repeat one another."[33] But it is quite possible that the task is not as hopeless as it seems to be if we are determined to work in that direction.[34]

[33] R. Champakalakshmi, 'Historiography of South India—New Directions', her Presidential Address to the Historiography Section, *Proceedings of the South Indian History Congress*, VII Annual Session, Madras, 1987, p. 47.

[34] Cf., for example, S. R. Goyal, *Dakshiṇa Bhārata kā Itihāsa*, in Hindi, Jodhpur, 1995. In this work, quite often, Goyal has illustrated how the writing of new political history of the Deccan and south India may be seriously attempted, at least in the case of some dynasties and some periods where our sources permit us to do so.

Section IV

Society and Religion

EIGHTEEN

S.R. Goyal's Contribution to the Study of Ancient Indian Social Ideas and Institutions

I

Social philosophy seeks to find out the philosophical implications, meaning and purpose of social phenomena. It is not only the study of social facts, it is also a study of social ideals and value systems. A student of social phenomena enquires into the significance of social values; but for this he must have an understanding of social values in general and also of the ultimate values of human life which a society seeks to achieve. In his writings S.R. Goyal has tried to examine the fundamentals of ancient Indian social system with a view to understanding their inner significance and meaning. Though mainly a scholar of political and religious history, he has shown equal brilliance in dealing with the history of Indian social ideas and structures specially of ancient period. He has written on these subjects primarily in connection with Indian religious and political history, but that does not minimise the originality and significance of his contribution to them. In his writings Goyal has covered almost all the aspects of ancient Indian society and basic concepts which have been accepted through the ages, quite frequently giving novel interpretations and suggestions. He has dealt with the concepts of man, society, community, *dharma*, caste, *karman*, *saṁsāra*, etc. and has also examined the role of religion as a factor of social change in ancient India. He has raised such problems as are discussed below and tried to provide their answer within the ambit of Indian historical and cultural tradition. His contribution to the study of Indian society and social philosophy is, therefore, quite significant.

II

Goyal begins his *A Religious History of Ancient India*, Vol. I,[1] with a discussion on the religious ideas and social strucures (whenever known) of various races which contributed to the formation of the population of India.[2] Then, in his study of the religion of the Indus civilization he has suggested with some reasons that most likely the supreme god of the authors of the Indus civilization was regarded as the brother and husband both of the mother-goddess most likely a form of Durgā and that probably this brother-sister incest had its social aspect also in the form of brother-sister marriages.[3] He connects this suggestion with the Yama-Yamī dialogue of the tenth maṇḍala of the *Ṛgveda* which refers to the currency of the brother-sister incest in an earlier period (whether the characters of this dialogue are regarded as human or divine), and the instances of brother-sister marriages mentioned in the Jātakas and elsewhere. Thus, he has endeavoured to show that there existed in the Indus society a social custom which was in the eyes of the Vedic Aryans 'against the moral laws of Varuṇa'.[4] It is one of his seminal contributions to ancient Indian social history which helps us to understand numerous references to brother-sister incest found in the Purāṇas and other texts which have baffled modern scholars for so long.

III

In his *Religious History*, Vol. I, Goyal has also made the remarkable suggestion that the migration of the Aryans into India imparted to their civilization the character of a 'frontier' civilization, the nature of which is so lucidly described by Laski in the context of the American civilization—"its sense of insecurity and robust optimism, its premium on 'success' and reliance on religion as a means unto that. Under such circumstances priests and warrior kings were naturally in the fore and led society."[5] The same features which Laski notices in the formative phase of American civilization are found in the Vedic society which spread from north-west to east. But the migrations of the Vedic tribes also produced another type of leaders, whom Goyal calls using the terminology of Robert Park, the 'marginal' men

[1] Meerut, 1984.

[2] Goyal, *A Religious History of Ancient India*, Vol. I, pp. 1-11; also reproduced in his *Pre-Paurāṇika Hinduism*, Jodhpur, 2008, pp. 1-10.

[3] *Religious History*, I, pp. 24-28; also see his 'Socio-ReligiousAspect of the Indus Civilization' in *Cultural Contours of India Dr. Satya Prakash Felicitation Volume*, New Delhi, 1981, pp. 35-38.

[4] *Ibid.*, pp. 27-28.

[5] Cf. H. S. Laski, *The American Democracy*, Chs. I-II, quoted by Goyal, *ibid.*, pp.89-90; for further details also see Goyal's *Pre-Paurāṇika Hinduism*, pp. 97-113.

of the Vedic age. According to Goyal, it were they who were the product of and responsible for the fusion of the Aryan and non-Aryan elements.[6] Goyal believes that 'marginal' men of the Vedic age came from both sides of the margin—Aryan and non-Aryan. They belonged to more than one *milieu* and more often than not found themselves in a sort of dilemma. Among them were included "non-Aryans who were attracted by the Aryan religious ideas but could not cut themselves off from their past. Similarly, there were Aryans who were inclined to accept some elements of non-Aryan religions or were impressed by the thinking of non-Aryan traditions but were proud of their Vedic heritage also. Such people were the product of the migrations of Aryan tribes (and also of the non-Aryan tribes which were forced by the Aryans to move onwards) and were part of and yet strangers to both the cultural worlds to which they originally belonged and by which they were influenced. They, therefore, belonged to the category of 'marginal' man of Robert Park and the 'stranger' of Simmel. It was in their minds that conflicting cultures of the age met and fused. In the lives of many this conflict of old and new cultures found expression in a moral dichotomy and inner turmoil something which was quite natural when one set of habits and ideas was being discarded and the other one was not fully adopted."[7] Goyal illustrates his theory by quoting numerous examples from the Vedic texts.

Goyal believes that the fusion of the Vedic and the non-Vedic ideologies created numerous social and moral problems for the Vedic society and even threatened the very basis on which it rested. The non-Vedic ideologies, on the one hand,[8] put *kāmāchāra*, the ideal of promiscuity, before the Aryans and, on the other hand, goaded them towards other-worldly or Śramaṇic outlook—*munivṛtti.* "It may appear as a strange phenomenon", Goyal points out, "but it is a fact that the thinkers responsible for both these rather contradictory appearing outlooks were associated with the Rudra-Śiva cult." But the curious contrast in the two outlooks, he concedes, is more apparent than real, for even in the historical period Śaivism in its Tāntrika form is found associated simultaneously with *nivṛtti dharma* as well as the grossest and crudest forms of sexual rites. The erotic images found on the Śaiva temples of Khajuraho and other places are the best evidence of this combination. The Purāṇas are full of the stories which narrate how Śiva used to go for begging alms in naked fashion making wives of ṛshis fall in love with him. That there was an atmosphere of sexual laxity among many tribes of the Vedic age is also a well-documented fact.[9]

[6] Robert Park, 'Human Migrations and Marginal Man', in *The American Journal of Sociology*, Vol. XXXIII; Goyal, *Pre-Paurāṇika Hinduism*, pp. 99-102.

[7] Goyal, *ibid.*, p. 101.

[8] *Ibid.*, p. 110.

[9] *Ibid.*

In the Aryan society the importance of the life of a householder was supreme. Their religion was this-worldly and its fulfilment depended upon the procreation of male progency. Therefore, when some Aryans were attracted by the *nivṛtti* ideal of munis, it became a problem for the tradition loving Aryans whether or not to denounce the philosophy of renunciation. That is why, on the one hand, our ancient literature is full of praise for munis, yatis and sannyāsīs, and, on the other, numerous passages denounce them roundly.[10] In his *Śramaṇism in Early Indian Religions and Religious Life* [11] Goyal points out that when Yudhishṭhira, the eldest Pāṇḍava, expressed the desire to lead the life of a sannyāsī, his brothers and wife Draupadī successfully persuaded him to give up the idea by emphasising the futility of renunciation and necessity of leading the life of a householder. According to Goyal,[12] all such cases point to the dilemma of those Aryans who were feeling attracted towards the life of renunciation but were at the same time finding it difficult to discard their heritage of looking at this world as something desirable.[13]

The mutual impact of various Aryan (belonging to both 'Vedic' and 'non-Vedic' categories) and non-Aryan (belonging to both 'Indus' and 'non-Indus' traditions) cultural currents, Goyal argues, produced not only their mixture but also a compound—not only a combination of various ideologies but something entirely new. It led to the emergence of the ideal of the Purushārtha as the goal of human life, of the āśrama theory as the ideal pattern for the life of the individual and the varṇa system as the ideal pattern for social organisation. All these three institutions aimed at arriving at a synthesis between the conflicting claims of the *pravṛtti* and *nivṛtti* ideologies. Much of this synthesis, specially the emergence of the āśrama and the Purushāṛtha doctrines, took place in the Later Vedic or the Upanishadic Age, or even later. But the varṇa system, which later on became transformed into the caste system, began to solidify in the Middle Vedic Age itself.[14] This analysis of Goyal is certainly quite unique and throws a new light on the evolution of social ideas and institutions in ancient India.

IV

In his *Śramaṇism* Goyal analyses in detail the origin and role of the concepts

[10] *Ibid.*, p. 111.

[11] Jodhpur, 2007, pp. 34 ff.

[12] Goyal, *Śramaṇism in Early Indian Religions and Religious Life*, Jodhpur, 2007, p. 35. On this, also see Shankar Goyal, *Investigating Indian Society*, Jodhpur, 2013, Intro., pp. xv-xxix.

[13] *Ibid.*

[14] *Ibid.*, pp. 43-44.

of *karman* and *saṁsāra* in Indian social philosophy.[15] The doctrine of *karman* implies that whatever action is performed by a person it leaves behind some sort of potency which has the power to ordain for him joy or sorrow in future in accordance with its good or bad nature. The Indian thinkers combined it with the doctrine of transmigration which implies that when the traits of actions are such that they cannot be enjoyed in this life, one has to take another birth in order to enjoy their fruits, good or bad. The act passes away as soon as it is done, but its moral impact is treasured in potency which fructifies in future. Some scholars see the origin of the doctrine of rebirth in accordance with *karman* in the eschatological speculations of the *Brāhmaṇa* texts. But following G.C. Pande, Goyal argues that the usual attitude of the *Brāhmaṇas* towards afterlife does not assume a belief in the doctrine of *saṁsāra*, the recurring cycle of death and birth. In the *Brāhmaṇas* the sacrificer is reborn after death in the midst of gods and enjoys an immortal existence imagined after the manner of the worldly life. On the other hand, the doctrine of transmigration presupposes a belief in an immortal conscious principle (*ātman*), recognition of the law of *karman* and a deep-seated urge for Mukti or Moksha. These ideas became part of the Vedic thought from a pre-existing stream of non-Vedic ideology which was represented by the munis and śramaṇas. By the Later Vedic age the Vedic thinkers had become prepared to receive these ideas and therefore we find a sudden appearance of them in the Upanishad texts. Their acceptance caused a veritable spiritual revolution in the Vedic society. The early Vedic religion was life-affirming; the post-Vedic attitude is much more of life-negating or *nivṛtti*. This change came about mainly through the change in the conception of life which the doctrines of *saṁsāra* and *karman* implied.

The *chaturāśramya* is regarded as the most important feature of ancient Hindu social order. According to G.C. Pande, whom Goyal follows closely, literally the word 'āśrama' means 'a hermitage' or 'resting place', but technically it means a stage in the life of a Hindu. The scheme of four āśramas was essentially socio-religious in nature. It accepted four stages, namely, *brahmacharya* (the stage of a student of the Vedas), *gṛhastha* (the stage of a householder), *vānaprastha* (the stage of an abandoner of all worldly concerns) and *sannyāsa*. Goyal suggests that the system of *vānaprastha* or hermit life was quite old in the Brāhmaṇa society. In the Āraṇyaka texts of the pre-Buddhist period we find references to a class of Brāhmaṇa hermits (and others also) who used to go to forest and were known as Vānaprasthīs. They studied the Vedic texts and performed yajñas (actually or only mentally). There is, however, no indication that they performed *tapas* also.

[15] *Ibid.*, pp. 36-43; also see G.C. Pande, *Śramaṇa Tradition : Its History and Contribution to Indian Culture*, Ahmedabad, 1978, pp. 12-13.

However, towards the close of the Upanishadic period Brāhmaṇic values underwent a change and some sections within the Vedic society tended to accept the pessimistic world-view which the doctrine of saṁsāra entails, with the result that the sannyāsa āśrama was now postulated. Actually, the victory of mendicancy over forest-dwelling was won quite late in the Vedic society. In the *Mahābhārata* we find that forest colonies preponderate over the parivrājakas. According to Śaṅkarāchārya, the hermits dwellings in the forests were distinguished by the practice of *tapas* or physical austerities, whereas the wandering mendicants were characterised by the practice of self-control, etc.[16] In the Upanishads the efficacy of the ritual is often replaced by that of *jñāna* (knowledge), *dhyāna* (meditation) and devotion (*bhakti*) and the moral rather than the ritual part of action is emphasized. In the *Gītā* and at some other places of the *Mahābhārata yajña* emerges as the second best in its struggle against the ideologies of renunciation, meditation and devotion. These changes, according to Goyal, led to the acceptance of *moksha* as the *summum bonum* of life. Now, moksha was added to the doctrine of Trivarga. The scheme of the Chaturvarga or Purushārtha thus became complete, and the Vedic religion became truly a synthesis of *pravṛtti* and *nivṛtti* ideals. This transformation found its social reflection in the formulation of the theory of the four āśramas in the Dharmasūtra and Dharmaśāstra texts.

V

Goyal has analysed the social philosophy of the Paurāṇika religion in detail in his *A Religious History of Ancient India*, Vol. II[17] and in chapter 7 of his *Fundamentals of Paurāṇika Hinduism* (Jodhpur, 2009). In these works he argues that the doctrines of *punarjanma* and *karman* had guadually but radically changed the picture of the Vedic religion. According to the Paurāṇika ideology, the end of human life is not to live a hundred autumns and 'see the sun looger' but to be released from the cycle of rebirth and not to see any autumn at all. As a result of the impact of the doctrines of rebirth and *karman* an element of fatalism also crept into the Indian attitude to life which acquired stranglehold on Indian psyche in subsequent ages. Despite the claim that man is the architect of his own fate, in real practice belief in gods as masters of human destiny became stronger.[18]

[16] Goyal, *Religious History*, Vol. I, pp. 157 ff.; vide also G.C. Pande, in *History of Punjab*, ed. L. M. Joshi, Patiala, 1977, p. 158.

[17] Goyal, *A Religious History of Ancient India*, Vol. II, Meerut, 1986, pp. 133-35; idem, *Fundamentals of Paurāṇika Hinduism*, Jodhpur, 2009, pp. 136-60.

[18] Goyal, *Religious History*, Vol. II, p. 10; idem, *Fundamentals of Paurāṇika Hinduism*, p. 15.

In the Paurāṇika age significant changes took place in Indian social organisation (e.g. caste system became more rigid in matters of food, marriage, social behaviour etc. and position of women and Śūdras declined). The Dharmaśāstras composed from time to time naturally reflect these changes giving rise to great conflict in socio-religious norms among themselves. But it was no problem for their writers because they believed that the Smṛtis have Veda as their source. The Smṛtis are generally regarded as the expanded and metrical versions of the Dharmasūtras. Some scholars even believe that each Smṛti was based upon a corresponding Dharmasūtra. As shown by Goyal in his *Literary Chronology of Ancient India*, the *Mānava Dharmaśāstra* or *Manusmṛti* is the oldest, the best known and the most respected work of this class. It was probably based upon a *Mānava Dharmasūtra* which is now lost but quotations from which have been traced in the *Vasishṭha Dharmasūtra.* As regards the date of the *Manusmṛti*, as external evidence we have citations from it by Aśvaghosha and in the *Dhammapada*, and an anonymous citation of a verse from it in the *Mahābhāshya.* An early Cambodian inscription cites Manu, II. 136 without naming him, and gives the gist of Manu, III, 77-80. And then there is Vātsyāyana's reference to Manu. For internal evidence, mention may be made to the reference in it of the Chinese, Parthians, Yavanas, and Śakas (X. 43-45) in the enumeration of Kshatriya tribes or people who had become *vṛshalas* by neglect of their enjoined duties (*kriyālopāt*). There are many other Smṛti texts of a more or less similar character of which those of Vishṇu, Yājñavalkya, Nārada, Bṛhaspati and Kātyāyana are regarded as more important than others. These were written between the first and the seventh centuries A.D. After them were composed the Smṛtis of Devala and Vyāsa. But for the commentators and authors of the digests on Smṛti law all the Dharmaśāstras that they consider are equally authoritative. For them the Dharmaśāstras themselves are the expression of eternal law though their ultimate source is the Veda. Therefore, according to the traditional view, despite the apparent contradictions and discrepancies that seemingly exist between them, complete consensus of opinion among the successive Smṛtis has to be assumed. This is the famous doctrine of *ekavākyatā* which the medieval commentators inherited from Mīmāṁsā.[19]

According to P. V. Kane, it would have been more honest if the Dharmaśāstra writers had said that the changed circumstances require that the words of the Veda and rules of the Smṛtis should be modified. But, in the opinion of Goyal, perhaps it was better what they did in the Indian situation. Placed as they were between the eternal law as represented by

[19] Robert Lingat, 'Time and Dharma', *Contributions to Indian Sociology*, Vol. VI, eds. Louis Dumont and D. Pocock, The Hague, 1962,pp.7 ff. quoted by Goyal, in his *Fundamentals*, p. 143.

the rules of Dharma and the innumerable customs and usages of this vast sub-continent that constitute the living positive law, the commentators were able to suggest a number of different, sometimes contradictory interpretations all based upon the same authority of the Dharmaśāstra. Thus, certain practices, often different from each other, could be recognised and legitimized. Their method had the advantage of conferring to their interpretation a pliancy which could never have been dealt with as temporal legislation. The complexity of the Indian world could hardly accomadate a more uniform law.[20] Thus, the Dharmaśāstras themselves became a great source of India's fundamental unity.

However, as Goyal hastens to add, the Smṛtis did not themselves believe in the doctrine of *ekavākyatā.* They do not try to reconcile their view with the views of earlier Smṛti authors. They were in favour of moral relativism in more than one ways. Firstly, they frankly admit that some people practise customs contrary to their teachings.. Secondly, Smṛti writers including Manu and Yājñavalkya prescribe that one should give up what was once deemed to be *dharma* if it has become unacceptable to the people. Thirdly, as early as Manu the theory of the decline of humanity and the withering of virtues in the course of the four yugas was postulated. Manu compared *dharma* to a bull who is deprived of one foot in each successive yuga.[21] The Smṛti of Bṛhaspati contains a passage wherein it is maintained that certain customs such as *niyoga* or the recognition of secondary sons other than the adoptive son are no longer possible or desirable in the Kali age owing to the spiritual decline of mankind. On the basis of such ideas was later on evolved the theory of Kalivarjyas according to which certain practices, even though admitted or prescribed by the Smṛtis, are forbidden in the Kali age.[22]

The Indian social thinkers used another device also to recognise social change without deviating from the past. It was the doctrine of Āpaddharmas—the duties permissible in the times of distress. The doctrine recognises that in the times of distress social and ethical rules become loose and *dharma* may assume the form of *adharma* and *adharma* may become *dharma.*[23]

The social thinking of the Paurāṇikas was based upon the theory of *karman* which had already become popular, or rather had become a part of the subconscious mind of the Indians in the age of the Upanishads, and on the doctrine of *karman,* depended the attitude regarding the expiation of sin

[20] Cf. Goyal, *Literary Chronology of Ancient India*, Jodhpur, 2009, p. 85.

[21] Goyal, *Fundamentals*, p. 144.

[22] *Ibid.*, p. 145.

[23] *Ibid.*, pp.145-47.

(*prāyaśchitta*). In the orthodox Vedic tradition the term *prāyaśchitta* meant expiation of *vidhi aparādha*, rectification of error in the performance of the Vedic ritual, though in some passages the word has nothing to do with sin and merely means 'doing something which would get rid of some accidental mishap'. Now, after the emergence of the doctrine of *karman, prāyaśchitta* came to mean atonement for *pātaka* (immoral action) involving a set of bodily mortificatory practices to neutralize the retributive potential of evil actions. Further, as Goyal points out, the Smṛtis evolved the doctrine that if a sinner did not undergo *prāyaśchitta* for his sins, he has to undergo immense suffering in hell and will be thereafter born as some insect or lower animal or tree on account of some remnants of his sins and then will be born as a human being afflicted with diseases or defects. The last two results are described as *karma vipāka* (the fruition of evil deeds) which implies that the human beings have to experience in Heaven or Hell the consequences of their deeds.[24]

The Mahākāvyas (Epics) and the Purāṇas were unmistakably in favour of *pravṛtti dharma* and gṛhasthāśrama. They eulogise the service rendered to one's parents and relatives. Obedience to one's parents is said to be productive of all fruits of *dharma*. In order to strengthen the basis of Hindu family organisation the Epics and Purāṇas give emphasis on chastity of women. They narrate numerous stories about the supernatural powers of *satīs*.

The Purāṇas believe that *moksha* is attainable only through *nivṛtti dharma*, but unlike the Buddhists and the Jainas they do not preach that anybody can and everybody should accept sannyāsa without caring whether he is fit for it or not. They also advocate that a person should generally pass through the different āśramas performing the duties enjoined by the Smṛtis in order to reach the stage of sannyāsa.

Goyal also discusses the place of social service in the Paurāṇika religion. Before the 20th century the term 'social service' meant philanthropy and charity. The Hindus of the Paurāṇika age also insisted on philanthropy and charity. The Purāṇas lay the greatest emphasis on what is called *pūrtadharma*, that is, works of public utility, charity,social service and relief to the poor and distressed. The new interpretations of rituals and sacrifices had a corresponding effect on ethical practices. It gave a wider and social meaning to religion. True religious life has a mission in the world. A truly religious person, according to the Paurāṇika religion, is always deeply interested in the welfare of all created beings. According to the *Gītā*, the seers whose sins have been washed away, whose doubts have been dispelled

[24] *Ibid.*, pp. 147-50.

by knowledge, whose mind is firmly established in God, and who are actively engaged in promoting welfare of all beings (*sarvabhūta hite ratāḥ*) attain Brahmanirvāṇa.[25] For such a person serving his fellow beings becomes a second nature.

VI

Buddhism did not concern itself much with the collective life of man on social and political level. But some social and political ideas are found scattered here and there throughout the Tripiṭaka or may be culled from the basic assumptions inherent in Buddha's teachings. In his *A History of Indian Buddhism* [26] Goyal provides a critical account of the social ideology of Buddhism. He first analyses the Buddhist account of the origin of the social orders. In this account the Kshatriyas take precedence over the Brāhmaṇas while the monks of high learning and character are assigned the foremost position in society. It also shows that the Buddhists explained the rise of class-divisions, not as in the Brāhmaṇical śāstras by the dogma of divine will but by the voluntary selection of occupations by the various classes concerned under the influence of their respective norms or standards. Goyal also argues that Buddhism cut man loose from the sense of dependence on gods and also struck a blow on the doctrine of social obligations. It replaced gods by the force of *karman*, what man receives he does not owe to gods but to his past *karmans*. Further, as man cannot avoid moral consequences of his actions, he must eschew egoism, violence, etc. which are, according to the Buddhist view, the main evils, and pursue morality. Therefore, it is in the corpus of monastic discipline that men can obtain concrete shape and form of their ideal of asceticism.[27]

It is usually argued that the Buddha was a great social reformer, a believer in the equality of all human beings, a democrat, and that his efforts for the emancipation of women and lower castes created a sort of social revolution in society. According to Ambedkar, "No caste, no inequality, no superiority; all are equal. That is what he (i.e. the Buddha) stood for." According to some recent historians, Buddhism produced the only consciously egalitarian social philosophy in ancient India. In order to examine his belief and find out whether or not the Buddha was a social revolutionary, Goyal suggests that one should not only analyse his stand on the various social problems of his time dispassionately, but also compare his ideas with those of other contemporary thinkers and religious leaders, and also compare

[25] *Gītā*, V. 25.

[26] Meerut, 1987, Ch. 15; idem, *Buddhism in Indian History and Culture*, Book Two, Part 2, Jodhpur, 2004, pp. 103-28.

[27] Goyal, *A History of Indian Buddhism*, p. 278.

them with the ideas of the thinkers of the preceding age. Without undertaking the last two excercises it will not be possible to determine whether or not he proposed something 'revolutionary' in social life. And after examining Buddha's social ideas from these angles Goyal has concluded that the Buddha had no particular respect for women as members of society and did not concern himself with the problems of the lay women at all. Goyal cites examples to prove that the Buddha cherished the ideal of the subservience of wife to her husband.

Goyal has also shown that the Buddha did not question the wisdom behind organising the society into the four varṇas. In his own scheme he only made Kshatriyas superior to the Brāhmaṇas; otherwise, he kept the Brāhmaṇical social divisions intact. In his partiality for the Kshatriyas Buddha had the good company of the Jainas who also claimed the highest status for the Kshatriyas. But he had nothing to offer to the last two varṇas so far as their social position was concerned. Thus, his whole exercise for social reorganisation boils down to one point only : the Kshatriyas are superior to Brāhmaṇas.[28] It is true that Buddhism reconised the right of and gave opportunity to even Śūdras to enter his Church. "But what was revolutionary about it ?", Goyal pointedly asks. The other ascetic sects of that period gave the Śūdras the same opportunities and rights. Even the *Gītā* accepts it as the right of everybody to achieve *moksha.* Further, it may be noted that the opening of the doors of the Buddhist saṅgha for the Śūdras and others did not have much significance for society, for those Śūdras who continued to remain in society as Śūdras, continued to suffer the lot of their forefathers. It appears that "the Buddhist protest was satisfied when the Buddhist *bhikshus* obtained a respectable position in society without reference to their caste origin." But anyone from the low castes who became a *bhikshu* acquired social respect not as a member of a low caste but as a monk. Therefore, so far as caste system was concerned, it was not at all shaken by the entry of the Śūdras in the Buddhist *saṅgha.*

Slavery was a well established institution in the age of the Buddha. The Buddhist literature itself is full of references to the pitiable condition of slaves and slave girls. In view of Goyal, early Buddhism did not at all appreciate the resentment among slaves on their pitiable condition. The entire *Tripiṭaka* is free from any suggestions for the betterment of their lot. On the other hand the Buddha is known to have consoled them with the argument that their condition was the result of their past actions and assured them the status of gods if they suffered their lot willingly.

It is also a fact that the Buddha did not see any 'suffering' in slavery

[28] *Ibid.*, pp. 266-73.

and for that matter in any evil social institution. It is noteworthy, Goyal points out, that none of the spectacles which led him to adopt the life of homelessness (viz., sickness, old age and death) was 'social' in nature; all these three represent 'individual' suffering. Actually, his concept of 'suffering' was not even individual; he was motivated by 'spiritual' suffering and scenes of sickness, old age and death were its symbolic representations. Similarly, his concept of *bahujana hitāya bahujana sukhāya* was not social in nature; the *hita* of others which he sought to achieve was spiritual or ethical, not social.[29]

Goyal also gives a critical expositon of the social philosophy of Buddhism as understood by Baba Saheb Ambedkar. Ambedkar believed, according to Goyal rather inaccurately, that the Buddha's gospel was essentially social. So is *dukkha*, the central Buddhist notion of suffering or sorrow. "The recognition of suffering (is) the real basis of religion", writes Ambedkar in his version of the Buddha's first sermon, and *dukkha* is the result of inequalities in human society. In this view the central insight of the traditional Buddhist vision of *dukkha* is omitted and suffering is interpreted as a social phenomenon. But if one's suffering is the result of social injustice from without, Goyal rightly argues, then its cause and removal do not relate directly to one's desire or craving as the Buddha had preached. In Ambedkar's version of the Buddha's first sermon, therefore, "the recognition of human suffering" and "the removal of this misery" are viewed as equivalents to the First and Fourth Noble Truths. But to the Second and Third Noble Truths, Ambedkar presents nothing substantial for no attention is given to the cause of suffering and no mention is made of craving or desire (*tañhā* of the *Chattāri Ariya Satyāni*).[30]

Goyal points out that one should not forget that the oppositon to caste system and social inequalities existed in India from very early times, both within the heterodox and orthodox traditions. An emphasis on *karma* rather than *janma* was given in the enlightened and liberal sections of the Brāhmaṇical society also. As early as the Upanishadic age the *Chhāndogya Upanishad* (IV.4) maintained that good conduct makes a man the best Brāhmaṇa. The *Gītā* accepts the existence of the Chāturvarṇya system but does not interpret it rigidly. It looks upon the four-fold order as the natural basis of social organisation and as a divine creation (*chāturvarṇyam mayā sṛshṭam*) to enable people to give their best to the society.[31]

[29] *Ibid.*, pp. 280-81.

[30] *Ibid.*, pp. 415-16; for more details also see his 'Ambedkar and Buddhism', in *Proceedings of the National Seminar on the Life, Mission, Contribution and Relevance of Baba Saheb Dr. B. R. Ambedkar*, New Delhi, 1991, Section IV, pp. 12-30.

[31] Cf. S.R. Goyal's foreword, 'Origin and Social Significance of the Medieval Bhakti' to Susmita Pande's *Medieval Bhakti Movement*, Meerut, 1989, p. xxiv; also see his

As Goyal points out, in the Ājagaraparvan of the *Mahābhārata* Yudhishṭhira is asked by the python, "Who, O King,is a Brāhmaṇa ?" (*Brāhmaṇaḥ ko bhaved rājan*) and the king answers, "A Brāhmaṇa is one who evinces truth, liberality, forbearance, virtue, mildness, austerity and piety." In the dialogue between the pedlar and Jājali (Śāntiparvan) also the profession of pedlary is held to be superior, if followed honestly. In the *Bhāgavata Purāṇa* Kṛshṇa tells Uddhava almost in the language of the *Gītā*: Devotion concentrated on He absolves even the Śvapākas (who cook and eat the flesh of dogs) from stigma attaching to their birth. Throughout the *Bhāgavata*, true devotees without wealth or status are contrasted with wealthy or high caste persons who reject *bhakti* and denounce its followers. It severely criticises those *dvijas* (twice-born) who have all the advantages and misuse them and who devote their time and energy to the acquisition of wealth. Thus, according to the *Bhāgavata*, the most desirable characteristics of a good person are compatible with devotion and these are independent of caste.

VII

A lucid exposition of the social outlook of the Tantras given by Goyal shows that these texts were also opposed to caste system. The Tantras not only reject the caste system, but also concede gender equality and criticize all external formalities in regard to spiritual quest. The Tantras offer to all, with freedom from Vaidika exclusiveness, the practical method which qualifies the *sādhaka* for the reception of the higher doctrine of the path of knowledge (*Jñānamārga*). The Śūdras and women are not, as in the case of Vaidikāchāra, under any ban. The *Gautamīya-tantra* says that people of all castes, whether men or women may receive its mantras. In the Chakra there is no caste at all; even the lowest Chāṇḍāla being deemed, while therein, higher than Brāhmaṇas. That is why, Goyal argues, the Tantras appear to have specially spread among the outcastes, voluntary outcastes, and carefree wanderers. In the *Kulārṇavatantra* caste is regarded as a *pāśa* which the *sādhaka* has to cut off. There are instances when Tāntrika priestly functions were performed by the people of low castes. In the works of the Siddhas Nairātmya is imagined as a ḍombī girl. A large number of the 84 Siddhas reportedly belonged to the lower castes— ḍomba, chamāra, chāṇḍāla, washerman, oilman, tailor, fisherman, wood-cutter, cobbler, and so forth. They cared little for social taboos and taught that for religious purposes all classes are one—there being no difference between a brāhmaṇa and a ḍomba, a king and a slave.

'Social Aspects of the Bhakti Movement', in *Viśvambharā : Probings in Orientology* (*Professor V.S. Pathak Festschrift*), Vol. II, eds. A. M. Shastri et al, New Delhi, 1995, pp. 431-44.

The Siddhas also stressed worship and devotion of the Guru, love for a pure and formless spiritual principal and the bliss of communion with it, inner cultivation of heart, disregard of Brāhmaṇical ritual and caste privileges, equal admission of lower castes and outcastes to spiritual life, etc. Goyal rightly believes that the participation of the low castes in the spiritual life of the society under the leadership of mendicants, poets, reciters, etc., independently of the Vedic Brāhmaṇical traditon was a tendency continuing from the days of the Buddhist social protect, through the South Indian saints, and then the Siddhas from the 10th century onwards.[32] Their doctrines were, in the words of Louis Renon, "esoteric as well as democratic as they do not recognise distinctions of caste or sect. They are a kind of free-masonry."[33]

VIII

Goyal has laid emphasis also on the social significance of the medieval bhakti movement. Most medieval bhakta saints supported the opening of the path of God-realization through bhakti to everybody. Further, quite a few of bhakta saints themselves belonged to the underprivileged classes. These facts have given rise to the generally accepted view that the medieval bhakti movement was by nature a radical social protest. But, according to Goyal, it would be exaggerating the radical potentialities of the bhakti movement to suggest that all the medieval saint-poets questioned the very existence of the social structure in which they lived, for a number of saint-poets such as Tulsidās, were quite orthodox and traditionalist in their social approach. Tukārām believed that we must recognise the differences of castes while we are living in this world. The difference, preached Tukārām, vanish only in the ecstatic state. The conservatism of the Chaitanya school is clearly seen in the recognition of caste restrictions in its ritualistic and devotional practices as codified by Gopāla Bhaṭṭa, one of the six Vṛndāvana Gosvāmīs, in his *Hari Bhakti Vilāsa.* Chaitanya never wanted to interfere with the established order. His sole concern with caste or other social restrictions was that they should not interfere with community of worship; but this did not imply community in eating or in other social concerns which should be governed by the established norms.[34] Gopāla Bhaṭṭa had great faith in caste system and his exaltation of the Brāhmaṇas and deprecation of Śūdras show that in his opinion Vaishṇavas are to be governed by the Smṛti rules in their social duties and relations. Tulsīdās was a supporter of the traditional, social system and did not subscribe to the concept of the equality of sexes. However, Kabīr and other similar preachers were critical of the Brāhmaṇa

[32] *Ibid.*
[33] *Ibid.*
[34] *Ibid.* p. xxii.

orthodoxy because they considered social and ritual regulations totally irrelevant to the attainment of the spiritual goal. But the appeal of Kabīr is to the independence of the individual person. He was not the supporter of one class or caste against another but pleads that personal spiritual freedom should not be restricted by caste or religion.

Contrary to the belief of some scholars that the social philosophy of the bhakti movement was the direct result of the influence of Islam on the traditional Indian society, Goyal is of the view that "the brotherhood of Islam did not extend beyond its own fold and can, by no stretch of imagination, be regarded as universal. In Islam Hindus were regarded as Kāfirs and occupied a distinctly inferior positon. Neither the theory nor the practices of Islam as regards the Hindus could appeal to the latter as bringing a new message of equality to them especially when they were forbidden to perform their own religious rites in public, denied political and civic rights on equal terms, and faced the prospect of the imposition of Islamic legal system upon them."[35]

[35] *Ibid.*

NINETEEN

S.R. Goyal's Studies in Religious History

The publication of *A Comprehensive History of Hinduism* of S.R. Goyal, my estemed papa, which it has been my good luck to bring out after his unfortunate demise on November 9, 2015, and fulfilling my promise made to him only a couple of days before his death that I shall publish all his incomplete books soon and his efforts will not go in vain, gives me immense satisfaction.[1] But his loss, which only I can experience, hurts me non-stop. How I wish he were alive today ! Professor Goyal was indeed a literary genius, an institution by himself. He belonged to that genre of historians whose contributions were not restricted to a single specialised field of study. He worked on a very wide canvas and published more than 50 scholarly works and over 175 research papers on a broad range of varied subjects relating to different branches of Indological studies. His researches that he published in his lifespan made such a great impact on the world of ancient Indian history that during the last five decades or so there has been hardly any important work which does not take note of his views and suggestions.[2] His researches have definitely altered the approach to ancient Indian history and also the

[1] After his demise so far I have published his three books : *Birth and Early Growth of Indian Society* (2016), *Paurāṇika Sects and Cults* (2017) and *A Comprehensive History of Hinduism* (2018).

[2] Such as 'in the Indus religion the supreme god was regarded as brother and husband both of the mother goddess'; 'the Paurāṇika date of the Bhārata War has become vitiated because these works have wrongly identified Janamejaya Pārikshita who flourished after the Dāśarājña with Janamejaya Pārikshita who flourished after the Bhārata War'; 'Rāma did not have any legitimate right over the ancestral throne'; 'the Brāhmī script was *invented* in the early Maurya period'; 'the pre-Aśokan society of India, barring the north-western regions, was largely illiterate'; 'Chāṇakya and Kauṭilya were two different persons, the former, a Jaina, was the *guru* and Prime Minister of Chandragupta Maurya while the latter, a Brāhmaṇa, who flourished in the third century A.D., was the author of the *Arthaśāstra*'; 'the personality of Heracles,

methods of its study. In fact the sheer volume of his writings and extensive range of their coverage, not to speak of their high quality and originality, have greatly amazed his contemporaries which include such great luminaries of Indology as G.C. Pande, R.S. Sharma, Romila Thapar, Irfan Habib, R. Champakalakshmi, David N. Lorenzen, Lallanji Gopal, A.M. Shastri and S.P. Gupta, to name only a few.

S.R. Goyal's interest in the study of religious history became pronounced in the eighties. However, in view of his all-pervasive activities in diverse fields of historical research this interest should not be thought of as sudden. A chronological observation on his publications show that he started writing in early sixties on subjects pertaining to ancient world history and Indian religions with which he became acquainted through primary and secondary sources.[3] In the next stage, as his works reveal, he was more interested in the study of the sources *in themselves*, both literary and

as described by Megasthenes with reference to Mathurā, mainly includes the legends connected with Manu Vaivasvata of the Indian tradition'; 'when Megasthenes visited India, Paurāṇika king-lists existed in more or less the same form as they are found in the present-day Purāṇas'; 'the imperial Guptas belonged to the Brāhmaṇa order'; 'the original home of the Guptas was located in eastern U.P. with Prayāga as its early capital'; 'King Chandra of the Meharauli inscription was no other than Samudragupta'; 'there flourished two sets of kings named Narasiṁhagupta Bālāditya and Kumāragupta Kramāditya, the former set just after Skandagupta and the second in the post-Bhānugupta period'; 'the Mālava *janapada* of the Later Guptas was located in Rajasthan'; 'the Maukharis were a branch of the Mālavas and belonged to the Lunar race'; 'the testimony of Yuan Chwang regarding the *personal* faith of Harsha in Buddhism is not reliable, for Harsha remained a Śaiva throughout his life'; 'the Jaina tradition has wrongly ascribed the elements of the personality of Nāgabhaṭa II Pratihāra *alias* Nāgāvaloka to Āma-Nāgāvaloka, the successor of Yaśovarman'; 'the Dīn-e-Ilāhi founded by Akbar was a new religion, and as such he did not remain a Muslim after its promulgation'; 'the unity in diversity of the Indian society is not the unity caused by the common elements in our cultural diversity, but the unity of the top of our social pyramid bound together by our religious tradition and the common bond of language—Sanskrit, Persian and English in different periods'; 'the adoption of adult franchise in our republican constitution has turned our social pyramid upside down, bringing the cultural elite bound by common language and religious tradition to the bottom and the masses at the top thus starting the process of deculturisation, at least temporarily', etc.

[3] In the early years of his academic career, that is in the early sixties, Goyal wrote numerous articles on the topics of religious interest. These include 'Paśchimī Eśiā meṅ Śivopāsanā' (*Bāsantī*, Varanasi, 1961, pp. 63-66); 'Rāmabhakta Akbar' (*Tripathagā*, Lucknow, April 1962, pp. 33-35); 'Atharvaveda meṅ Rudropāsanā' (*Aaj*, Feb. 16, 1963, pp. 12-13); 'Kṛshṇa bhakti ka Eka Akhyāta Sampradāya : Sahajayāna' (*Bhāratī*, Bombay, July 1964, VIII, xxiii, pp. 50-53); 'Brāhmaṇa Granthoṅ meṅ Rudra

epigraphic, in course of which he increasingly realized that religious elements are inextricably blended with the materials he has been handling all through. This mastery over the sources pertaining to religious history induced him to write on the subject. His first work came out in two volumes, published respectively in 1984 and 1986, under the title *A Religious History of Ancient India*, the first dealing with the pre-Vedic, Vedic, Jaina and Buddhist religions and the second with Smārta and epic-Paurāṇika religions, Tāntrika Hinduism, Christianity and Islam. The subject is not new. Earlier the history of Indian religions was written in broad perspective by scholars like Monier-Williams, Barth, Hopkins, Louis Renou and others. But Goyal brought a more modern mind to work on the same subject. Wherever possible he discussed the role of various factors—cultural, economic, political etc. —operating in society in giving shape to different facets of a religion and also the role of that religion as a factor of social change. Goyal's second work *Harsha and Buddhism* came out in 1986. Before him it was usually believed that Harsha was a Buddhist. This conjecture chiefly rests on the evidence of Yuan Chwang. On the other hand, three known inscriptions giving a genealogy of the Pushyabhūti kings describe his elder brother as a Buddhist and Harsha himself as a Māheśvara. This contradiction has never received much attention. Goyal not only collected the entire evidence on this problem, both Indian and Chinese at one place, including the Chinese and Uigur versions of the letters exchanged between Yuan Chwang and the Indian priests of Mahābodhi, but also analysed it thoroughly and came to the conclusion that though extremely liberal in his religious outlook Harsha never adopted Buddhism as his *personal* religion and remained a Śaiva all through his life. Goyal's third work on religious history *A History of Indian Buddhism* was published in 1987. Though there is no dearth of scholarly works on Buddhism even in its historical aspects, most of them stop with its so-called disappearance after the establishment of the Turkish rule. But Goyal studies the fortunes of this religion in India down to the modern times. It is an encyclopedic study of the history of Indian Buddhism against the background of Indian cultural evolution and delineates its impact on and contribution to the various facets of Indian culture. Another publication of S.R. Goyal, *A Comprehensive History of Hinduism*, was published after his demise runs into 678 pages and is divided into three parts. Its *first part* deals with the earliest phase of Hinduism beginning with the contribution of prehistoric people of India and the Indus civilization to her religious heritage

kā Svarūpa' (*Aaj*, May 3, 1964, pp. 13-14); 'Ṛgveda meṅ Rudropāsanā' (*Aaj*, March 4, 1964, pp. 13-14); 'Rāsalīlā kā Aitihāsika Vikāsa' (*Parishad Patrikā*, July 1955, pp. 57-60); 'Kṛshṇa Vallabhā Śrī Rādhā kā Āvirbhāva' (*Bhāratī*, Bombay, 1965, pp. 55-59); and 'Sītā ke Janma kī Vichitra Kathāyeṅ' (*Tripathagā*, Lucknow, pp. 17-22).

along with a detailed picture of the Vedic and Upanishadic religion which gradually gave way, though not wholly, to the Paurāṇika religion which is by and large still the dominant form of Hinduism. The *second part* of the work seeks to delineate the fundamental features of the Paurāṇika phase of Hinduism which acquired dominant place in the life of the Hindus only gradually in the post-Upanishadic era which was earlier enjoyed by the Vedic religion. As a result of this change the two great Epics, the *Gītā*, Dharmaśāstras and the Purāṇas became the chief texts of Hindu religion though a belief in the *apaurusheyatva* of the Vedas was never fully given up. In the Paurāṇika age new schools of Hindu philosophy, specially Vedānta, evolved. The pantheon of the Paurāṇika religion in many respects was different from the pantheon of the Vedic age. One of its main characteristics was *avatāravāda*, the doctrine of incarnation, which was almost unknown in the Vedic age. Similar was the case with the Paurāṇika form of worship which gave emphasis on bhakti and image worship (*pūjā*). With these new features Paurāṇika Hinduism advocated a different social philosophy. In the *third part* Goyal comprehensively discusses various sects and cults of the Paurāṇika Hinduism. After the Vedic age Hinduism was greatly influenced by the Smṛtis, Epics and Purāṇas, and was divided into various sects, sub-sects and cults, each dominated by a major god or goddess. The main sects of Hinduism included Vaishṇava, Śaiva, Shākta, Saura and Gāṇapatya. In many instances the sects worshipping the multifarious *avatāras*, and their associates, such as Hanumāna, also acquired prominence and sub-sects grew around them as well. Most of these sects and sub-sects also developed their own philosophy. Goyal has discussed the rise and growth of these Paurāṇika sects and cults equably.

The work of S.R. Goyal on Hinduism is quite different from many other existing works on the subject and has its own distinguishing features. Here, Goyal does not look upon the history of Hinduism as only a part of the 'superstructure'; he believes that *sādhanā*, that is the pursuit of spiritual values embodied in the concept of *dharma*, has remained the basic component of Indian culture through the ages and the Indian psyche has revealed itself through various modes of *sādhanā* in different ages—*karma*, *jñāna*, *bhakti*, etc. That is why in the Indian context he gives greater emphasis on the role of ideas. Of course, he concedes that material conditions did play a significant role in the determination of the pattern of Indian culture and seeks to understand and evaluate the Indian experience in the totality of its various aspects; he only insists that in India ideas played a greater and more significant role than material conditions. Goyal adopts a wider approach, for wherever possible he discusses not only the role of the various factors—cultural, political, economic, etc.—operating in society behind the origin, nature and evolution of every religion, but also delineates the role of that religion as a factor of social change. I therefore feel that this work follows a new, something more than what is usually described as sociological, approach. Importantly he also incorporates the results of his own researches in this work so that, quite obviously, they may be considered by a wider readership and it may be examined as to how far his suggestions change the generally accepted account of Hindu religion. For example, he suggests that in the Indus civilization the Supreme God was regarded as husband and brother both of the Mother Goddess, that the Indus people worshipped *aśvattha* for procuring male progeny and victory over enemies, that the concept of the divine Vāsudeva was originally distinct from and chronologically older than the concept of Vāsudeva-Kṛshṇa, that the personality of Heracles as described by Megasthenes in connection with Mathurā is nearer to the personality of Vaivasvata Manu of the Vedas and Purāṇas rather than Vāsudeva-Kṛshṇa, that the Indian Dionysus described by Megasthenes represented not one but several gods and legendary personages, and that Rāma did not have any legitimate right over the ancestral throne, and so forth. He thus himself raises controversies in the spirit of a true researcher in his work. He also incorporates, critically examines and synthesizes the results of the researches of other scholars in the field published till recently. While discussing the various topics he has also made critical and detailed references to the recent-most books and research papers.

S.R. Goyal also published a number of research articles and forewords to learned works on subjects concerning Indian religions.[4] Some of them were based on his researches on the topics discussed in them. For example, in one of his significant papers entitled 'Studies in Early Kṛshṇa Worship' on the Christian bias in the historiography of Kṛshṇa worship

[4] Some of them are : 'Śaktivāda kā Udaya' (*Purākalpa*, Varanasi, 1974, IV, ii, pp. 36-50); 'Vedottara Kāla meṅ Śaktivāda kā Vikāsa' (*Purākalpa*, 1974, IV, iii, pp. 38-49); 'Christian Bias in the Historiography of the Early Kṛshṇa Worship' (in *Bias in Indian Historiography*, ed. D. Devahuti, New Delhi, 1980, pp. 120-39); 'Did Harsha Ever Embrace Buddhism as His *Personal* Religion' (*JBRS*, Dr. K. P. Jayaswal Commemoration Volume, 1981, pp. 373-93); 'A Socio-Religious Aspect of the Indus Civilization' (*Cultural Contours of India*, Dr. Satya Prakash Felicitation Volume, 1981, pp. 35-38); 'Hindu Dharma meṅ Śaktivāda' (Foreword to *Prāchīna Bhārata meṅ Śakti Pūjā*, by N. K. Sharma, 1986, pp. v-viii); 'Jainācharya Hemachandra' (Foreword to *India as Known to Haribhadra Sūrī*, by R.S. Shukla, 1989, pp. ix-xiii); 'Origin and Social Significance of Medieval Bhakti' (Foreword to *Medieval Bhakti Movement*, by Susmita Pande, 1989, pp. ix-xxxiii); 'State of Buddhism as Revealed in the Inscriptions of Western India' (Foreword to *Buddhism in Western India*, by Gindallian Mangvung, 1991, pp. ix-xxiii); 'Prāchīna Bhārata meṅ Yaksha Pūjā' (Foreword to *Yakshoṅ kī Bhārata ko Dena*, by Arun, 1991, pp. vii-xxxiii), 'Mīrā kī Bhakti' (Foreword to *Bhakti Kāvya kī Paramparā meṅ Mīrā*, by Rama Bhargava, 1991, pp. vii-xix).

published in the *Bias in Indian Historiography* (ed. D. Devahuti, New Delhi, 1980, pp. 120-39), he has shown that despite the rebuttal by H. C. Raychaudhuri and others of the views of early Western scholars, who believed that early Kṛshṇa worship was a plagiarism of Christianity, some European scholars, such as Allan Dahlquist (*Megasthenes and Indian Religion*, Uppsala, 1962), are still trying to prove that no Indian source of pre-Christian period makes a reference to Kṛshṇa bhakti and, therefore it originated and developed as a result of the impact of Christianity. Goyal is the first, and probably the only Indian scholar, to answer the arguments of Dahlquist in detail. In this paper he points out that many pre-Christian epigraphs and literary works prove that the god mentioned by them is no other than Kṛshṇa. The Besnagar records of Heliodorus and Gautamīputra, the Ghosundi inscription of Sarvatāta and the Nanaghat record of Nagannikā, as well as Pāṇini's *Ashṭādhyāyī*, Patañjali's *Mahābhāshya*, the *Gītā*, the *Mahābhārata* and the Buddhist works *Niddesa* and the *Ghaṭa Jātaka* provide enough evidence of Kṛshṇa bhakti in the pre-Christian period.

Goyal's another significant contribution to the religious history of ancient India was in the form of a foreword to *Yakshoṅ kī Bhārata ko Dena* by Arun (Jodhpur, 1991, pp. vii-xxxiii) in which he discussed almost all the aspects connected with the Yaksha worship in various religious systems of India.

It will not be out of place to mention two of Goyal's more significant forewords which are based on his researches and throw new light on the subject discussed in them, pertain to the medieval bhakti movement. In one of them, written for Susmita Pande's *Medieval Bhakti Movement* (Meerut, 1989, pp. ix-xxxiii), he criticised the view that medieval bhakti was influenced by Christianity, Islam or Sufism in any appreciable degree. He also argued against the view of those historians who seek to establish a link between bhakti and feudalism and look upon the *Gītā* itself as a manual of feudalism. He pointed out that the characteristics of a true bhakta (devotee) in the *Gītā* are those of a fairly strong person and not of a docile feudal tenant. Similarly, voluntary offering of leaf, flower, fruit or water to the deity can hardly be equated with the payment of tribute by vassals to the lord. Moreover, such gods as are named in the *Gītā* fail to form a pyramidical structure as would befit the feudal age. The most significant discussion in this foreword is however on the social significance of the medieval bhakti movement. He showed that though the medieval bhakta saints almost unanimously opened the path of God-realization through bhakti to all the sections of society, yet many of them were quite conservative and traditionalist in their social approach, and not social revolutionaries as they are sometimes made out to be by modern historians.

Another important contribution of Goyal to the study of medieval bhakti movement was in the form of his foreword to the *Bhakti Kāvya kī Paramparā meṅ Mīrā* by Rama Bhargava (Jodhpur, 1991, pp. viii-xv). In this foreword he discussed the nature and sources of Mīrā's bhakti and comes to the conclusion that her bhakti was not derived from one source. It can be understood only with reference to the entire medieval bhakti movement, specially its *madhura* school the elements of which were then popular throughout the country.

To sum up, S. R. Goyal's contribution to the religious history of ancient India and the history of Hinduism is by any yardstick simply stupendous. To his credit, it must be pointed out that he has not restricted himself to conventional sources alone, but has roamed comprehensively in all areas of studies concerning Hindu religious systems, discriminating facts from fiction and presenting before us a reliable and connected account on the basis of which further researches may be constructed.

TWENTY

Indian Religions and Religious Life in Yuan Chwang

I

With his fundamental concern in Buddhism, Yuan Chwang provides more space to those regions and kingdoms which were associated with Buddhism in one way or another. Although he speaks with full magniloquence of its doctrinal developments and strict observance of a rigid code of conduct among the brethren, one fact becomes quite clear from his records that Buddhism was declining in India. Gandhāra, for example, had produced many scholars of Buddhist *śastras.* Among them were Asaṅga, Vasubandhu, Nārāyaṇadeva, Dharmatrāta, Manoratha, and Pārśva. The first two were regarded as Bodhisattvas. There were about 1,000 monasteries in Gandhāra[1] but all deserted and in ruins; the *stupas* were mostly decayed.[2] The kingdom of Mathurā was significant in its own way. There were about twenty monasteries with 2,000 monks who studied equally the Mahāyāna and the Hīnayāna. Three *stupas* were ascribed to Aśoka with very many 'traces' of the four past Buddhas. There were *stupas* to commemorate the holy followers of the Śākya Buddha, such as, Sāriputra, Mudgalaputra, Pūrṇamaitriyāniputra, Upāli, Ānanda, Rāhula, and Mañjuśrī. There were *stupas* of other Bodhisattvas too.[3] Magadha was exceptionally significant for Yuan Chwang. The first of its 84,000 *stupas* was built in the palace of Aśoka at Pāṭaliputra. Its foundation wall had sunk, and it was in a

[1] Such figures regarding the number of Buddhist monasteries and Deva temples, strength of students and monks in a monastery, followers of other sects, etc., are obviously wrong.

[2] T. Watters, *On Yuan Chwang's Travels in India* (hereafter *Travels*), I, Delhi, 1961, pp. 198-24.

[3] *Ibid.* pp. 301-13.

leaning, disastrous condition.[4] The pilgrim appears to have been impressed with the people of Magadha who were honest in character; esteemed learning and reverenced Buddhism.[5] There were above fifty Buddhist monasteries, and more than 10,000 ecclesiastics, for the most part adherents to Mahāyāna system.[6] Yuan Chwang also refers to Śaśāṅka's abortive attempt to have the image (of Buddha) removed and replaced by one of Śiva.[7]

Other 'countries' were not so important as Magadha or Gandhāra. Though the monasteries in Takshaśilā were numerous, many of them were desolate and the brethren who were very few, were all Mahāyānists.[8] As regards the religious beliefs of the inhabitants of Sthāṇvīśvara the Chinese pilgrim regretfully notes that non-Buddhists were numerous, and that there were in the capital only three Buddhist monasteries, with over 700 professed Buddhists, all Hīnayānists, as against over 100 Hindu temples.[9] In Śatadru were ten monasteries, but they were desolate, and the brethren were not many.[10] Rāma or Rāmagrāma was deeply connected with Buddhism but when the pilgrim visited the site, it had been waste and wild for a long time, its towers were heaps of ruins and there was a scanty population.[11] About Kapilavastu, Yuan Chwang mentions the remains of above 1,000 Buddhist monasteries; but he refers to only one existing monastery with above 30 inmates adherents of Sammatīya School.[12] There were some hundreds of Buddhist monasteries in Śrāvastī, of which the most were in ruins, the brethren who were very few, were Sammatīyas.[13] In Prayāga there were only two Buddhist establishments and a very few brethren, all Hīnayānists.[14] In Kauśāmbī there were more than ten Buddhist monasteries, but all in complete ruins, and the brethren, who were above 300 in number, were all followers of Hīnayāna School.[15] Kuśīnagara was once a flourishing centre

[4] *Ibid.*, II, pp. 86-178.

[5] *Ibid.*, p. 86.

[6] *Ibid.*, p 87.

[7] *Ibid.*, p. 116. On this, cf. also Shankar Goyal, 'Śaśāṅka and Buddhism', in *Studies in Indian History and Culture*, edited by T. P. Verma and O. P. Tandon, Varanasi, 1988, pp. 45-50.

[8] *Ibid.*, I, p. 240.

[9] *Ibid.*, p. 314; also see Shankar Goyal, *The Significance of Yuan Chwang in the Context of the Seventh Century : A Critical Assessment*, New Delhi, 2018, pp. 72 ff.

[10] *Ibid.*, p. 299.

[11] *Ibid.*, II, p. 20.

[12] *Ibid.*, p. 1.

[13] *Ibid.*, I, p. 377.

[14] *Ibid.*, p. 361.

[15] *Ibid.*, p. 365.

of Buddhism but when the pilgrim visited this place he found it deserted.[16] In Champā there were some tens of monasteries, mostly in ruins, and there were above 200 brethren, all Hīnayānists.[17] Referring to the religious establishments in Vaiśālī, Yuan Chwang tells us that the Buddhist monasteries, of which there were some hundrends were with the exception of three and four, dilapidated and deserted, and the brethren were very few.[18] Kāmarūpa was one of those territories where Buddhism was not introduced. According to the Chinese pilgrim, the people of this province did not believe in Buddhism.[19] In Karṇasuvarṇa there were fifty Deva temples, but only ten Buddhist monasteries, and above 2,000 brethren, who were all adherents of Sammatīya School.[20] In Tāmralipti also there were more than fifty Deva temples, but only ten Buddhist monasteries, with 1,000 brethren.[21] According to Yuan Chwang, in Kaliṅga there were only a few Buddhists, the majority of the people being of other religions.[22] About south Kosala the pilgrim tells us that there were above 100 Buddhist monasteries, and above 10,000 brethren, all Mahāyānists.[23] In Ujjain there were some tens of Buddhist monasteries, of which the majority were in ruins, and only three or four were in a state of preservation.[24] The monasteries in the Chola country were in ruins and the monks were dirty. There was a *stupa* attributed to Aśoka and connected with the Tathāgata's preaching of the law to the heretics and guiding both men and Devas. An old monastery was associated with Deva Bodhisattva's discussion with a Buddhist monk who recognized his superiority.[25] Buddhism was no longer important in the Chola country. This was not true of Draviḍa in the far south which had about a hundred monasteries and 10,000 monks. They all studied the teachings of Sthavira School of Mahāyāna. Tathāgata was believed to have frequented this country much, and Aśoka had built *stupas* over all the sacred spots. The city of Kāñchipura was the native place of Dharmapāla Bodhisattva. In the south of the city was a monastery in which men, well known for talent and learning, congregated and stayed. There was a *stupa* attributed to Aśoka built on a spot where Tathāgata was believed to have

[16] *Ibid.*, II, p. 25.
[17] *Ibid.*, p. 181.
[18] *Ibid.*, p. 63.
[19] *Ibid.*, p. 185.
[20] *Ibid.*, p. 191.
[21] *Ibid.*, p. 189.
[22] *Ibid.*, p. 198.
[23] *Ibid.*, p. 200.
[24] *Ibid.*, p. 250.
[25] *Ibid.*, pp. 224-26.

converted both men and Devas.[26] There were twenty monasteries and about 3,000 monks in Andhra. A monastery near Veṅgī was beautifully carved and ornamented, with a figure of the Buddha portrayed with great artistic power. A *stupa* of stone was several hundred feet high.[27] In Maharashtra there were about a hundred monasteries and 5,000 monks who followed both the Hīnayāna and the Mahāyāna. Five *stupas* built by Aśoka marked the spots where the four Buddhas walked and sat. There were many other *stupas* made of brick or stone.[28] In Sindh there were several hundred monasteries and about 10,000 monks who studied Hīnayānist Sammatīya School. The pastoral people in Sindh wore robes of monks and, holding to their narrow views, they attacked the Mahāyāna.[29]

As is apparent, the 'countries' taken up here for illustration represent only a small number. But the Chinese pilgrim's detailed account gives us an idea of the nature of his concern : the prevalence or disintegration of Buddhism, its monasteries and *stupas* and their architecture and sculpture, scholars of Buddhism, the affiliation of monks to Hīnayāna or Mahāyāna, their mutual relations, the Buddhas and Bodhisattvas and the myths and legends related with them, Aśoka and Kanishka as the legendary patrons of Buddhism, and the superstitious lore and miracles associated with several Buddhist places.[30]

II

Yuan Chwang noticed Deva or Brāhmaṇical temples almost everywhere in India. Many of these belonged to the worshippers of a female deity and the worshippers of Maheśvara. He found a Deva temple outside the western gate of Puśakalāvatī in Gandhāra. The image of the god was imposing and worked 'constant miracles'. The temple of Bhīmā Devī, the wife of Īśvara Deva, was on the top of a mountain about ten miles from the city. The temple of Maheśvara Deva was below the mountain. The heretics who came here to offer sacrifice covered themselves with ashes.[31] In Ṭakka many people sacrificed to Devas and heavenly spirits, and there were hundreds of temples. There were nine Deva temples in Chīnapati and three in Jālandhara with 500 cinder-sprinkled Pāśupatas. There were eight Deva temples in Multan. The one dedicated to the sun was very magnificent and profusely

[26] *Ibid.*, pp. 226-28.

[27] *Ibid.*, pp. 209-14.

[28] *Ibid.*, pp. 239-41.

[29] *Ibid.*, p. 252.

[30] For details, see J.S. Grewal, 'Hiuen Tsiang's India', in *India—Studies in the History of an Idea*, New Delhi, 2005, pp. 75-80.

[31] *Travels*, I, pp. 214-15, 221-23. On this, also see J.S. Grewal, *op.cit.*, p. 72.

decorated.[32] Of the Deva temples in Kapiśa there were some tens, and above 1,000 professed sectarians, Digambaras and Pāśupatas, and those who wear wreaths of skulls as head-ornaments.[33] In Lampa the non-Buddhists had a score or two of temples and they were numerous.[34] There were five Deva temples in Nagar and above 100 professed non-Buddhists.[35] Of Deva temples in Udyāna, Yuan Chwang writes, there were above ten and the various sectarians lived pell-mell.[36]

Yuan Chwang uncertainly refers to an ancient battle fought near Sthāṇvīśvara which accounted for the country being called 'the field of religious merit'. There were a hundred Deva temples here. There were ten Deva temples in Pāriyātra (northern Rajasthan) with 1,000 followers of different sects. In Mathurā there were five Deva temples of all kinds of sectaries. In the Rohilkhand region there were some nine Deva temples with 300 sectaries. They sacrifice to Īśvara, Yuan Chwang writes, and belong to the company of "ashes-sprinklers" (Pāśupatas). In Kanauj there were more than 200 Deva temples and the non-Buddhists were several thousands in number.[37] On the eastern bank of the Ganges near Kanauj was a Deva temple with towers and storeyed turrets remarkable for their skilfully carved work.[38] In Śrāvastī there were 100 Deva temples and the non-Buddhists were numerous.[39] In Ayodhyā there were ten temples and the non-Buddhists were few.[40] In Kauśāmbī there were more than fifty Deva temples and the non-Buddhists were numerous.[41] We are told that there were hundreds of Deva temples in Prayāga and the majority of the inhabitants were non-Buddhists.[42] A temple in the city was beautifully ornamented, and it was celebrated for its numerous miracles. In Vārāṇasī there were about a hundred Deva temples and about 10,000 sectaries. The majority worshipped Maheśvara. Some cut their hair off and others tied their hair in a knot, and went naked. They covered their bodies with ashes and practised all sorts of austerities to escape the cycle of birth and death. In the capital itself were twenty Deva temples.[43]

[32] *Ibid.*, II, pp. 254 ff.
[33] *Ibid.*, I, pp. 122-30.
[34] *Ibid.*, p. 181.
[35] *Ibid.*, p. 182.
[36] *Ibid.*, p. 225.
[37] *Ibid.*, p. 340.
[38] *Ibid.*, pp. 340 ff.
[39] *Ibid.*, p. 377.
[40] *Ibid.*, p. 354.
[41] *Ibid.*, p. 365.
[42] *Ibid.*, pp. 361-65.
[43] *Ibid.*, II, pp. 46-47.

In Bengal and Kāmarūpa there were hundreds of Deva temples for sectaries of all kinds who lived together. There were fifty Deva temples in Utkal for sectaries of all sorts. In Kaliṅga there were about a hundred Deva temples with very many 'unbelievers' of different sorts. About seventy temples in south Kosala were frequented by heretics of various beliefs.

In Amarāvatī there were a hundred Deva temples and the people who frequented them were numerous and of different persuasions. In the Chola country there were tens of Deva temples. In Draviḍa there were about eighty Deva temples.

In Kachchha there were tens of Deva temples with very many sectaries. In north of Kachchha the people worshipped heavenly spirits in hundreds of temples. Sectaries of different characters assembled in these. In Valabhī there were several hundred Deva temples and very many sectaries of different kinds. In Surashtra there were about a hundred temples occupied by sectaries of various sorts. Sectaries of different denominations had tens of Deva temples in Gurjara. There were tens of Deva temples in Ujjain occupied by sectaries of diverse kinds. The principal heretics in Maheśvarapura were Pāśupatas and there were tens of Deva temples in the kingdom.[44] The heretics in Malwa were plentiful, especially the Pāśupatas.[45]

III

Yuan Chwang does not give the same sort of information about the Jainas as about the Buddhists. His interest in the Jaina 'heretics' was as minimum as his interest in other non-Buddhist religious systems in the country. The use of the term 'heretic' for all of them indicates that he believed Buddhism alone as the true religion. But he was certainly a vigilant Buddhist traveller. Even in Kapiśa he noticed naked ascetics who could have included the Digambara Jainas who went naked.[46] He noticed the white-robed 'heretics' in Simhapura. "The laws of their founder", he states, "are mostly filched from the principles of the books of the Buddha. These men are of different classes, and select their rules and frame their practices accordingly. The great ones are called Bhikshus; the younger are called Śramaṇeras. In their ceremonies and modes of life they greatly resemble the priests (of Buddha), only they have a little twist of hair on their heads, and they go naked. Moreover, what clothes they chance to wear are white. Such are the slight differences which distinguish them from others. The figure of their sacred

[44] For details, see *ibid.*, pp. 179, 183-84, 186-87, 190-91, 193, 196, 198, 214-19, 224, 226, 242, 245-46, 248-51.

[45] *Ibid.*, p. 242.

[46] Samuel Beal, *Si-Yü-Ki* or *Buddhist Records of the Western World* (hereafter *Records*), I, Delhi, 1969, p. 55; *Travels*, I, p. 123.

master they stealthily class with that of Tathāgata; it differs only in point of clothing; the points of beauty are absolutely the same."[47] There were numerous followers of the Nirgranthas in Vaiśālī.[48] *A stupa* in Magadha was virtually taken over by the naked heretics (Nirgranthas) who frequented the place in great numbers to practise penance night and day without intermission, and from morn till night walked round (*the stupa*) and contemplated it with respect.[49] The Nirgrantha heretics were also noticed in Kajaṅgala, Karṇasuvarṇa, Prāgjyotishapura, Puṇḍravardhana, Samataṭa, Oḍra, Koṅgoda and Kaliṅga.[50] There were many Nirgrantha heretics in Chola country, and in the far south there was a crowd of heretics mostly belonging to the Nirgranthas.[51]

[47] *Travels*, I, p. 251.
[48] *Ibid.*, II, p. 63.
[49] *Records*, II, p. 158.
[50] *Travels*, II, pp. 182, 185, 187, 191, 193, 198, 200.
[51] *Ibid.*, pp. 224, 226, 228.

TWENTY ONE

Bhakti Movement in South India

I

In south India till about the fifth century A.D. harmony and tolerance characterized the relations between the different religious sects. But thereafter a great change came about particularly in the Tamil region and people began to entertain fears of the whole land being converted to Jainism and Buddhism. Consequently, missionary parties of the devotees of Vishṇu and Śiva under the leadership of gifted saints called the Āḷvārs (Vaishṇavas) and Nāyanārs (Śaivas) began to traverse the country singing, dancing and debating all through their way. This great wave of religious enthusiasm attained its peak in the middle of the seventh century A.D. and had not fully spent itself by the middle of the ninth. The Chinese pilgrim Yuan Chwang, who visited south India in 642 A.D. when the Hindu devotional revivalism was just gathering momentum, failed to notice the new movement. He indeed regrets that Buddhism was on the decline, but remarks repeatedly that it was yielding to Digambara Jainism.[1] It seems that the triumph of the Hindu revivalism was largely achieved in the two centuries that followed him. Public disputations usually led rulers to transfer their allegiance from one creed to another, but more significant was the impact of the soul-stirring compositions of the Śaiva Nāyanārs and the Vaishṇava Āḷvārs and the fact that these were set to simple popular tunes. The Nāyanārs and Āḷvārs, especially the earlier ones, were simple-hearted bhaktas rather than philosophical or theological scholars. They were god-intoxicated people who transmitted their divine infatuation to millions of their contemporaries. But some of them were talented singers also and have left behind them an imperishable legacy of devotional poetry which has rarely been equalled anywhere else in quantity and quality.[2]

[1] Cf. S.R. Goyal, *Fundamentals of Paurāṇika Hinduism*, Jodhpur, 2009, p. 115.

[2] K.R. Srinivasa Iyengar, in *The Classical Age*, eds. R. C. Majumdar and A.D. Pusalker, Bombay, 1954, p. 327.

We owe the collection and preservation of the devotional songs of the Śaiva and Vaishṇava saints to the labours of two religious leaders, Nambi-Āṇḍār-Nambi and Nāthamuni. The former arranged the available Śaiva hymns into eleven *Tirumuṛais.* The first seven of these (collectively called *Tevāram* or *Devāram*), bring together the hymns of Sambandar, Appar and Sundarar. The eighth (called *Tiruvāchakam*) is the work of Māṇikkavāchakar, the ninth is a miscellaneous collection, the tenth brings together the mystic outpourings of a sixth century Śaiva yogī, Tirumūlar, and the eleventh and the last *Tirumuṛai* is another miscellany of poems from Nakkīrar to Nambi-Āṇḍār-Nambi. Similarly, Nāthamuni, the Vaishṇava counterpart of Nambi-Āṇḍār-Nambi, arranged the extant Vaishṇava hymns into a colossal collection, called *Nāḷāyira Divya Prabandham,* which is a veritable treasure-house of devotional poetry. The four thousand hymns included in this collection are the work of twelve Āḷvārs including a woman mystic, Āṇḍāl.

II

Śaiva bhakti became widespread throughout the Tamil land because of the zeal of the Nāyanārs, the Śaiva mystics and bhaktas. Their movement reached its peak in the seventh century A.D. and had not spent itself entirely by the middle of the ninth century.[3] Their hymns are full of and noble sentiments of devotion, but their main emphasis is on the majesty and greatness of God and the feeling of submission, self-abnegation and surrender to God. Later tradition counted sixty-three Nāyanārs, individual and collective, as the most prominent leaders of this revival. The individuals included a woman Kāraikāl Ammaiyār (the woman of Kāraikāl) and a pariah, Nandan from Āḍanūr, besides a general of the Pallava forces, Śiruttoṇḍar. Their main contribution lay in the creation of a firm foundation of Tamil mysticism and bhakti philosophy. They made no distiction of caste, creed or sex in the cause of devotion.

The relationship of the Nāyanārs to the Śaiva Āgamas is somewhat similar to that of the Āḷvārs to the Pāñcharātra Āgamas. Tirumūlar, the author of the tenth *Tirumuṛai*, whom a myth makes a permanent door-keeper (*dvārapāla*) of Śiva, refers to the Āgamas being as divine as the Vedas. He enunciates in his work called *Tirumantiram* the Śaiva Siddhānta doctrine of three *padārthas*—Pati, Paśu and Pāśam. *Pati* or Śiva is the creator of the universe and the saviour of the soul. *Paśu* or soul is distinct from *Pati* but is eternal, individual consciousness having the powers of cognition and activity. *Pāśam* is ultimately rooted in *mala* which binds the soul to ignorance, passions and sufferings. Since *mala* is a substance it cannot totally disappear

[3] K. A. N. Sastri, *Development of Religion in South India*, Madras, 1963, pp. 40-41.

without the action of God's grace. Tirumūlar believed that the spirit no less than the matter must be accepted as real, for it is impossible to conceive of one quite independently of the other.

About a century after Tirumūlar, Māṇikkavāchakar and the other three great Śaiva Samayāchāryas—Appar, Sambandar and Sundarar— flourished in the Tamil land. It is now generally agreed that Appar and Sambandar were contemporaries, and that Sundarar lived two or three decades after Appar's death in 681A.D.[4] But whether Māṇikkavāchakar preceded or came after the three *Tevāram* singers is not certain.

Tirunavukkaraśu or Appar is generally believed to have been a contemporary of the Pallava ruler Mahendravarman I. Though born in an orthodox Śaiva family he was attracted to Jainism in his early years, and joined the Jaina monastery at Pāṭaliputra (Cuddalore) as a monk with the adopted name of Dharmasena. His elder sister, a devout Śaiva, who had watched his change of faith with extreme anguish and dismay, implored Śiva's help. As if in answer to her prayer, Dharmasena became afflicted with an incurable abdominal disorder. When all his fellow Jainas failed him, he was compelled to go and seek his sister's help. She succeeded in securing his cure by the grace of Śiva. But because of his defection, the Jainas poisoned the mind of the Pallava ruler of the country against him. According to the tradition, he was subjected to many trials and tortures which, however, by the grace of Śiva he easily surmounted. Finally, the king himself was convinced of the superiority of Śaivism, and embraced it. A verse in a Trichinopoly inscription of Mahendravarman's time does indeed suggest that the king turned to Śaivism from some other creed.[5] The rest of Appar's life was spent in pilgrimages during which he met many contemporary Nāyanārs, of whom Sambandar was the most notable, indeed the greatest of them all.

Appar's contribution to *Tevāram* consists of 313 hymns. He conceives a personal relationship with God — who is mother, father, and a relative for him. Every perfection in man and nature is a sign of God's love for man. Appar also had a profound sense of sin and hence his bhakti is marked by humility, penitence and repentance.[6] But in spite of all this he is optimistic about salvation through the Divine Grace.

Jñānasambandar or Sambandar was a Brāhmaṇa of the Kauṇḍinya *gotra* from Shiyali in the Tanjore district. According to a legend, as a child

[4] C.V. Narayana Ayyar, *Origin and Early History of Śaivism in South India*, Madras, 1936, p. 642.

[5] K. A. N. Sastri, *A History of South India*, Madras, 1966, p. 424.

[6] Susmita Pande, *Birth of Bhakti in Indian Religions and Art*, New Delhi, 1982, p. 132.

of three he got the milk of the divine knowledge from Pārvatī herself and narrated this incident to his father in a song. At that time the Pāṇḍya country was almost completely overrun by Jainism. Sambandar betook himself to Madurā, foiled the conspiracies of the Jainas against him, vanquished them in debate and converted the king and his subjects to Śaivism. It is said that on this occasion 8,000 Jainas were put to death by impalement. This, however, according to K.A. Nilakanta Sastri, is a little more than an unpleasant legend and cannot be treated as sober history.[7]

Sambandar is said to have been absorbed into the god-head at the age of 16 only. Probably it only means that he died in the prime of his life. He is reputed to have composed 10,000 hymns, though only 384 of these are now extant.

Some decades later than Sambandar came Sundarar, or Sundaramūrti Nāyanār. He was the last of the four great Śaiva Samayāchāryas. He was born of poor Brāhmaṇa parents. His beauty as a child was such that he attracted the attention of a local chieftain who, with the consent of the parents, brought him up. When his marriage with a girl of his own caste was about to take place it was stopped, it is said, by the mysterious intervention of Śiva who claimed him as his slave. A little later Sundarar fell in love with two women, one a dancing-girl and the other a Śūdrā. Their jealousies were resolved by Śiva himself. Like the other Nāyanārs, Sundarar is also credited with many miracles, and the contemporary Chera ruler, Cheramān Perumāl, is said to have been his friend. Sundarar's devotion to Śiva was that of an intimate friend (*sakhyabhakti*) so that he was given the title *Tambirān-Toḷan* ('Friend of God'). During his incredibly short life of only eighteen years, he crowded a career of astounding service in the cause of the Divine. Of the tens of thousands of songs said to have been composed by him hardly one hundred have survived which are included in the seventh book of the *Tirumuṛai.* In these God is conceived as madly in love with his devotees. Sundarar's hymns are on every devout Tamil bhakta's lips to this day, and are sung by the musicians in temples and maṭhas.

About a century after Sundarar came the illustrious Māṇikkavāchakar who was also born of Brāhmaṇa parents. Legend makes him the minister of a Pāṇḍyan king; and on his account Śiva, the presiding deity of Madurā, is said to have performed many miracles. He is said to have debated with the Buddhists who came from Ceylon at Chidambaram and to have utterly vanquished them. The collection of fifty-one hymns known as *Tiruvāchakam* is, as if, Māṇikkavāchakar's spiritual autobiography. Mystical writings reached their climax, it is said, in the writings of Māṇikkavāchakar. They melt the heart and purify all sins. He who remains unmoved by them is

[7] Sastri, *op. cit.*

called a veritable stone. *Tiruvāchakam* seems to bring out the quintessence of Tamil Śaivism — especially by its doctrine of self-surrender to the Supreme God — even more completely than *Tevāram.*[8]

III

The Āḷvārs[9] (meaning 'divers into the qualities of God' or 'those who delved deep in wisdom') represented the Vaishṇava wing of the Bhakti movement. They were looked upon as 'wise seers who exercised spiritual sovereignty over the hearts of men'.[10] Their bhakti was certainly more intense than the bhakti advocated in the *Gītā.* Hooper calls them the morning stars of the medieval bhakti movement.[11] They had before them a tradition of the Upanishads and the *Gītā* which helped them form their own basic philosophy concerning God. Their theology was completed by accepting the ideas of the Pāñcharātra Āgamas and the Purāṇas. They may not have succeeded in making much positive contribution to philosophical thought, but their revelation of a depth of fervour produced by the idea of Deity as incarnating Himself out of love for His creatures, and desiring in return their whole-hearted devotion, is worth noting.

The Āḷvārs hailed from different parts of the Tamil land. The Pallava country contributed the first four Āḷvārs, namely, Poygai, Bhūtattār, Pey, and Tirumaliśai; Chola Deśa was the home of Toṇḍaraḍippoḍi, Tiruppān, and Tirumaṅgai; the Chera country produced Kulaśekhara; while to the Pāṇḍya Nāḍu belonged the rest, notably, Nammāḷvār, and also Āṇḍāl, one of the supreme women mystics. It is also worthy to note that the twelve Āḷvārs, like the sixty-three Nāyanārs, were a cosmopolitan group, and came from all castes and various strata of the society. Nammāḷvār, like Appar,

[8] *The Classical Age*, p. 331.

[9] Cf. D.C. Sircar, 'Early History of Vaiṣṇavism', in *The Cultural Heritage of India*, Vol. IV, ed. Haridas Bhattacharyya, Calcutta, 1969, pp. 143 ff.; H.V. Sreenivasa Murthy, 'Revival of Bhakti Movement in the Tamil Country by the Āḷvārs', in *The Bhakti Cult and Ancient Indian Geography*, ed. D. C. Sircar, Calcutta, 1970, pp. 82-87; R.N. Saksena, *Indian Social Thought*, Meerut, Year not given, pp. 92-93; K. Rajayyan, *Tamil Nadu : A Real History*, Madurai, 2005, pp. 75-86; Sastri, *op. cit.*, pp. 422-36; Pande, *op. cit.*, pp. 111-29; Goyal, *op. cit.*, pp. 115-20.

It is an interesting and significant fact that the Nāyanārs and Āḷvārs have been studied intensively by some Hindi scholars also. Cf., for example, Yaduvamshi, *Śaiva Mata*, Patna, 1955, pp. 139-64; Hazari Prasad Dvivedi, *Madhyakālīna Dharma-sādhanā*, Allahabad, 1956, pp. 38-48; Parashuram Chaturvedi; *Madhyakālīna Prema-sādhanā*, Allahabad, 1957, pp. 53-74; idem, *Bhakti Sāhitya meṅ Madhuropāsanā*, Allahabad, 1962, pp. 35-42; Munshi Ram Sharma, *Bhakti kā Vikāsa*, Varanasi, 1958, pp. 352-60.

[10] Pande, *op. cit.*, p. 114.

[11] J. S. M. Hooper, *The Hymns of the Āḷvārs*, Oxford, 1929, p. 6.

was a Veḷḷāḷa by caste, Tirumaṅgai came from a robber's family, Kulaśekhara was a princely ascetic while Periāḷvār was a Brāhmaṇa.

There are three main sources for the study of Āḷvārs — (1) legendary lives of the saints narrated in the Guruparamparās, (2) contemporary inscriptions on stone or metal, and (3) collections of their hymns called *Nāḷāyira Divya Prabandham*, compiled by Nāthamuni. Of these Guruparamparās are not of much historical importance. They mix facts and fiction so liberally that they are of little value for the historian. However, they provide religious and mythological colour to the lives of the saints. Contemporary inscriptions furnish authenticity to the meagre data available to us while the *Nāḷāyira Divya Prabandham* acquaints us with the essence and soul of the Āḷvārs' teachings. There cannot be two opinions about its poetical and spiritual fervour.

Tradition found in the Guruparamparās arranges the Āḷvārs into three groups and gives them precise but impossible chronology:[12]

(1) *Ancient* group of Poygai, Bhūtattār, Pey and Tirumaliśai Āḷvārs which is placed in 4203 B.C.

(2) *Middle* group of Nammāḷvār, Madhurakavi, Kulaśekhara, Periāḷvār and Āṇḍāl. It is placed between 3102 and 3005 B.C.

(3) *Last* group consisting of Toṇḍaraḍippoḍi, Tiruppān and Tirumaṅgai Āḷvārs (2814-2706 B.C.).

These seemingly precise dates are, however, of no use whatsoever as historical data. According to the traditional accounts, the earliest of the Āḷvārs, Poygai, Pey and Bhūtattār and also their contemporary Tirumaliśai were born in the Dvāpara yuga in Toṇḍaimaṇḍalam and lived at the time of the Pallava domination over that region. But it is impossible to believe that the Āḷvārs flourished in the Dvāpara age because of the following reasons :

(1) Now we know that the Pallavas first came to Kāñchī not earlier than the second century A.D.[13] Therefore, the early Āḷvārs who lived at the time of the Pallava domination cannot be placed there earlier than that.

(2) Tirumaliśai Āḷvār mentions the Śramaṇas (obviously the Jainas), the Bauddhas and the Śivabhaṭṭārakas. But Buddhism and Jainism had not come into being in the Dvāpara yuga. Therefore, the Āḷvārs who refer to these religions cannot have lived earlier than the Buddha who belonged to the sixth century B.C.

(3) A verse of Tirumaliśai seems to be an adaptation from the famous *Tirukkuṛal*, a work which belonged to the Saṅgam period, variously dated from the 2nd to the 6th century A.D.

(4) Bhūtattār Āḷvār refers to Māmallai as his own birth place which is the same as the modern Mahābalipuram. This town did not probably exist

[12] Vide Iyengar, in *The Classical Age*, pp. 332-33.

[13] Sircar, in *The Classical Age*, pp. 275 ff.

before the time of Narasiṁhavarman I, for it was this king who is said to have founded or at least enlarged it and gave it the name of Māmallapuram after his own name Māmalla. Therefore, Bhūtattār and his contemporaries cannot be assigned to a period earlier than the middle of the seventh century of the Christian era, the date of this king, before whom this city, even if existed, could not be known as Māmallai.

(5) Some facts contained in an Anaimalai inscription first brought to notice by T.A. Gopinatha Rao[14] records many things which are in striking consonance with those found in the Guruparamparās regarding Nammāḷvār. For example, it mentions a disciple of Nammāḷvār who was known as Madhurakavi.

(6) In one of his verses Nammāḷvār also shows his acquaintance with the famous *Tirukkuṛal*, a work composed in the Saṅgam age.

(7) Kulaśekhara Āḷvār was, according to the tradition, next to Nammāḷvār in point of time. In his work there is a reference to a historical incident which alludes to the defeat and death of a Pallava king at the hands of Kulaśekhara Āḷvār. After discussing the history of the Pallavas of that period, Gopinatha Rao has suggested that the Pallava contemporary of Kulaśekhara was someone later than Nandivarman Pallavamalla and that Kulaśekhara probably joined the Pāṇḍya king in assailing and probably also killing the Pallava king Dantivarman sometime about 825 A.D. It is perhaps this event that is alluded to in the *Perumāl Tirumoḷi*.[15]

(8) Apart from the *Tirukkuṛal*, the Āḷvārs were familiar with several other Tamil classics. In the *Tirumālai* of Toṇḍaraḍippoḍi, for instance, there occur two feet of a verse which is identical with two feet of a verse belonging to the work of the Śaiva saint Appar. Since we know that Appar lived about the middle of the seventh century A.D., we must hold that Toṇḍaraḍippoḍi could not belong to the twenty-ninth century B.C.

For reasons such as these, modern scholars do not believe in the tradition that the Āḷvārs flourished in 4203-2706 B.C. According to S. Krishnaswamy Aiyangar, the earliest of the Āḷvārs must have flourished in the second century A.D., but most of the other scholars place the earliest Āḷvārs about the sixth or seventh century A.D. In any case, the Āḷvārs cannot be placed earlier than the Gupta age. Nilakanta Sastri also argues from the non-sectarian simplicity of their hymns, style and metre that the earlier Āḷvārs could not have been later than the fifth or sixth century A.D. On the other hand, all the Āḷvārs almost certainly flourished before Vaishṇava Āchārya Nāthamuni (10th or 11th century A.D.). In the present state of our knowledge one cannot be surer and more exact than this.

[14] Cf. T.A. Gopinatha Rao, *Sir Subrahmanya Ayyar Lectures on the History of Śrī Vaiṣṇavas*, Madras, 1923, pp. 18 ff.

[15] *Ibid.*, p. 22.

IV

The twelve Āḷvārs came from diverse social groups and backgrounds. Though some of them were Brāhmaṇas, one was a Chāṇḍāla (Tiruppān); though most were men, one was a woman (Āṇḍāl); though one was a king (Kulaśekhara of Travancore), one was a thief and a brigand (Tirumaṅgai). But despite such differences in their social and cultural background, they were accepted by the tradition as saints.

The first three Āḷvārs — Poygai, Bhūtattār and Pey are known to have had miraculous origin as they are believed to have been born out of flowers.[16] Poygai, according to a tradition, was born in Kāñchī from a golden lotus; Bhūtattār in Mahābalipuram, just outside Chennai, again from a lotus; and Pey, in the suburb of the present-day Chennai known as Mylapore, again from a lotus, though in a well. All of them are said to have been incarnations of important Vishṇu symbols, Poygai of Vishṇu's conch named Pāñchajanya, Bhūtattār of Vishṇu's mace, and Pey of Vishṇu's sword Nandaka.[17]

The three early Āḷvārs did not know one another until Vishṇu simultaneously induced in each of them a desire to visit his shrine at Tirukkovalur (Koval).

Poygai, Bhūtattār and Pey were early voices in the evolution of a personal poetry of devotion in Tamil. By that time the age of classicism in Tamil literature was coming to a close, therefore the classical influence is not pervasive in their poems. Nevertheless, many of their verses display or extend classical motifs and techniques.[18]

The first three Āḷvārs contributed one hundred verses each in praise of the Lord. Their poems are embroidered with references of Vishṇu's sports in His various *avatāras* ; but their key-note is a mystical longing for Him. Their bhakti was gentle simple dovotion, altogether free from a sectarian outlook. This fact, and their employment of the *veṇbā* metre in their songs, are regarded as pointers to an early date for them.

Poygai Āḷvār was fascinated by various myths, such as, the myth of ocean-churning, and the Vāmana myth, and speaks of the measureless qualities of the Lord revealed in those myths.

Bhūtattār was also greatly impressed by the various *avatāras* of Vishṇu. He enumerates the exploits of Vāmana, Trivikrama, Varāha and

[16] *Ibid.*, pp. 2-3.

[17] *Ibid.*

[18] A. K. Ramanujan and Norman Cutler, 'From Classicism to Bhakti', in *Essays on Gupta Culture*, ed. Bardwell L. Smith, Delhi, 1983, p. 194. For the contribution of the Nāyanārs and Āḷvārs to the Bhakti movement in south India, also cf. Shankar Goyal, *Studies in the History of Deccan and South India*, Jodhpur, 2009, pp. 132-50.

Nṛsiṁha *avatāras.* The various episodes from the life of Kṛshṇa held particular interest for him, e.g. the Pūtanā incident and the episode of Kṛshṇa getting down from the chariot to kill Bhīshma in spite of his vow not to take a weapon in his hands in the Bhārata War. This incident, Bhūtattār believed, shows the utmost love of God for His devotees. Bhūtattār claimed a constant vision of the Divine in sleep as well as in the waking state and emphasized the importance of constant remembrance. This is reminiscent of the *Dhruvā Smṛti* of Rāmānuja.

The greatness of Pey lay in his knowledge and vision of the Divine from a deeper perception of God's eternal divinity as the Divine Two, comprising Nārāyaṇa and his consort Śrī.[19] He mentions numerous exploits of the Lord especially the incidents of Dantavaktra, Pūtanā, Hiraṇyakaśipu and Gajendramoksha. The Trivikrama exploit is the one which he most frequently refers to.

After the early Āḷvārs came Tirumaliśai or Bhaktisāra born in Chingleput district. He became famous after the name of the village where he was born. He is said to have been an incarnation of the Sudarśana Chakra of Vishṇu. Most probably he was an elder contemporary of the Pallava ruler Mahendravarman I. It is said that at birth he was a shapeless mass of flesh abandoned by his parents and was brought up by a Śūdra. He is said to have practised Jainism, Buddhism and Śaivism in turn before he became a Vaishṇava yogī. His poems show a more controversial tone than those of the first three Āḷvārs, and this was quite natural for his age. He gives a more personal description of God and describes His *vibhavas* and *vyūhas.* According to him, God runs after His devotees and grants them grace if they adopt the path of *śaraṇāgati.*[20]

Tirumaliśai appears to have been ideologically a militant Vaishṇava extremely hostile to the Buddhists, Jainas and Śaivas. He was also uncompromising in his monotheism, and his learning was prodigious. The single-minded devotion, that is *ekāntika* bhakti, of Tirumaliśai finds expression in assertions like this : "Be it today or tomorrow or some future day, Your grace is surely mine; I shall take refuge in none other than you, Neither will you ever abandon me, O Nārāyaṇa."[21]

Tirumaṅgai, who may be placed after Tirumaliśai, is variously described as 'a petty chieftain', 'leader of a big gang of robbers', and 'a military chief who was weaned away from his worldly career by the redemptive grace of God'. His life seems to have been highly colourful. He was skilful versifier, though as a mystic poet he is usually rated below Nammāḷvār. There is a story

[19] Pande, *op.cit.*, p. 119.
[20] Cf. *The Classical Age*, p. 332.
[21] *Ibid.*, p. 335.

that Tirumaṅgai was a contemporary of the Śaiva saint Tirujñāna- sambandar or Sambandar who was himself a contemporary of the Pallava king Narasiṁhavarman I (630-68 A.D.) of Kāñchī. But K. A. Nilakanta Sastri says that Tirumaṅgai mentions the siege of Kāñchīpuram by Vairamegha, who is usually identified with the first Rāshṭrakūṭa ruler Dantidurga (mid. 8th century A.D.). However, there are many resemblances in literary form and religious sentiments between Sambandar and Tirumaṅgai. According to the legends, he became a highwayman in order to carry off and marry the daughter of a higher caste Vaishṇava for whom he also changed his religion. He is said to have stolen a solid golden image of the Buddha from a monastery in order to pay for renovation of the temple of Śrīraṅgam.

Tirumaṅgai's hymns are full of good poetry and attack Jainism and Buddhism. To Śaivism he shows a friendlier attitude. His hymnal collection comprises the *Periya Tirumoḻi* and constitutes almost one-third of the *Nāḻāyira Divya Prabandham.* He sings passionately of his seeking for the Lord and of His grace which gives refuge to all, however lowly.[22]

A little later than Tirumaṅgai, about the close of the eighth and the beginning of the ninth century, came a number of Āḻvārs. Periyāḻvār, also known as Vishṇuchitta, was a Brāhmaṇa by caste. He is said to have won a religious disputation in the court of the Pāṇḍya king Śrīmāra Śrīvallabha (815-62 A.D.). In his verses he assumes the role of Kṛshṇa's parents or associates showing *vātsalya* and *sakhya bhāva.* Renunciation for him meant renunciation of everything except the service of God. He contributed about five hundred hymns to the 'Four Thousand'. He also composed the *Tirumoḻi,* a splendid imaginative recreation of Lord Kṛshṇa's life.

Āṇḍāl or Kodai (Skt. Godā) was the real or adopted daughter of Periyāḻvār. She is deemed to have been a form of Vishṇu's consort Lakshmī. According to the tradition, Periyāḻvār found a child Āṇḍāl at the foot of a tree and brought her up with more than a fatherly affection.

From the outset Āṇḍāl or Godā thirsted for the Divine, and poured forth her divine love into some of the finest poetry she wrote. She regarded herself as one of Kṛshṇa's gopīs, sought Him with singular fervour and determination, and is believed to have achieved union with Him at last at Śrīraṅgam. In her intense devotion to Vishṇu she dreamt of her marriage with him, and described her experience in her hymns. This mystical union was the only one she knew.

The devotion of Āṇḍāl shows *mādhurya bhakti* in the most intense form like that of the gopīs of the *Bhāgavata* and of Mīrā of Rajasthan. Her two works *Tiruppāvāi* and *Nāchchiyār Tirumoḻi* are full of hymns showing this aspect of bhakti. Śrī or the Divine mother is sought by her as the supreme

[22] Pande, *op. cit.*, p. 121.

teacher, companion and guide who also acts as a mediator between the soul and the Divine. Her *Tiruppāvāi* is a lyrical essay on the dynamics of true devotion. In her *Nāchchiyār Tirumoḷi* she constantly dreams of her beloved and prays sleeplessly for the fulfilment of her desire. She seems to be lost in dreaming about her dalliance with God. Vedāntadeśika in his *Godāstuti* declares that all the other Āḷvārs have transmuted their bhakti into *śṛṇgāra* taking their cue from Godā. Her hymn '*varaman ayiram*', etc. speaking of her dream-marriage with Vishṇu is still sung at all Vaishṇava, Brāhmaṇa marriages.

Tiruppān was responsible for only ten verses. He belonged to the Chāṇḍāla caste, and was not permitted to enter the temple of Lord Raṅganātha at Śrīraṅgam and was thus a Vaishṇava counter-part of Nandan. But so great was his devotion to Raṅganātha that the Lord is said to have asked the Brāhmaṇa priest of the temple to bring Tiruppān on his shoulders to His presence. He is said to have been fond of his *vīṇā* to abstraction. It is said that he often fell into deep *samādhi* whilst playing it. Being a Chāṇḍāla he could not enter any temple, so he would pray and sing on the banks of the Kāverī.[23] In his verses God is described as taintless, origin of all, resplendent, immaculate and holy and upholder of the right. He refers to the Trivikrama and Rāma *avatāras* of the Lord.[24]

Toṇḍaraḍippoḍi ('the dust of the feet of the devotees') was a Brāhmaṇa from Tanjore district whose real name was Vipranārāyaṇa. His intolerance of Buddhism and Jainism was as great as that of Tirumaṅgai. He sang of the nature of God, His beauty and His grace. Fifty verses of his are extant. He lived for a time with a courtesan and got into trouble, but was ultimately saved by Raṅganātha. According to Toṇḍaraḍippoḍi, God is the First Being and has three functions of creation, preservation and destruction of the world. His beauty is beyond description. Even if a sinful person utters His name, he attains the highest state. 'There is no other God than He to save'. He slew Rāvaṇa in order to save the world from *adharma*. He revealed Himself in the temple at Śrīraṅgam. This is the *archā* form of the Lord in which he has descended for the sake of his devotees.

Toṇḍaraḍippoḍi says that he does not even want Indraloka, but longs to address the Lord forever on this earth. He says that his purpose of being born will not be fulfilled if he will not spent all his time offering flowers at the feet of the Lord, and will not speak faultless words describing His qualities. He remembers that even monkeys and squirrels helped the Lord when he was crossing the sea to reach Laṅkā and therefore he feels the

[23] I. Kesarcodi-Watson, in *Bhakti Studies*, eds. G.M. Bailey and I. Kesarcodi-Watson, New Delhi, 1992, p. 115.

[24] Pande, *op. cit.*, p. 123.

necessity of doing his bit too.[25] He prays to the Lord to take away the food of those who do not take His name and give it to dogs.

Kulaśekhara was a king of Travancore. He was proficient in Sanskrit and Tamil both. His hunger for the Divine made him more and more unworldly till at last he renounced the throne and devoted himself wholeheartedly to the service of the Divine.

The works of Kulaśekhara are known as *Perumāḷ Tirumoḷi* and *Mukundamālā.* The latter is often compared with the *Gīta-govinda* of Jayadeva. His *Tirumoḷi* consists of 105 hymns and is divided into ten sections. He fancies all sorts of relationships with the Lord — mother-child, child-mother, beloved-lover, father-child, etc. and prays for His grace.

Nammāḷvār was born in a Veḷḷāḷa family. He was one of the greatest god-intoxicated men. His personal name was Māṛan and he seems to have gained the name Śaṭhakopa as well on the occasion of his initiation. He renounced the world in his thirty-fifth year to practise yoga. His hymns, the largest in number after those of Tirumaṅgai, are rightly regarded as embodying the deepest religious experience and philosophic thought of one of the greatest seers of the world as is evident from his following declaration : "My tongue sings to me divine songs. My body dances as if it is possessed by a Deity, worships the Lord and turns back to Him. ... He does not take a few deserving only. He does not leave off the undeserving. He is not vexed with wrong-doers nor does He love the good only. He is unseconded nectar to those who join and love him."[26]

Nammāḷvār is venerated as the super mystic of Vaishṇavism, and as the founder of the *prapatti* school. The *prapanna* bhaktas are those who advocate utter surrender to Vishṇu as the only or at least the most ideal way to *moksha.* He is held in high esteem by the Vaishṇavas so much so that he has become a symbol of the Divine experience. Later, his icon was placed in every temple.

Nammāḷvār was considered so devout that tradition holds that he sat in deep *samādhi* under a tamarind tree for sixteen years right from his birth. His four major works—the *Tiruviruttam, Tiruvāśiriyam, Tiruvāymoḷi,* and *Periyatiruvantādi* — are often spoken of as Śrī Vaishṇavas' four Vedas. His *Tiruvāymoḷi* has been called *Dramiḍopanishad* by Vedāntadeśika. In this work love poetry, mythology, philosophy and heroic poetry alternate with one another and blend together in new ways. It consists of 1102 stanzas. It has been described as the 'universal compendium' (*saṁhitā sārvabhaumī*) of the essence of the Vedic and Paurāṇika lore.

Madhurakavi was a Brāhmaṇa by caste. He was a disciple of

[25] *Ibid.*, p. 125.

[26] Quoted in Saksena, *op. cit.*, p. 93.

Nammāḷvār. He was highly devoted to his *guru* and adored him as God incarnate. His short hymn in praise of Nammāḷvār is sung even now by the Vaishṇavas. He claims that he understood the inner meaning of the Vedas from his *guru* and had become a realized soul by having sought refuge with his *guru*. It has to be remembered that although the importance of the teacher is an ancient tradition it came to be one of the most striking features of the medieval Indian mysticism.

From the tradition of these saints emerged the teachers or Āchāryas including Nāthamuni (born in Tanjore district, 824 A.D.) who is credited with compiling the Āḷvār canon.

V

The bhakti of the Nāyanārs and Āḷvārs was socially an all-embracing movement in the sense that it knew no barriers of caste. Therefore, there has been a general assumption among historians and sociologists that the concept of bhakti, as expressed in the Āḷvār and Nāyanār hymns, initiated a movement of protest and reform particularly aiming at caste hierarchy and Brāhmaṇa exclusiveness in Tamil society. But, as R. Champakalakshmi points out, 'this view represents an inadequate understanding of their hymns'.[27] According to her, the bhakti hymns are dominated by three major themes. First, the idea of devotion to a personal god; second, a protest against orthodox Vedic Brāhmaṇism and the exclusiveness of the Brāhmaṇas in their access to divine grace and salvation, that is, against an elitism in the religious sphere; and, third, a vehement denunciation of the Jainas and Buddhists as non-believers and heretics. In other words, the theistic and pietistic religion of the Śaiva and Vaishṇava saints was also at least partly a reaction against the impersonal and atheistic tendencies of the two ascetic religions.[28]

[27] R. Champakalakshmi, 'From Devotion and Dissent to Dominance : The Bhakti of the Tamil Āḷvārs and Nāyanārs', in *Religious Movements in South Asia 600-1800*, ed. David N. Lorenzen, New Delhi, 2006, p. 54.

[28] M.G.S. Narayanan and Veluthat Kesavan have also written on the bhakti movements in south India, especially in the Tamil region. According to them, these represent a new wave of Aryan or Hindu influence which was basically a religious phenomenon albeit with a social content that reflects the elements of dissent, protest and reform. Beginning with a framework of definitions and concepts, they have analyzed the apparent religious movement against its socio and political and economic background, also within the larger perspectives of Indian civilization (M.G. S. Narayanan and Veluthat Kesavan, 'Bhakti Movement in South India', in *Indian Movements : Some Aspects of Dissent, Protest and Reform*, ed., S.C. Malik, Simla, 1978, pp. 33-66).

The hymns of the Āḷvārs and the Nāyanārs reveal that the general nature of their bhakti was similar, i.e., of dispassion in relation to the world and intense longing for personal union with God, the sense of despair and ecstasy and a claim for a personal relationship between the bhakta and the Lord. "The general metaphysical assumption of an individual soul as lying midway between the world and God seeking to move from the world to God, and of a God who as the Supreme Soul creates and governs the universe determining the destiny of souls in accordance with their deeds and yet conferring grace on them by its own miraculous and mysterious power—these are common assumptions of the Āḷvārs and Nāyanārs and also of the Pāñcharātra and the dualistic Śaiva Āgamas."[29] One marked difference, however, is in relation to the concept of incarnation. For the Vaishṇava saints God is more recognizably human and historical, and there is a better scenario for the *līlā* of the Lord and the possibility of a greater synthesis with matters and events of ordinary life.[30]

There is a great similarity between the Upanishadic teachings and hymns of the Āḷvārs. We can glean in the hymns of Poygai Āḷvār, for example, the teachings of *Īśopanishad.* He says that he will not hanker after anyone's wealth, and that everything belongs to Him, which reminds one of *Īśāvāsyamidaṁ sarvaṁ yatkiñcha jagatyāṁ jagat*, etc. of the Upanishads. Poygai says that those who meditate on the name of God do not tread the path of pain. The *Īśopanishad* also states, "For him who has seen himself in God and God in himself where is the delusion, where is fear." When Pey Āḷvār says, 'To such a God who has completely occupied me both within and without, have I become a slave', he also echoes the Upanishadic saying that 'the Divine is in all, pervading both inside and outside'.[31] In the *Bhagavadgītā* the supreme spirit is humanized in the concept of the incarnation. This places the relationship between man and God in the centre of worship. In the *Gītā*, however, it is simultaneously realized that God's approach to man as an incarnation also facilitates man's approach to him.[32]

Almost all human relationships which are based on love are conceived of by the Āḷvārs — mother-child, slave-master, and lover-beloved. This makes their love very intense and a personal one. The Āḷvārs accepted the five-fold manifestations of God described in the Pāñcharātra Āgamas, especial importance being given by them to the *archā* form. For them the icon is not a mere symbol of God, but God himself.

The grace of God is an important aspect of the Pāñcharātra Āgamas. The Āḷvārs also accepted this. We attain Him through His grace and not by

[29] Pande, *op. cit.*, p. 134.
[30] *Ibid.*
[31] *Ibid.*, p. 116.
[32] *Ibid.*, p. 112.

our works, efforts, intellect or charity. Service to the Lord is, therefore, more important than liberation. This is suggested by numerous verses especially those of Vishṇuchitta. In such a view the ultimate aim for a devotee is a perfect union with God and not a complete merging in Him. Here again, the Āḷvārs seem to have been impressed by the Pāñcharātra philosophy. However, as Hooper says, the goal of the Āḷvārs is seen to vacillate between two alternatives as is the case with mystics of every country and every period. Firstly, there is a normal human longing for a relation of conscious love and trust between man and God, and secondly, there is the goal of complete absorption as suggested in the stories of Āṇḍāl and Tiruppān.

It is the second theme, namely, protest against orthodox Vedic Brāhmaṇism, that needs to be specially examined from the point of view of the social significance of the Nāyanārs and Āḷvārs. Their hymns made bhakti a well-established ideal for all and sundry and thus carried an earnest message of personal religion to all the people. But that created a situation in which some conflict between the saints and the established social order became inevitable. Champakalakshmi finds hints of this struggle between the privileged Brāhmaṇas on the one hand and the saints on the other in the bhakti literature. And indeed there was an element of protest or dissent in the Āḷvār and Nāyanār poetry, representing an attempt to provide avenues of social acceptance and even mobility to less privileged castes and economic groups. A certain reformatory zeal characterizes some of the bhakta saints or religious teachers like Rāmānuja.[33] Madhurakavi says that the Chaturvedins (those who recite the four Vedas) regarded him as vile and that he accepted only Nammāḷvār (a Śūdra) as his teacher. This is an expression of the solidarity of the bhakta community with the down-trodden against the orthodox Vedic Brāhmaṇas. Hence, their opposition seems to be against orthodox religious attitudes. "It stemmed primarily from the need to defend the bhakti tradition not by denying the superiority claimed by orthodox *brāhmaṇas* but by hailing the devotee's status as higher than even that of the *brāhmaṇa*. In other words, to be a *bhakta* was more important than being a *brāhmaṇa*."[34] Toṇḍaraḍippoḍi asserts that even those who recite the Vedas and know the six *aṅgas*, if they speak ill of the devotees of Vishṇu, are equal to the *pulaiyar* (outcastes).[35] He further holds that even the Chaturvedins become slaves if they are not devotees of Vishṇu, whereas even those actually born among the *kuṭis*, who work on the lands of others, are better than the Brāhmaṇas (if they are His devotees). The *Bhāgavata Purāṇa* also reiterats this position when it says that even a chāṇḍāla or a śvapāka (dog-eater), who is a true devotcc, is better than a 'virtuous'

[33] Champakalakshmi, *op. cit.*, p. 55.

[34] *Ibid.*, p. 56.

[35] *Ibid.*

[36] *Ibid.*, p. 57.

Brāhmaṇa who has turned away from Vishṇu's feet. The story of Tiruppān, who was of low caste, and who was carried to the temple by a Brāhmaṇa on his shoulders, implies such a struggle between the authors of these hymns and the Brāhmaṇical priests. "The relation between the *bhaktas* and the *varṇa* system is represented here as one of tension. ... If anything like a direct rejection of caste can be recognized in the Śaiva hymns, it is only in the hymns of Appar, as in the following verse: 'O rogues who quote the Law Books: Of what use are your *gotra* and *kula* (clan). Just bow to Māṛperu's lord as your sole refuge'." Appar says that he would worship even the 'leper with rotting limbs, the outcaste, even the foul *pulaiyan* who skins and eats cows, even these men, if they are servants of Him (that is, Śiva) who shelters the Ganges in his long hair'.[36]

Section V

Art and Culture

TWENTY TWO

On the Free-standing Sculptures of the Gupta Age

ORIGIN AND TYPES OF FREE-STANDING PILLARS

In ancient India, pillars were used not only as the integral part of a structure but also as free-standing sculptures usually to meet some religious or political need. The erection of free-standing pillars was undertaken on a large scale by Aśoka. However, it could not have been the result of the Persian impact as some early scholars surmised. According to D.R. Bhandarkar, "the erection of pillars independent and not forming part of any edifices seems to have originated in India alone and is not found in Western Asia or Europe before the time of the Roman emperors."[1] In India the tradition of erecting pillars to commemorate a victory (*jayastambha*), or sacrifice (*yūpa*), or in honour of a deity (such as *garuḍadhvaja*), is a very ancient one. Though no pre-Mauryan column has yet been found, references to *yūpas* are abundant in the Vedic literature. Their earliest stone specimens found from Nandsa, Barnala, Badva and Bichpuria in Rajasthan go back only to the third century A.D.,[2] probably because in the earlier days the *yūpas* were made of wood, as laid down in the *Śrauta-* and *Gṛhya-sūtras.*

The earliest specimen of a pillar erected in honour of a Brāhmaṇical deity (*dhvajastambha*) is the famous monolithic column at Besnagar set up in the second century B.C. in honour of Vāsudeva by Heliodorus, a Greek, who calls himself a Bhāgavata or a worshipper of Bhagavata or Kṛshṇa-Vishṇu. As for *jayastambhas* or victory pillars, we have no definite archaeological evidence of their existence at such an early period. According to S.P. Gupta, it is likely that the very idea of raising victory columns may have originated out of the *yūpas.* There are sacrifices like the *Rājasūya* and

[1] *MASI,* No. 4.

[2] For these *yūpas* and the records engraved on them cf. S.R. Goyal, *Prāchīna Bhāratīya Abhilekha Saṁgraha,* Jaipur, 1982, pp. 275-92.

Aśvamedha which only a *Chakravartī* monarch was authorized to perform. Such sacrifices necessarily followed an extensive conquest made by a ruler, and the *yūpas* erected for them had a special significance. S.R. Goyal thinks it quite possible that the Aśokan pillar on which the Prayāga *praśasti* is engraved was used as a *yūpa* in the Aśvamedha of Samudragupta.[3] In the course of time, however, with the popularity of Buddhism (among other reasons), such sacrifices became less and less common, and the idea of raising pillars in commemoration of such events seems to have grown more popular, with or without the sacrifices. Even at the time of Kālidāsa the word *yūpa* had not lost its significance as a *jayastambha.*[4]

Jayastambhas, that is the pillars raised to celebrate or associated with the victory of a king, were also called *kīrtistambhas.* The Aśokan pillar at Allahabad, on which the eulogy of Samudragupta is engraved, has been described as the raised arm of the earth (*bhuvo bāhur-ayam-uchchhritaḥ stambhaḥ*) indicating the spread of his fame (*kīrti*) in both the worlds.[5] In other words, it is claimed that it was his *kīrtistambha.*

The free-standing lofty pillars in front of the chaitya-halls at Karle, Kanheri, etc. were also called *kīrtistambhas.* As pointed out by V.S. Agrawala, "such pillars formed an integral part of the earliest *chaitya-prāsāda* architecture. This is borne out by the description of the *prāsāda* in Laṅkā, of which a monumental pillar formed a distinguishing land-mark :..... (Sundara. 43.17).

"We may go even earlier, and we find that the stūpa monument, when standing under the open sky, had also its free standing pillars. The mounds of thick yellow clay rammed as hard as stone, at Lauriya Nandangarh offer typical examples. Their contents indicate that they were burial mounds. In the particular mound in which a piece of gold-leaf with the figure of the Earth Goddess was found, a little below that level was discovered a long hollow shaft 10" in diameter showing that once a wooden pillar was placed there. In another adjoining mound the shaft of the wooden pillar was found *in situ.* We have another instance in the Aśokan pillar installed in front of one of the Gateways of the Great Sāñchī Stūpa. Probably reference to a wooden pillar (*sthūṇā*) associated with a mound of earth raised over the relics of the departed ones may be traced to the *Ṛigveda* X.18.13. The Sabhāparvan refers to such a pillar erected on the top of a *śmaśāna chaitya* as *chaityayūpa,* the two together invoked as a befitting *upamāna* in point of loftiness to Vishṇu riding on Garuḍa.

[3] S.R. Goyal, *A History of the Imperial Guptas,* Allahabad, 1967, p. 188; also see his *The Imperial Guptas : A Multidisciplinary Political Study,* Jodhpur, 2005, pp. 240 ff.

[4] S.P. Gupta, *The Roots of Indian Art,* Delhi, 1980, p. 41.

[5] *Corpus,* III, revised ed., p. 215.

"Thus in accordance with a well-established old custom the *chaitya-prāsāda* was provided with its associative column. This explains the existence of *kīrtistambhas* in front of *kīrti* excavations."[6]

That even Aśokan pillars were erected before *chaitya prāsādas* is now conceded by many scholars. Earlier it was generally supposed that Aśoka erected his pillars along the highways. But A. Ghosh and N.P. Chakravarty have argued[7] that Aśokan pillars were meant to commemorate the important events in the lives of the Buddhas, present and past, as also to form part of the stūpa complexes. Long ago S.P. Gupta systematically analysed the entire evidence and came to the conclusion that by and large, wherever they are found, the Aśokan pillars form part of the *stūpa* or *chaityagṛha* complex. Presently, in some of the examples, if they are not found along with a *stūpa* or *chaityagṛha*, it appears to be due to some other reasons, such as vandalism and ravages of time. As a corollary, pillars are likely to have been erected along with the *stūpas* and *chaityagṛhas* by Aśoka himself, presumably in the beginning without any kind of inscription over them; since these pillars were regarded as sacred, his edicts were engraved on some of them later. May be, erecting pillars in front of a *stūpa* or *chaityagṛha* was an older practice; may be in the pre-Aśokan times wooden pillars were installed in front of the *stūpas*, but there is no proof for this practice in the Buddhist literature. The Kanakamuni's *stūpa* which Aśoka enlarged (Nigali Sagar) received a pillar at the hands of Aśoka himself.[8]

The practice of erecting free-standing pillars called *dhvajastambhas* in the courtyard or outside the sanctuary was adopted in the Brāhmaṇical sects and some examples of such pillars of the Gupta age are now extant. For example, in Udaigiri Cave 19 there were originally two tall columns well to the front, although now only one survives. They were possibly *dhvajastambhas* or free-standing supports for emblems of the divinities.[9]

BIJAYAGADH YŪPASTAMBHA OF THE GUPTA AGE

The practice of erecting sacrificial *yūpas* continued in the Gupta age. The Bijayagadh (near Bayana, in Rajasthan) monolithic red sandstone pillar which contains an inscription of the year (Mālava era) 428 (=371 A.D.) stands on a rubble masonry platform which is about 13'6" high and 9'2" square at the top. The height of the pillar above the plinth is 26'3". The base of the pillar is square to a height of 3'8" and above it, it is octagonal for

[6] V.S. Agrawala, *Studies in Indian Art*, Varanasi, 1965, pp. 242-43.

[7] Quoted by S.P. Gupta, *op.cit.*, p. 37.

[8] *Ibid.*, pp. 46-47.

[9] Joanna G. Williams, *The Art of Gupta India*, New Delhi, 1983, pp. 87-88 (fig. 8, pl. 116).

a length of 22'7" and then tapers off to a point. The extreme top is broken off but a metal spike, which projects from it, indicates that it was surmounted by a capital. According to the inscription engraved on it, it was set up as a *yūpa* on the occasion of the ceremony of Puṇḍarīka sacrifice performed by Vishṇuvardhana of the Varika tribe.

USE OF AŚOKAN PILLAR AS KĪRTISTAMBHA OF SAMUDRAGUPTA

More than half a dozen *dhvajastambhas* that support (or once supported) an emblem or image of the deity, and *kīrtistambhas* that were erected for engraving the eulogy (*praśasti*) of the kings, belonging to the Gupta age are still extant. To some extent they are like the Maurya pillars and their sculptors were evidently influenced by the Maurya pillars which were standing at places like Sarnath and Sāñchī for everybody to see. The fact that the very number of the columns erected in the Gupta age is as great as under any post-Maurya dynasty proves that the kings of the Gupta age also followed the policy of proclaiming their deeds and glory by such means. The statement of Harisheṇa that the pillar (Allahabad pillar of Aśoka) on which the *praśasti* of Samudragupta was engraved, was, as if "the raised arm of the earth, proclaiming as it were, that the fame (of Samudragupta) having pervaded the entire surface of the world with (its) rise caused by the conquest of the whole earth, has... repaired from here (i.e. from this world) to the abode of (Indra)"[10] clearly brings out the psychology of the Gupta rulers towards such pillars and suggests that they recognised such pillars as imperial symbols.

MEHARAULI VISHṆUDHVAJA OF CHANDRA

The best example of the Gupta *dhvajastambhas* is the Vishṇu *dhvaja*, an iron pillar, now standing near the Qutb Mīnār at Meharauli, just outside Delhi. It stands 22 ft. above the ground, and as its depth under the pavement is only 20 in., its total height is 23 ft. 8 in. Its diameter at the base is 16.4 in., and at the capital 12.05 in. The capital is 3'6" high, and is sharply and clearly wrought into the lotiform. Many of the older foreign travellers supposed the pillar to be a casting made of brass or bronze, but the discovery that the material is pure malleable iron, which must have been forged, filled experts with admiration for the mechanical skill capable in accomplishing so great a work.[11] In 1897 Smith observed: "It is not many years since the production of such a pillar would have been an impossibility in the largest foundries of the world, and even now there are comparatively few where a similar mass

[10] *Corpus*, III, pp. 218-19.
[11] V.A. Smith, in *JRAS*, 1897, pp. 1 ff.

of metal could be turned out."[12]

The questions whether or not the Iron Pillar occupies its original position, and if not, where was it originally erected, are intriguing. The inscription engraved on it expressly states that the pillar was erected as the lofty standard of the divine Vishṇu on a hill (*giri*), known by the name of Vishṇupada. This implies that the monument was erected in a conspicuously commanding position on the summit of a hill sufficiently isolated to bear a distinctive name. The pillar now stands in a practically level courtyard, situated in a depression with rising ground on each side. Consequently it must be supposed that the pillar was moved from its original site on a hill to its present site in a hollow. The place where the hill known as Vishṇupada existed must have been a well-known spot frequented by Vaishṇava pilgrims, within the Gupta dominions, and not very remote from Delhi. All the conditions of such a position are satisfied by Mathurā. That city is less than hundred-twenty kilometers from the Qutb Mīnār, was within the boundary of the Gupta empire, has many hills and mounds in or adjoining the city precincts, is one of the most ancient cities of India, and has been from time immemorial the site of famous temples of Vishṇu, and a centre of Vaishṇava worship. Inscriptions of Chandragupta II and of his son Kumāragupta I have been found at Mathurā. For these reasons it seems to be extremely probable that the pillar was originally erected at Mathurā. The Katra mound, where the magnificent temple of Vishṇu under the name of Keśava once stood, may have been the *Vishṇupadagiri* mentioned in the inscription.[13]

A major problem that this inscription presents is the identity of the ruler called Chandra, whose exploits from "beyond the seven mouths of the Indus" to Vaṅga (Bengal) and upto the Southern Sea, are described in this epigraph. Most scholars of the older generation identified him with Chandragupta II but S.R. Goyal has very cogently argued that it is likely that these exploits are those of Samudragupta, a view with which now scholars like B.Ch. Chhabra, Munish Chandra Joshi, S.B.Deo and a host of others agree.[14]

The Meharauli capital in many ways reminds one of the Maurya capitals. It consists of seven parts, namely, a reeded bell, a thin plain disc,

[12] *Ibid.* For metal sculptures of the Gupta age, cf. P.K. Agrawala, *Gupta-kālīna Kalā evaṁ Vāstu*, Varanasi, 1994. The general impression, which is found repeated even in research works, that the iron of the Meharauli pillar has not rusted at all, is not quite accurate, for parts of its portion buried in the ground and the cavity in the square portion of the capital have become somewhat rusted.

[13] Smith, *op.cit.*

[14] For their observations vide, Munish Chandra Joshi, S.K. Gupta and Shankar Goyal (eds.), *King Chandra and the Meharauli Pillar*, Meerut, 1989.

three discs with serrated edges, another thin plain disc and a square block. As observed by Joanna Williams : "The capital, lotiform here as on all these pillars of the Gupta period, demonstrates that the Aśokan model remained in force for this *genre* in a way it did not for architectural columns. The form of the lotus on the Mehrauli capital is relatively close to Maurya ones, except that the petal edges are all rounded (rather than round alternating with angular ones) and the 'neck' or constricted portion above is not as deeply inset as on Aśokan originals. This neck consists of a twisted band found also as early as the Sāñcī Maurya Lion Capital.[15] Above this rise three fluted forms, each slightly different in profile. The lower one, precedented by a Śuṅga-period capital from Besnagar,[16] suggests the broad-grooved version of the *āmalaka* form that was to serve as a capital at Mukuṅdara and in the western Deccan. The upper cogged elements in the Mehrauli capital, taken together, may form a vase, fluted on its rim, a member occurring at Besnagar at roughly this same time.[17] Together these shapes suggest the rich ambiguity of connotations inherent in elements treated with formal harmony. Above the topmost square block, an emblem of the god Viṣṇu would presumably have completed the capital."[18] This emblem was presumably Garuḍa.

FREE-STANDING GUPTA AGE PILLARS OF SĀ-CHĪ, BHITARI, LATHIYA, KAHAUM AND ERAN

Another *dhvaja* pillar, that may be assigned to the reign of Kumāragupta I, was found at Sāñchī.[19] This was inscribed with the name of an unidentified donor in fifth-century script. Thus, the pillar was not a royal dedication. Comparing it with the Maurya pillars Joanna Williams states: The lotus, abacus, and lions are all so close to the Maurya capital of the same site that it is clear that this directly emulated that Aśokan model, rather than those of the south gateway of Stūpa 1 or of Sāñchī 17. There are, of course, differences from the Maurya sources here, particularly a softer carving and loss of articulation (such as in the lions' legs and manes). Minor changes are wrought in the twisted band above the lotus, which becomes the common twisted garland. Moreover, the disc at the top rests on a block covered with foliage of the Gupta type, in particular so similar to that of the four Buddhas of Stūpa 1[20] that a date close to theirs is probable. Thus the Sāñchī capital shows a general but not slavish fidelity to the Maurya model of the same site.

[15] Marshall and Foucher, *Monuments of Sāñchī*, pl. 107.
[16] Cunningham, *ASI*, X (1874-1877), pl. xiv.
[17] Joanna Williams, *op.cit.*, pl. 47.
[18] *Ibid.*, p. 96.
[19] *Ibid.*, pl. 141.
[20] *Ibid.*, pl. 110.

Bhitari (Ghazipur dist., U.P., 25 km. north-east of Varanasi) is well known for its inscribed red sandstone *dhvajastambha* of Skandagupta. Discovered probably in 1834 it records the installation of an image of god Śārṅgin (Vishṇu) under the name of perhaps Kumārasvāmin called after Kumāragupta I and allotment to the idol, of the village in which the column stands.

The Bhitari pillar clearly indicates that the Maurya tradition was not yet altogether extinct. The Maurya lotus here, as at Sāñchī, is followed with general integrity, although angular and rounded edges are not differentiated as on the originals. The flattened profile, with neck and curve of the lotus relatively little indented and with a squarish upper bulge, likewise betrays the fact that this is a post-Maurya work.[21]

At the village of Lathiya (about 50 km. east of Varanasi, in Zamania dist., U.P.) there stands a sandstone column which is supposed to be a sister-column of the Prahladpur inscribed pillar now in the Sanskrit University, Varanasi. The Lathiya column shows a yet flatter version of the lotus petals.[22] "The straightness of the profile is increased by the outset band immediately below the lotus and by the ring above. The upper surviving member of the Latiya column consists of eight addorsed lions,... apparently surmounted by a Janus carving of two human torsos with arms raised, now on the ground. Too little is clear for identification, although a Garuḍa is at least one possibility."[23]

At Kahaum (Deoria dist., U.P.) is found another *dhvaja* pillar of the time of Skandagupta dated G.E. 141 (=460 A.D.). The inscription mentions Skandagupta, but it records not his exploits but rather the motivation of the donor Madra, who dedicated this column with five images of Tīrthaṅkaras 'when the world's troubles led him to seek religious merit'. Thus a personal and private twist is given to the concept of the *kīrtistambha.*[24] The column contains five standing naked figures. These are distinctly Jaina images probably of Ādinatha, Śāntinātha, Neminātha, Pārśvanātha and Mahāvīra. They are in all probability the five images of the Ādikartṛs or Jaina Tīrthaṅkaras referred to in the inscription. "The column differs from Maurya ones in its extremely tapered form and in the division of the shaft into a series of differentiated sections (eight-sided, sixteen-sided, and round), the uppermost marked with a foliate band. ... On the whole, the Kahaum pillar transmutes significantly both the form and the content of earlier *stambhas.*"[25]

[21] *Ibid.*, pl. 142, p. 97; P.K. Agrawala, *op.cit.*, p. 38.
[22] Joanna Williams, *op.cit.*, pl. 143.
[23] *Ibid.*, p. 97.
[24] *Ibid.*
[25] *Ibid.*, pp. 97-98; P.K. Agrawala, *op.cit.*, p. 39.

The Eran (Sagar dist., M.P.) pillar[26] is a large monolith red-sandstone column which stands near the well-known group of temples about half a mile to the west of the village. It contains an inscription of the Gupta year 165 (=484 A.D.) referring to Mahārāja Suraśmichandra, a feudatory of Budhagupta and the local Mahārāja Mātṛvishṇu and his younger brother Dhanyavishṇu. The inscription itself describes the pillar as a *dhvajastambha* of Janārdana (Vishṇu). The inscription is engraved on the lower square part of the 43' long monolithic column. "The column rises from a square shaft,... above this is a short octagonal section. The next member has almost entirely lost its lotiform character, with no indication that the bottom represents petals at all. The curve of this capital is moreover very flaccid, the twisted band at the top only slightly inset. Above this occurs a second small octagonal section (the kind of logical sequence we have seen in the columns of Sāñcī), followed by three square members. Lions remain at the top, their faces more grotesque than any seen so far. At the very summit is the emblem of Viṣṇu, apparently a Janus image of the Garuḍa bird holding a snake. The wheel above lends itself to three interpretations : Viṣṇu's discus, a sun disc appropriate for the solar Garuḍa, and possibly the *cakra* of the *cakravartin* (although that claim on the part of the local rulers would seem pretentious). Perhaps several subjects were originally intended, for ambivalent imagery was entirely in keeping with Maurya capitals themselves, notably that of Sārnāth."[27]

As observed by Joanna Williams : "At Eran, the strong curves of the snake and of the legs and the tightly curling hair are consonant with images of Mathurā and Sārnāth at this point, although the canon of proportions is slightly heavier here. The images also resemble the symmetrical but equally strong and curvilinear Viṣṇu at Eran. On the whole, this area, while slipping from Gupta political control, seems not markedly out of touch with the style at Sārnāth and its hinterland."[28]

KĪRTISTAMBHAS OF YAŚODHARMAN-VISHṆUVARDHANA

A pair of monolithic columns of sandstone were found lying in a field in the village Sondani situated about four km. to the south-east of Mandasor. Both of them contain the inscriptions of the Mālava emperor Yaśodhar- man-Vishṇuvardhana (known date 532 A.D.).[29] One of the pillars is 39'3" in length and originally had a lion capital. It is possible that the capital was surmounted by a statue or statues, now lost. The second column is now

[26] Joanna Williams, *op.cit.*, pl. 145.
[27] *Ibid.*, p. 98.
[28] *Ibid.*; P.K. Agrawala, *op.cit.*, p. 36.
[29] P.K. Agrawala, *ibid.*, p. 42.

broken and its full length cannot be determined. It was also topped by a lion capital which was also probably surmounted by a statue or statues. The finish at the top of both the pillars suggests that they were not connected by a beam after the fashion of a *toraṇa* or arched gateway and there are no traces of a temple to which they could have belonged. They therefore must be put under the category of *jayastambhas* or *kīrtistambhas.*[30]

[30] On this, also see my chapter in *Indian Art of the Gupta Age : From Pre-Classical Roots to the Emergence of Medieval Trends*, eds. S.R. Goyal and Shankar Goyal, Jodhpur, 2000, pp. 139-49.

TWENTY THREE

Art and Architecture of the Age of Harsha as Known from the Literary Sources

The age of Harsha cannot be regarded as a separate chapter in the sphere of Indian art. It is so closely associated with the age of the imperial Guptas that one finds it difficult to draw a line between the Gupta art and the art of the age of Harsha. Like the Guptas, Harsha also gave patronage to all creeds and faiths—Vaishṇavism, Śaivism, Jainism and Buddhism and, therefore, images and temples and monasteries associated with these faiths shaped the artistic activities of his age.

HOUSES AND BUILDINGS

Yuan Chwang, who visited the greater part of India, has left a detailed account of the Indian houses and buildings. He found similarity of styles between the houses and buildings of India and those of China. According to him, houses were made of stone, brick, or wood, and their flat roofs were covered with planks, thatching, or burnt or unburnt tiles.[1] Like Bāṇa, he also refers to walls plastered with lime and painted or carved doors, walls, and ceilings. The floors, when unpaved, seem to have been coated with a mixture of straw, clay and cowdung, as is still done in some villages, and, as Yuan Chwang writes, 'strewn with flowers of the season'. Of the houses of the Buddhist laity the pilgrim says they were 'sumptuous inside and economical outside'. He states that the people of lower castes such as "butchers, fishermen, public performers, executioners and scavengers were not allowed to live among the people of the higher castes. They were forced to live outside the cities and towns" and "their habitations were marked by a distinguishing sign". Alms-houses, rest-houses, gardens, and fresh-water tanks were common features of a city. The city streets apart from the

[1] T. Watters, *On Yuan Chwang's Travels in India* (*A.D. 629-645*), I, eds. T. W. Rhys Davids and S. W. Bushell, New Delhi, 1961, p. 147.

highways seem to have been narrow and zigzag.[2] Yuan Chwang was also impressed by the height of the structures. The Nālandā structures seem to have been exceptionally tall.[3] The pilgrim speaks of the four-storeyed outside courts at the establishment.[4] The Nālandā inscription describes the *vihāras* with 'spires (that) lick the clouds... like a garland hanging up high'.[5] A legend preserved in a Tibetan history, written in the eighteenth century, records the presence of a nine-storeyed library building at Nālandā called the Ratnodadhi.

The description in the *Harshacharita* refers mainly to Prabhākara's capital, where houses appear to have been single or multistoreyed, whitewashed or plastered with stucco. There is a reference to the polishing of 'mosaic floors of red lead', apparently in the king's palace, as well as to the painting of pictures obviously on the walls.

According to Yuan Chwang, the monasteries had the most remarkable architecture. They had a tower at each of the four corners of the quadrangle and three high halls in a tier. The rafters and roof beams were carved with strange figures and the doors, windows, and walls were painted in various colours. The inner rooms and the central hall varied in their dimensions. Their "doors opened to the east," and the throne also faced the east.[6] It is strange to note that the pilgrim is silent about the temples though their number must have been larger than that of the monasteries. In the course of his accounts he himself mentions a number of temples along with that of the monasteries.

As regards furniture, people used "corded benches," obviously, modern cots and beds. We are told that "the royal families, the grandees, officials and the gentry adorned their benches in different ways but all had the same style (or *form*) of seat." Yuan Chwang states that the frames of the seats were carved in different ways and adorned with precious substances.[7] Bāṇa gives a beautiful description of the bed specially decorated

[2] S. Dutt, *Buddhist Monks and Monasteries in India*, London, 1962, p. 343, n. 2; D. Devahuti, *Harsha : A Political Study*, Second edn., New Delhi, 1983, p. 171; for further details, cf. Shankar Goyal, *The 'Medieval' Factor and the Age of Harsha : A Cultural Study*, Jodhpur, 2016, pp. 189-96.

[3] For the hugeness and magnificence of the buildings of the Nālandā Mahāvihāra, see S.R. Goyal, *A History of Indian Buddhism*, Meerut, 1987, pp. 174-80.

[4] Samuel Beal, *The Life of Hiuen Tsiang*, Second edn., New Delhi, 1973, pp. 111-12; Shankar Goyal, *The Significance of Yuan Chwang in the Context of the Seventh Century : A Critical Assessment*, New Delhi, 2018, pp. 84-86.

[5] *EI*, XX, p. 45.

[6] *Travels, op.cit.*

[7] *Ibid.*, pp. 147-48.

for the honeymoon chamber, *Vāsagṛha* of Rājyaśrī.[8]

PALACE ARCHITECTURE

No actual remains of palaces or forts of the age of Harsha are now available. However, literary sources such as the *Harshacharita* and *Kādambarī* of Bāṇa and the *Si-Yü-Ki* of Yuan Chwang describe these buildings of that period, sometimes in detail. The most important unit of the palace complex was known as the *skandhāvāra*. It contained the *rājakula* and the *rājakula* included the royal palace known as *dhavalagṛha*, the White House.[9] *Skandhāvāra* was a term for the entire military encampment which included the area for the horse and elephant wings, camel corps, encampments of guest kings and miscellaneous establishments relating to the army. These various portions were assigned special places for them in the vast extensive area outside the *rājakula*. The *rājakula* proper was entered through the main entrance known as *rājadvāra*. Inside the *rājakula* was the palace containing the living apartments of the kings and queens, and that was known as *dhavalagṛha*.

Skandhāvāra

In the *Harshacharita* we find a description of the *skandhāvāra*, *rājakula* and *dhavalagṛha*. Bāṇa had his first meeting with Harsha in the temporary palace built for the king on the bank of Ajiravatī (modern Rāptī) in the village named Maṇitārā. The area necessary for the army encampment (*skandhāvāra*) was very extensive. The whole army was stationed there. The *skandhāvāra* was planned in two portions, the army encampment and the royal palace. The outer area of encampment had extensive grounds for horses on the one side, and for elephants on the other. The area for horses (*mandurā*) also had stables of camels. After this there were camps of kings and other royal guests who came on state business. This area was known as *śivira*. It had its own market and shops to which admission was unrestricted for the public. While returning from his march Harsha first passed through its *bāzār*. This was called *vipaṇivartma* and later on in the Muslim period known as *Urdū Bāzār*, i.e., the market place of the army hordes. When the present writer was young and lived in Gorakhpur, he found that the main *bāzār* of that city (which was originally the market of Gorakhpur cantonment area) was known as *Urdū Bāzār* which was later on under the nationalist impact rechristened as *Hindi Bāzār*. The very extensive area in front of the Red Fort in Old Delhi

[8] *The Harṣa-carita of Bāṇa*, trans. by E.B. Cowell and F. W. Thomas, Delhi, 1968, pp. 131-32.

[9] Interestingly, in the United States of America, the Presidents' residence is also known as the White House.

was also once known as *Urdū Bāzār*, which was but a translation of *Vipaṇivartma*. This wide plot of ground accommodated the camps for kings and rulers and feudatories who came to meet the emperor.

In the *skandhāvāra* area of Harsha there were various kinds of encampments. These included encampments for kings from many countries, enemy kings and feudatory kings defeated in battles, embassies from many foreign lands, Mlechchhas or barbarians who came from across the ocean and probably included the rulers of Śaka, Yavana, Hūṇa, Pārasīka and other Mlechchha races; and principal representatives from amongst the people and also religious heads and teachers who especially came to see the king. There was additional open area all of which was known as *ajira*.[10]

Rājakula

At the end of the *skandhāvāra* was situated the *rājakula*. It was also called *rājabhavana*, *rājaprāsāda* or *rājamandira*. Its entrance was known as *rājadvāra*. The palace was well-guarded. The entry into it was restricted and strictly controlled. The entrance of the *rājakula* was guarded by the *bāhya-pratīhāras* (chamberlains posted outside the palace). The first portion of the *rājadvāra* on both sides of the entrance consisted of several rooms in one or more storeys known as *dvāraprakoshṭha* or *alinda*. It is stated that at the time of Rājyaśrī's marriage goldsmiths were seated in the *alinda* portion for making golden ornaments.

Inside the *rājakula* there used to be a series of courts (*kakshyās*). The palace of Harsha was planned in *three courts*. In the *Kādambarī* the palace of Tārāpīḍa, father of Chandrāpīḍa, was divided into seven courts. In the *Rāmāyaṇa* the palace of Daśaratha is stated to have five courts. The palace of Rāma as the crown-prince (*yuvarāja-bhavana*) had only three courts. In the *first court* of Harsha's palace on the left side of the *rājadvāra* was an extensive pavilion (*avasthānamaṇḍapa*) for the royal elephants (*ibhadhishṇyāgāra*) in which the king's own elephant, Darpaśāta, was kept. On the right side opposite to it was the stable (*mandurā*) for the king's own horses. Bāṇa often refers to the king riding on the royal elephant or horse entering the entrance, crossing the four courts and dismounting near the big staircase (*mahāsopāna*).

In the *second court* at the centre was situated the *bāhyāsthāna-maṇḍapa*, i.e., the hall of public audience, also called *sabhā* or *sadas*, from ancient times and also known as *āsthāyikā* or *sarvāvasara*. As stated by V.S. Agrawala, in the Mughal palace architecture this was known as *Darbār-i-*

[10] See V.S. Agrawala, *The Deeds of Harsha*, Varanasi, 1969, pp. 240-55 for more details.

ām.[11] In front of it was the extensive *first court*, also called *ajira*. Up to this point the king had the privilege to mount his horse, or elephant. In order to gain access into the audience hall the king had to dismount at the foot of the staircase. After mounting the steps one entered the audience hall. Chandrāpīḍa took the decision of his military conquest in the *āsthānamaṇḍapa*. In the *Kādambarī* it is described as the *sabhāmaṇḍapa*. In the Delhi fort there is an open court in front of the *Darbār-i-ām* which may be identified as *ajira*. At the time of Prabhākaravardhana's illness his friendly kings and feudatories assembled in the *ajira* to express their sympathies. When the king used to convene a *Darbār* or hold assembly or court of justice, it was always in the *Darbār-i-ām* or *bāhyāsthānamaṇḍapa*. After the death of Rājyavardhana, Harsha took counsel with his Senāpati Siṁhanāda and marshal of the elephants Skandagupta in the *bāhyāsthānamaṇḍapa*. In the *rājakula* there were two *āsthānamaṇḍapas* or audience chambers. One was the *bāhyāsthānamaṇḍapa* or *Darbār-i-ām*, the other was inside the *rājakula* in the *dhavalagṛha* portion, usually at the end of the series of courts which was known as *bhuktvāsthānamaṇḍapa* corresponding to the *Darbār-i-khās* of the Mughal period. The difference between the outer and the inner *āsthānamaṇḍapas* is clear both in the *Harshacharita* and the *Kādambarī*. In the *bhuktvāsthānamaṇḍapa* the king used to take rest. He also had consultation with his select friends, ministers and inmates of the harem there. This was also known as *pradoshāsthāna-maṇḍapa*, i.e., the place where the king gave audience in the evening. In the *Kādambarī* the Chāṇḍāla girl carrying the parrot in the cage saw the king in the *bāhyāsthānamaṇḍapa*.

Bāṇa has given an elaborate description of the *dhavalagṛha* or the palace which was situated in the *third court*. Round the *dhavalagṛha* there used to be a contingent of other buildings which included: 1. *Gṛhodyāna* (the palace garden), also known as *bhavanodyāna* or *mandirodyāna*. 2. *Gṛhadīrghikā* (a flowing canal which derives its name from its length), water ponds (*krīḍāvāpī*) containing lotuses and Haṁsas, where the inmates of the palace enjoyed themselves. The *dīrghikā* is mentioned not only in Indian literature in the age of Kālidāsa and Bāṇa but it was also a feature of the palace architecture in Iran in the time of Khushru Parves. This feature of the palace architecture continued during the medieval times also. Vidyāpati in his *Kīrtilatā* has mentioned *krīḍāśaila*, *dhārāgṛha*, *pramadavana*, *pushpavāṭikā* and also *kṛtrima-nadī*, i.e., an artificial canal of flowing water, which was the another name for *bhavanadīrghikā*. In the palace named Hampton Court of the Tudor Henry VIII this was known as 'Long Water',

[11] *Ibid.*, p. 242.

which seems similar to the Indian *Dīrghikā.*[12] 3. *Vyāyāmabhūmi* (the king's gymnasium). In the *Kādambarī* it is stated that the king Śūdraka dismissing his court went to his *vyāyāmabhūmi* or gymnasium, where he took routine exercises. That the Indian kings observed such a routine is also mentioned in the *Kauṭilīya Arthaśāstra.* 4. *Snānagṛha* or *yantradhārāgṛha* (the fountain and the swimming pool). 5. *Devagṛha.* Inside the *dhavalagṛha* there used to be *devagṛha* with an image of the deity worshipped by the king and other inmates of the palace. Kshemendra names it as *devārchana-maṇḍapa.* 6. *Toyakarmānta.* The place for storage of drinking water which was placed in the charge of an officer named *toyakarmāntika,* i.e., the Superintendent of Waterworks. 7. *Mahānasa* or the royal kitchen. 8. *Āhāramaṇḍapa* (the dining hall or the pavilion where the king took his meals).

In addition to the above, we also find in the *Kādambarī* a reference to *saṁgītabhavana* or the music hall, *āyudhaśālā* or the armory, ground for the practice of archery and *adhikaraṇamaṇḍapa* or the court of justice. These were located in the different portions of the palace.

Dhavalagṛha

Besides the above component parts of the palace the main portion was the *dhavalagṛha* in which the king and his female inmates resided. It was the palace proper forming the residential quarter. In Hindi, it is called *dhaurāhara,* literally the 'White House'. According to Bāṇa, the entrance to the *dhavalagṛha* was known as *gṛhāvagrahaṇī* in which *gṛha* signified *dhavalagṛha* and *avagrahaṇī* the *dehalī* or threshold, i.e., the point where strict checking was made by the chamberlains posted for the purpose. The doorkeepers appointed here were much more experienced and trustworthy. In the *Rāmāyaṇa* this portion of the palace is named *pravivikta-kakshyā,* i.e., the secluded court, where Rāma with Sītā was given accommodation as prince-regent and where only trustworthy persons were allowed to enter.

The *dhavalagṛha* was architecturally planned in two or more storeys. The king and the queens usually lived in the upper storeys. Just after entering the *dhavalagṛha* one found two staircases on right and left leading to the upper floor. At the time of his illness Prabhākaravardhana was occupying the upper floor of the palace. It is also said that the chamberlains angrily forbade the noise or the sound produced by treading on the staircase. Harsha is said to have gone to see his father several times in the upper storey. There used to be an extensive court in the middle of the *dhavalagṛha* and round which were series of rooms or *śālās* because of which that portion was named *chatuḥśāla.* The Hindi derivative of *chatuḥśāla* is *chausallā* which is

[12] *Ibid.*, p. 245.

still current in the dialect of Vārāṇasī.[13] Prabhākaravardhana himself was in the upper storey of the palace but his servants were assembled on the ground floor in the *chatuḥśāla*.

In the middle portion of the *chatuḥśāla* there was a pavilion supported on pillars and known as *suvīthī* which was enclosed by triple screens (*triguṇa-tiraskariṇī*). This was separated from the rooms of the *chatuḥśāla* by a pathway all around open to the sky. The *suvīthī* portion was entered into by side entrances (*pakshadvāra*). The middle portion of the *suvīthī* was like a platform known as *vitardikā* which was a covered pavilion.

In the upper storey of the *dhavalagṛha*, on the front side, the central portion was called *pragrīvaka* and the two side portions were called *saudha*, and *vāsabhavana* or *vāsagṛha*. In the *vāsagṛha* was located the *śayanagṛha* or the sleeping chamber. There were wall paintings in the *vāsabhavana*. Hence, this particular room was known as *chitraśālikā*. Queen Yaśovatī used to sleep in *vāsabhavana*. Harsha also took his nightly rest in the *vāsabhavana*. The *saudha* portion was exclusively occupied by the queens. It had an open roof on which queen Yaśovatī used to enjoy moon light by putting off her upper garment. The central portion was called *pragrīvaka* because it occupied the *grīvā* or neck portion of the palace. It was also known as *mukhaśālā*. Corresponding to it the back portion on the upper storey was known as *chandraśālikā*, which was a roofed pavilion supported on pillars in which the king and queens enjoyed the moon light. The two long verandahs on right and left connecting the *chandraśālikā* and the *pragrīvaka* were known as *prāsādakukshi* furnished with ventilators or latticed windows (*vātāyana*).

The Mughals inherited the older building traditions of the Hindus which they adopted in their palaces and at the same time introduced several features of their own. That is why one finds so much similarity between the ancient Hindu palaces and the medieval Mughal palaces.

Significantly, as Agrawala points out, the Rāshṭrapati-bhavana at New Delhi also has the following planning : central vista up to India Gate (*skandhāvara*), secretariat (*adhikaraṇamaṇḍapa*), main gate (*rājadvāra*), fore-court (*bāhyakakshyā*), grand staircase (*prāsāda-sopāna*), Darbār Hall (*bāhyāsthānamaṇḍapa*), military secretary's wing (*pratīhārabhavana*), audience room (*bhuktvāsthānamaṇḍapa*), banqueting room (*āhāramaṇḍapa*), ball room (*prāsādakukshi* for *antaḥpurasaṁgīta*), Mughal Gardens (*gṛhodyāna*), flower area (*kamalavana*), pond (*krīḍāvāpī*), fountain and long canal (*dīrghikā*) showing the continuation of the ancient tradition of Hindu architecture.[14]

[13] *Ibid.*, p. 247.
[14] *Ibid.*, p. 255.

TWENTY FOUR

India and Iran : The History of Relations in the Age of Harsha

BUDDHISM AND HINDUISM IN IRAN

As in earlier periods, India's cultural and commercial contacts with Iran in the age of Harsha were quite close. Yuan Chwang attests to the thriving state of Hinduism and Buddhism in Lāṅgala or Lang-kie-ka-lo (to the west of India bordering on the ocean) which was "under the government of Persia." The script used by its people, and with some differences the spoken language also, were like those of India. It had above one hundred saṅghārāmas and 'perhaps 6000 priests' and also 'several hundred deva temples' and very many professed Pāśupatas.[1]

According to the Chinese pilgrim, Po-la-sse (Persia) also abounded in deva temples. He generally uses this term for Hindu sanctuaries. The presence of several hundred Buddhist monks and two or three saṅghārāmas in Iran is also recorded by him and their preference for the Hīnayānist Sarvāstivādin school noted.[2] He also informs us that a *pātra* of the Buddha was in the palace of the king of this country. The Persian contact with Buddhism is revealed by several other evidences. We have from Dandanuliq, in the Chinese Turkistan, a picture of eighth century A.D., of a Bodhisattva in the garb of a Persian. The picture may be a specimen of the Buddhist art as it developed in the seventh century A.D. Here, it may also be recalled that it was a Parthian prince An-Shih-Kao (second century A.D.) who had made the first organised efforts to translate the Buddhist canon into Chinese. The tenth-eleventh century Muslim scholar Alberuni records the presence

[1] S. Beal, *Si-Yü-Ki* or *Buddhist Records of the Western World*, II, Delhi, 1969, p. 277.

[2] *Ibid.*, p. 278.

of Buddhism, in former times, in Khorasan, Iran, Iraq and neighbouring countries up to the borders of Syria. These facts prove that Yuan Chwang's statement about the existence of the Buddhist monks in Iran in the seventh century A.D. may be correct and that in the age of Harsha Hinduism and Buddhism were living forces in that country.

INDO-IRANIAN COMMERCIAL AND CULTURAL RELATIONS

Trade relations of India with Iran were also in a flourishing condition in the age of Harsha. Amianus Marcellinus tells us that Indian wares were sent to the great annual fair at the mart of Batne, not far from the bank of the Euphrates, about the second half of the fourth century A.D.[3] The Chinese annals refer to a brisk trade by land route between China and Western countries like Arabia and Persia which must have passed through India.[4] The Arabs and Iranians sent a large number of merchant ships to China which passed through Indian ports. I-tsing, the Chinese pilgrim, came to India in a Persian ship, and Vajrabodhi, who went to China in 720 A.D., is said to have seen thirty-five Iranian ships in a port of Ceylon.[5] Arab and Iranian historians also make numerous references to Indian ships in the Persian Gulf and the Red Sea and the first Muslim fleet is said to have appeared in the Indian waters in 636 A.D.

Several other aspects of India's cultural relations with Iran in the post-Gupta age may also be briefly noted here. The westward journey of the *Pañchatantra*,[6] the great Sanskrit book of stories, began in the sixth century A.D. with its translation into Pahlavi, and then into Syriac. Similarly, Persian and Arabian writers state that chess or Śatarañja (Sanskrit *Chaturaṅga*) came to Persia from India. From Iran the game passed to the Arabians and from them, directly or indirectly, to various parts of Europe.[7] Hindu sciences, notably Āyurveda and Arithmetic, were highly prized in Iran. It is on record that Barzouhyeh, a subject of the Iranian Sassanid king Khusru I, who ruled between 531 and 579 A.D., came to India to learn Indian medicine and other sciences.[8]

[3] R.C. Majumdar and A.D. Pusalker (ed.), *The Classical Age*, Bombay, 1954, p. 638; also see Haripada Chakraborti, *Trade and Commerce in Ancient India*, Calcutta, 1966, p. 338.

[4] *Ibid.*

[5] *Ibid.*

[6] M. Winternitz, *A History of Indian Literature*, Vol. III, repr., Delhi, 1963, pp. 294 ff. According to Philip Khuri Hitti (*History of the Arabs*, originally published in 1937, repr., MacMillan, 1949, p. 404), the basis of the famous work entitled *Thousand and One Nights* was a Persian book which contained several stories of Indian origin.

[7] H.J.R. Murray, *A History of Chess*, 1913, quoted in *CA*, p. 639, n. 2.

[8] *CA*, p. 640.

It is thus evident that economic and cultural relations of India with Iran were quite close in the sixth-seventh centuries. Sometimes these relations found reflection in the political sphere also. Interestingly, Tabari records that Nashīrwan (Khusru I) dispatched an expedition to India which resulted in the gain of some provinces for the Persians. According to Sykes, there does not seem to be any certainty about the reality of this campaign but it is also not impossible that Khusru I did make such an attempt in this direction.[9] Therefore, the question which we pose before ourselves is "did Indo-Iranian economic-cultural relations assume political overtones in the age of Harsha ?"

THEORY OF EXCHANGE OF EMBASSIES BETWEEN KHUSRU II AND PULAKEŚIN II

The most interesting evidence of a close contact between India and Iran in the age of Harsha is preserved by the Persian historian Tabari (838-923 A.D.). He informs us that in the thirty-sixth year of the reign of the Persian emperor Khusru II (590-628 A.D.). i.e. in 626 A.D. when Harsha was ruling over northern India and Pulakeśin II was the Lord of the Deccan, a king of India, named Prmesh, sent to the Persian ruler ambassadors carrying a letter and presents for him and his sons. The account of Tabari is in the form of a reply of Khusru II to the charges brought against him by his son Shiruyieh. It runs as follows :

> Two years ago, Pulakeśi, king of India, sent to us, in the thirty-sixth year of our reign, ambassadors carrying a letter imparting to us various news, and presents for us, for you, and our other sons. He also wrote a letter to each of you. To you he presented—don't you remember it ?—an elephant, a sword, a white falcon and a piece of gold brocade. When we looked at the presents and at the letters, we remarked that yours bore the mark "Private" on the cover in the Indian language. Then we ordered that the presents and other letters should be delivered to each of you, but we kept back your letter, on account of the remark written on the outside. We then sent for an Indian scribe, got the seal broken, and the letter read. The contents were :— "Rejoice and be of good cheer, for on the day Dai ba Ādhar, of the thirty-eighth year of reign of Chesroés, thou will be crowned king and become ruler of the whole empire. Signed, Pulakeśi." But we closed this letter with our seal, and gave it into the keeping of our consort Shirīn.[10]

The name of the Indian king, as written by Tabari, reads Prmesh. Noldeke, the translator of this passage, rendered it as Pulakesha or Pulakeśi. He argued

[9] Percy Sykes, *History of Persia*, I, London, 1958, p. 456.

[10] Quoted by R.C. Majumdar, *Readings in Political History of India*, ed. S. P. Gupta, Delhi, 1976, p. 155.

that as *R* and *L* are written with the same sign in Pahlavi, *R* is to be taken as a false mode of expressing *L*. Further, *M* may be substituted for *K*(*Q*) in the Arabic or in the Pahlavi. It, therefore, follows that the name may be read as Pulakesha, obviously, Pulakeśin II of the Chālukya dynasty of Badami, who was a contemporary of Khusru II.

EVIDENCE OF THE AJANTA PAINTINGS

The suggestion of Noldeke was used by Fergusson to support his interpretation of the paintings found in the Cave 1 at Ajanta.[11] Four of these paintings are found on the four corners of the central square of the principal design of the roof. They are replicas of the same design. The principal figure in these four pictures is a stout burly foreigner who is sitting cross-legged on a cushion with a female companion or his wife. He is holding a drinking cup in his right hand and two femal figures are shown offering fruits or food; in other two they are omitted.

Besides these paintings on the roof there is a very remarkable fresco on the wall of this cave which represents an Indian king on his throne receiving an embassy or deputation of people who are also foreigners, most likely, though not certainly, of the same nationality to which the foreign personage depicted in the paintings of the roof belongs. They are bearers of a letter and are being dismissed with return present.

Fergusson assigned the Cave No. 1 to the period between 610 and 630-40 A.D. He also believed that the foreigners depicted in these paintings were Persians. With these facts he combined the suggetion of Noldeke that Pulakeśin II sent an embassy to Khusru in 626 A.D. Therefore it was easy for him to suggest that the drinking scene depicted on the roof or the Bacchanalian scene in the paintings, as it is called, represents Khusru II and his queen Shirīn and that the Persian emperor must have sent a return embassy to the court of Pulakeśin II, the ceremonial reception of which is depicted in the fresco on the wall. Thus the theory of the exchange of embassies between Khusru II and Pulakeśin II was postulated. It was accepted by Smith and many subsequent historians.

However, the theory is open to serious objections. As pointed out by Ettinghausen and R. C. Majumdar Noldeke overlooked the fact that Prmesh is a good transliteration of the Indian word Parameśa or Parameśvara, a title often used by the Indian kings. There is therefore no need to transliterate the original Prmesh conjecturally into Pulakeśi. As regards the paintings of the Cave No. 1 at Ajanta it is not at all certain that the cave or its paintings definitely belong to the age of Pulakeśin II. Yazdani

[11] *JRAS*, 1879, pp. 155 ff.

ascribed these paintings to the fifth century A.D.[12] But in my view the monuments of the Gupta and post-Gupta age cannot be so precisely dated since it merges at both ends in the continuous development of earlier and later periods.[13] The nationality of the foreigners depicted in these paintings is controversial. As regards the foreigners depicted in the so-called 'embassy scene', some scholars, such as Smith[14] and Rajendra Lal Mitra,[15] agree with Fergusson in believing that they are Persians, but Yazdani thought them to be of Turkish origin,[16] while Motichandra[17] hesitatingly and M. K. Dhavalikar[18] rather confidently suggest that they are Syrian merchants. So far the foreigners of the drinking or the Bacchanalian scene are concerned it is usually conceded that they are Persians, but the assertion that the chieftain and his wife shown in it are Khusru II and his queen Shirīn has been doubted by Foucher,[19] Dhavalikar[20] and others. As pointed out by Foucher their costume is common enough in these paintings and its knowledge to the Ajanta painters is easily explained by the nearness of Ajanta to the western coast. Therefore there is no reason to assume that the couple in question are Khusru II and Shirīn. Dhavalikar's suggestion that the scene represents a Persian nobleman and his wife[21] may therefore be correct.

IDENTIFICATION OF HARSHA WITH THE KING OF INDIA MENTIONED BY TABARI

But the negation of the relevance of the Ajanta paintings for the theory of the exchange of embassies between Khusru II and Pulakeśin II does not solve the problem of the identity of Parameśa or Parameśvara, the king of India who, according to Tabari, sent an embassy to Khusru II in 626.

[12] *JBORS*, XXVII, 1944, p. 14.

[13] Shankar Goyal, *175 Years of Vākāṭaka History and Historiography*, Jodhpur, 2009, p. 30; also see, my *The Classical Age : A Study in Feudalization*, New Delhi, 2022, Ch. 3.

[14] V.A. Smith, *The Early History of India*, Oxford, 1924, pp. 442-43.

[15] *JASB*, XLVII, 1878, pp. 66-68.

[16] G. Yazdani, *Ajanta*, Part I, Text, London, 1930, p. 46.

[17] Motichandra, *Bhāratīya Veśabhūshā*, Prayāga, Saṁ. 2007, p. 21.

[18] M. K. Dhavalikar, 'Foreigners in the Ajanta Paintings', in *Foreigners in Ancient India and Lakshmī and Sarasvatī in Art and Literature*, ed. D. C. Sircar, Calcutta, 1970, p. 14.

[19] *Journal of the Hyderabad Archaeological Society*, 1919-20, p. 99.

[20] Dhavalikar, *op. cit.*, p. 16.

[21] However, the argument of R. C. Majumdar that there was no reason for a scene of a political embassy finding a place amidst religious surrounding in a cave is not valid. After all, even if it does not depict the scene of an embassy, the painting is patently secular and so are the drinking scenes depicted on the roof and all of them do find place amidst religious surrounding.

Cunningham suggested the pos1sibility that he was a certain Indo-Sassanian prince, Vāsudeva, whose existence as the ruler of Multan and adjoining regions is known from coins bearing legends in Pahlavi and Nāgarī, or Shahi Tigin, who is called master of Tukān and Khurāsān in the Pahlavi legend and "Supreme Lord of India and Iran" (*Hitvi cha Airan cha Parameśvara*) in Nāgarī.[22] B. Ghosh is inclined to agree with him.[23] But the date of these rulers is not known. Further it has been rightly pointed out that correspondence between an Indo-Sassanian prince and Khusru must have been in Pahlavi. It is therefore unlikely that the former should have used his Indian title Parameśvara and not its Pahlavi equivalent in his letter.[24]

The theory that the Indian embassy received by Khusru II was sent by Harsha was advanced by R.C. Majumdar.[25] To me it appears to be the best solution of the problem. It may be pointed out that Harsha exerted a great influence in the north-western part of the sub-continent[26]—even more than Majumdar was ready to concede. His hold over Rajasthan is indicated by the prevalence of his era in this region.[27] His political influence in Gujarat is proved by his victory over the king of Valabhī recorded in the inscription of Gurjaras of Lāṭa. His invasion of Sindh has been explicitly recorded by Bāṇa, while his political hold over some parts of the Punjab is proved by the testimony of Yuan Chwang and the Tibetan historian Tārānātha. According to Yuan Chwang Harsha was able to assign the task of taking him safely across the Indian border to the king of Jālandhar. Tārānātha has recorded the story of the persecution of the Mlechchhas near Maulasthāna or Multan at the hands of Harsha.[28] The Mlechchhas of this story were undoubtedly Persians. The story, if correct, makes it highly likely that Harsha might have had some dealings with the Persian court.

Secondly, Harsha was not only an immediate neighbour of the Iranian emperor, there is also a likelihood that the former had economic and political

[22] A. Cunningham, *Later Indo-Scythians*, repr. from the *Numismatic Chronicle*, London, 1893-95, p. 123.

[23] *JBRS*, XXX, p. 189.

[24] *Ibid.*, p. 190.

[25] See Majumdar, *Readings in Political History of India*, pp. 156-57.

[26] For a detailed discussion on this problem see my paper, 'Yuan Chwang's India and the Problem of the Extent of Harsha's Empire and Sphere of His Influence', in the *Proceedings of the Papers from the Aligarh Historians Society*, ed. Irfan Habib, 77th Session, Indian History Congress, Kerala University Thiruvananthapuram, 28-30 December, 2016, pp. 104-16.

[27] Cf. S.R. Goyal, 'Harsha and Rajasthan', *PRHC*, Jaipur, 1979, pp. 14-19; idem, *Harsha Śīlāditya*, Meerut, 1987, pp. 137-41.

[28] Tārānātha, *History of Buddhism,* trans. by A. Schiefner, St. Petersburg, 1869, p. 94.

relations with the latter. Bāṇa says that the conquest of Iran was regarded by Harsha's *sāmantas* as not so difficult. They boasted that "the land of the Turuṣkas is to the brave but a cubit; Persia is only a span."[29] Tārānātha's story of the persecution of the Mlechchhas near Maulasthāna or Multan at the hands of Harsha, even if false, suggests quite a close relationship between India and Persia during his rule. Bāṇa refers to the fact that Harsha's horses were imported, among other countries, from Persia also.[30] In the *Kādambarī* also we are informed that a horse named Indrāyudha, which was of exceptionally good breed, was sent by the monarch of Iran for the hero of this work.[31] Tārānātha confirms the existence of such contacts by stating that a Persian king presented horses to the king of Madhyadeśa (probably Harsha) and the latter sent to the former in return a few elephants. The story reminds one of a similar return present of elephants by Chandragupta Maurya to Seleucus and may be indicative of more intimate commercial relations.

Lastly, it may be pointed out that in the story recorded by Tabari the Persian king refers to the Indian monarch as the king of India. As Iran is closer to north India than to the Deccan, *prima facie* one should infer that the term 'king of India' means the king of north India. In view of all these facts it should be regarded as more legitimate to hold that the king of India who sent an embassy to Khusru II of Iran was Harsha, and not Pulakeśin II.[32]

[29] *Harshacharita* of Bāṇa, trans. by E.B. Cowell and F.W. Thomas, 2nd edn., Delhi, 1968, p. 210.

[30] *Ibid.*, p. 50.

[31] *Kādambarī* of Bāṇa, ed. Pt. Ramtej Shastri, Kāśī, Saṁ. 2020, pp. 164-65.

[32] Shankar Goyal, *Harsha : A Multidisciplinary Political Study*, Jodhpur, 2006, pp. 231 ff.

Bibliography

Agrawal, Jagannath and Goyal, Shankar, eds., *S.R. Goyal : His Multi-dimensional Historiography*, New Delhi, 1992.

Agrawala, P.K., *Gupta Temple Architecture*, Varanasi, 1968.

—, *Gupta-kālīna Kalā evaṁ Vāstu*, Varanasi, 1994.

Agrawala, V.S., *Harsha Charita —Eka Sāṁskṛtika Adhyayana* (in Hindi), Patna, 1953.

—, *Kādambarī—Eka Sāṁskṛtika Adhyayana* (in Hindi), Varanasi, 1958.

—, *India as Known to Pāṇini*, Varanasi, Second edn., Varanasi, 1963.

—, *Prāchīna Bhāratīya Loka Dharma*, Ahmedabad, 1964.

—, *Studies in Indian Art*, Varanasi, 1965.

—, *The Deeds of Harsha*, Varanasi, 1969.

Aiyangar, S.K., *Some Contributions of South India to Indian Culture*, Calcutta, 1923.

—, *Ancient India and South Indian History and Culture*, Vol. I, Poona, 1941.

Allan, J., *Catalogue of the Coins of the Gupta Dynasties and of Śaśāṅka, King of Gauḍa (in the British Museum)*, London, 1914.

—, *Catalogue of the Coins of Ancient India*, London, 1936.

Altekar, A.S., *The Coinage of the Gupta Empire*, Varanasi, 1957.

—, *State and Government in Ancient India*, Delhi, 1977.

Arthaśāstra of Kauṭilya, Eng. tr. R. Shamasastry, Bangalore, 1950; edn. of R.P. Kangle, in 3 Parts, Bombay, 1960, 1963, 1965.

Āryamañjuśrīmūlakalpa, ed. and trans. by K.P. Jayaswal as *An Imperial History of India*, Lahore, 1934.

Ayyar, C.V. Narayana, *Origin and Early History of Śaivism in South India*, Madras, 1936.

Bagchi, P.C., *She-Kia-Fang-Che*, Calcutta, 1959.

Bailey, G.M. and Kesarcodi-Watson, I., eds., *Bhakti Studies*, New Delhi, 1992.

Bakker, Hans T., *Ramtek*, Leiden, 1989.

—, *The Vākāṭakas : An Essay in Hindu Iconology*, Groningen, 1997.

—, ed., *The Vākāṭaka Heritage : Indian Culture at the Crossroads*, Groningen, 2004.

Banskhera Copper Plate of Harsha, *Epigraphia Indica*, IV, pp. 208-11.
Basham, A.L., *The Wonder that was India*, London, 1954.
—, ed., *A Cultural History of India*, London, 1975.
Beal, S., *Si-Yü-Ki* or *Buddhist Records of the Western World*, Delhi, 1969.
—, *The Life of Hiuen-Tsiang*, New Delhi, 1973.
—, *Chinese Accounts of India*, Vol. II, Calcutta, n.d.
Beni Prasad, *The State in Ancient India*, Allahabad, 1928.
Bhandarkar, D.R., *Lectures on Ancient Indian Numismatics*, Calcutta, 1921.
Bhati, Nagendra Singh, 'Shankar Goyal on the Problems of the Decline of Political Theory and History', in *Shankar Goyal : Marching with History* ', ed. Radhika Seshan, New Delhi, 2021, Ch. 9.
Bhati, P.S., *Political Theory and Organisation*, Lucknow, 1989.
—, *The Normative Traditions in Political Theory*, Jodhpur, 1998.
Bindoff, S.T., 'Political History', in *Approaches to History*, ed. H.P.R. Finberg, London, 1962.
Bṛhatsaṁhitā of Varāhamihira, ed. H. Kern, Calcutta, 1865.
Buddha Prakash, *Aspects of Indian History and Civilization*, Agra, 1965.
Byrski, M.C., 'Some Remarks about King Harṣavardhana Śīlāditya', *Bhāratī*, 5, i, 1961-62, pp. 75-85.
Catlin, George, *A History of Political Philosophers*, London, 1950.
Chakrabarti, Kunal and Sinha, Kanad, eds., *State, Power and Legitimacy : The Gupta Kingdom*, Delhi, 2019.
Chakraborti, Haripada, *Trade and Commerce in Ancient India*, Calcutta, 1966.
Chakrabortty, S.K., *A Study of Ancient Indian Numismatics*, Calcutta, 1931.
Chakravarti, Ranabir, *Exploring Early India up to c. AD 1300*, 3rd edn., Delhi, 2016.
Champakalakshmi, R., *Trade, Ideology and Urbanization : South India 300 BC to AD 1300*, New Delhi, 1999.
—, 'Historiography of South India—New Directions', her Presidential Address, in *PSIHC*, VII Annual Session, Madras, 1987.
Chatterjee, Bhaskar, ed., *History and Archaeology, Professor H.D. Sankalia Felicitation Volume*, Delhi, 1989.
Chatterji, G.S., *Harshavardhana* (in Hindi), 2nd edn., Allahabad, 1950.
Chattopadhyaya, B.D., *The Making of Early Medieval India*, New Delhi, 1997.
Chattopadhyaya, S., *Early History of North India*, Calcutta, 1958.
Chaturvedi, Parashuram, *Madhyakālīna Prema-sādhanā*, Allahabad, 1957.
—, *Bhakti Sāhitya meṅ Madhuropāsanā*, Allahabad, 1962.
Chhabra, B.Ch., *Catalogue of the Gupta Gold Coins of the Bayana Hoard in the National Museum*, New Delhi, 1986.
Chhabra, B.Ch., Agrawala, P.K., Agrawal, Ashvini and Goyal, Shankar, eds., *Reappraising Gupta History for S.R. Goyal*, New Delhi, 1992.

Chhabra, B. Ch. and Gai, G.S., eds., *Corpus Inscriptionum Indicarum*, Vol. III, *Inscriptions of the Early Gupta Kings and their Successors*, revised by D.R.Bhandarkar, New Delhi, 1981.

Choudhary, G.C., *Political History of North India from Jaina Sources*, Amritsar, 1954.

Coker, F.W., *Readings in Political Philosophy*, New York, 1962.

Craig, Gordon, 'Political History', in *Daedalus*, Cambridge, Mass., Winter 1971, pp. 323-38.

Cunningham, A., *The Ancient Geography of India*, Varanasi, 1963.

—, *Coins of Mediaeval India*, Varanasi, 1967.

—, *Coins of Ancient India*, London, 1891, repr. Varanasi, 1971.

Daedalus : The Historian and the World of the Twentieth Century, Cambridge, Mass., Spring 1971.

Daṇḍin, *Daśakumāracharita*, ed. M.R. Kale, Bombay, 1917.

Das, A.C., *Ṛigvedic India*, Vol. I, Calcutta, 1921.

Dasgupta, S.N., *A History of the Sanskrit Literature*, Vol. 1 : *Classical Period*, Second edn., Calcutta, 1975.

De, S. K., *History of Sanskrit Literature*, Calcutta, 1947.

Deo, S.B. and Joshi, Jagatpati, *Pauni Excavations (1969-70)*, Nagpur, 1972.

Devahuti, D., *Harsha : A Political Study*, 2nd edn., Oxford University Press, New Delhi, 1983; 1st edn., Oxford, 1970.

—, ed., *Problems of Indian Historiography*, Delhi, 1979.

—, ed., *The Unknown Hsüan-tsang*, New Delhi, 2001.

Dhavalikar, M.K., 'The Beginning of Coinage in India', *World Archaeology*, Vol. 6, No. 3, London, 1975.

—, 'The Golden Age and After : Perspectives in Historical Archaeology', his Presidential Address delivered to the Diamond Jubilee Session of the Indian History Congress, Calicut, 1999.

Dikshitar, V.R.R., *The Mauryan Polity*, Madras, 1932.

—, *The Gupta Polity*, Madras, 1952.

—, *The Purāṇa Index*, 2 Vols., Madras, 1951, 1952.

Dubey, D. P. and Dubey, A.K., 'Uttar Pradesh, Bihar and Uttarakhand', in *25 Years of Indian Epigraphy* (A Bird's Eye-view of the Progress of Epigraphy in Different States of the Country), ed. Shrinivas V. Padigar, Dharwad, 2016, pp. 301 ff.

Dubey, S.R., ed., *Ābhilekhika Adhyayana kī Pravidhi evaṁ Itihāsa-Lekhana*, Delhi, 2004.

Dubreuil, J., *Ancient History of the Deccan*, tr. from French by V.S.S. Dikshitar, Pondicherry, 1920.

Dvivedi, Hazari Prasad, *Madhyakālīna Dharma-sādhanā*, Allahabad, 1956.

Elliot, W., *Coins of South India*, London, 1886.

Elton, G.R., *Political History : Principles and Practice*, London, 1970.

Ettinghausen, M.L., *Harṣa Vardhana : Empereur et Poète, etc.*, London, 1906.
Finberg, H.P.R., ed., *Approaches to History*, London, 1962.
Fleet, J.F., *Corpus Inscriptionum Indicarum*, III, Calcutta, 1888.
—, *Dynasties of the Kanarese Districts*, Bombay, 1899.
Freeman, Donald, M., ed., *Foundations of Political Science : Research Methods and Scope*, New York, 1977.
Ghoshal, U.N., *Studies in Indian History and Culture*, Second revised edn., Calcutta, 1965.
Ghurye, G.S., *Caste and Class in India*, 2nd edn., Bombay, 1957.
Giles, H.A., *The Travels of Fa-hsien*, London, 1923.
Goff, E.G., 'Is Politics Still the Backbone of History ?', *Daedalus*, Cambridge, Mass., Winter 1971, pp. 1-19.
Gopal, S. and Thapar, R., eds., *Problems of Historical Writing in India*, New Delhi, 1963.
Goyal, Shankar, *History and Historiography of the Age of Harsha*, Jodhpur, 1992.
—, *Aspects of Ancient Indian History and Historiography*, New Delhi, 1993.
—, *History Writing of Early India*, Jodhpur, 1996.
—, *The Image of Classical India*, Jodhpur, 1997.
—, *Recent Historiography of Ancient India*, Jodhpur, 1997.
—, *Ancient Indian Numismatics*, Jodhpur, 1998.
—, *Marxist Interpretation of Ancient Indian History*, Poona, 2000.
—, *Problems of Ancient Indian History : New Perspectives and Perceptions*, Jaipur, 2001.
—, *Contemporary Interpreters of Ancient India*, Jaipur, 2003.
—, *Harsha : A Multidisciplinary Political Study*, Jodhpur, 2006.
—, *Ancient India : A Multidisciplinary Approach*, Jodhpur, 2006.
—, *175 Years of Vākāṭaka History and Historiography*, Jodhpur, 2009.
—, *The 'Medieval' Factor and the Age of Harsha : A Cultural Study*, Jodhpur, 2016.
—, *Harsha Revisited : A Re-interpretation of Existing Data*, Delhi, 2018.
—, *The Significance of Yuan Chwang in the Context of the Seventh Century : A Critical Assessment*, Delhi, 2018.
—, *The Classical Age : A Study in Feudalization*, New Delhi, 2022.
—, *Prāchīna Bhārata : Itihāsa, Itihāsa-Lekhana aura Vichāradhārāyeṅ*, Varanasi, 2022.
—, ed., *Political History in a Changing World*, Jodhpur, 1992.
—, ed., *S.R. Goyal : His Multidimensional Historiography*, New Delhi, 1992.
—, ed., *Prāchīna Bhārata kā Ādhunika Itihāsa-Lekhana*, Jodhpur, 2000.
—, ed., *Reconstructing Indian History for S.R. Goyal*, 4 Vols., Jaipur, 2003.
—, ed., *History and Politics*, Jodhpur, 2015.
—, 'Social *Milieu* of the Pushyabhūtis : Significance of Some Hitherto

Unnoticed Passages of the *Harshacharita* ', *Essays in Indian History and Culture*, ed. Y. Krishan, New Delhi, 1986, pp. 167-70.

—, 'Śaśāṅka and Buddhism', in the *Proceedings of the Indian History and Culture Society*, 10th Annual Conference, 1986, Varanasi, 1988, pp. 45-50.

—, 'Political History : The Loss of Innocence', in *Political History in a Changing World*, eds. G.C. Pande et al, Jodhpur, 1992, pp. 290-99.

—, 'Political Ideology of the Early Imperial Guptas', in *Reappraising Gupta History for S. R. Goyal*, eds. B. Ch. Chhabra, P. K. Agrawala, Ashvini Agrawal and Shankar Goyal, New Delhi, 1992, pp. 215-23.

—, 'A Critique of Professor D.N. Jha's Evaluation of the Classicism of the Gupta Age', in *Reappraising Gupta History for S.R. Goyal*, eds. B. Ch. Chhabra, et al, New Delhi, 1992, pp. 61-73.

—, 'Coins of Prabhākaravardhana Pratāpaśīla and Harsha Śīlāditya', *Journal of the Numismatic Society of India*, Vol. LIV, Pts. 1-2, 1992, pp. 65-69.

—, 'Rise of Medievalism in Indian History', *Vishveshvaranand Indological Journal*, Vol. XXX, Pts. 1-2, June-Dec. 1992, pp. 233-60.

—, 'Recent Historiography of the Age of Harsha', *Annals of the Bhandarkar Oriental Research Institute*, Vol. LXXII-LXXIII, 1993, pp. 331-61.

—, 'The Rājyavardhana Murder Case', *Heritage of India : Past and Present* (Professor R.K. Sharma Felicitation Volume), eds. P.K. Mishra and S.K. Sullerey, Delhi, 1994, pp. 579-90.

—, 'Historiography of the Imperial Guptas : Old and New', *VIJ*, Vol. XXIX, Pts. I-II, 1991 (1995), pp. 239-74.

—, 'Voices of Protest and Dissent in the Works of Bāṇa', *Śrījñānāmṛtam* (A Commemoration Volume dedicated to Professor Shri Niwas Shastri), ed. Vijaya Rani, Delhi, 1996, pp. 650-60.

—, 'Prabhākaravardhana : A New Assessment', in *Sri Venkateswara University Oriental Journal*, Volume XLIII, Parts 1 and 2, 2000, pp. 9-31.

—, 'Harsha's Relations with the Deccan and the Far South: Some Problems and Suggestions', in the *Proceedings of the Twenty-second Annual Session of the South Indian History Congress*, Thiruvananthapuram, 2002, pp. 135-37.

—, 'Political History as an Integral Study of Political Life and Institutions', *Annals of the Bhandarkar Oriental Research Institute*, Vol. LXXXIV, 2003, pp. 135-42.

—, 'On Dr. P.L. Gupta's Contribution to Gupta History and Coinage', *JNSI*, LXIV-V, 2003, pp. 24-28.

—, 'Factors in the Making of Early Medieval Society in India', *Journal of Indian History and Culture*, Vol. XI, 2004, pp. 25-52.

—, 'Psycho-Sociological Analysis of Harsha's Personality', *Journal of Indian*

History, Vols. LXXVI-LXXVIII, 2004, pp. 7-14.

—, 'Harsha ke Abhilekha : Kuchha Samasyāyeṅ aura Sujhāva' (in Hindi), in *Ābhilekhika Adhyayana kī Pravidhi evaṁ Itihāsa-Lekhana*, ed. Sita Ram Dubey, Delhi, 2004, pp. 183-89.

—, 'Professor Ajay Mitra Shastri's Contribution to Ancient Indian Numismatics', *JNSI*, LXVI, 2004, pp. xl-xliv.

—, 'A.S. Altekar and the Bayana Hoard', *JNSI*, Vol. LXVII, Pts. i-ii, 2005, pp. 80-84.

—, 'The Vākāṭakas in the History of the Deccan : A Fresh Appraisal in the Light of Recent Discoveries and New Interpretations', The Loyola College Endowment Lecture delivered at the XXVI Annual Session of the South Indian History Congress, held at the Bangalore University, March 3-5, 2006, pp. 1-21.

—, 'Professor V.S. Pathak's Contribution to Numismatic Studies', *JNSI*, LXVIII, 2006, pp. 121-25.

—, 'The Recently Discovered Kurukshetra-Varanasi Grant of Harsha : Year 23', *East and West*, Vol. 57, 1-4, 2007, pp. 193-203.

—, 'Religious Analysis of Harsha's Personality', *Proceedings of the Indian History Congress*, 68th Session, Delhi, 2007 (Delhi, 2008), pp. 136-48.

—, 'The Myth of the Vākāṭaka Coins', *IHR*, Vol. XXXIV, No. 2, July 2007, pp. 1-15.

—, '*Harshacharita* as a Source of History', in the *Papers from the Aligarh Historians Society*, ed. Irfan Habib, 69th Session, Indian History Congress, Kannur University, Kannur, 2008, pp. 122-52.

—, 'The Authenticity of the Plays Ascribed to Harsha', *Proceedings of the Indian History Congress*, 69th Session, Kannur University, Kannur, 2008 (Kolkata, 2009), pp. 86-93.

—, 'Caste System as Reflected in the Works of Bāṇa and Yuan Chwang', in the *Papers from the Aligarh Historians Society*, ed. Irfan Habib, 71st Session, Gaur Banga University, Malda, 2011, pp. 124-47.

—, 'Harsha-Pulakeśin II Struggle : A Collated Study of Epigraphic and Literary Evidence', in *JESI*, XXXVII, 2012, pp. 100-05.

—, 'An Investigation into the Feudal Nature of the Vākāṭaka Economy : A Study of the Epigraphic Evidence', our Presidential Address, The Epigraphical Society of India, published in the *Journal of the Epigraphical Society of India*, Vol. XXXVIII, 2012, pp. 1-38.

—, 'Feudalization of Polity in the Age of Harsha : An Analysis', in *History and Politics*, ed. Shankar Goyal, Jodhpur, 2015, pp. 143-67.

—, 'Yuan Chwang's India and the Problem of the Extent of Harsha's Empire and Sphere of His Influence', in the *Papers from the Aligarh Historians Society*, ed. Irfan Habib, 77th Session, Indian History Congress, Kerala University, Thiruvananthapuram, 2016, pp. 104-16.

—, 'Some Observations on India's Intercourse with Iran in the Seventh Century A.D.', in the *Papers from the Aligarh Historians Society*, ed. Irfan Habib, 78th Session, Indian History Congress, Jadavpur University, Kolkata, 2017, pp. 11-16.

—, 'Harsha : A Retrospective', our Presidential Address, Section I : Ancient India, 78th Session, Indian History Congress, Jadavpur University, Kolkata, 28-30 December, 2017, *PIHC*, Delhi, 2018, pp. 27-41.

—, 'The Rāmṭek Prabhāvatīguptā Memorial Fragmentary Inscription', in *Epigraphic Studies*, Selected Papers from the Panel on Epigraphy at the 16th World Sanskrit Conference, 2015, Sanskrit Studies Centre, Silpakorn University, Bangkok, Thailand, ed. D.P. Dubey, New Delhi, 2018, pp. 129-37.

Goyal, S.R., *A History of the Imperial Guptas*, Allahabad, 1967.

—, *Gupta evaṁ Samakālīna Rājavaṁśa*, Allahabad, 1969.

—, *Prāchīna Nepāla kā Rājanītika aura Sāṁskṛtika Itihāsa*, Varanasi, 1973.

—, *Prāchīna Bhāratīya Abhilekha Saṁgraha*, Vol. I, *Prāk-guptayugīna*, Jaipur, 1982.

—, *Guptakālīna Abhilekha*, Meerut, 1984.

—, *A Religious History of Ancient India*, 2 Vols., Meerut, 1984, 1986.

—, *Harsha and Buddhism*, Meerut, 1986.

—, *Harsha Śīlāditya*, Meerut, 1986.

—, *Gupta Sāmrājya kā Itihāsa*, Meerut, 1987.

—, *Maukhari-Pushyabhūti-Chālukyayugīna Abhilekha*, Meerut, 1987.

—, *Māgadha-Sātavāhana-Kushāṇa Sāmrājyoṅ kā Yuga*, Meerut, 1988.

—, *Gupta aura Vākāṭaka Sāmrājyoṅ kā Yuga*, Meerut, 1988.

—, *Maukhari-Pushyabhūti-Chālukya Yuga*, Meerut, 1988.

—, *Indigenous Coins of Early India*, Jodhpur, 1994.

—, *An Introduction to Gupta Numismatics*, Jodhpur, 1994.

—, *The Dynastic Coins of Ancient India*, Jodhpur, 1995.

—, *The Coinage of Ancient India*, Jodhpur, 1995.

—, *Dakshiṇa Bhārata kā Itihāsa*, Jodhpur, 1995.

—, *Ancient Indian Inscriptions : Recent Finds and New Interpretations*, Jodhpur, 2005.

—, *The Imperial Guptas : A Multidisciplinary Political Study*, Jodhpur, 2005.

—, *A History of the Vākāṭaka-Gupta Relations*, Jodhpur, 2006.

—, *Birth and Early Growth of Indian Society*, Jodhpur, 2016.

—, *Paurāṇika Sects and Cults*, Jodhpur, 2016.

—, *A Comprehensive History of Hinduism*, Jodhpur, 2018.

—, 'Political History : A Reconsideration', in *Jijñāsā*, Volume 2, Number 2, April 1975, pp. 9-26.

—, 'Need of a Ṇew Approach to the Writing of Political History of Ancient India', in *Political History in a Changing World*, eds. G.C. Pande et al,

Jodhpur, 1992, pp. 1-17.
—, 'The Myth of the Golden Bird : An Investigation into the Belief of Material Opulence of Ancient and Early Medieval India in the Light of Her Gold Coinage', his Presidential Address, The Numismatic Society of India, published in the *Journal of the Numismatic Society of India*, Vol. LXIX, Parts I and II, 2007, pp. 1-24.
Goyal, S. R. and Goyal, Shankar, eds., *Indian Art of the Gupta Age*, Jodhpur, 2000.
Grewal, J.S., 'Hiuen Tsiang's India', in *India — Studies in the History of an Idea*, ed. Irfan Habib, New Delhi, 2005, pp. 60-81.
Gupta, P.L., *Punch-Marked Coins in the Andhra Pradesh Government Museum*, Hyderabad, 1960.
—, *The Amarāvatī Hoard of Silver Punch-Marked Coins*, Hyderabad, 1963.
—, *Coins*, New Delhi, 1969.
—, *Gupta Sāmrājya*, Varanasi, 1970.
—, *The Imperial Guptas*, Varanasi, 1974.
Gupta, S.P., *The Roots of Indian Art*, Delhi, 1980.
—, ed., *Readings in Political History of India*, Delhi, 1976.
Habib, Irfan, ed., *India — Studies in the History of an Idea*, New Delhi, 2005.
Handa, Devendra, ed., *Oriental Numismatic Studies*, Volume I, New Delhi, 1996.
Harshacharita of Bāṇa, ed. Kasinatha Pandurang Parab, 5th edn., Bombay, 1925.
—, ed. P.V. Kane, 2nd edn., Delhi, 1965.
—, tr. E.B. Cowell and F.W. Thomas, 2nd edn., Delhi, 1968.
—, ed. Jagannath Pathak, 6th edn., Varanasi, 1998.
Hauser, Arnold, *The Social History of Art*, Vol. I.
Heras, H., 'The Royal Patrons of the University of Nālandā', *JBORS*, XIV, 1928.
Hiralal, *Inscriptions of the Central Provinces and Berar*, Nagpur, 1932.
Hitti, Philip K., *History of the Arabs*, first published in 1937, revised 10th edn., Palgrave Macmillan, 2002.
Hooper, J.S.M., *The Hymns of the Āḷvārs*, Oxford, 1929.
Huart, C., *Ancient Persia and Iranian Civilization*, tr. M. R. Dobie, London, 1927.
Jayaswal, K.P., *History of India, 150 A.D. to 350 A.D.*, Lahore, 1933.
Jha, D.N., *Ancient India : An Introductory Outline*, New Delhi, 1977; revised and enlarged edn. as *Ancient India in Historical Outline*, New Delhi, 1998.
—, *Prāchīna Bhārata, Sāmājika, Ārthika aura Sāṁskṛtika Vikāsa kī Paratāla*, Delhi, 2009.
Jha, D.N. and Shrimali, K.M., eds., *Prāchīna Bhārata kā Itihāsa*, Delhi, 1981.
Jha, J.S., ed., *K.P. Jayaswal Commemoration Volume*, Patna, 1981.

Joshi, L.M., *Studies in the Buddhistic Culture of India*, Delhi, 1967.
Joshi, Munish Chandra, Gupta, S.K. and Goyal, Shankar, eds., *King Chandra and the Meharauli Pillar*, Meerut, 1989.
Kādambarī of Bāṇa, tr. C.M. Ridding, London, 1896; Indian repr., Bombay, 1956.
—, ed. P.V. Kane, Bombay, 1920.
—, ed. Pt. Ramtej Shastri, Varanasi, 1952.
Kalhaṇa, *Rājataraṅgiṇī : A Chronicle of the Kings of Kashmir*, 2 Vols., tr. Sir M.A. Stein, Westminster, 1900 ; tr. R.S. Pandit, Allahabad, 1935.
Kālidāsa, *Kumārasambhava*, in *Kālidāsa Granthāvalī*, ed. Sitaram Chaturvedi, Aligarh, 1950.
—, *Raghuvaṁśa*, in *Kālidāsa Granthāvalī*, ed. Sitaram Chaturvedi, Aligarh, 1950.
Kaliyugarājavṛttānta of *Bhavishyottra-purāṇa*, quoted in *History of Classical Sanskrit Literature* by M. Krishnamachariar, Madras, 1937.
Kāmandakīya-nītisāra, ed. Ganapati Sastri, Trivandrum, 1912.
Kāmasūtra of Vātsyāyana, ed. D.L. Goswami, Banaras, 1929.
Kane, P.V., *History of Dharmaśāstra*, Vol. III, Poona, 1973.
Kathāsaritsāgara, ed. Durga Prasad and Parab, Bombay, 1930.
Kaumudī-mahotsava by Vijjikā (?), ed. Shakuntala Rao Shastri, Bombay, 1952.
Kāvya-mīmāṁsā of Rajaśekhara, eds. C.D. Dalal and R.A. Sastry, Baroda, 1934.
Keith, A.B., *Sanskrit Drama*, Oxford, 1924.
—, *History of Sanskrit Literature* (Hindi edn.), Delhi, 1960.
Kosambi, D.D., *An Introduction to the Study of Indian History*, 2nd revised edn., Bombay, 1975.
—, *The Culture and Civilisation of Ancient India in Historical Outline*, 7th edn., New Delhi, 1982.
Krom, N.J., 'The First Hindu Coin from Java', *JNSI*, Vol. XXX, 1968, pp. 200-01.
Kurukshetra-Varanasi Copper Plate Inscription of Harsha, *East and West*, Vol. 57, 1-4, 2007, pp. 193-203 ; *Epigraphia Indica*, XLIII, i, pp. 40-51.
Kuṭṭanīmata of Dāmodara, ed. M. Kaul, Calcutta, 1944.
Kuvalayamālā, ed. L.B. Gandhi, Baroda, 1927.
Law, B.C., *Buddhistic Studies*, Calcutta, 1931.
Legge, J.H., *A Record of the Buddhist Kingdoms, etc.*, being an account of the Chinese monk Fa-hien's travels in India, Oxford, 1886.
Liu, Xinru, *Ancient India and Ancient China, Trade and Religious Exchanges A.D. 1-600*, Oxford, 1988.
Lorenzen, David N., ed., *Religious Movements in South Asia 600-1800*, New Delhi, 2006.

—, 'Professor S.R. Goyal's Suggestion on Political History Writing in the Light of Historians and Political History of the Gupta Empire', in *Political History in a Changing World*, eds. G.C. Pande, S.K. Gupta and Shankar Goyal, Jodhpur, 1992, pp. 53 ff.

Macdonell, A.A., *A History of Sanskrit Literature*, Delhi, 1962.

Madhuban Copper Plate Inscription of Harsha, *Epigraphia Indica*, I, pp. 67-75.

Mahābhārata, Critical Text, 7 Vols., Poona, 1877-97.

Mahalingam, T.V., *South Indian Polity*, Madras, 1967.

—, *Kāñcīpuram in Early South Indian History*, Bombay, 1969.

Maitland, F.W., *Political Theories of the Middle Age*, Cambridge, 1927.

Majumdar, R.C., *Readings in Political History of India*, ed. S.P. Gupta, Delhi, 1976.

—, ed., *The History of Bengal* (Vol. I : Hindu Period), Dacca, 1943.

—, ed., *A Comprehensive History of India*, Vol. III, Pt. I (A.D. 300-985), New Delhi, 1981.

—, 'Ideas of History in Sanskrit Literature', *Historians of India, Pakistan and Ceylon*, ed. C.H. Philips, London, 1961.

Majumdar, R.C. and Altekar, A.S., eds., *A New History of the Indian People*, Vol. VI : *The Vākāṭaka-Gupta Age (Circa 200-550 A.D.)*, Lahore, 1946.

Majumdar, R.C. and Dasgupta, K.K., eds., *A Comprehensive History of India*, Vol. III, Pt. II, New Delhi, 1982.

Majumdar, R.C. and Pusalker, A.D., eds., *The Classical Age*, Bombay, 1954.

Malik, S.C., ed., *Indian Movements : Some Aspects of Dissent, Protest and Reform*, Simla, 1978.

Mammaṭa, *Kāvyaprakāśa*, Eng. tr. Ganganatha Jha, Allahabad, 1925.

Mānavadharmaśāstra or *Manusmṛti*, ed. J. Jolly, London, 1887.

Maxey, C.S., *Political Philosophies*, New York, 1956.

Mayūra, *Sanskrit Poems by Mayūra*, ed. G. Quackenbos, New York, 1917.

McCrindle, J.W., *Ancient India as Described by Megasthenes and Arrian*, Calcutta, 1877.

Mirashi, V.V., *Corpus*, V, *Inscriptions of the Vākāṭakas*, Ootacamund, 1963.

—, *Vākāṭaka Rājavaṁśa kā Itihāsa tathā Abhilekha* (in Hindi), Varanasi, 1964.

—, *Literary and Historical Studies in Indology*, Delhi, 1975.

—, *Indological Research Papers*, Vol. I, Nagpur, 1982.

Mitchiner, M., *The Origins of Indian Coinage*, London, 1973.

Mookerji, R.K., *Harsha*, London, 1926.

Motichandra, *Bhāratīya Veśabhūshā*, Prayāga, Saṁ, 2007.

Mukherjee, S.N., ed., *India : History and Thought*, Calcutta, 1982.

Murray, H.J.R., *A History of Chess*, published in 1913, repr., Oxford, 1962.

Murray, R.H., *The History of Political Science from Plato to the Present*, London, 1926.

Nāgānanda of Harsha, tr. P. Boyd, London, 1872.

—, ed. R.D. Karmarkar, Poona, 1919.

Nālandā Seals, *Epigraphia Indica*, XXI, pp. 74-76.

Narain, A.K., 'Writing a New History of Ancient India : A Study of Problems, Sources and Methods', in *Problems of Historical Writing in India*, New Delhi, 1963, pp. 1-10.

Nītisāra of Kāmandaka, ed. Rajendralal Mitra, Calcutta, 1884.

Oakeshott, Michael, *Rationalism in Politics*, Oxford, 1962.

—, *On Human Conduct*, Oxford, 1975.

Om Prakash, *Prāchīna Bhārata kā Itihāsa*, New Delhi, 1987.

Padigar, Shrinivas V., ed., *25 Years of Indian Epigraphy*, Dharwad, 2016.

Padmagupta, *Navasāhasāṅkacharita*, ed. V.S. Islampurkar, Bombay, 1895.

Pañchatantra, tr. A. Williams, *Tales from the Pañchatantra*, Oxford, 1930.

Pande, G.C., *Śramaṇa Tradition*, Ahmedabad, 1978.

Pande, G.C., Gupta, S.K. and Goyal, Shankar, eds., *Political History in a Changing World*, Jodhpur, 1992.

Pande, Susmita, *Birth of Bhakti in Indian Religions and Art*, New Delhi, 1982.

—, *Medieval Bhakti Movement*, Meerut, 1989.

Pandey, R.B., *Historical and Literary Inscriptions*, Varanasi, 1962.

—, *Prāchīna Bhārata*, Varanasi, 1971.

Panikkar, K.M., *Śrī Harsha of Kanauj*, Bombay, 1922.

Pargiter, F.E., *The Purāṇa Text of the Dynasties of the Kali Age*, London, 1913.

Patañjali, *Mahābhāshya*, Rohtak, 1961-63.

Pathak, V.S., *Ancient Historians of India*, Bombay, 1966.

Philips, C.H., ed., *Historians of India, Pakistan and Ceylon*, London, 1961.

Pirenne, Jacques, *The Tides of History*, Allen and Unwin.

Pocock, D. and Dumont, Louis, eds., *Contributions to Indian Sociology*, The Hague, 1962.

Prinsep, J., *Essays on Indian Antiquities*, Vol. I, ed. E. Thomas, London, 1858.

Priyadarśikā of Harsha, ed. Jivanand Vidyasagar, Calcutta, 1874.

—, tr. G.D. Nariman, A.V. William Jackson and C.J. Ogden, New York, 1923.

Problems of Historical Writing in India, Proceedings of the Seminar held at the India International Centre, New Delhi, 1963.

Raghuvaṁśa of Kālidāsa, ed. G.R. Nandargikar, Bombay, 1897.

Rai, Jaimal, *The Rural-Urban Economy and Social Changes in Ancient India*, Varanasi, 1974.

Rāmacharita of Sandhyākara Nandī, eds. R. C. Majumdar, R. G. Basak and N. G. Banerji, Rajshahi, 1939.

Rao, T.A. Gopinatha, *Sir Subrahmanya Ayyar Lectures on the History of Śrī Vaiṣṇavas*, Madras, 1923.

Rapson, E.J., *Indian Coins*, Strassburg, 1897.
Rathore, L.S., *In Defence of Political Theory*, New Delhi, 1986.
Ratnāvalī of Harsha, ed. K.M. Joglekar, Hedvi, 1907.
—, ed. and tr. C.R. Devadhar and N.G. Suru, 2nd edn., Poona, 1954.
Raychaudhuri, H.C., *Political History of Ancient India*, Calcutta, 1953; with a *Commentary* by B.N. Mukherjee, Oxford, 1996.
Ray, S.C., *Stratigraphic Evidence of Coins in Indian Excavations and Some Allied Issues*, Varanasi, 1959.
Ṛgveda, ed. F. Maxmüller, 1890-92; edn. of T. H. Griffith, Banaras, 1896-97; Poona edn., 4 Vols., 1933.
Roy, U.N., *Gupta Samrāṭ aura Unkā Kāla*, Allahabad, 1971.
Śabdakalpadruma of Radhakant Dev, 5 Vols., Delhi, 1961.
Sabine, George H., *A History of Political Theory*, New Delhi, 1963.
Sampurnanand, *Samrāṭ Harshavardhana* (in Hindi), Bombay, V.S. 1977.
Sankalia, H.D., *The University of Nālandā*, Madras, 1934.
Saraswati, S.K., *A Survey of Indian Sculpture*, Calcutta, 1957.
Sastri, K.A.N., *Development of Religion in South India*, Madras, 1963.
—, *A History of South India*, Mạdras, 1966.
—, *The Cōlas*, repr., Madras, 1975.
—, *The Pāṇḍyan Kingdom*, Madras, 1982.
Schwartz, Benjamin, 'A Brief Defence of Political and Intellectual History with Particular Reference to Non-Western Cultures', *Daedalus*, Cambridge, Mass., Winter 1971, pp. 98-112.
Sen, Surendranath, *India through Chinese Eyes*, Madras, 1956.
Seshan, Radhika, ed., *Shankar Goyal : Marching with History*, New Delhi, 2021.
Shamasastry, R., ed., *The Arthaśāstra of Kauṭilya*, 3rd edn., Mysore, 1922.
Sharma, B.N., *Harṣa and His Times*, Varanasi, 1970.
Sharma, D., 'Harṣa : A Buddhist', *Indian Historical Quarterly*, XXXII, Nos. 2 and 3, 1956, pp. 168 ff.
Sharma, Munshi Ram, *Bhakti kā Vikāsa*, Varanasi, 1958.
Sharma, R.S., *Śūdras in Ancient India*, Delhi, 1958.
—, *Indian Feudalism*, Calcutta, 1965.
—, *Perspectives in Social and Economic History of Early India*, New Delhi, 1983.
—, *Urban Decay in India (c. 300-1000 A.D.)*, New Delhi, 1987.
—, *Ancient India*, New Delhi, 1995.
—, *Aspects of Political Ideas and Institutions in Ancient India*, 4th revised edn., Delhi, 1996.
—, *Early Medieval Indian Society : A Study in Feudalisation*, Kolkata, 2001.
—, *India's Ancient Past*, Oxford, 2015.
—, ed., *Indian Society : Historical Probings in Memory of D.D. Kosambi*, 3rd edn., New Delhi, 1984.

Shastri, A.M., *Early History of the Deccan : Problems and Perspectives*, Delhi, 1987.
—, *Inscriptions of the Śarabhapurīyas, Pāṇḍuvaṁśins and Somavaṁśins*, New Delhi, 1995.
—, *Vākāṭakas : Sources and History*, New Delhi, 1997.
—, ed., *The Age of the Vākāṭakas*, New Delhi, 1992.
She-Kia-Fang-Che, ed. P.C. Bagchi, Calcutta, 1959.
Shrimali, K.M., *Agrarian Structure in Central India and the Northern Deccan (c. A.D. 300-500) : A Study of Vākāṭaka Inscriptions*, New Delhi, 1987.
Shrivastava, B.N., *Harshavardhana and His Times*, Varanasi, 1974.
Sinha, B.P., *Readings in History and Culture*, Delhi, 1978.
Sinha, G.P., *Post-Gupta Polity (500-750 A.D.)*, Calcutta, 1972.
Sircar, D.C., *Select Inscriptions*, Calcutta, 1943.
—, ed., *Foreigners in Ancient India and Lakshmī and Sarasvatī in Art and Literature*, Calcutta, 1970.
Smith, Bardwell L., ed., *Essays on Gupta Culture*, Delhi, 1983.
Smith, V.A., *Early History of India*, 4th edn., Oxford, 1924.
Soḍḍhala, *Udayasundarīkathā*, ed. C.D. Dalal and E. Krishnamacharya, G.O.S., Baroda, 1920.
Somadeva, *Kathāsaritsāgara*, tr. C.H. Tawney, 2 Vols., Calcutta, 1880-84.
Sonepat Seal of Harsha, *Corpus Inscriptionum Indicarum*, III, ed. J.F. Fleet, pp. 231-32.
Subandhu, *Vāsavadattā*, Bibliotheca Indica, Calcutta.
Subrahmanian, N., *Tamilian Historiography*, Madurai, 1988.
Sykes, Percy, *History of Persia*, I, London, 1958.
Takakusu, J.A., *A Record of the Buddhistic Religion as Practised in India and Malaya Archipelago (A.D. 671-695) by I-tsing*, Delhi, 1966.
Tārānātha, *History of Buddhism*, tr. A. Schiefner, St. Petersburg, 1869.
Thakur, V.K., *Social Roots of Buddhism*, Patna, 2000.
Thapar, Romila, *A History of India*, Vol. I, Harmondsworth, 1966.
—, *Ancient Indian Social History*, Hyderabad, 1978.
—, *Aśoka and the Decline of the Mauryas*, Oxford, 1997.
—, *The Penguin History of Early India*, New Delhi, 2003.
—, *The Past Before Us : Historical Traditions of Early North India*, New Delhi, 2013.
—, *Readings in Early Indian History*, Oxford, 2013.
Thaplyal, K.K., *Inscriptions of the Maukharīs, Later Guptas, Puṣpabhūtis and Yaśovarman of Kanauj*, Delhi, 1985.
Thomas, E., *Ancient Indian Weights*, London, 1885.
Trautmann, T.R., *Kauṭilya and the Arthaśāstra*, Leiden, 1971.
Tripathi, R.S., *History of Kanauj to the Moslem Conquest*, Delhi, 1959.
Vaidya, C.V., *History of Mediaeval Hindu India*, Vol. I, Poona, 1921.

Vākpati, *Gauḍavaho*, ed. S.P. Pandit, Bombay, 1887; 2nd edn. by N.B. Utgikar, Poona, 1927.
Varma, S.P., *Modern Political Theory*, New Delhi, 1976.
Vikramāṅkābhyudaya, ed. G. Bühler, Bombay, 1875.
Vikramāṅkadevacharita of Bilhaṇa, ed. G. Bühler, Bombay, 1875.
Warder, A.K., *An Introduction to Indian Historiography*, Bombay, 1972.
Watters, T., *On Yuan Chwang's Travels in India*, Delhi, 1961.
Whalley, Paul, 'Place Names in U.P., of Agra and Oudh', *Journal of the Uttar Pradesh Historical Society*, II, Pt. 2, 1921, pp. 19-29.
Williams, Joanna Gottfried, *The Art of Gupta India*, New Delhi, 1983.
Wilson, H.H., *Ariana Antiqua*, repr., Delhi, 1971.
Winternitz, M., *History of Indian Literature*, 3 Vols., Delhi, 1981; 1983, 1985.
Yaduvamshi, *Śaiva Mata*, Patna, 1955.
Yazdani, G., *Ajanta*, Part I, Text, London, 1930.
—, ed., *The Early History of the Deccan*, London, 1960.

Journals

Annals of the Bhandarkar Oriental Research Institute, Poona.
Bhāratī, Varanasi.
Bulletin of the Gorakhpur University, Gorakhpur.
Bulletin of the School of Oriental and African Studies, London.
Daedalus, Cambridge.
East and West, Rome.
Epigraphia Indica, New Delhi.
History Today, New Delhi.
Indian Antiquary, Bombay.
Indian Coin Society Newsletter, Nagpur.
Indian Culture, Calcutta.
Indian Historical Quarterly, Calcutta.
Indian Historical Review, New Delhi.
The Indian Journal of Political Science, Jodhpur.
Indian Numismatic Chronicle, Patna.
Indica, Bombay.
Itihāsa-Samīkshā, Jaipur.
Jijñāsā, Jaipur.
Jñāna-Pravāha, Varanasi.
Journal of Ancient Indian History, Calcutta.
Journal of the Asiatic Society, Kolkata.
Journal of the Asiatic Society of Bengal, Calcutta.
Journal Asiatique, Paris.
Journal of the Bihar and Orissa Research Society, Patna.
Journal of the Bihar Purāvid Parishad, Patna.
Journal of the Bihar Research Society, Patna.

Journal of the Bombay Branch of the Royal Asiatic Society, Bombay.
Journal of the Epigraphical Society of India, Mysore.
Journal of the Ganganath Jha Research Institute, Allahabad.
Journal of Indian History, Trivandrum.
Journal of Indian History and Culture, Chennai.
Journal of the Numismatic Society of India, Varanasi.
Journal of Oriental Institute, Baroda.
Journal of Oriental Research, Madras.
Journal of the Royal Asiatic Society of Bengal, Calcutta.
Journal of the Royal Asiatic Society—Bombay Branch, Bombay.
Journal of the the Royal Asiatic Society of Great Britain and Ireland, London.
Journal of the U.P. Historical Society, Lucknow.
Memoirs of the Archaeological Survey of India, Delhi.
New Indian Antiquary, Bombay.
Numismatic Digest, Nasik.
Panjab University Research Bulletin (Arts), Chandigarh.
Prāchī-Jyoti, Kurukshetra.
Proceedings of the Indian History Congress.
Proceedings of the Indian History and Culture Society.
Proceedings of the Oriental Conference.
Proceedings of the Papers from the Aligarh Historians Society, Aligarh.
Proceedings of the South Indian History Congress.
Quarterly Review of Historical Studies, Calcutta.
Social Scientist, New Delhi.
South Indian Epigraphy, Annual Reports.
Sri Venkateswara University Oriental Journal, Tirupati.
Studies in Indian Place Names.
Vishveshvaranand Indological Journal, Hoshiarpur.

Index